345

The Field is Won

A

Other books by the same author

SAINT THOMAS MORE

SAINT JOHN FISHER

THREE CARDINALS
(Newman—Wiseman—Manning)

MARGARET ROPER

JOHN SOUTHWORTH

THE TRIAL OF ST THOMAS MORE

THOMAS MORE AND ERASMUS

The author has also edited

THE HEART OF THOMAS MORE

Daily readings from his works

Stapleton's LIFE OF SIR THOMAS MORE

Hallett's translation

LIVES OF SIR THOMAS MORE

Roper and Harpsfield

Everyman's Library

SIR THOMAS MORE

THE FIELD IS WON

The Life and Death of Saint Thomas More

by

E. E. REYNOLDS

Son Roper, I thank Our Lord, the field is won

—thomas More

LONDON

BURNS & OATES

BURNS & OATES LIMITED

25 Ashley Place, London S.W.1

First published 1968

Nihil obstat: LIONEL SWAIN, S.T.L., L.S.S., Censor.

Imprimatur: ✠ PATRICK CASEY, Vicar General.
Westminster, 18 May 1968.

The Nihil obstat and Imprimatur are a declaration that a book or
pamphlet is considered to be free from doctrinal or moral error. It is
not implied that those who have granted the Nihil obstat and
Imprimatur agree with the contents, opinions or statements expressed.

© E. E. Reynolds 1968
SBN: 223 97628 8

Made and printed in Great Britain by
The Ditchling Press Ltd, Ditchling, Hassocks, Sussex
Set in 'Monotype' Bembo

To the Abbé
GERMAIN MARC'HADOUR
Université Catholique, Angers
in friendship
and gratitude

Contents

Illustrations

granted him by the King. The central figure represents the
Speaker, Sir Thomas More.

These are the only two separate portraits (in addition to that of
Thomas More) that have survived of those that, presumably,
Hans Holbein painted.

In the text

ACKNOWLEDGEMENTS

The Holbein (Windsor) drawings and No. 6 are reproduced by gracious
permission of H.M. The Queen.

Grateful acknowledgements for permission to reproduce are made to
the following: No. 1, the Warburg Institute, London; No. 2, Galleria
Nazionale d'Arte, Rome; No. 3, the Earl of Radnor, No. 4, J. R.
Chichester-Constable, Esq.; No. 7, Kunstsammlung, Basle; No. 8,
Lord St Oswald; No. 18, Lord Methuen, R.A.; No. 19, Lord Sack-
ville; Nos. 20 and 21, the Metropolitan Museum of Art, New York;
No. 23, the Trustees of the British Museum; and the Frontispiece, the
Trustees of the National Portrait Gallery, London.

CHIEF REFERENCES TO SOURCES

Allen   *Opus Epistolarum Des. Erasmi Roterdami*, ed. P. S. and H. M. Allen. Reference to letter number.

Apologye   *The Apologye*, ed. A. I. Taft (E.E.T.S., 1930).

Bridgett   *Life and Writings of Blessed Thomas More* (1891).

Cresacre More   *Life*, ed. J. Hunter (1878).

Dialogue of
Comfort   Everyman Library Edition.

E.W.   *Works of Sir Thomas More* (1557).

Gibson   *St Thomas More: A Preliminary Bibliography*, ed. R. W. Gibson (Yale, 1961). Reference to number of entry.

Hall   *Henry VIII*, ed. C. Whibley, 2 vols (1904).

Harpsfield*   *Life*, ed. E. W. Hitchcock and R. W. Chambers (E.E.T.S., 1932).

Herbrüggen   *Neue Briefe* (Münster, 1966).

L.P.   *Letters and Papers of the reign of Henry VIII.*

Richard III   Yale edition, ed. R. S. Sylvester (1963).

Rogers   *Correspondence of Sir Thomas More*, ed. E. F. Rogers (Princeton, 1947). Reference to letter number. Where a number is given in brackets, the reference is to *St Thomas More: Selected Letters* (Yale, 1961).

Roper*   *Lyfe*, ed. E. W. Hitchcock (E.E.T.S., 1935).

Span. Cal.   *Calendar of State Papers: Spanish.*

S.P.   *State Papers of the reign of Henry VIII.*

Stapleton   *Life*, trans. Hallett; ed. Reynolds (1966).

Utopia   Yale edition, ed. E. Sturz, s.j., and J. H. Hexter (1965).

*The lives by Roper and Harpsfield are published in one volume in Everyman's Library.

Preface

THIS BOOK IS NOT a revised edition of my *Saint Thomas More* (1953) but a new work. The need for it arises from the considerable attention given by scholars during the past decade not only to all that directly relates to Sir Thomas More's life and work, but to the period in which he lived. The adjustment of our attitudes towards the Renaissance and Reformation may be illustrated by comparing the two volumes of those titles in the *Cambridge Modern History* published at the beginning of the century with those in the *New Cambridge Modern History* of 1957-58. The old labels are still serviceable provided they are no longer given their former black and white meanings. The Tudors continue to fascinate historians; this is not a romantic attraction, but a recognition of the complex nature of the problems—religious, economic, constitutional—of that period. These extensive studies have inevitably led to a better appreciation of Thomas More's relation to his own times.

Some additions have been made to the documentation of More's life. Dr. H. S. Herbrüggen's *Neue Briefe* (Munster, 1966) brings together some hitherto unprinted official letters concerning the negotiations in the Low Countries in which More took part. Professor Geoffrey Bullough, of King's College, London, identified at Valencia the holograph manuscript of the Latin *Passion* written by More in the Tower; the notes and drafts bound up with this throw light on his methods of composition. In 1963 I found in the Record Office the earliest report of the More-Rich conversation. Each of the successive volumes of the *Yale Edition of the Works of St Thomas More* adds to our knowledge. The studies that led to my own books, *Margaret Roper* (1960), *The Trial of St Thomas More* (1964), and *Thomas More and Erasmus* (1965), gave me, I hope, a more perceptive appreciation of the man and his contemporaries.

The growth of the fame of Thomas More continues. It might have been thought that the outstanding contributions to the study of his life made some thirty years ago by R. W. Chambers, E. V. Hitchcock, and A.W. Reed and others would have sufficed for some time, but, in fact, this impetus, far from being exhausted, has led to an expanding interest in all that concerns Thomas More. One sign of this was the formation of the Amici Thomae Mori following a More Exhibition in Brussels in December 1962. My friend the Abbé Germain Marc'hadour of the Université Catholique, Angers, was the prime mover in this development and he continues to direct its quarterly journal *Moreana*. His own *L'Univers de Thomas More* (1963) is an essential tool for workers in this field. A glance through the pages of *Moreana* reveals the wide range of research that is being carried on in the many aspects of the life, thought and writings of Thomas More.

The Amici Thomae Mori is not a Catholic organization, though it may be called catholic as its members are to be found in many countries. Nor was the Yale Edition of the Works a Catholic project. Again, the initiative to erect a statue to Sir Thomas More in Chelsea did not come from Catholics. Even more striking is the success of Robert Bolt's play *A Man for all Seasons* (1961), which has crossed the English Channel and the Atlantic and found appreciative audiences in many countries. The film version has proved equally popular.

Mr Bolt has written, "I am not a Catholic nor even in the meaningful sense of the word a Christian. So by what right do I appropriate a Christian Saint to my purposes?" Mr Bolt's answer should be read in the printed version of his play. One quotation must suffice.

What first attracted me was a person who could not be accused of any incapacity for life, who indeed seized life in great variety and almost greedy quantities, who nevertheless found something in himself without which life was valueless and when that was denied him, was able to grasp his death.

The nearest parallel to this universal praise is the popular

appreciation of St Francis of Assisi; he is famed for the things
he would have regarded as unimportant, whereas the one thing
that mattered to him—his religious faith—is ignored and even
disliked by some of his admirers. So St Thomas More's deep
religious convictions, the motive of his life and death, are too often
minimized or even discounted as a kind of amiable eccentricity.
Yet it is meaningless to write about a saint and leave out God. At
the same time, I trust that, to borrow a phrase from Newman, I
have not been guilty of "mincing a saint into virtues".

*   *   *

For the bibliography of Thomas More's writings, the reader
should consult R. W. Gibson, *St Thomas More: A Preliminary
Bibliography* (Yale, 1961). It is impossible after so many years in
the study of a subject to trace all one's obligations, but I hope the
footnotes will indicate the more important ones; they will also
serve as a guide to sources. Comprehensive lists of books and
articles will be found in *Moreana: Material for the Study of St
Thomas More*, by E. & S. Sullivan (Loyola University, Los Angeles).

E. E. R.

CHAPTER I

The Period

THE NAMES of Thomas More and Henry VIII are so linked in our minds that we are apt to forget that More was born towards the end of the reign of Edward IV and came to maturity during that of Henry VII. John More, his father, was a boy when the first battle of the Wars of the Roses was fought in 1455. Henry VIII was Thomas More's junior by fourteen years.

The reigns of Edward IV and Henry VII were one of the formative periods in English history. The failure of Henry VI to govern resulted in a generation of lawlessness; the Wars of the Roses, as we have come to call these faction-fights, were not so much a cause as a result of the lack of firm central government. The comparatively small armies involved did not create widespread havoc; there were no battles, for instance, in East Anglia nor south of the Thames, yet, in East Anglia, as we know from the Paston Letters, powerful magnates such as the Dukes of Norfolk and Suffolk could harry their neighbours with impunity. Even in remote Cornwall there was much turbulence.[1] It was no wonder then that people longed for stable government under an effective king. Edward IV, during the twenty-two years of his reign, began the work of restoring law and order, but he was too easy-going to complete the task; moreover, his rule was interrupted by the rebellion of the Earl of Warwick who met his death at Barnet in 1471; he has been well called "The Last of the Barons", and his death may be regarded as a sign of the end of feudalism which had been disintegrating during the hundred years since the Black Death and the subsequent economic depression. The great magnates with their warring factions had destroyed one another and the second half of Edward's reign saw their eclipse and the conditions established for the restoration of stable government. Richard III's brief rule brought the final clash at Bosworth Field

[1]See Chapter V of A. L. Rowse, *Tudor Cornwall* (1941).

in 1485. Had he come to the throne in less discreditable circumstances, he might have proved a better king than his brother, but he was fortunately followed by Henry Tudor who, during the twenty-four years of his reign, re-established the monarchy. As a statesman he was perhaps the greatest of his line, but as a personality he was the least attractive. Lambert Simnel and Perkin Warbeck were not serious threats to the throne and Henry's son was able to follow him in security. The executions of pretenders and possible contenders by both Henries removed the few residual dangers to the dynasty.

The English shared with the peoples of other countries a growing sense of nationalism, but, whereas in the others there was a soil favourable to absolute monarchy, in England this was kept in check by the two centuries' tradition of Parliament as an integral part of the State. Not that there was a defined constitutional theory, nor was any attempt made to delimit the areas of authority; it was a growth out of custom. The description of Tudor government as despotic needs qualifying. Henry VIII declared in 1543, "We be informed by our judges that we are at no time so highly in our estate royal as in the time of Parliament".[2] This was not a piece of flattery addressed to the Commons; it was a Tudor recognition of the place of Parliament. Both Edward IV and Henry VII had called seven Parliaments during their reigns. We must not think of these in the same way in which we think of Parliament today. The usual occasion for a summoning was to grant exceptional supplies or meet the needs of war. The people did not clamour for frequent Parliaments; they were expensive gatherings and there was little competition to become a Member. Henry VIII's words were a recognition that the king was not above the law. This belief was derived partly from the feudal system that implied a contract between the overlord and his vassals who claimed the right to be consulted. Chief Justice Fortescue in the fifteenth century declared that "the king of England cannot alter nor change the laws of the realm at his pleasure. For why, he governeth his people by power not only royal but politique", that is constitutionally. There was a second

[2]Holinshed, Chronicles, III, p. 956.

principle that was assumed to underlie the government of the country. Henry of Bracton in the thirteenth century put it in the famous words, "the king is under God and the Law". *Rex est sub Deo et sub lege.* By "law" is not here meant the law of the land only for there was little statute law in those days; it meant the Natural Law, the Law of Reason, the Wisdom of God. It would be absurd to claim that such ideas were formulated in the minds of the mass of the people; yet there was an undoubted sense that the king could not do just what he liked. He was set apart, anointed, and there was a certain aura about him that marked him as chosen by God to rule justly.

> Not all the water in the rough rude sea
> Can wash the balm from an anointed king.[3]

The coronation service emphasized this sanctification, but this did not free him from the obligation, included in the coronation oath, to govern according to law and custom. The duty of the subject was obedience and that was a generally accepted obligation though the long-suffered disputes over the throne had somewhat weakened the sense of duty. It is hard for us to appreciate all that this attitude towards kingship meant, but we must keep it in mind as we study the relations between Sir Thomas More and Henry VIII.

The Tudors were careful to keep within the terms of this unwritten obligation. The crying need for settlement meant that Edward IV and Henry VII had to govern the country in person until more efficient organs of government could be developed. By the time of his death Edward had laid the foundations on which Henry was able to build more securely. This did not mean that they did not make use of councillors, but that there was as yet no regularly constituted council; choice of whom to consult lay with the king and both Edward and Henry were handicapped by a lack of trustworthy noblemen; so it came about that they made more use of bishops and of the lawyers. The country's finances remained in the charge of the royal household and the exchequer. The judiciary, though still subject to royal favour,

[3]Shakespeare, *Richard II*, III, 3, 54-5.

maintained a large degree of independence in the administration of the law; fees were exacted that were often hardly distinguishable from bribes as we should think. The common law survived all changes. The Tudors observed the traditional conventions. Thus Henry VII had his title confirmed by Parliament before he married the daughter of Edward IV; moreover, he obtained from Pope Innocent VIII a Bull recognizing him as King of England, a fact of which his son prematurely boasted to Sir Thomas More.

While the great nobles and their henchmen were engaged in mutual self-slaughter, changes were taking place in the social structure and in economic life. The merchant and the trader were rising in prestige and influence and the lawyer accompanied them. The greater trading towns such as London, Norwich, York and Bristol, took advantage of the disturbed state of the country to play off one contestant against another and so win greater privileges in self-government. London had become almost an *imperium in imperio* with its strongly entrenched government of mayor and alderman, its powerful livery companies and its pre-eminence as a port with a flourishing and vital foreign trade. No king could risk alienating the City; he depended on its wealth for the loans he needed until he had consolidated his position. Edward IV was a firm friend of the merchants—and of their wives! The clothiers and woolmen of the country were growing richer and we can see some of the result of their generosity and fine taste in the churches and houses they built. They were buying up land and inter-marrying their sons and daughters with the long-established aristocratic families. Nor did the younger sons of the nobility scorn to enter trade. Both Edward IV and Henry VII engaged in commerce and their profits contributed to the great fortunes they left behind them.[4] A new kind of landed gentry was forming and from its ranks and from the lawyers were to be drawn increasingly the councillors of the king, the Members of the Commons, and the local justices of the peace. On the countryside itself, the need to raise money for warfare, followed by its

---

[4]It is interesting to speculate how our history might have differed if Henry VIII had had the money-sense of his father and grandfather. With his inherited wealth plus the spoils of the monasteries he could have made himself independent of Parliament.

disastrous effects, forced some magnates to sell land or to rent it instead of cultivating it themselves; so the yeoman as well as the new landowner became more prominent.

At the end of the fifteenth century the Church in England seemed impregnable, and the country had been singularly free from heresy. The Lollardism of the fourteenth century had a brief period of influence and, as an organized body, had been suppressed; a few groups of adherents lingered on but their tenets had deteriorated into garbled expressions of doctrine. They were certainly not the precursors of the Reformation though the soil they had prepared was ready for cultivation. The Catholic faith was firmly established. Side by side with this doctrinal loyalty, there were sound reasons for the growing criticism of the Church as an institution and of some of the clergy for irregular living. Even such a sober observer as Bishop John Fisher could warn his congregation in 1508 to "take heed and call to mind how many vices reign nowadays in Christ's Church, as well in the clergy as in the common people".[5] It is possible to indicate some causes. The Church had become unbalanced. At one extreme was a wealthy hierarchy; at the other an impoverished clergy. Bishoprics increasingly became rewards and provided emoluments for clerics engaged in State affairs; such bishops might be strangers to their sees until they decided to think about the welfare of their souls in their old age. Between the two extremes came those clerics who had been fortunate enough to collect several benefices or lucrative appointments. The non-resident pluralists were content to leave their pastoral duties to ill-paid curates. It was not that the Church temporal was poor; with the monasteries it owned about a fifth of the land and any reasonable system of distribution would have ensured every priest an adequate living. Monastic fervour was on the decline; abbots were more often like landed gentry than fathers of their monks. The cares of their extensive property played too large a part in monastic economy. Convents had shown the same falling away from original ideals and many had become hostels for unmarriageable daughters with no vocation. The friars too had deteriorated and some were little

[5]*English Works* (E.E.T.S.), p. 170.

better than parasites on society, as were the many chantry priests who had no cures of souls, nor even glebes to cultivate. Grave as these defects undoubtedly were, we must keep a sense of proportion. There were numerous priests and monks and friars and nuns who had true vocations and were dedicated to the service of God. Nor should we forget the work done by the Church in education, in hospitals and in the relief of the poor; all this amounted to a considerable benefit to the community, a service that otherwise would not have been done.

It is easy to paint a dark picture of the Church at the end of the fifteenth century for, as is customary in human affairs, abuses and scandals get a more prominent place in the records than sincere devotion and good works. As Sir Thomas More wrote, "For men use if they have an evil turn, to write it in marble: and whoso doth us a good turn, we write it in dust".[6]

Chaucer's pilgrims were a cross-section of fourteenth-century society and could equally be transferred to the fifteenth. Against his over-fastidious prioress with her three chaplains, the hunting monk who had forgotten the Rule of St Benedict, the wanton friar and the bamboozling pardoner, must be set his poor parson, who

> . . . Christ's lore, and his apostles twelve,
> He taught, and first he followed it himself.

We are warned by commentators that this is an ideal portrait, but it is impossible to believe that the Church could have continued to hold men's loyalty at all if such good men were not to be found in all parts of the country; in addition there must have been many who were adequate for their duties and free from scandal. One of the degenerative factors was that there were too many priests without enough work to keep them busy or to maintain them. Out of a population of some three million, there were perhaps 30,000 secular clergy with about the same number of monks, nuns and friars. One serious deficiency was that the standard of education among the clegy was low; there was no regular system of training for the priesthood and some were

[6]*Richard III*, p. 57.

admitted to orders who were not sufficiently instructed to be able to teach their people.

There seems to have been no noticeable decline in outward observances, but it is impossible to assess how far this was an expression of true religion. The ease with which religious changes, now in this direction and now in that, were soon to be accepted suggests a superficial acquiescence rather than a well-grounded belief. Nostalgia for the old ways lingered for a generation or so, but it was a sentiment that gradually faded except for a handful of convinced Catholics who kept the faith alive. The use of English instead of Latin reconciled many to the changes. We should be wary of making wrong deductions from the attention that has been given in recent years to the writings of Richard Rolle and other English mystics of the late Middle Ages. Their influence was very limited and certainly did not reach out to the majority of ordinary folk.

The Venetian who observed in 1497 that "they attend Mass every day and say many Paternosters [the beads] in public—the women carrying long rosaries in their hands" was no doubt basing his report on a limited range of contacts, but he was not inventing. He added, "any who can read take the Office of our Lady with them, and with some companion recite it in church, verse by verse, in a low voice after the manner of churchmen. They always hear Mass every Sunday in their parish church and give liberal alms." We must not assume from this that everyone attended Mass regularly; diocesan records tell of many who through laziness or indifference stayed away. The Venetian could have added the love of pilgrimages to shrines in England, or, for the more venturesome, to Compostela in Spain or to Jerusalem itself. We should be shocked at people's behaviour at Mass and at the familiar way in which they treated their churches. Visitors to Italy today have similar surprises. The church was the hub of the life of the parish. People's knowledge of doctrine may have been small, but that too is a modern characteristic. If the parish priest was a true priest he saw to it that the children learned the paternoster and the creed. He could use simply written explanations provided for him in instructing the grown-ups. Wandering

friars gave sermons of a lively character that must have lingered
in their hearers' memories. Of course superstition crept in as in
every religion, but this was not surprising in an age when even the
educated believed in astrology, demonology and witchcraft.

The complaints and grumblings about the Church that grew in
volume during the century were not against beliefs or forms of
worship. There was, for instance, no demand for an English
Bible outside the small groups of residual Lollards. Attacks were
directed against the temporal powers of the Church that closely
affected men's everyday lives, such as the delays and costs of the
ecclesiastical courts and the local exactions of tithes and fees.[7] The
Church courts could alone grant probate of wills and that could
mean tiresome journeys and the payment of fees and bribes to
several officials. The Church had complete control over marriages.
The Consistory courts dealt with offences against morals, an ill-
defined field, and this too could be a long drawn-out business and
expensive. Here were good grounds for complaints, though some
applied equally to the civil courts. We must try to strike a
balance. The Church courts could protect as well as menace.
Thus they enforced by fines and penances the keeping of workless
Sundays and Feast Days, and though they could achieve little
against turbulent nobles, they held the power of excommunica-
tion, a terrible penalty, over all who transgressed the Canon Law.
Many had cause to be grateful for the protection of the bishop's
court.

Two important privileges brought the Church and the State
into conflict; one was the right of sanctuary, and the other the
benefit of clergy, both of which could lead to abuses. Churches
were places of sanctuary and a criminal or fugitive could gain
protection, or at least a breathing space, by taking shelter in the
nearest one. Sometimes the privilege, as at Westminster Abbey,
covered a considerable area round the church.[8] Rules varied from
place to place but the clergy firmly defended the privilege; it

[7]The Reformation did not do away with the ecclesiastical courts nor with their pro-
tracted and expensive operation.

[8]The name Broad Sanctuary is a reminder of this privilege. There is a discussion by
Buckingham on sanctuaries in More's *Richard III*, pp. 28-33; see also Cardinal Morton's
reference in *Utopia*, p. 81.

could be a genuine act of mercy, but rogues can always find ways of taking advantage of the compassion of others, and there were undoubtedly abuses. Henry VII obtained a Bull from Pope Innocent VIII to restrict the right. The objection was that criminals could evade and thereby weaken the law.

Benefit of clergy was more open to abuse. A cleric accused of any crime more serious than a misdemeanour could claim to be tried by the ecclesiastical courts where he could expect more lenient treatment than in the civil courts. "Cleric" did not mean exclusively priests; it included anyone who had received the tonsure but had not gone further to orders. To prove himself a cleric, the offender had at one period to show his tonsure, and any barber could provide that! Later the test was ability to read; this came to be conventionalized into saying what came to be known as the "neck-verse", the first verse of Psalm 51: "Have mercy on me, O God". An illiterate rogue escaped punishment by learning the words by heart. The stormy dispute between Henry II and Thomas Becket had been partly on this church privilege and subsequent kings had thought it unwise to raise the subject again. Edward IV had even relaxed what few limitations there were. Henry VII, however, was not inclined to tolerate an abuse that operated against law and order, but, as was his manner, he went cannily to work and avoided rousing clerical antagonism; convicted clerks in minor orders were to be burned in the hand, and those who claimed to be deacons or priests had to prove their titles. It was a first step towards reform and was so reasonable that the clergy acquiesced.[9]

Relations with Rome were comfortable during the fourteen century. Over the years Kings and Popes had found working compromises to such problems as appointments to bishoprics and the right of appeal to Rome. Not much money went to Rome as the greater part that was collected either stuck to the fingers of the collectors or found its way into the royal treasury. The Babylonish Captivity of Avignon followed by the Great Schism

[9]Benefit of clergy did not disappear with the Reformation. Thus in 1578, Ben Jonson, the dramatist, successfully pleaded benefit of clergy when arrested after killing a fellow actor. He was burned in the hand. The privilege was not abolished by statute until 1827.

of the fourteenth century did immeasurable harm to the prestige
of the papacy. The lavish splendour of the papal court, the
extravagances of the cardinals and above all the deplorable
morals of some of the Popes made Rome a by-word. The end of
the century was to see the reign of Alexander VI; how could
devout Catholics hold in honour him and his Borgia family?
That Pope died when Thomas More was twenty-five years old.
A further loss of spiritual influence was the development of the
Popes into Italian Princes with political ambitions and warlike
methods inconsistent with their positions as Vicars of Christ.

The fifteenth century saw a marked increase in the number of
schools; the endowment of a new Grammar (Latin) School was
regarded as a public benefaction; bishops and wealthy merchants
were proud to establish schools in their native towns, and local
gilds might also support schools. The part played by the Church
in education had been important but it had been a restricted one;
now the new trading class helped to spread schools through the
land. This largely explains the rapid increase in literacy in that
century; when printed books became available after 1476, they
were eagerly bought because there was a reading public and the
books in their turn encouraged literacy. Thomas More claimed
that in his day more than half the population could read.

Five new colleges were founded at Cambridge during the
century and three at Oxford. These were an indication of a
growing demand for a university education; it is true that only a
small number of the students, who went up at the age of fifteen
or so, completed the course of studies; many were content with
sufficient knowledge to enable them to follow clerical careers and
opportunities for these were increasing. The universities were at a
low ebb intellectually during the century and showed little
enterprise. Individual scholars went to Italy to study Greek or
Canon Law, or medicine; they imbibed something of the spirit
of the Renaissance but they were too few to have much influence
on their return. They formed a small nucleus and slowly they
passed on their fresh knowledge to younger men. There was no
enthusiasm in England for the New Learning.

The increasing importance of the Inns of Court should also be kept in mind in estimating educational opportunities. They came to be regarded, not unjustly, as a third university to Oxford and Cambridge and indeed had a greater prestige until the universities freed themselves from the strait-jacket of the Old Learning. The Inns were of special importance for the training they gave to the country gentry and landowners who were to man the Commissions of the Peace. As in the universities, only a small proportion of the students completed the long course of study. The local Justice of the Peace was to become under the Tudors the key agent in the administration of law in his county, and to him even a smattering of law was helpful especially at a period when litigation might be described as a gentleman's pastime.

So much has been charged against the "overmighty subject" that two deserve to be singled out for their services to learning, though neither was a reputable person. Duke Humphrey of Gloucester (d. 1447) and John Tiptoft, Earl of Worcester (d. 1470), had both been to Italy and had acquired some learning there, and both had a love of books. Duke Humphrey's Library at the Bodleian, Oxford, is that noble's memorial, and Tiptoft also left books to that university. He died a few years before William Caxton brought printing into England in 1476. It has already been noted that increasing literacy had prepared a welcome for the printed book. Among Caxton's patrons were Edward IV and his brother-in-law, Earl Rivers. Caxton's output before his death in 1491 was prodigious; it included religious books such as *The Golden Legend* (1483), English poetry such as Chaucer's *Canterbury Tales* (1478), and romances such as Malory's *Le Morte Darthur* (1485). Many of Caxton's books were his own translations or adaptations and it was in this way, as well as by his prologues and prefaces, that he had an important part in the shaping of modern English. One of the crucial developments of the century had been the establishment of the vernacular language, and, as nearly all books were printed in London, it was southern English that won the day. The full effect of all this could not be seen at the time but with the coming of the sixteenth century it was possible for our language to flower.

The disturbances of the dynastic wars did not stifle the arts.

Surviving wall-paintings, illuminated manuscripts and ecclesiastical embroidery are evidence of taste and skill; it was in architecture, however, that the age was most distinguished. Its notable
buildings range from King's College Chapel at Cambridge to
such parish churches as at Lavenham in Suffolk, to manor houses
as Icomb Place in Gloucestershire as well as to town houses as
Crosby Place in London.

It was an age of extreme contrasts. Wealth was concentrated in
a small section of the community; at the other end was the dire
poverty of the masses; in between came the growing middle-class
of small traders, craftsmen, shopkeepers, clerks and lawyers whose
ambition it was to rise higher in the social scale. Landless peasants
struggled to keep alive while discharged soldiers and other ne'er-
do-wells roamed the countryside. The towns had their throngs of
beggars, hangers-on and vagabonds. They took refuge in hovels
on the outskirts of towns, living in wretched conditions that
added to the prevalent insanitary state which brought the recurrent
plagues that were a scourge wherever people were closely herded
together. The sweating sickness, said to have come in with
Henry Tudor's army, broke out five times between 1485 and
1551 when it disappeared as mysteriously as it had come. There
is no record of the deaths from plague and this sickness, but each
visitation meant that thousands perished. Leprosy was another
curse and leper-spitals were built to segregate the victims; there
were several outside London as at Highgate and St Giles-in-the-
Fields. We are reminded of the religious origins of the hospitals
by the names of St Bartholomew's and St Thomas's in London.
Medical science was still, as we should think, rudimentary and
some of the remedies, such as cautery, seem worse than any
disease. The doctors and physicians were often men of considerable attainments who went to great trouble to learn the best that
was known, going, as some did, to famous medical schools such
as those at Padua and Montpellier. Most people had to rely on
traditional herbal lore and were probably none the worse off for
it; indeed, the "old wives" remedies were often effective. Some,
of course, and by no means only the ignorant, took themselves to
sorcerers and witches.

There are no vital statistics for the fifteenth century; the death rate was certainly appallingly high; perhaps two or three out of every five children died at birth or in infancy. The expectation of life may be indicated by the ages of those kings who died in the course of nature: Henry V, 34; Edward IV, 41; Henry VII, 53. To reach the age of fifty was to be an old man. The constant child-bearing of the women led to the early deaths of many, but those who survived often became the masterful managers of their households with the oversight of all the careful planning and provisioning the times necessitated. Such women were the equals of men. Margaret Paston, for instance, would stand no nonsense.

Life was hard and was held cheap, and there was an insensitiveness to pain, especially to the pains suffered by others. Quarrels that ended fatally were not uncommon. Murders were not rare. Robbery with violence was an everyday affair. People kept their doors bolted and barred at nights. Penalties for discovered crimes were harsh; the gallows with its "fruit" was a familiar sight. For some offences, in addition to heresy, the sentence was death by burning. For minor crimes, the penalty could be the amputation of a hand, or exposure in the pillory and stocks, or a savage flogging at the cart's tail. Such punishments excited no feeling of horror; they were an everyday occurrence. It was in the same spirit of acceptance that a public execution became a public occasion. If the victim showed cowardice, then the onlookers were indeed shocked.

What then of Merry England? Romantic notions fostered during the nineteenth century gave a highly-coloured and false idea of the late Middle Ages. If we could be taken back to those days we should be horrified at some of the commonplace features of the time; the filth and stench of the streets and of many houses would appal us; men's habits were far from refined; they hawked and spat and relieved themselves where they would. Personal cleanliness, as we know it, was rare. Yet there was a Merry England—an England in which vigorous life walked with sudden death. One of Thomas More's favourite words was "merry", but he could also write with grim realism of the Four Last Things.

Here it must suffice to note some of the many things people

enjoyed: strolling entertainers, Punch and Judy shows, running the quintain, dancing, river sports, the Feast of Fools, miracle plays and interludes, hunting, May Day festivities, bull baiting, tennis, dicing, jousts, football, the Lord of Misrule, cock-fighting, the Boy-Bishop, pageants, buffoonery, acrobats and jugglers, music making—a rich catalogue that could be extended. Some of these were the preserve of the nobles and the wealthy, and others were organized by fraternities and gilds. The countryman laboured all the hours of daylight for a pittance but he too had his fun; feast days brought relaxation with a church ale or other junketing, and there was always the chance that a wandering gleeman would find his way to the village.

We must keep in mind that England was a predominantly rural society. Nine-tenths of the population (a total of three million perhaps) lived on the land, many in secluded villages and hamlets with little intercourse with the outside world. The small market town was more typical than the large city. York had a population of some 25,000; Norwich, Bristol and Exeter were, apart from London, the only other cities with more than 5,000 inhabitants.

Thomas More's home was to be in the City of London for over forty-five years; it is as well to recall this as we have come to associate him so closely with Chelsea where he lived for only ten years. In 1500 the population of the City itself was perhaps over 50,000. The "Square Mile", as we sometimes call the City, lay mainly between the river and the old wall with its outer ditch, but London as a unit of government covered a greater area especially to the west (Farringdon Without), going as far as Temple Bar, and to the north-east to take in Smithfield. Part of Cripplegate was "without" the wall, and there was a narrow extension from the Bishops Gate towards Hoxton. Even so, the greater part of the population was concentrated within the walls. While all were justly proud of the main east-west thoroughfare, Cheap, there were innumerable narrow alleys and courts mostly unpaved with filthy "kennels" down each side. Many orders were made from time to time for the cleaning of the streets, for the removal of laystalls and heaps of refuse, and for the preventing of pigs from rooting about, but these orders were more often ignored than obeyed. There was also a law that houses should be roofed with tiles, but thatch was still common and was a constant danger from fire. Most of the houses and shops were of wood and it is surprising that the Great Fire did not come two centuries earlier. London presented the usual extreme contrasts of the Middle Ages; crowded tenements and the hovels built outside the walls to shelter the many poor and indigent folk—that was the seamy side of City living; at the other extreme came the fine mansions of the wealthy merchants. An Italian traveller in the reign of Henry VII could marvel at the riches displayed in Cheap with its "fifty-two goldsmiths' shops, so rich and full . . . that all the shops in Milan, Rome, Venice and Florence put together"[10] could not rival such magnificence. London was pre-eminent as a trading port and the Pool (from the famous Bridge to Cuckold's Point) was always crowded with shipping and the wharves were piled high with the produce of many lands.

Seen from the heights around, London was a city of spires. There were the churches of more than ninety parishes as well as those of fifteen or more religious houses. The remittent ringing of bells was part of the sound of London. Rising over all was St Paul's with its five hundred foot spire.[11] The precincts of the cathedral were then surrounded by a wall and the easiest way from Ludgate to Cheap was through the church itself which became a kind of business exchange for merchants and a place for consultations with lawyers. The Cross[12] with a stone pulpit in the northeast of the enclosure was the most noted place for public sermons. Thomas Carlyle called it, not inaptly, "a kind of *Times Newspaper*, but edited partly by heaven itself".[13] It stood appropriately on the site of the ancient folkmoots. On the north side of the Cathedral were the cloisters on whose walls was painted the Dance of Death, or "Dance of Paul's", showing how old and young, rich and poor, all have to join, willy-nilly, this universal dance.

All this may suggest a town dense with buildings, but there were many gardens and orchards. It is true that the graveyards

[10]*Italian Relation* (Camden, 1847), p. 42.
[11]Burned down in 1561 and not replaced.
[12]The site is marked by a Cross erected in 1910.
[13]*Cromwell*, Intro., p. 50.

gave much of the open space and were a serious cause of infection, but the religious houses and the mansions of the merchants had spacious gardens with trees and even smaller dwellings had their garden plots.[14] Within half an hour a Londoner could walk into the country. Just beyond the wall at the north lay Moor Fields and Finsbury Fields where the citizens could walk and the young disport themselves. Sport too was provided by the unpolluted Thames which was more of a highway to Westminster than Fleet Street and the Strand.

The fact that the Sovereign still halts at Temple Bar for leave to enter the City is evidence of a tradition of jealously-guarded privileges. It was governed by the Mayor and Aldermen and Common Council. As the Aldermen were irremovable, it might have become a self-perpetuating oligarchy, but the Common Council, elected by the freemen of the sixteen Wards, checked any such tendency. The Mayor (it was not until after 1540 that the term "Lord Mayor" became usual) served for one year; he selected one of the two Sheriffs, the other being elected by the Aldermen and Common Council who also chose the Mayor. Under-sheriffs were appointed, not elected. The City was dominated by the twelve great Livery Companies; each had control over the trading activities and workmanship of its members under the supervision of the City. By 1500 the Companies had members who were not practising traders or craftsmen of the named Company. Thus John More and his son after him were members of the Mercers' Company. There were frequent disputes among the Companies and between the less powerful craft gilds; some of these we should call "demarcation" problems. Such disputes were brought before the City and often led to litigation. In addition the City was closely concerned with trade negotiations with other countries. All such matters provided the lawyers with a large field of operation. One special problem was that the German merchants of the Hanse towns had gained privileges, for substantial consideration, from the king. By the

---

[14] Almost the last vestige of London's greenery is the tiny garden of the Drapers' Hall. This was once part of the garden of Thomas Cromwell's house, and may be the piece he filched from John Stow's father. See *Survey* (ed. Kingsford), I, p. 179.

fifteenth century they had established themselves in a walled enclave on the banks of the Thames known as the Steelyard.[15] This was like a sore thumb to the City and there was much ill-feeling against the German and other foreign traders.

We find it hard to project ourselves back into times so different from our own, but, to appreciate Thomas More's life, we must make the effort to see him in the society in which he grew up, matured and worked. The many aspects touched on in this chapter were part of his world and influenced his way of thought. Our problem is to keep in mind the apparently conflicting characteristics of the age. We must avoid the romanticism that sees the later Middle Ages as through a stained-glass window, but we must not go to the other extreme and think of it as a period little removed from the so-called Dark Ages.

One thing we must not forget. The Christian faith, even if but dimly understood and sometimes manifested in what we regard as superstition, lay behind all the diversity and bound men into one society. It gave meaning to their joys and sorrows, their hardships and pleasures, to life and death. Thomas More's story is largely of the breaking up of that one society. Our modern scepticism and indifference were unknown. A man of those days could repeat even on the scaffold, or with the noose round his neck, the words of Everyman in the morality play that was composed when Thomas More was a young man.

> Into thy hands, Lord, my soul I commend;
> Receive it, Lord, that it be not lost;
> As thou boughtest me, so me defend,
> And save me from the fiend's boast,
> That I may appear with that blessed host
> That shall be saved at the day of doom.

[15]Cannon Street station stands on part of the site.

B

CHAPTER II

Boyhood

THE FIRST DATE in Thomas More's life that can be given with certainty is 12 February 1496 when he was admitted to Lincoln's Inn. For the date of his birth we have to choose between 6 or 7 February 1477 or 1478.[1] His father was John More, a lawyer of London, who was born about 1450. He was the son of William More, citizen and baker of London, who had married Johanna the daughter and heiress of John Joye, citizen and brewer of London. Her grandfather on her mother's side was John Leycester, also of London and a Chancery clerk. He died in 1455.[2] The repetition of "London" is to be noted. The Mores and their relatives were all Londoners, and it was in the City that Thomas More had his home for some forty-five years before he moved to Chelsea. In his epitaph he described himself as of a family that was "not illustrious but of honourable standing".[3] It was such families of substance who were the sinews of the City's life.

William More, the baker, died in 1465 leaving his eldest son John, aged sixteen or so, and three other sons and two daughters; only one of the brothers, Christopher, is mentioned in later years. It is not known how well-off the widow was left, but there was property in her mother's family and, though her husband's will does not mention any of his own, it does include the statement that the Earl of Northumberland owed him £87 16s. 2d. "for bread bought of me". Her eldest son, John, was admitted to Lincoln's

[1]For discussion of this problem, see Ap. I. In these pages the year 1478 will be assumed (without prejudice) as that of birth; this will avoid the awkwardness of giving alternative ages.

[2]These facts are based on Dr Margaret Hastings' *The Ancestry of Sir Thomas More* (London Guildhall Miscellany, July 1961). While there are still some outstanding problems, the main conclusions seem established. Here it may be noted that the name More was not uncommon, and John and Thomas were the most popular Christian names, so not every Thomas was our Sir Thomas.

[3]See Epitaph, below, p. 258. Also Harpsfield, pp. 279-281, for original text.

Inn in the Hilary Term of 1475.[4] There is no complete record of
his career. He was counsel to the City in connection with the
management of London Bridge from 1485 to 1517, and this may
be typical of the legal work he did. It was not until 1503, when
he was about fifty, that he was called to the degree of serjeant-at-
law, "the order of the coif". This unusual delay may have been
because his practice was mainly in the City with the Livery
Companies. Yet there are indications that he found a patron in
Edward IV. John More, according to the heralds' records of
Henry VIII's reign, received a grant of arms in the reign of
Edward IV;[5] this would imply a recognition of social status and
the possession of an estate of free tenure. It was from his mother's
grandfather, John Leycester, that he inherited an estate in North
Mimms, Hertfordshire, known as Gobions or More Park.[6] A
second link with Edward IV was probably John Morton, then
Bishop of Ely and Master of the Rolls; only some such association
would explain how John More could later find a place for his
son in Archbishop Morton's household. Finally, in his will,[7] dated
24 February 1527, John More, now Sir John, provided for prayers
for the soul of Edward IV; this was more than forty years after
the death of that king and eighteen after that of Henry VII who is
not mentioned in the will.

Thomas More described his father as "affable, sweet-tempered,
inoffensive, placid, compassionate, just and uncorrupted",[8] an
ideal portrait, but Holbein's drawing of the old judge suggests a
shrewd, kindly and witty man who had come to terms with life.
His son recorded some of his father's sayings. The first refers to
his experience of marriage for he had been widowered three
times and his fourth wife survived both father and son.

I have heard my father merrily say every man is at the choice of his

[4]Two John Mores were admitted on the same day to Lincoln's Inn; the elder of them
had been butler and steward. He has been confused with Thomas More's father.
[5]*Argent a chevron engrailed between two moorcocks sable crested gules.* In Chelsea Old Church
this is quartered with the Colt arms, i.e. *Argent, a fess between three colts courant sable.* The
More crest was a moor's head (*affrontée sable*) with two gold ear-rings.
[6]On the southern boundary of the present Brookman's Park. The name lingers in
Gobions Fish Pond and Gobions Wood.
[7]P.C.C. Jankyn (24).
[8]Epitaph. "Homo civilis, suavis, innocens, mitis, misericors, aequus, et integer."

wife, that ye should put your hand into a blind bag of snakes and eels together, seven snakes for one eel, ye would I ween reckon it a perilous choice to take up one at adventure though you had made your special prayer to speed well.[9]

Another saying on the subject of wives reads:

I would that we were all in case with our own faults, as my father saith we be with our wives. For when he heareth folk blame wives, and say that there be so many of them shrews, he saith that they defame them falsely. For he saith plainly that there is but one shrewd wife in the world, but he saith indeed that every man weeneth he hath her, and that that one is his own.[10]

John More's first wife, the mother of Thomas, was Agnes Granger, the daughter of Thomas Granger, an Alderman who became Sheriff of the City in November 1503, and there is a glimpse of him in Stow's *Chronicle* when he dined at Lambeth Palace with the Mayor and the newly appointed serjeants-at-law, among whom was his son-in-law. The marriage took place on 24 April 1474 in the parish of St Giles without Cripplegate.[11] Their first child, Johanna (Joan), named after her paternal grandmother, was born on 11 March 1475; she was to marry a lawyer, Richard Staverton, who made his career in the City. Thomas, the eldest son, named after his maternal grandfather, was born in the first week of February 1477 or 1478. A second daughter, Agatha, was born on 31 January 1479; she may have died in infancy as nothing more is known of her. The second son, John, was born on 6 June 1480; he seems to have become his brother's secretary or scribe and is last mentioned in 1511.[12] A third son, Edward, perhaps named after Edward IV, was born on 3 September 1481, and, presumably, died young. The last child was Elizabeth, who was born on 22 September 1482; she may have been named after Edward IV's queen; she was to marry John Rastell, a lawyer of Coventry and later printer in London. There are no records of where the More children were christened.

[9]E.W., p. 165.   [10]E.W., p. 233.
[11]The church was rebuilt after a fire in 1545; it survived the Great Fire but not the Great Blitz. Oliver Cromwell was married there in 1620, and John Milton buried there in 1675.
[12]Allen, 246.

The family tradition[13] was that Thomas More was born in Milk Street, a short street that runs up from Cheap to Catte Street (now Gresham Street). A century later John Stow said of Milk Street, "there be many fair houses for wealthy merchants and others".[14] Evidently John More was prosperous enough to live in a good residential quarter. The only church in the street itself was near Cheap, St Mary Magdalen, but as John More wished to be buried in the Lady Chapel of St Lawrence Jewry, near the upper end of Milk Street, that was probably his parish church and it was there that his son was to lecture on St Augustine.

Only conjectural dates and ages can be given for the first eighteen years of Thomas More's life. If the customary practice of the day was followed, he would go to his first school when he was six or seven; before admission he would have learned to read and write. He went to St Anthony's School[15] which was attached to the hospital of that name on the north side of Threadneedle Street. The school was considered among the best in London. John Stow recorded that in his own schooldays (c. 1530) St Anthony's "commonly presented the best scholars"[16] in the annual competition between the London Grammar Schools. More's master may have been Nicholas Holt[17] who had a reputation as a sound scholar. Latin was the main subject of instruction; the boys wrote it and spoke it. They were also taught the rudiments of rhetoric through disputation. It is not known how long the boy remained at St Anthony's; perhaps five or six years.

From school he joined the household of Archbishop (later Cardinal) John Morton at Lambeth Palace. A foreign visitor was shocked at the English custom of sending children away to be brought up in other households. He thought it was to learn better manners—hardly a compliment to their own parents! It was not to learn better manners but the kind of manners needed in mixing

[13]Cresacre More, p. 14.
[14]Survey (ed. Kingsford), I, p. 295.
[15]Roper, p. 5.
[16]Survey, I, 74.
[17]The only authority for this is Stapleton, p. 2. Some doubt has been expressed. See a correspondence in The Times Literary Supplement, Dec. 1953.

with society other than one's own and of a higher standing. Habits of good breeding were important. A second motive, perhaps stronger, was to secure the patronage of an influential man of rank; in those times this was the best way of furthering a young man's career, and as much might depend on his patron as on his own merits. In some households the emphasis would be on field sports and the use of arms. Here it may be noted that there is no hint in his writings that Thomas More had any interest in outdoor activities. In Morton's household the emphasis would probably be on social decorum and a chaplain-tutor would supervise the boys' studies. The experience of living at Lambeth Palace, where the leading ecclesiastics and statesmen would be visitors, was itself an education quite apart from the good talk the boy would hear as he waited at table. This meant that in later life Thomas More could move with ease among men of higher social status. In his *Richard III* he described Morton as "a man of great natural wit, very well learned, and honourable in behaviour lacking in no wise to win favour . . . thus living many days in as much honour as one man might well wish, ended them so godly at his death, with God's mercy, well changed his life".[18] There is probably as much of John More's judgment there as his son's. The tribute in *Utopia* is better known. "In his speech he was polished and pithy. He had a profound knowledge of the law; in wit he was incomparable and he had a remarkable memory. These outstanding natural qualities had been developed by learning and practice."[19] The account that follows in *Utopia* of a discussion at dinner was not the record of an actual occasion, but More would not have chosen such a setting unless serious discussion had not been appropriate. It tells us something of the kind of talk this intelligent boy heard as he went about his duties. According to Roper, the Archbishop once declared, "This child here waiting at table, whosover shall live to see it, will prove a marvellous man".

We are also told that Thomas More would "at Christmas tide suddenly sometimes step in among the players, and never studying

[18]*Richard III*, pp. 90-1.
[19]*Utopia*, p. 59.

for the matter, make a part at his own there presently [immediately] among them, which made the lookers on more sport than all the players beside".[20] Fortunately an interlude or play of this kind has survived. *Fulgens and Lucrece* was "compiled by Master Henry Medwall, late chaplain to the right reverend father in God, John Morton, Cardinal and Archbishop of Canterbury".[21] In this interlude two youths step out from the audience to take part. They are distinguished from the other characters by being named A and B.

> B. Now have I spied a meet office for me
>   For I will be of counsel, an I may,
>   With younder man—
>
> A.   Peace, let be!
>   By God, thou wilt destroy the play.
>
> B. Destroy the play, quotha? nay, nay,
>   The play never began till now.

We do not know the dates of Medwall's chaplaincy but it is conjectured that his play was written about 1500; it was first printed by More's brother-in-law, John Rastell, about 1515. What prompted him to print this interlude? As the dates are uncertain, some speculation is permissible. May there not be here a link with More's revived memories of Lambeth as he wrote *Utopia*? More must have met Medwall when he was visiting his old patron, the Cardinal, and he could have seen *Fulgens and Lucrece* acted at Lambeth one Christmas. He may have suggested that his brother-in-law should print it. The Cardinal died in 1500 and Medwall a few years later.

It was at Morton's suggestion that John More sent his son to Oxford University. It is not known with certainty which college the boy of about fourteen entered. This seems an early age to us, but it was not then unusual. Family tradition said that he went to Canterbury College (now absorbed in Christ Church).[22] Neither Roper nor Harpsfield named the college though the latter was an

[20]Roper, p. 15.
[21]Printed in *Five Pre-Shakespearean Comedies*, ed. F. S. Boas (1934). See also A. W. Reed, *Early Tudor Drama* (1926), pp. 94ff.
[22]Cresacre More, p. 18.

Oxford man. Canterbury College[23] had been established as a house of studies from Christ Church priory, Canterbury; it was thus a Benedictine foundation. The Warden and Fellow were monks. The "poor scholars" were expected to spend five or six years there. Anthony à Wood (1632-95) said that Cresacre More was wrong and that his great-grandfather had been a member of St Mary's, the Austin Canons. There may be a confusion here. Erasmus, as an Austin Canon, stayed at St Mary's when he was at Oxford and his later close friendship with Thomas More may have led to the belief that he too had been there. Harpsfield tells us that More was at Oxford for "not fully two years", too short a period to have a determinative effect on a boy, but, if he was at Canterbury College, he came under Benedictine influence. The College was vigorous, but Oxford had not yet been radically influenced by the new interest in classical studies, especially Greek, that came from Italy. The University was still a centre of scholastic learning just as Paris was at that time. A knowledge of even the elements of Greek was exceptional among Oxford scholars, and its study was not promoted; interest grew as scholars returned from Italy. Greek would not have been part of the *trivium* (grammar, rhetoric, logic and dialectic) that formed the curriculum for the first two years; Thomas More may not have completed this stage.

It should be unnecessary to confute again the notion of the young Oxford scholar being a member of a group intent on pursuing humanistic studies and looking to a reform of the Church,[24] but that this idea has taken root and must be torn up. Thomas More was too young to consort with scholars who were his seniors in age and standing. Some of those usually named were not even at Oxford during his two years. John Colet, by ten years his senior, may have been known to More as the son of a former Mayor of London, but we cannot be certain of his Oxford dates.[25] It seems likely that he left to travel in France and Italy in

[23]For the history of the College, see W. A. Pantin, *Canterbury College* (1947-50). For a brief period the monks shared the fellowships with secular priests; in 1365 the Warden was a secular—John Wycliffe. A later Warden was Edward Bocking, who was condemned with the Nun of Kent.

[24]As so persuasively put in F. Seebohm's *Oxford Reformers* (1867).

[25]See Sears Jayne, *John Colet and Marsilio Ficino* (1963).

1492 and did not return until 1496. Thomas Linacre (b. 1460?) became a Fellow of All Souls in 1484 but left for Italy three years later in the suite of William Selling, Prior of Canterbury. Linacre remained in Italy for several years. William Latimer (b. 1460?) became a Fellow of All Souls in 1489 and, almost immediately, went to Italy with William Grocyn (b. 1446?) of Magdalen, who returned alone to Oxford in 1491 leaving his companion in Italy. Grocyn's godson, William Lily (b. 1468?), who was to be one of More's closest friends in London, was also at Magdalen from 1486 and later journeyed to Jerusalem and Rhodes before spending a few years in Italy to perfect his Greek. A contemporary of More's at Oxford was Cuthbert Tunstal (b. 1474) who was at Balliol for a brief period before going on to Cambridge. Neither More nor Tunstal made any mention, as far as the records go, of having known one another at Oxford. Indeed, More rarely mentioned his Oxford days. In a letter to the University in 1518 he recalled that "it was at your University that my education began". In his bantering talk with his family after his resignation of the Chancellorship, he spoke of the meagreness of Oxford fare.[26] It may be noted that, in his account of More's scholarship, Erasmus, writing in 1519, made no mention of Oxford. The impression is that More's Oxford days were more of an interlude than an important stage in his development.

What was his future career to be? Two courses were open to a scholar who had to earn his living outside the University. He could go into the Church or into the law. It was no doubt John More who made the decision for his young son.

A tentative chronology of these early years is all that can be given.

1485 St Anthony's School
1490 Lambeth Palace
1492 Oxford
1494 London

The year before Thomas More went to Oxford, the Yorkshire

[26]Rogers, 60. Roper, pp. 53-4.
B*

born John Fisher (b. 1469) had taken his M.A. at Cambridge and had been ordained. In 1494 he became Senior Proctor and made his first contact with Henry VII's mother, the Lady Margaret Beaufort, Countess of Richmond and Derby.

CHAPTER III

Vocation

THOMAS MORE entered New Inn to begin his training in the law. This was one of the eight Inns of Chancery that might be called preparatory schools for the four Inns of Court. Little is known of the early histories of the Chancery Inns. They grew up in response to a need for giving a basic training to youths who were not old enough or sufficiently educated to undertake the rigorous courses of study that lay before them. It seems that the curricula of the Chancery Inns were of a general character and included divinity, history, music and dancing. Thomas More remained at the New Inn until he was admitted to Lincoln's Inn on 12 February 1496[1] at the same time as his future brother-in-law, Richard Staverton. At the request of John More, both were excused "four vacations". The exact significance of this is not known as the practice has long been dropped. It was essential that, unless excused, a student should "keep his vacations". Nor is it certain how long the course was. The earliest recorded Calls to the Bar at Lincoln's Inn are dated 1515 when ten members were called. Their periods of training varied from six to eight years.

In some respects the course of studies at the Inns was more exacting than at the two universities. The students lived a communal life with every day mapped out for them. During term time they attended the courts at Westminster to listen to cases. On returning to their Inns, they were questioned on what they had heard and difficulties were discussed. In moots they argued points of law put to them by the Reader and commented on by the Benchers. The Reader also gave lectures expounding the law.

---

[1] At the same period another Thomas More was at the Middle Temple. He has been confused (I plead guilty!) with our Thomas More. The Middle Temple Thomas was a frequent member of the Commission of the Peace for Hampshire (where he lived) from 1502 to 1518. It was he, and not our Thomas, who was appointed to the Commission inquiring into enclosures in Hampshire in May 1517. (Herbrüggen, No. 37A, is here mistaken.)

There were four terms: Hilary (mid-January to mid-February), Easter (a month following Easter), Trinity (June to mid-July), and Michaelmas (end of September to end of November). The Learning Vacations were between the terms except that that between Trinity and Michaelmas was a "mesne" or "dead" vacation without instruction. The Learning Vacations were fully occupied with lectures and moots and what we should call seminars. Allowance should be made for the Greater Feasts of the Church (nearly fifty in the year) which were obligatory holy-days but were not strictly kept except by the devout. Thomas More's "four vacations" would not shorten the number of years of study, but presumably freed him from attendance for those periods.

If it is assumed that he took the shortest period recorded, six years, this would bring him to 1502 before he "was made and accounted a worthy utter-barrister".[2]

Here it will be convenient to give More's later appointments within the legal university. For "three years or more" he was Reader at Furnivall's, one of the Chancery Inns. The dates are not known, but such work would not come until he was within a year or so of his Call, say 1503 to 1506. He was Autumn Reader in his own Inn in 1511; this may indicate the date of his call to the Bench. He was Lent Reader in 1515. Only the more learned lawyers were given the responsibility of directing the students' studies.

Thomas More's interests ranged outside his legal training. He crowded so much into these early years that he must have had exceptional powers of application, a characteristic that was to be shown again in the later period of his controversial writings. His visits to his patron, now Cardinal Morton, brought him the friendship of John Holt[3] who was a Fellow of Magdalen when Thomas More was at Oxford. John Holt was appointed tutor in the household of the Cardinal in 1495, and his teaching experience led him to write an elementary Latin grammar which was first printed in Antwerp just before the Cardinal's death in September

[2]Roper, p. 5. An Utter (Outer) Barrister was at the first stage of his professional practice.
[3]Perhaps the son of Nicholas Holt who may have been headmaster of St Anthony's. See above, p. 21.

1500; the book was dedicated to him; several editions were later printed in London. The title was *Lac puerorum, or mylke for children*,[4] and its interest to us is that it contained the first verses by Thomas More to appear in print. He composed introductory and closing verses in Latin elegiacs. The first are headed, "Thomae Mori adolescentuli diserti Epigramma", and invited the pupils to push open the door that John Holt had unlocked for them as "a first gate to grammar". The closing verses gave a glimpse of the pleasures that lay ahead.

John Holt also received the first extant letter written by Thomas More.[5] This can be dated as it refers to the arrival of Catherine of Aragon in London on 12 November 1501 for her marriage to the heir to the throne, Prince Arthur. The letter ends, "I do hope this much talked-of marriage will prove auspicious for England".

It was shortly after his return to London from Oxford that More had a love affair. The girl was named Elizabeth and she was by two years his junior. Our knowledge of this is given in one of his Latin poems, "Gratulator, quod eam repererit incolumen, quam olim ferme puer amaverat". The date of composition is fixed by the fact that the poem first appeared in the 1520 edition of his *Epigrammata* and not in the 1518 edition. In the poem he states that "five long lustres" have passed since they had first met.

> Many a long year, since first we met, has roll'd:
> I then was boyish, but now am old.
> Scarce had I bid my sixteenth summer hail,
> And two in thine were wanting to the tale;
> When thy soft mien—ah mien for ever fled!—
> On my tranc'd heart its guiltless influence shed. . . .
>
> For one, who knew with what chaste warmth you burn'd,
> Had blabb'd the secret of my love return'd.
> Then the duenna and the guarded door
> Baffled the stars, and bade us meet no more.[6]

Erasmus tells us that, "When he was of age for love, he showed no

---

[4]Gibson, 360.
[5]Rogers, 1 (1).
[6]Translated by Francis Wrangham, 1808.

aversion to women, but he destroyed no one's good name. In fact he was always rather the tempted than the tempter and found more pleasure in the intercourse of mind than of body."[7]

Nothing further is traceable of his early romance when the duenna kept the young law-student at arm's length. He could not have had much time for such dalliance. Indeed, it is difficult to fit all his activities into his time-table. In his letter to John Holt he wrote, "I have laid aside my Latin books to take up the study of Greek", and he went on to say that William Grocyn was his instructor; he had become rector of St Lawrence Jewry in 1496 but he did not move to London until 1500. It may be assumed that he was the Mores' parish priest and this would bring him into touch with Thomas, though there is just the possibility that they had met at Oxford. William Lily also helped the young student. On his return from Italy (the year is uncertain) he settled in London. He had been admitted to minor orders and had received a benefice in Northamptonshire, but he resigned this in 1495 and was afterwards married. Minor orders did not bind to celibacy. He made his living as a tutor in London until he became the first high master of St Paul's School in 1512. Although he may have been ten years older than Thomas More, they became close friends, and, when More had gained some proficiency in Greek, they vied with each other in translating epigrams from the Greek Anthology.[8] A third scholar also helped More in his studies; this was Thomas Linacre who, after taking his doctorate in medicine at Padua, had come to London in 1499. A letter from More to John Colet, which may be dated before 1504, brings his friends together.

> Meanwhile I pass my time with Grocyn, Linacre and our dear friend Lily. The first, as you know, is the sole director of my life during your absence; the second my master in letters, and the third the beloved confidant of all my affairs.[9]

Here it may be noted that Thomas More's friends were nearly all senior to him in age, several of them, such as Erasmus, Colet and

[7] Allen, 999.
[8] See below, p. 132.
[9] Rogers, 3 (2).

Fisher by ten years. A fellow student named Arnold flits across the scene and is gone. This suggests an early maturity of mind.

John More was worried by his son's new-found enthusiasm for Greek and other non-legal subjects. Erasmus tells us:

> As a young man he applied himself to the study of Greek literature and philosophy; this distressed his father, who, though otherwise an upright and clear-headed man, decided to check these studies by cutting down his son's allowance; in fact, More was all but disowned for apparently deserting his father's profession.

Erasmus may have been exaggerating, but we need not accept his view and regard this as the action of a heavy-handed and obtuse father. John More knew the importance to his son's career of a thorough knowledge of law and neither he, nor anyone else at that time, could have realized Thomas More's intellectual powers. His progress at Lincoln's Inn and the responsible work he was given by the Benchers showed that he was able to master both the law and other subjects at the same time.

His studies were not seriously affected. The appointment of his son as Reader at Furnivall's Inn must have satisfied John More that all was well. This was perhaps about 1503, but the chronology is uncertain as Roper, in default of Lincoln's Inn records our only informant, is vague in his statements. He was writing many years later. Our difficulty is that there is so much to be packed into a few years. In writing to John Holt in 1501, More mentioned the lectures being given at St Paul's by William Grocyn on *De Ecclesiastica Hierarchia* attributed to Dionysius the Areopagite; Grocyn demonstrated that the work could not have been by Dionysius.[10] More gives an amusing account of the audience: "a group of students, whose numbers, unfortunately, are greater than their learning, but it also includes a large number of educated people".[11] Later on, Grocyn invited More to give readings on St Augustine's *De Civitate Dei*; the lectures, according to Stapleton,[12] dealt with the historical and philosophical, rather than the theo-

---

[10]This opinion had already been advanced by Lorenzo Valla (d. 1457), the Roman but not very Christian humanist; his work had not yet been published.

[11]Rogers, 1 (1).

[12]Stapleton, p. 7.

logical, aspects of that great work. It was probably Grocyn who
also encouraged More in this study for we are told that in Grocyn's
library the works of St Augustine were "lavishly represented".[13]
More continued his study of the Early Fathers but St Austin (to
use the popular form) remained his mainstay with St Jerome as a
near favourite. How far he progressed in the study of theology
can only be assessed by occasional references. Stapleton (writing
in 1588) noted that More had closely read the works of St
Thomas Aquinas and he added the following testimony from
John Harris, More's secretary in his later years. While the two of
them were going down the Thames from Chelsea one day, More
was reading a new controversial pamphlet; his comment was:

> The arguments which this villain has set forth are the objections
> which St Thomas puts to himself in such and such a question and
> article of the Secunda Secundae, but the rogue keeps back the good
> Doctor's solutions.[14]

It is interesting to note that More's admiration of Aquinas was not
shared by John Colet who even went so far as to say that Aquinas
had "corrupted the whole teaching of Christ by mixing it with his
profane philosophy". Indeed, on this point he and Erasmus all
but quarrelled, for although Erasmus had little use for scholasticism
in its later phases, a view he had in common with More, he praised
Aquinas's "thoroughness, soundness of mind, and solid erudition".

Most of More's study of the Early Fathers lay in the future, but
the foundations were laid under the guidance of William Grocyn.

Roper tells us that after More's "three years or more" as a
Reader at Furnivall's Inn, "he gave himself to devotion and
prayer in the Charterhouse of London, religiously living there
without vow, four years".[15] The earliest date for the end of the
Readership would be 1505; by then More was married. We are
in a chronological impasse. Cresacre More recorded the family
tradition that More, during the period to which Roper refers, was
"dwelling near the Charterhouse, frequenting their spiritual

[13]D.N.B.
[14]Stapleton, p. 35.
[15]Roper, p. 6.

exercises".[16] This suggests a possible way out of the difficulty. May it not have been that for several years he shared in the devotional life of the monks whenever his leisure allowed him? As a Reader he would have more time than as a law student, and there were also the holy-days and the vacations. Even so, it is not easy to fit in his Greek and Augustine studies in addition to his work as a lawyer, and he could not have afforded to marry in 1505 unless he had already built up a sound practice. I think we must regard Roper's statement as a misunderstanding of some confused information; it seems unlikely that Thomas More would have talked with a young man such as Roper about this very personal experience. Stapleton makes things more complicated by writing, "He debated with himself and his friend Lily the question of becoming a priest. For the religious state he had an ardent desire, and thought for a time of becoming a Franciscan."[17] Stapleton does not mention the Charterhouse. Here perhaps we can see again a reflection of a confused and vague recollection of something heard. Erasmus tells us of the period at which More was giving his lectures on St Augustine.

> At the same time with all his powers he turned towards the religious life by watching, fasting, prayer, and similar tests, preparing himself for the priesthood; more wisely than the many who rush blindly into that arduous calling without first making trial of themselves. And he had almost embraced this ministry, but, as he found he could not overcome his desire for a wife, he decided to be a faithful husband rather than an unfaithful priest.[18]

This testimony from Erasmus is important and carries more weight than Roper's much later statement. As we shall see, the friendship between More and Erasmus was of the most intimate and was sealed by the many hours they spent together at More's home and elsewhere. To no one does More appear to have revealed his inmost thoughts more fully than to this older friend who was himself a priest. Erasmus published his account in 1519

[16]Cresacre More, p. 25.

[17]Stapleton, p. 8. This has been interpreted as meaning that both More and Lily were considering their vocations to the priesthood, but Lily was married about 1496.

[18]Allen, 999. Margaret Paston on her son's future wrote, "I will love him better to be a good secular man, than to be a lewd priest." 18 Jan. 1473.

and, as far as is known, More took no exception to what his friend wrote. Roper was recording nearly forty years later what he had had heard of something that happened when he was a child. I think it best to accept Erasmus' version without trying to particularize the form of More's testing of his vocation. The important fact is that Thomas More was drawn to the religious or priestly life but, after testing his vocation, decided that he was called to the world.

He himself left no account of this spiritual trial. He was reticent about his inner life, but, in a letter to John Colet, which may have been written in 1503,[19] he said, "By following your footsteps I had escaped almost the very gates of hell, and, now, driven by some secret but irresistible force, I am falling back again into gruesome darkness". He is using the somewhat rhetorical language of a youngish man, but we get here a hint of the spiritual anguish he suffered out of which Colet had rescued him. Perhaps it was Colet who brought his young friend to see that he was not intended for the religious life.

The first meeting of More and Erasmus became the matter of legend. In one form the story was that when Lord Chancellor More was dining at Guildhall, a stranger asked to speak to him. After some conversation, the stranger, who was Erasmus, declared, "Aut tu es Morus aut nullus" (You are More or no one). To this More replied, "Et tu es Deus aut daemon aut meus Erasmus" (Either you are God or the devil or my Erasmus). Another version describes how they met at a meal as strangers and got on to the subject of the Real Presence; this led to a similar exchange of exclamations. The Elizabethan authors of *The Booke of Sir Thomas More* set the meeting in More's house at Chelsea when he was Lord Chancellor. To test

> . . . if great Erasmus can distinguish
> Merit and out ward ceremony[20]

More arranges for a servant to play the part of the Lord Chancellor

[19]Rogers, 3 (2). The date 23 Oct. 1504 is there suggested, but I think it should come earlier, 1503 or even 1502; it suggests that More had not yet made his great decision, and he was married at the end of 1504 or, at latest, at the beginning of 1505.
[20]Act III, 2.

when the Earl of Surrey brings Erasmus to be introduced. The
servant bungles his role and the deception is uncovered. In the
margin of the manuscript are written the words, "et tu Erasmus
an Diabolus".

The circumstances of these folk-tales are wide of the truth, but
they are evidence of the place held in common repute by both
More and Erasmus. They first met in 1499, thirty years before
More became Lord Chancellor and twenty-five years before he
left the City for Chelsea. Neither of them was well known, still
less famous, at the time of that meeting; More was then just over
twenty years of age and Erasmus was his senior by some ten
years.

Erasmus had come to England as the guest of his pupil Lord
Mountjoy who was to prove his life-long patron. Mountjoy
took him to stay at Bedwell, a manor in Hertfordshire belonging
to Sir William Say whose daughter Mountjoy may already have
married. Later they moved to Sir William's house near Deptford.[21]
He knew the Mores sufficiently well for the father and son to
become trustees of his property in 1515. The opening sentence of
the account Erasmus wrote in 1523 of an incident in their early
association suggests that they were already on intimate terms.
"Thomas More," he wrote, "who, while I was staying in the
country house of Mountjoy, had paid me a visit, took me to a
neighbouring village."[22] This was Eltham, Kent, and, to the
surprise of Erasmus, the purpose of their walk was to pay their
respects to the children of Henry VII at the palace that had been
built by Edward IV. We may note that More had the entrée to
the royal palace; this was doubtless due to his connection earlier
with Cardinal Morton. Prince Arthur was not at Eltham but
they were presented to his brother, Henry, Duke of York, who
was then eight years old. Mountjoy was in attendance as he was
studying history with the child Prince whose schoolmaster, John
Skelton, Poet Laureate, would also be there. Erasmus was put
out at not having been warned that he was going to meet the

[21]Sayes Court; it became the home of John Evelyn in the seventeenth century.
[22]Allen, Vol. I, p. 6. More may have been staying with the Ropers at their country
house at Well Hall, Eltham, only a mile from the palace and four miles from Sayes Court.

Duke as it was customary on such an occasion to present a complimentary set of verses; the Duke himself pointed this out with all the assurance of his eight years! As soon as he could, Erasmus composed his *De Laudibus Britanniae*, a conventional production that served its turn. In it he took the opportunity to praise "Stelkon", as he named him, as "that incomparable light and ornament of British Letters". As Erasmus could not read English, this was an empty compliment, but Skelton was proud to recall it in later years.

It is not extravagant to say that the meeting of More and Erasmus was a case of love at first sight. In a letter from Oxford a few months later, Erasmus could call his new friend, "the best-natured of men, and one who, I am persuaded, has no little love for me". It was not a friendship that could have been predicted for there were considerable differences in their circumstances.

Erasmus was illegitimate and was born in Rotterdam about 1469.[23] He was orphaned in boyhood and his guardians persuaded him to enter the Augustinian monastery (Austin Canons) at Steyn, Gouda. He was ordained priest in 1492. He found communal life irksome; this gives point to his warning, just quoted, against hasty acceptance of the religious life. At school under the Brethren of the Common Life and at his monastery he laid the foundations of his wide learning but without more than a smattering of Greek. He longed to go to Italy but could not get the necessary funds, so he went to Paris for his further studies and it was there that he met Mountjoy. He seems then to have resolved at all costs to preserve his independence and not to return to Steyn.

By contrast, Thomas More belonged to an established family with all the sense of security that went with it and he had an assured future. Erasmus' future, unless he returned to his monastic life for which he admittedly had no vocation, depended on the uncertain support of patrons. Yet, in spite of these differences, the two formed a friendship that was to last as long as they both lived

[23]One romantic version of his parentage is the basis of Charles Reade's *Cloister and the Hearth* (1861). Erasmus may not himself have known the full details; it is not the kind of information parents give to their children; hence the variations in his accounts of his birth. The year is disputed, ranging from 1466 to 1469.

—a friendship without a shadow of disagreement. The initial attraction may have been the younger man's facility in Latin (did he act as Erasmus' interpreter at times?), his wide reading and his quickness of intellect. They shared a ready sense of humour and a lively appreciation of the ridiculous and a dislike of cant and humbug.[24]

---

[24]It will be useful here to give the dates of Erasmus' visits to England. May 1499-Jan. 1500 (Oct.-Dec., at Oxford); April 1505- June 1506; July 1509-April 1511 (London, etc.); Aug. 1511-Jan. 1514 (Cambridge); May 1515; June 1516; Aug. 1516; April 1517.

CHAPTER IV

"*Picus*"

THOMAS MORE put himself to school with four scholars who were his seniors in age: Grocyn by nearly forty years, Linacre by some fifteen, and Colet and Lily by about ten. Each of them had studied in Italy. We cannot say when their closer association began. They were all in London from about 1503. Grocyn left in 1506 for his living at Maidstone where he died in 1519 shortly after the death of Colet. Linacre was appointed a royal physician in 1509. It was therefore with Colet and Lily that More enjoyed the longest period of personal relations, and it was William Lily who became his great friend but, without doubt, it was John Colet who had the greatest influence over him at his most formative period. The arrival of Erasmus in 1499 was the beginning of a notable friendship but it did not mature until his return in 1505 and from then onwards it developed into a fertile contact of mind and spirit.

This small circle of friends was not consciously intent on the revival of classical studies in England nor on a reformation of the Church. Colet, it may be noted, was not an enthusiast for the new learning but he was something of a prophet in his call for the reform of clerical shortcomings. Three of those who had been in Italy—Grocyn, Linacre and Lily—had gained a mastery of Greek and it was with the study of Greek that they inspired their young friend. Neither they nor Colet were tainted with the neo-paganism that had disfigured the classical revival in Italy.

John Colet stands somewhat apart from the others. He did not study Greek in Italy but theology and philosophy. He left England in 1492, as Erasmus wrote, "like a merchant seeking goodly wares . . . and devoted himself to the study of the sacred writers". Unfortunately hardly anything is known of his stay in Italy and France.[1] He seems to have been chiefly influenced by the

[1]The standard biography is still that of J. H. Lupton (1887), who also translated several volumes of Colet's lectures and notes. Our knowledge has been increased by Sears Jayne, *Colet and Marsilio Ficino* (1963).

writings of Marsilio Ficino of Florence, the translator of Plato, though the two did not apparently meet. The writings of Pico della Mirandola were also part of Colet's reading. When he returned to Oxford in 1496, he gave lectures on the Epistles of St Paul; in these he showed how much he had profited during his absence abroad by new ways of studying the Scriptures. He was a discriminating reader for he rejected ideas that verged on the unorthodox in religion and adopted those that could help to elucidate Christian doctrine. One feature of his lectures was the emphasis he placed on historical and grammatical factors. To us his digressions are more interesting than his exegesis and they revealed the moralist that was stronger in him than the scholar; thus he denounced the litigious habits of the clergy and their over-eagerness to exact their tithes and to collect benefices. His Platonism he owed to a study of Ficino's Latin translation and his *Theologia Platonica*. This liking for Plato was passed on to Thomas More in spite of Grocyn's more traditional preference for Aristotle. "I think", he once wrote, "the difference between these great philosophers Aristotle and Plato is simply between a man of science and a man of myths."[2]

We have seen that Colet was not a disciple of St Thomas Aquinas. He was equally scornful of the Franciscan Duns Scotus and to all "quibbling with terms"; but his own treatment of Scripture may have owed something to that other Franciscan, William of Ockham, one of those scholars who had made the Oxford of the twelfth and thirteenth centuries a centre of en-lightened scholarship, but this earlier revival of learning was soon stifled by ecclesiastical censure.

Colet was suspicious of the influence of the great classical writers such as Cicero; it may be that he had witnessed in Rome some of the excesses of the neo-pagans. His own Latin was not of classical standard, much to the regret of Erasmus. In this he again showed not only his independence of judgment and his devotion to orthodox teaching, but his difference from the accepted con-ception of a humanist.

[2]Oxford Historical Society, *Collectanea*, II, p. 319.

The short visit of Erasmus to Oxford at the end of 1499 proved a turning-point in his life. This was due to John Colet. Hitherto Erasmus' delight in pure scholarship had lacked a clear purpose. He thought of himself as a man of letters or a poet, and he was shaken from this position when Colet reproached him for arguing for the sake of argument like a rhetorician taking any side for the fun of it. After Oxford, Erasmus became a scholar with a mission. He stayed at St Mary's, a house of his own Order, where Prior Charnock was a man of culture and a friend of learning. It may have been as a result of meeting Erasmus that Prior Charnock soon afterwards went to Italy. Erasmus attended Colet's lectures which were, of course, in Latin, and was at once captured by the earnestness and originality of the lecturer who was so unlike those by whom he had been bored in Paris. He had unconsciously been prepared for this break with tradition by his own training under the Brethren of the Common Life at Deventer and 's-Hertogenbosch and by the all-pervading influence in the Low Countries of the *devotio moderna* of which the *Imitatio Christi* of Thomas à Kempis was the fine flower. It is possible to draw many parallels between that spiritual classic and the writings of Erasmus. The mark of the *devotio moderna* was its emphasis on personal sanctification through disciplined training in prayer and meditation and the study of the New Testament. Its followers did not put the customary value on popular devotions, pilgrimages and the veneration of relics, nor were they interested in the institutional side of the Church.[3] There was no sign of this spirit in the University of Paris when Erasmus studied theology there, and it must have come as a happy surprise to find that John Colet had moved away from the established dry teaching. The two soon formed a close friendship and Colet tried to persuade Erasmus to remain at Oxford to lecture on the Old Testament or on some secular subject. Erasmus replied, "I know well how imperfectly I am equipped for such a task, nor do I lay claim to sufficient learning to justify my undertaking it".[4] Colet did not capture Erasmus for Oxford, but he achieved something that was

[3]For an adverse view, see Philip Hughes, *The Reformation in England*, I, p. 101.
[4]Allen, 108.

far more fruitful. Erasmus could now focus his mind on the study of the New Testament and for this he saw the need for a thorough knowledge of Greek. As he still lacked the means to get to Italy, he returned to Paris and, for several years, devoted himself to study in conditions that were at times little short of penury. Just before he left England, he wrote to a former pupil, Robert Fisher:[5]

> I have found here a climate as delightful as it is wholesome, and so much learned culture, not of the out-of-date, superficial sort, but both deep and accurate in Latin and Greek, that I now hardly regret not having seen Italy. Listening to my friend Colet is like listening to Plato. Who would not marvel at Grocyn's wide range of knowledge? What could be more searching, profound or refined than Linacre's judgement? Has nature ever fashioned a character more gentle, endearing or happier than Thomas More's?[6]

Erasmus took a roseate view of English scholarship, and of English weather, during his first short visit. The omission of Lily's name suggests that they had not yet met. Yet, how many names could he have added to his list? Cuthbert Tunstal would be one of them but he does not seem to have been much in London until 1511. It was a younger generation that was to carry forward the new learning, a movement to which Erasmus was to contribute. Nor does he seem yet to have met three patrons of learning who were not themselves classical scholars in the humanist sense but who had a true sense of the value of the new emphasis on the classics. William Warham, who became Archbishop of Canterbury in 1503 and Lord Chancellor in 1504, had been in Rome in 1490 on ecclesiastical affairs but had not studied there; he numbered Thomas More among his younger friends; thus the old association with Lambeth Palace was resumed. Warham was to prove Erasmus' constant patron. John Fisher was Master of Michaelhouse in 1497 and took his D.D. in 1501 when he was already closely concerned with the Lady Margaret Beaufort, Henry VII's mother,

[5] After leaving Paris he studied in Italy for seven years. He has been described as a cousin or relative of Bishop John Fisher, but there is no clear evidence of this.

[6] Allen, 118. It is interesting to compare this list with one in a dedicatory letter from Johan Froben, the Basle printer, to More in Nov. 1518: Colet, Linacre, Grocyn, Latimer, Tunstal, Pace, Croke and Sixtin. The last four were of More's own generation. Rogers, 67.

in promoting the study of divinity. It is doubtful if he knew Thomas More at this period. He became Bishop of Rochester and Chancellor of Cambridge in 1504. He had not been to Italy nor did he know Greek. With the third future patron, Richard Fox, then Bishop of Durham and later of Winchester, the link would be Richard Whitford who had accompanied Lord Mountjoy to Paris in 1496 as his tutor; Erasmus was to know them both well at that time. Whitford became chaplain to Bishop Fox but the date is not known; it may have been about 1500. The Bishop was a leading counsellor of Henry VII and was away in Scotland on a diplomatic mission in the latter part of 1499. Fox was to be the founder of Corpus Christi College, Oxford, in 1515; among the provisions was a Greek lectureship. It was probably during his second visit to England in 1505 that Erasmus gained the friendship of these three patrons.

There are indications that John Colet was active at St Paul's for a year or so before he became Dean.[7] His predecessor, Robert Shirburn, was busied with state affairs, being absent in Rome in 1502, Scotland in 1503, and Rome again in 1504. Colet may have acted as Dean-designate until Shirburn was prepared to forgo the emoluments in 1505. One of the indications of Colet's influence was the revival of preaching at St Paul's. Colet bore the expenses of sermons and lectures by the Carmelite, John Sowle, and by a learned divine, John Major. It is evident too that before he was officially Dean Colet was delivering those "powerful sermons" to which Thomas More referred in his letter. We have already noted the part, perhaps the decisive part, that Colet played in determining More's vocation. Their close association covered twenty years and was to include Colet's call for the correction of abuses in the Church, as well as his foundation of St Paul's School. To these topics we must return in later pages.

It may have been Colet who first drew More's attention to the life of Pico della Mirandola, the young Italian Christian humanist whose death, while Colet was in Italy, caused wide grief. Colet would have seen the similarities between the problems Pico had

---

[7]When Colet resigned the prebend of Goodeaster on 26 Jan. 1504, Thomas More was one of the witnesses.

to face and those confronting More. Pico's nephew had published his uncle's works in 1496 and added a short biography to the next edition of 1498; this was the edition More used. It may have come into Colet's hands, or have been brought back by Linacre on his return from Italy.

Pico della Mirandola (1463-1494) had studied in the leading universities of Italy and at Paris before settling in Florence where he came under the influence of Ficino and later of Savonarola. He learned Hebrew as well as Greek. His inquiring mind led him to study the Cabbala—the mystical system of theology and metaphysics said to have been handed down from Moses to the Jews. Pico wished to reconcile Plato with Aristotle and both with Christian doctrine; this attempted syncretism produced in him a deepened Christian faith and a desire to attain personal sanctity. An extract from a letter by Lorenzo de' Medici to Lanfredini, dated 14 June 1489, shows us the characteristics of Pico that must have appealed to Thomas More:

> The Earl of Mirandola has taken up his residence here [Florence], and lives as devoutly as if he were a monk. He has written, and continues to write, theological works of great value; he comments on the Psalms, says the office regularly, fasts and is continent. He lives very simply and expects only the minimum of service. He seems to me a model for everyone.

Of himself, Pico wrote, "I prefer my own room, my studies, the pleasure I get from books, and the peace of my soul, to the palaces of princes, public affairs, hunting, and the favours of the Roman Curia". Such a brief notice can do little more than suggest why Thomas More was fascinated by Pico; to us the Italian seems a remote historical personage of minor interest, but to More he was a contemporary, living in the same religious and intellectual atmosphere and excited by the opening up of fresh paths by the new learning.

Stapleton said that More "determined, therefore, to put before his eyes the example of some prominent layman, on which he could model his life".[8] Cresacre More elaborated this by adding,

[8]Stapleton, p. 9.

"when he determined to marry . . .",[9] but that was an unwarranted gloss. Pico, to quote More, "appointed to profess himself in the order of Friars Preachers [Dominicans]". One would have thought that a study of Pico's life would have strengthened and not weakened a desire for the cloister. Nor would it seem appropriate that, with marriage in mind, More should have addressed his book to a nun or one who was about to take vows. In his letter to Joyeuce Leigh he gave as reason for his labours the example set by Pico of "temperance in adversity", and his belief that Pico's works "be such that for the goodly matter (howsoever they be translated) may delight and please any person that hath any mean [moderate] desire and love to God".

Joyeuce Leigh, or Lee, and her brother Edward (the future Archbishop of York) were the grandchildren of a Lord Mayor of London and they seem to have been playmates of the young Mores. She became a Poor Clare of the House of Minoresses in Aldgate,[10] and More's words "his right entirely beloved sister in Christ" suggest that she was already a nun, and we may see a hint here that he had still not come to a final decision and that he might follow her example and dedicate himself to God.

The *Lyfe of Johan Picus*[11] was first printed by More's brother-in-law, John Rastell, before 1510. The little book must have proved popular for a pirated edition was brought out in 1510 by Wynkyn de Worde.

More did not make an exact translation of the biography of Pico; he left out parts he considered would be of small interest to the general reader, and, for examples of the writings of Picus, he selected three letters, and an interpretation of the Psalm "Conserva me Domine" (Vulgate, 15). To these he added verse translations or adaptations of "Twelve Rules partly exciting, partly directing a man in spiritual battle" and a prayer composed by Picus. He himself wrote original verses on "The Twelve weapons of spiritual battle", with his own caption, "The Twelve

[9]Cresacre More, p. 27.

[10]The Minories, near the Tower of London, preserves the name. When the House was surrendered in 1539, it was worth £418 a year. Twenty-seven of the nuns, perhaps including Joyeuce Leigh, died in the plague of 1515.

[11]Gibson, 67, 68.

Weapons have we more at length declared as followeth". The play on his own name may be noted.

The opening paragraph is not from the original biography and part of it will serve as a specimen of More's early prose. He dismisses the need for giving an account of the noble ancestry of Picus on the grounds that "his learning and his virtues" were more important. He goes on:

For these be the things which we may account for our own, of which every man is more properly to be commended than of the nobleness of his ancestors, whose honour maketh us not honourable. For either they were virtuous or not; if not, then had they none honour themselves, had they never so great possessions: for honour is the reward of virtue. And how may they claim the reward that properly belongeth to virtue, if they lack the virtue that the reward belongeth to? Then, if themselves had none honour, how might they leave to their heirs that thing which they had not themselves? On the other side, if they be virtuous and so, consequently, honourable, yet may they not leave their honour to us as inheritants, no more than the virtue that themselves were honourable for. For never the more noble be we for their nobleness, if ourselves lack those things for which they were noble. But rather the more worshipful that our ancestors were, the more vile and shameful be we, if we decline from the steps of their worshipful living, the clear beauty of whose virtue maketh the dark spot of our vice the more evidently to appear and to be more marked.

Thomas More's own verses in this book need not detain us here as they can more suitably be considered in the next chapter with his other early poetry.

When was the book written? There is no clear indication in the text. It has been noted that he used the 1498 edition, so the volume may have been in his hands by the following year. The dates 1504-5 have been suggested, but, for the considerations stated above, it could be put somewhat earlier, perhaps soon after 1500, especially as the book does not tend towards marriage but to the life of the cloister.[12]

[12]There is a good introduction to J. M. Rigg's edition of 1890. Walter Pater's essay in *The Renaissance* (1875) is well known. See also L. Gautier Vignal, *Pic de Mirandole* (Paris, 1937).

CHAPTER V

Early Verses

THE 1557 FOLIO of the *English Works* opens with sixteen un-numbered pages of verses. It would seem that these did not come into William Rastell's hands until the main text had been set up, so he put them before the first numbered page. They are headed: "These four things here following Master Thomas More wrote in his youth for his pastime". They are: "A merry jest how a sergeant would learn to play the friar", nine rhymes for tapestries in his father's house, "a rueful lamentation of the death of Queen Elizabeth", and, lastly, verses for the Book of Fortune. The last two were copied by Richard Hill, a contemporary of More's, in his Commonplace-book.[1]

The "Merry Jest" was the only one of these rhymes to be published during More's lifetime; Julian Notary of the sign of St Mark in Paul's Churchyard brought it out in 1516.[2] It has been suggested that the poem was made for the feast at Lambeth Palace on 13 November 1503 for the newly-made sergeants-at-law of whom John More was one.[3] The theme is that every man should stick to his own trade. This is illustrated by the tale of a sergeant (not at-law, but in the office of a constable) who was ordered by the mayor to arrest a bankrupt merchant who stayed indoors and refused to admit any callers. The sergeant dressed himself as a friar, and in this charitable guise, was allowed to offer spiritual comfort to the self-imprisoned merchant. The sergeant then threw off his disguise and tried to drag the merchant off to the Counter [prison]. A struggle followed that is described with much gusto.

> They rent and tere,
> Eche others here,
> And clave togyder fast,

[1] *Songs, Carols*, etc. (E.E.T.S., 1907). Balliol MS., 354.
[2] Gibson, 69.
[3] See above, p. 19.

> Tyll with luggyng,
> And with tuggyng,
> They fell downe bothe at last,
> Than on the grounde,
> Togyder rounde,
> With many a sadde stroke,
> They roll and rumble,
> They turne and tumble,
> As pygges do in a poke.

The wife and the servant-girl join in, the first using her distaff and the second the battledore with which she pounded the washing. They got the counterfeit friar down, and then,

> Up they hym lift,
> And with yll thrift,
> Hedlyng a long the stayre,
> Downe they hym threwe,
> And sayd adewe
> Commaunde us to the mayre.

So to the moral and a welcome to the guests at the feast.

> Now make good chere,
> And welcome every chone.

Good, knock-about stuff, written with great spirit.

The verses composed for the tapestries in Sir John More's house are written in Chaucer's seven-line stanza; this was favoured by More and was used frequently by him. The first will serve as a specimen.

CHYLDHOD

> I am called Chyldhod, in play is all my mynde,
> To cast a coyte, a cokestele,[4] and a ball.
> A toppe can I set, and dryve it in his kynde.
> But would to god these hatefull bookes all,
> Were in a fyre brent to pouder small.
> Than myght I lede my lyfe alwayes in play:
> Which lyfe god sende me to myne endyng day.

Thomas More's most considerable poem was his "Rueful lamentation of the death of Queen Elizabeth, mother to King

---

[4]coyte = quoit; cokstele = short stick for cockshying.

Henry the Eighth, wife to King Henry the Seventh, and eldest daughter to King Edward the Fourth". She died on her thirty-eighth birthday, 11 February 1503. If the title is More's and not his nephew's, the poem was not written until after the death of Henry VII in April 1509. In the poem she is imagined as speaking from her death-bed, and her thoughts turn to her husband, to her dead son, Arthur, to her younger son, Henry and to others of the family. She recalls the King's new buildings at Richmond and Westminster.

> Where are our Castels, now where are our Towers,
> Goodly Rychmonde[5] sone art thou gone from me,
> At Westminster that costly worke of yours,
> Myne owne dere lorde now shall I never see.
> Almighty god vouchsafe to graunt that ye,
> For you and your children well may edefy.
> My palyce bylded is, and lo now here I ly.

> Adew myne owne dere spouse my worthy lorde,
> The faithful love, that dyd us both combyne,
> In mariage and peasable concorde,
> Into your handes here I cleane resyne,
> To be bestowed uppon your children and myne,
> Erst wer you father, & now must ye supply,
> The mothers part also, for lo now here I ly.

The fourth "thing" was printed in 1540 by Robert Wyer in a book entitled, *The Boke of the feyre Gentywoman, that no man shulde put his truste, or confidence in: that is to say, Lady Fortune.*[6] Thomas More's name was not on the title-page; it would have been unwise at that date to give it. Only one copy of this edition has survived the constant thumbing every copy probably received from the devotees of Fortune. This copy contains More's verses, "The words of Fortune to the people" but not the other verses given in the 1557 folio. It was part of an elaborate fortune-telling device by which, after a throw of dice, the seeker tracked

[5]Shene Palace, where Edward III died, was rebuilt after a fire in 1499 by Henry VII, who renamed it Richmond after his earlier title. He himself died there, as did his grand-daughter, Queen Elizabeth I. Only a gateway remains near Richmond Green. The "costly worke" at Westminster was what we now know as Henry VII's Chapel.

[6]Gibson, 47.

down his fortune through the pages headed "Here findeth Lady Fortune". Some of the verses, not included, however, in this unique copy, are among More's best.

> The rollyng dyse in whome your lucke doth stande,
> With whose unhappy chaunce ye be so wroth,
> Ye knowe your selfe came never to myne hande.
> Lo in this pond be fysshe and frogges both.
> Cast in your nette: but be you liefe or lothe,
> Holde you content as fortune lyst assyne:
> For it is your owne fishyng and not myne.

To the "four things" printed in the folio must be added the original verses More includes in his *Picus* on subjects suggested by counsels given by Pico. It is all but impossible for true poetry to break through the restrictions of didacticism. Here are the two stanzas on the Fourth Property of a Lover: "To suffer long, though it were death, to be with his love".

> If love be strong, hote, mightie, and fervent,
> There maye no trouble, grief, or sorow fall,
> But that the lover would be well content
> All to endure, and thinke it eke to small,
> Though it wer death, so he might therewithall
> The joyful presence of that parson get,
> On whom he hath his heart and love yset.
>
> Thus should of god the lover be content
> Any distres or sorow to endure,
> Rather then to be from god absent,
> And glad to die, so that he maye be sure
> By his departing hence for to procure,
> After this valey darke, the heavenly light,
> And of his love the glorious blessed light.

More's preference for the Chaucerian stanza of seven lines (later known as rime-royal) suggests that he found Chaucer much to his liking; nor would this be surprising for both had a lively sense of humour, and we can catch here and there in More's works echoes of Chaucer as well as direct references.[7] This stanza

[7]For examples see below, pp. 217, 322.

C

was also favoured by John Skelton whose "Bouge of Court" was printed by Wynkyn de Worde before 1500. The author's name was not given, but Skelton was far from diffident and copies of his poems were circulating in the manner of the times. More's "Merry Jest" is written in a verse form more regular than Skelton's later "breathless rimes" that have been labelled "Skeltonic". It is tempting to think that More and Skelton were more closely acquainted than the records show. We have seen them both at Eltham Palace, and there is one popular tale that brings them together again but this time in a Westminster tavern. There may be a connection between More's "Rueful Lamentation" and Skelton's poem on the death of Edward IV. Each verse of this ends with the Latin line, "Et, ecce, nunc in pulvere dormio!" More imagined Queen Elizabeth lying on her death-bed and each verse of his poem ends with the words, "for lo now here I lie". Skelton had the more macabre idea of imagining Edward IV speaking from his grave.

The two men had in common a command of Latin. Caxton had highly praised Skelton's Latin and it was his learning that commended him to the Lady Margaret Beaufort who was responsible for his appointment as tutor to Prince Henry. There was a raffish strain in Skelton that would not have commended him to Thomas More. There is, however, one other possible link; in 1533 John Rastell printed Skelton's interlude *Magnificence*, warning the king against lavish expenditure and bad counsellors.

CHAPTER VI

Parliament and Marriage

WILLIAM ROPER is the only authority for the statement that Thomas More was a member of the last Parliament of Henry VII's reign.[1] It met on 20 January 1504 and was dismissed at the end of March. Unfortunately the usual records of membership, such as sheriffs' returns, are not extant for this Parliament so it is not known for which county or borough More sat, except that it was not for London. Although Roper's report cannot be confirmed, there is no reason for doubting its substantial accuracy; in the course of years, the facts may have got twisted. There was no point in inventing such a story as he gives us.

We have to adjust our ideas of Parliament to visualize its working under the first two Tudors. The Parliament chamber at Westminster was used by the Lords—two archbishops, nineteen bishops, twenty-eight mitred abbots and only twenty-nine lay peers, thus giving the clergy the preponderant voice. The knights and burgesses who formed the Commons numbered about three hundred. They could approach the King or the Lords only through their Speaker (who had a fee of £100), except on special occasions, such as the opening of Parliament, when they all crowded at the bar. (See Plate 5.) They had already won the right to control grants of money; such indeed was the usual purpose of calling a Parliament. That of 1504 was no exception; Henry wanted feudal aids for the knighting of Prince Arthur in 1489 and for the marriage of the Princess Margaret to James IV of Scotland in 1503. The Prince had died in 1502 and the Commons may have felt that it was rather late in the day to demand the feudal dues. The King asked for two fifteenths and tenths. The fifteenth was levied on the shires and the tenth on the boroughs; the basis of assessment was property but it was a rough and ready business.

[1] Roper, pp. 7-8.

Normally a fifteenth and tenth brought in about £30,000. The Commons proved reluctant to make the full grant and offered £40,000, of which the King graciously remitted a quarter, so he got half what he wanted. He was shrewd enough to keep the goodwill of the Commons by such concessions when he sensed opposition.

According to Roper, it was Thomas More who effectively voiced the opposition to the full demand. As a result, the King "conceiving great indignation towards him, could not be satisfied until he had some way revenged it". It would have offended the Commons if this young member had been penalized, so instead, the story goes, John More was imprisoned until he had paid a fine of £100. Here credulity is rather strained. John More could have paid £100 without going to prison. Be that as it may, Roper supports his account by recording an incident involving More's friend Richard Whitford, who may have been alive when Roper wrote his memoir. On one occasion, when More was making suit to Bishop Richard Fox, then Lord Privy Seal and a leading counsellor, the Bishop took the opportunity to suggest that, with his help, More could regain the King's favour. Whitford, who was now the Bishop's chaplain, advised his friend not to have any further dealings with the Bishop as "my lord, my master, to serve the King's turn, will not stick to agree to his own father's death". This is the kind of story that cannot be checked; there is a touch of maliciousness about it that makes it suspect. Roper averred that, as a result, Thomas More seriously thought of going abroad to escape the King's anger, a move that would have disrupted his legal career. There is no supporting evidence for this. More's first known journey to the Continent was when he went to Paris and Louvain about 1508 for a brief visit to study the working of the universities. Stapleton adds a curious incident.[2] When Edmund Dudley, who had been Speaker of the 1504 Parliament, was being escorted to his execution on 18 August 1510, More approached him and asked, "Well, Master Dudley, in that matter of the exactions, was I not right?" To this Dudley replied that More had been wise to keep out of the King's way or he would certainly

[2]Stapleton, p. 25.

have lost his head. Such conversations on the way to execution seem to us somewhat callous, but at that period hangings and executions were common hazards and excited little comment. Shakespeare made good use of such dramatic encounters.

Roper went on to say that the death of Henry VII "soon after" removed the threat to Thomas More, but, in fact, the King lived for five years after that Parliament during which More made steady progress in his profession. It may be noted that in 1506 he dedicated some translations to Thomas Ruthall who was secretary to Henry VII.[3] It is a friendly letter that in no way suggests that the writer was seeking the secretary's favour.

More's appointment to the 1504 Parliament shows that although he had not yet been called to the bench at Lincoln's Inn, he had already gained a reputation as an advocate. It seems probable that he was the spokesman for the merchants of London and that they arranged for his election. It must be concluded that by the end of 1504, or even earlier, he had reached a firm decision on his vocation. Certainly his courting must have followed soon after Parliament was dismissed, and this again casts doubt on the seriousness of the threat that Roper declared hung over him at this period. In those days a prospective father-in-law would not have encouraged a suitor who was under the royal displeasure.

John Colt was to be that father-in-law. He owned extensive properties in East Anglia but he lived at Netherall, near Royden, on the Herts.-Essex border and within riding distance of John More's country house, Gobions, at North Mimms. John Colt's father, Thomas, had been Chancellor of the Exchequer to Edward IV and so may have come to know John More when he was a rising lawyer. There were eighteen children in the Colt family, eleven of them girls. Roper's story was that Thomas More would have preferred the second daughter, but, lest the eldest, Jane, should feel slighted, he chose her. That may well have been so at a period when marriages were rarely based on passionate emotion. Jane Colt and Thomas More were married towards the end of 1504 or very early in 1505. They had four children: Margaret (b. 1505) Elizabeth (b. 1506), Cecily (b. 1507) and John (b. 1509). To these

[3] Rogers, 5. See below, p. 58.

must be added Margaret Giggs (or Gyge) who seemingly was Margaret More's foster-sister and was brought up as one of the family. They settled at the Old Barge, Bucklersbury; Stow

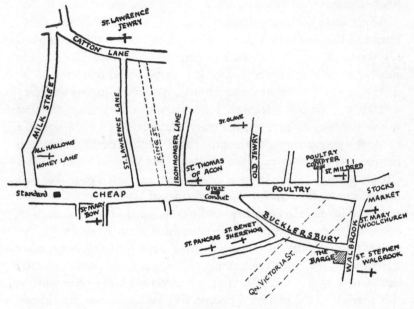

Bucklersbury in Sir Thomas More's time

described it in Elizabethan times as "one great house builded of stone and timber". Perhaps at first the Mores rented only part of it. It was not until December 1513 that they leased the whole house from the Hospital of St Thomas of Acon which had close associations with the Mercers' Company.[4]

Erasmus returned to England in April 1505 and spent much of his time at the Old Barge; he stayed for over a year and paid visits to Grocyn and Mountjoy and to Colet at Stepney where he made a conquest of Colet's mother. He also spent a short time at Cambridge. He came to know Jane More, though conversation

[4]See J. Watney, *The Hospital of St Thomas of Acon* (1892), pp. 263-71. The pre-blitz Barge Yard preserved the name. The site is now covered by Bucklersbury House. The Old Barge was at the Walbrook end and More's garden may have been over the Temple of Mithras uncovered in 1954.

between them must have been limited to smiles and a few words as she did not speak Latin (though probably learning it from her husband) and Erasmus never bothered to learn fluent English. In his account of Thomas More, he wrote:

> He married a young girl of good family, who had been brought up with her sisters in their parents' home in the country; he chose her as she was untrained so that he might the more readily mould her to his liking. He had her taught literature and trained her in every kind of music; and she was just growing into a charming life's companion for him, when she died young.

Erasmus may have been referring to Thomas and Jane More in his Colloquy on "The Discontented Wife" (first published in 1523), in which he gave this picture of a newly wedded couple.

> I have the honour to be acquainted with a gentleman of good family, learned and of unusual refinement and ability. He married a young lady of seventeen years of age who had been brought up entirely in the country in her father's house. He had a mind to have a fresh, inexperienced maid that he might form her more easily to his own tastes. He began to instruct her in literature and music and to practise her by degrees in repeating the heads of sermons that she heard. Now these things being wholly new to the girl, she soon grew weary of this kind of life and she absolutely refused to submit to what her husband required of her.

This tallies in several particulars with the account quoted above from Erasmus, but it would be a mistake to see an exact record in the story of the Colloquy where the author would allow his imagination some play. Our sympathies are surely with Jane More; her young husband seems to have been rather heavy-handed, but, if this is a portrait of Jane More, it shows that she had the firmness of spirit that was part of her eldest daughter's inheritance. The story goes on to say that the young couple paid a visit to her father in the country and while there, the husband complained of her obstinacy to her father. After a talk with him, she proved more amenable.

The Erasmus of 1499 had been an unknown struggling scholar. The Erasmus who returned six years later had already made his name. He had not only worked hard at Greek, but he had

produced the *Adages* (1500), a book that was to go on selling long
after his death. This first collection of brief quotations from Latin
authors contained 818 entries; edition followed edition and soon
Greek quotations were added; the last edition of 1536 contained
4,139 passages.[5] Then in 1504 he published a miscellany under the
title *Lucubratiunculae aliquot*; included was the *Enchiridion* that
was to become one of his best-known works. Among the tasks he
carried out in London was a new translation of the Greek New
Testament into Latin; this was made at the suggestion of John
Colet who lent him two old codices from the Chapter Library of
St Paul's. It is not known how early these were as they perished
in the Great Fire of 1666 when the library was destroyed.

It was during this year that Erasmus won the patronage and
friendship of Archbishop Warham, Bishop Fox and Bishop John
Fisher. The last had become Chancellor of Cambridge and it was
no doubt at his invitation that Erasmus paid his first visit to that
university. He was entered at Queens' College (of which Fisher
was then Master) with the intention of qualifying for a doctorate
of divinity; he was described as a B.D. of Paris. Just when he was
settling down (if he could ever settle down) an opportunity came
for him to go to Italy as bear-leader to two young men; he left
England in June 1506.

Was it Erasmus who introduced Thomas More to the satires of
Lucian? There was certainly no one among the later Greek
writers so akin in spirit with Erasmus whose comment on Lucian
might be applied to his own writings, particularly to the *Colloquies*.
"Such is the grace of his style, the felicity of his invention, the
elegance of his wit, the sharpness of his satire, that no comedy, no
satire that was ever written, can be compared with his dialogues,
either for the pleasure or for the instruction they afford."[6]

These translations into Latin were one of the ways in which
Erasmus, after the manner of the times, solicited the patronage of
influential men. Thomas More had not the same need; for him,
it was a means of consolidating his knowledge of Greek with

---

[5] See *The "Adages" of Erasmus*, by M. M. Phillips (1964).
[6] Dedication to Christopher Urswick of the translation of *Micyllos*. See, C. R. Thompson, *The Translations of Lucian by Erasmus and St Thomas More* (1940).

Erasmus at his side. Lucian's laughing scepticism was congenial to More at that period and he never lost the Lucianic touch. Yet in those earlier years he had other, more censorious, moods. In two of his letters, he showed the impatience of youth with what seemed to him the shortcomings of his fellows. Part of his letter of 1501 to John Holt has already been quoted.[7] The description of the audience at Grocyn's lectures continued, "Most of those who think themselves clever, keep away lest they seem to admit their ignorance of subjects of which they are in fact ignorant". And in his letter to John Colet, he wrote, "Wherever you turn, what do you see around you? Pretended friends and the sweet poison of smooth flatterers, fierce hatreds, quarrels, rivalries and contentions." Such scornful comments are appropriate to youth, but the indignation had yet to be touched with humour before it could be the material for satire. Erasmus played his part in bringing out his friend's capability; Lucian was one medium. The two could enjoy Lucian and then apply the same kind of criticism to the contemporary scene.

Thomas More translated *Cynicus*, *Philopseudes*, and *Necyomantia* (or *Menippus*). He and Erasmus both translated *Tyrannicida*, and then each wrote a rhetorical declamation on the same theme. The problem was that in a country where tyrannicide was rewarded by the state, a man killed a tyrant's son, and the tyrant, in despair, committed suicide. The question was, "Is the assassin entitled to the reward?" Both Erasmus and More argued that he was not so entitled. While they disliked the logic-chopping of the later school-men, they approved of the method of declamation, and, in their later writings, they showed a strong dislike of tyranny in all its forms.

In a dedicatory letter to Richard Whitford of the declamation of the *Tyrannicida*, Erasmus paid a tribute to their friend Thomas More:

> He is writing on the same subject and in such a way as to thresh out and dissect every part of it. For I do not think, unless the vehemence of my love leads me astray, that Nature ever formed a mind more alert, ready, discerning and penetrating, or, in a word, more com-

[7]See above, pp. 29-30.

C*

pletely furnished with every kind of faculty. Add to this a power of expression equal to his intellect, a singular cheerfulness of character and an abundance of wit, but only of the good-humoured kind, and you miss nothing that should be found in a perfect advocate. I have therefore not undertaken this task with any idea of either surpassing or matching such an artist, but only to break a lance as it were in this tourney of wits with the sweetest of all my friends, with whom I am always pleased to join any employment grave or gay. I have done this all the more willingly because I very much wish this kind of exercise to be used in schools where it should be of the greatest value.

This method was in fact used by Thomas More when his children and their companions were old enough to learn the classical languages. The praise Erasmus lavished on his friend may seem extravagant and we must make allowance for his enthusiasm. One reason, without in any way discounting this tribute, may have been that at the Old Barge Erasmus for the first time found himself living on the closest terms with a family. It was typical of him that he praised his friends fervently without showing any sign of envy of their talents or merits.

How far did John Colet approve of his friends' labours on Lucian? In the statutes for his school the Latin authors he recommended were Christians such as Sedulius, Juvencus, and Baptiste Mantuanus (Shakespeare's "good old Mantuan"), but at the same time he wanted his pupils to learn the classical Latin of Cicero, Virgil and Sallust. His dilemma was that too great a concentration on such authors might encourage a pagan outlook, yet to acquire a pure Latin style, they had to be studied. Lucian was a pagan-agnostic, but the argument put forward by some of his apologists was that by exposing the absurdities of the myths of the gods, he cleared the ground, so to speak, for true religion. This justification is hinted at by More in his dedicatory letter to Thomas Ruthall, but, it will be seen, he carries the war against myth into Christian territory.

No wonder if simple folk are affected by the fictions of those who think they have done a lasting service to Christ when they have invented a fable about some saint or a tragic description of hell which either reduces an old woman to tears or makes her blood run cold. There is scarcely any life of a martyr or virgin in which some falsehood of this kind has not been inserted; an act of piety no doubt considering the risk that truth would be insufficient in itself unless propped up by lies! Thus they have not scrupled to corrupt with fiction that religion which was founded by truth herself and ought to consist of naked truth alone. They have failed to see that such fables are so far from promoting religion that nothing can be more injurious to it. . . . Therefore while the histories commended to us by divinely inspired scripture ought to be accepted with undoubted faith, the others tested by the doctrine of Christ should either be received with caution or rejected if we would avoid both vain belief and superstitious fear.[8]

There was one characteristic of Lucian that went to shape More's future writings; this was the Greek's love of dialogue and his skill in composing it in a lively style in contrast with the more formal manner of Plato. It may have been in making these translations that More discovered the form that was to suit his own genius.

Erasmus arranged for these translations to be printed by Badius in Paris under the title *Luciani . . . opuscula . . . ab Erasmo Roterodamo et Thoma Moro . . . traducta*. It was published in November 1506 and was reprinted at least thirteen times during More's lifetime.[9] Erasmus added translations of other dialogues to later editions but More did not increase his share.

[8]Rogers, 5.   [9]Gibson, 78-94.

CHAPTER VII

The Accession of Henry VIII

THOMAS MORE'S SISTER, Elizabeth, was married perhaps a year or so before her brother. His eldest sister, Johanna (Joan), had married Richard Staverton who had been admitted to Lincoln's Inn on the same day as Thomas More; he became protonotary of the City court. Elizabeth married John Rastell of Coventry where he succeeded his father as coroner in 1506. He must have moved to London within a few years for, as we have seen, he printed his brother-in-law's *Picus* before 1510. It was no doubt during his years in London at the Middle Temple (no details of his career are recorded) that he came to know the Mores. One official record connects him with them. In 1500 with John More, his son Thomas and another, John Rastell repaid a loan or debt of a hundred marks to the Crown.[1]

John Rastell (b. 1475)[2] was a man of astonishing versatility—lawyer, litigant, printer, voyager, pageant master, decorator, military engineer, writer of interludes and histories and law-books; whatever he undertook was done with gusto. He appears to have been a man of restless ambition but of doubtful prudence. His family must have had an exciting life.

It was perhaps in 1506 that Thomas More paid a visit to the Rastells at Coventry. There he had an encounter with a friar which he described some years later in a letter to an anonymous monk who may have been John Batmanson[3] of the London Charter-house. The friar had declared that anyone who recited daily Our Lady's Psalter would never be damned.[4] The parish priest warned his people in vain that they should not believe such nonsense. When More was asked for his opinion, he tried to laugh it off as he had no wish to get involved in the argument, but he was

[1]King's Book of Payments, E. 415/31.
[2]For John Rastell, see A. W. Reed, *Early Tudor Drama* (1926).
[3]Rogers, 83 (26). See, D. Knowles, *The Religious Orders in England*, III, ap. I.
[4]Our Lady's Psalter was the rosary of one-hundred-and-fifty Hail Marys.

soon to find that this was a burning local question that could not be ignored. The friar turned up to dinner. More tells us what happened:

> In comes an old friar, dryasdust, severe and sour; a boy follows him with some books. I saw that I was in for an argument. We sat down, and, so as to lose no time, the question was at once put by our host. The friar answered just as he had preached. I said nothing as I do not like to meddle in annoying and fruitless disputes. At last they asked my opinion. As I was obliged to speak, I told them what I thought, briefly and moderately. Then the friar poured out a long prepared speech which might have made two sermons. His whole argument depended on certain miracles he read from a Mariale[5] and from other books of that kind. When he had at last finished, I quietly answered that he had said nothing in his whole discourse capable of convincing whose who did not admit the truth of those miracles which they might deny without abjuring the Christian faith, and that even if they were absolutely proved, they had little to do with the question. . . . I have not related this in order to impute crime to any body of religious, since the same ground produces herbs both wholesome and poisonous. Nor do I wish to find fault with the custom of those who salute Our Lady, than which nothing could be more beneficial, but because some trust so much in their devotions that they draw from them boldness to sin.

We too may be inclined to laugh off the friar's claim, but it was a symptom of a serious distemper within the Church that was not cured until it was too late. In the printed Primers of the time, incredible indulgences were attached to the saying of some prayers, such as assuring the petitioner that his soul would not go to hell if he repeated the correct number of prayers; this was but one example of what had become a common perversion that degenerated into superstition among the credulous. Too often the emphasis was put on the indulgence and not enough on the prerequisite of true contrition for sin, and on subsequent penance.

Henry VII died on 21 April 1509, and, three weeks later, Bishop John Fisher preached the dirge, "the body being present", in St Paul's. The Bishop selected for praise those characteristics of the late King that historians have recognized as his outstanding qualities.

[5] A commentary on the five Joyful Mysteries of the rosary.

His politic wisdom in governaunce it was singular, his wit always quick and ready, his reason pithy and substantial, his memory fresh and holding, his experience notable, his counsels fortunate and taken by wise deliberation.

The greater part of the sermon was in effect a call to repentance. The Lady Margaret Beaufort died two months after her son. Bishop Fisher preached her "month's mind",[6] but it is not recorded where this was; perhaps it was at Cambridge where the University owed so much to that great lady. This sermon was far more of a panegyric than that on Henry VII which was marked by its restraint. Was this a reflection of the unpopularity into which the King had fallen in his last years? His irascibility, his parsimony and avarice had increased with the years and his exactions had become a burden.

The accession of Henry VIII was welcomed not only as a relief, as it was vainly hoped, from financial demands, but with the rejoicing that always comes when an old, tired man gives way to a vigorous youth. And Henry was a prince to capture public enthusiasm. Physically he was a magnificent creature with the tall, handsome, powerful frame of his grandfather Edward IV. His skill in the tourney, on the hunting field and in all sports was universally acknowledged and admired. For the most part he retained his father's advisers, with Archbishop Warham as Chancellor, but within a year he showed that he could be ruthless when it seemed expedient. Richard Empson[7] and Edmund Dudley[8] were executed on a trumped-up charge of treason; they had been the too effective instruments of the late King's financial policy, and, though they were doubtless guilty of unjust extortion and of lining their own pockets, in the manner of the times, they had not plotted against the Crown; indeed, it might be said they plotted with it. The executions were welcomed by the populace

---

[6]An anniversary Mass a month after the day of death. Both sermons were printed by Wynkyn de Worde in 1509. See *English Works of John Fisher* (E.E.T.S., 1876).

[7]The unpopularity of Empson was not a passing emotion. A satirist (c. 1512) declared he would need the pen of Skelton, of Cornysh, or "Master More" to do justice to the theme. Wm Cornysh was Master of the Children of the Chapel under Henry VIII. *Great Chronicle of London* (ed. 1938), p. 361.

[8]His grandson was Robert Dudley, Queen Elizabeth's Earl of Leicester.

but the way in which they were condemned set a dangerous precedent which was not forgotten by the new King.

When Henry came to the throne, he was some two months short of his eighteenth birthday. He married Catherine of Aragon, his brother's widow, at Greenwich on 11 June 1509, and they were crowned at Westminster on 24 June. As Catherine had been married to Prince Arthur, she and Henry were in the first degree of affinity and only a papal dispensation could remove what was a canonical impediment. Julius II granted the necessary dispensation in a brief in 1504.

The coronation produced one long Latin poem and four short ones from Thomas More.[9] The presentation copy of these is now in the British Museum. The *Carmen Gratulatorium* welcomed the coming of a new age. The day should be marked with a pure white stone for it was the beginning of an epoch of freedom. The references to the extortions of Henry VII were unequivocal.

> Now no one hesitates to show the possessions he has hitherto hidden from sight. Now it is possible to enjoy any profit that escaped the sly, grasping hands of many thieves.

Yet the merits of the dead King were not overlooked. Addressing the new King, the poet wrote:

> You, Sire, have the wisdom of your father, your mother's kindly strength, the intelligence of your paternal grand-mother [the Lady Margaret Beaufort], and the noble heart of your mother's father [Edward IV]. What wonder then if England rejoices since she has such a King as never before?

Thomas More was here reflecting the mood of the nation at the beginning of the new reign.

There is ample testimony to this expectation of a new age of glory about to break under the young King's inspiration. Lord Mountjoy, who was one of his close companions, at once wrote to Erasmus who was then in Italy:

> What may you not promise yourself from a prince with whose extraordinary and almost divine character you are well acquainted, and to whom you are not only known but intimate, having received

[9] Published in *Epigrammata* (1518). See below, p. 132.

from him (as few others have done) a letter traced with his own hand? But when you know what a hero he now shows himself, how wisely he behaves, what a lover he is of justice and goodness, what affection he bears to the learned, I will venture to swear that you will need no wings to make you fly to behold this new and auspicious man.[10]

This flowery letter was probably composed by Andrea Ammonio, an Italian Latinist, who had been sent to England as apostolic notary; he soon became one of Mountjoy's circle and was employed later by Henry VIII as a Latin secretary. Ammonio lodged for some time with the Mores, where Erasmus joined them on his arrival in England in August 1509 having set out from Italy as soon as he got Mountjoy's paean. He was almost at once prostrated by an attack of the stone, but he found happy occupation in carrying out a brilliant idea that had been bubbling in his head on the long journey from Rome. It was to find expression in his little book variously known as *Moriae Encomium*, *Stultitiae Laus*, *Moria*, or, in English, *The Praise of Folly*. In the dedication to his host, Thomas More, the author wrote:

In my late travels from Italy to England, so as not to trifle away my time in repeating old wives' tales, I thought it more to the point to employ my thoughts in reflecting upon some past studies, or calling to remembrance several of those highly learned, as well as witty, friends I had left behind here, among whom you were the chief; whose memory, while absent at this distance, I respect with no less satisfaction than when I could enjoy your more intimate conversation, which last gave me the greatest pleasure I could possibly expect. Having therefore resolved to do something and thinking my journey not suited to anything serious, I thought it a good idea to amuse myself by drawing up a panegyric on Folly. "What maggot", you say, "put this into your head?" Why the first hint was your own surname More, which comes as near the literal sound of the word *moria* as you are distant from its meaning and, that in all men's judgments, is very wide. In the next place, I supposed that this kind of sportive wit would be more especially acceptable to you who are accustomed with this kind of jocose raillery (such as, if I am not mistaken, is neither dull not impertinent)

[10]Allen, 206, 215.

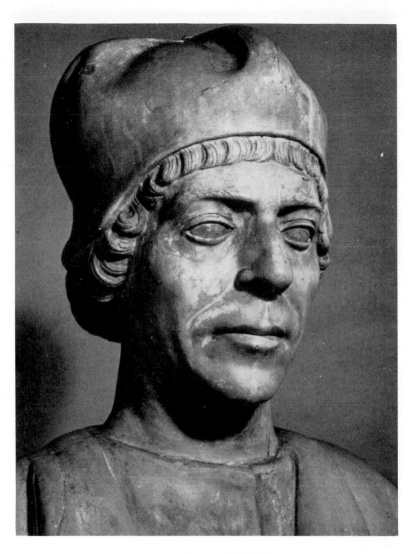

1. JOHN COLET

2. ERASMUS

3. PETER GILLES

4. CUTHBERT TUNSTAL

5. THE PARLIAMENT OF 1523

7.   THE MORE FAMILY GROUP

FAMILY GROUP

to be greatly delighted, you who in your ordinary talk show yourself a Democritus junior. For truly, as you do from a singular vein of wit very much differ from the common herd of mankind, so, by an incredible affability and easiness of temper, you have the art of suiting your humour to all kinds of company.

Democritus, "the laughing philosopher", came to Erasmus' mind when thinking of Thomas More, and not, as one might expect, Lucian. *The Praise of Folly* itself is certainly Lucianic in tone and treatment.

We can imagine with what delight More listened as his friend read to him each portion of the book as it was written. Other friends no doubt joined in the listening. Ammonio would be there as a lodger at the Old Barge, and perhaps Lily. Would Colet have entered into the joke? More liked the play on his own name and he used *Moria* as the title when he mentioned the book. It is well to remember the spirit of fun that brought the book into being, and not overburden it with too great a weight of serious purpose. This is not to say that it lacks significance. Erasmus was deeply concerned with the need to send people back to the Gospels as the sources of our knowledge of the wisdom of Christ, and he and More were alive to the abuses that had gradually come to obscure that teaching. The latter part of the book makes Erasmus' intention clear. "Through his whole course of life the pious man, without any regard to the baser materials of the body, spends himself wholly in a fixed intentness upon spiritual, invisible and eternal subjects." Yet it is probably true to say that the majority of those who laughed as they read, remembered the fun that is poked at monks and ecclesiastics and all pompous persons rather than the underlying seriousness of the jester.

Erasmus was to be disappointed; he had been urged to come to England in the belief that the young King would prove an eager patron, but though vague promises were made and goodwill shown, nothing substantial was ever offered to the scholar.

From our distance of time we can see how mistaken those hopes were. Henry's learning was not negligible for a prince, but a young athletic king could not acquire more than superficial knowledge of any one subject. Perhaps to us his most attractive

trait was his devotion to music as listener, performer and com-
poser. He was credited with a knowledge of theology; it is true
that he had a liking for discussing theological problems and had
gained sufficient knowledge to talk intelligently, but this was a
long way from a true understanding of all that was involved. A
more important question may be posed. Was Mountjoy mistaken
when he urged Erasmus to hurry back to England because the
new King loved learning and was a patron of scholars?

Henry's grandmother, the Lady Margaret Beaufort, under the
guidance of John Fisher, had used her great wealth to promote
learning at Cambridge. This, however, was not directed towards
the spread of the revived classical studies; she and her mentor
were chiefly concerned with the training of priests and of good
preachers, and no more important purpose could have inspired
their efforts, for the welfare of the Church, their paramount
concern, depended on a more soundly educated clergy. The
tragedy was that time was not on their side, and St John's College,
instead of proving a seminary of orthodox priests, became a
nursery of protestants. It is not without significance that John
Fisher had to fight hard to try to keep out of Henry's hands the
munificent bequests the Lady Margaret intended for this new
college, and thereby the Bishop incurred the lasting resentment
of the King.

Henry VII had not been deeply concerned with the encouragement of learning though his accounts show that he bought books,
mostly French. His appointment of the Italian Pietro Carmeliano
as Latin Secretary was not a tribute to scholarship as such but a
practical measure to meet the need for someone who could write
the classical Latin then being more widely used in diplomatic
correspondence. It was, in fact, a recognition of the low state to
which classical learning had sunk in England. Another indication
was that in 1491 Cambridge University had to engage an Italian
scholar to compose Latin orations as there were no residents
capable of doing so in classical style.[11] Henry's invitation to the
papal sub-collector, Polydore Vergil, to write a history of
England was not a deliberate move to promote the new learning,

[11] C. H. Cooper, *Annals*, I, p. 240.

but it was a happy choice and Vergil soon became one of the More circle of scholars.

Henry VIII was a better educated man than his father, but his learning did not carry him very far, and, after his accession, he does not seem to have continued his studies. He knew sufficient to enjoy talking with a cultured man such as Sir Thomas More but their conversation could hardly have been an exchange of full minds. Catherine of Aragon had been well taught during her girlhood in Spain which she left at the age of fifteen. She had learned to have a respect for scholars but neither she nor Henry could be regarded as serious patrons of learning. Perhaps the final comment on Henry's attitude towards learning is that, had he been truly appreciative of its value, he would not have allowed priceless libraries to have been dispersed or wantonly destroyed when the monasteries were dissolved, nor would he have thrown away the opportunity to endow learning with the funds he gathered in, nor would he have stood idle while great monuments of medieval architecture were pulled down. It can be argued that the want of royal patronage was a contributory cause to the slow progress made by the new learning in England.

We do not know how long Erasmus stayed with the Mores in 1509, nor how much time he gave to the revision of his book. He liked to give the impression that it had been thrown off within a few weeks, but it was not until he was back in Paris in May 1511[12] that he arranged for the printing. It has been suggested that he delayed publication lest the book might spoil his chances of preferment in England, but it is just as likely that he did not want it to go into print until it was as perfect in style as he could make it. The little book was frequently reprinted in Cologne, Strassburg and Basle but without the author's supervision. A French translation was made in 1520 and an Italian in 1539. Ten years later came an English translation by Sir Thomas Chaloner, the friend of William Cecil, Lord Burghley.

At first there was little outspoken criticism of Moria; readers

[12]In his letter to Dorp (Rogers, 15 (3)), More said that Moria had been available "for more than seven times in seven years" (he was writing in 1515). This goes back to 1508, which is impossible; it does suggest that there might have been an earlier edition than that of 1511.

were content to enjoy its mockery, and it is said that the Pope chuckled as he read it. The Louvain theologians, however, scented doubtful doctrine and resented the implied censure of themselves and their kind of learning. They induced a young colleague, Martin van Dorp (1485-1525), to criticize *Moria* and, at the same time, voice their objections to Erasmus' declared intention of editing the Greek text of the New Testament. Dorp was well known to Erasmus and indeed had undertaken to see his *Lucubratiunculae* through the press in 1504. Dorp's letter was therefore worded in friendly vein though perhaps the instigators may have wished for something more trenchant. Here we are concerned only with the part in which *Moria* was criticized. Dorp complained of the flippant tone of the book with its mocking of sacred subjects; he suggested that a counterbalance should be provided by "The Praise of Wisdom". Erasmus made a courteous but firm reply. Dorp again took up his pen and this time Thomas More wrote a reply; this was probably in 1515. He pointed out that *Moria* had delighted many scholars and was decried only by disgruntled theologians whom the cap fitted. As for a "Praise of Wisdom", that would not appease these angry men for Erasmus would have to exclude them from the company of Wisdom having already included them in the company of Folly.

CHAPTER VIII

The City Lawyer

THE INCREASING USE of Thomas More's services in the City of London dates from the accession of Henry VIII. This may have been a coincidence; the shadow of the displeasure of Henry VII would have been sufficient to deter the City merchants from employing the young lawyer. On 21 March 1509, to quote the entry in the records of the Mercers' Company, "Master Thomas More, gentleman, desired to be free of this fellowship, which was granted by the whole company to have it frank and free".[1] His admission would be by patrimony as his father was a Mercer. John Colet was also a freeman of the Company by patrimony.

In September 1509 Thomas More was engaged as Latin interpreter and orator when the Pensionary (chief magistrate) of Antwerp came to discuss some difficulties that had arisen between that city and the Merchant Adventurers of London.[2] This was a company of traders, chiefly in cloth, with Flanders, and included representatives of several of the Livery Companies, but the lead seems to have been yielded to the Mercers, and it was they who asked Thomas More to be their Latin speaker. A full account of the matters in dispute would be out of place here; the part played by More has its importance as showing his rising prestige both as lawyer and as a Latinist. One passage from the records tells of the decorum of the proceedings in the Mercers' Hall; the church mentioned is that of St Thomas of Acon.

> Then was there assigned Master Governor and three Wardens of divers Companies to go down into the Church and for to bring up the said Pensionary, and so it was done, and after he was comen up and made his obeisance, Master Governor brought him to the north end of the table and caused him to sit down his face towards the south. Then Master More sitting on the south bench next the window began

[1] Lyall and Watney, *Acts of the Court of the Mercers' Company* (1936), pp. 320, 334-5.
[2] Thomas Cromwell may have been working with the English Antwerp merchants at this period, but the dates in his early career are uncertain.

69

to declare unto him the mind and pleasure of the Company in Latin.

The Pensionary was satisfied with the answer and said that to please the Company he would be content to stay twice as long.

Then when that he had declared as is aforesaid in Latin, Master More did interpret the same in English to the company, and then they arose and every man went his way.

In 1510 Thomas More was chosen as burgess to represent the City in the Parliament that was called on 21 January and was dismissed a month later. There is a reference to this appointment in Richard Hill's *Commonplace Book*; he mentioned "Young More, burgess of the parliament for London".[3] He was usually distinguished in this way from his father. He may have been in the Parliament for only part of the month during which it met as he replaced James Yarford, another Mercer, who resigned as burgess when he became an Alderman. Yarford and Young More often worked together for the Mercers. The other burgesses were the Recorder and two more Mercers, John Tate and John Bruges, an indication of the influence of the Company at that period. Thomas More did not represent London in any later Parliament. This may be explained by his appointment as an Under-Sheriff on 3 September 1510,[4] in place of Richard Brooks who had been elected Recorder. The Sheriffs had two courts in which the Under-Sheriffs served as magistrates to deal with civil cases and cases of debts. More was assigned to the Poultry Compter (or Counter) which was also the prison.[5] Erasmus gave this account:

In the City of London, his birthplace, he has been for some years, [i.e. before 1519] a judge in civil causes: an office which entails little work, as the court only sits on Thursday mornings till dinner-time, but the position is one of honour. No one has disposed of more cases than he nor acted with greater integrity; indeed he usually remits the fee charged to litigants which is three shillings deposited by each beforehand. By such conduct he has made himself much beloved in the City.[6]

[3]Balliol MS. 354, fol. 236 v.
[4]*Journal* (Common Council), II, 118.
[5]The Poultry Compter was between the Grocers' Hall and Poultry.
[6]Allen, 999.

While Erasmus was no doubt right in his description of the work in the court, he could have added that the position of Under-Sheriff carried with it many other obligations such as serving on committees for arbitration, for the care of London Bridge, or for inquiries into disputes between the Livery Companies or the Crafts. On several occasions More accompanied delegations to the King's Council or to Parliament.[7] These appearances on official business would attract notice to the young lawyer whose reputation was steadily rising. At the same time he had his own professional work to do and this would mean attending the courts at Westminster on behalf of his clients. Roper tells us that More's total income at this period was about £400.[8]

The More circle during the first decade of the sixteenth century must have had many discussions on two subjects—education, and the state of the Church. Both centred on John Colet for he was planning his new school, and, at the same time, he was trying to bring about improvements at St Paul's in the conduct of the services and in the quality of the preaching. On the death of his father, Sir Henry, in the autumn of 1505, Colet inherited considerable wealth as the only survivor of twenty-one children! He decided to devote much of this patrimony to the foundation of a grammar school on new principles. Other rich men of the City had founded schools in their native towns but none did so with such purposive care. It seems probable that Colet was experimenting with a school at St Paul's several years before the final statutes were made. He then placed it in the trusteeship of the Mercers' Company; as Erasmus put it, "he set in charge not a bishop, nor a chapter, nor dignitaries, but married citizens of established reputation".[9] During the preliminary period, Colet discussed his ideas with Erasmus and indeed, at one time, tried to persuade him to become the first high master. Erasmus had definite notions on how boys should be taught, but he himself does not seem to have had any taste for teaching; he did, however, write *Copia* for the

[7]For a list of these and other duties, see Harpsfield, pp. 312-3.

[8]A substantial sum before Henry VIII began to debase the coinage which his father had stabilized. It would be misleading to suggest a modern equivalent as our way of life is radically different.

[9]Allen, 1211.

use of the new school; this was designed to give the pupils a wide choice of words in Latin composition. Another book by Erasmus, *Institutum Christiani hominis*, was also recommended in the school statutes, and a prayer composed by Erasmus in honour of the Child Jesus was used in the school. Colet invited Linacre to write a new Latin Grammar, but what he produced was far above the heads of young pupils. It was published by John Rastell in 1525 with the title *Progymnasmata grammatices Vulgaria*, with a short commendatory poem by Thomas More. In its place Colet wrote an accidence and Lily added a syntax which Erasmus revised. This book had a remarkable history; it became the national Latin Grammar and, eventually, the famous Eton Grammar.[10] William Lily was chosen by Colet to become the first high master of St Paul's School, and among the early pupils were John Clement who became tutor to More's children, and Thomas Lupset. Both became lecturers in Greek at Wolsey's new college at Oxford, Cardinal College, now Christ Church. More must have joined in many of the discussions about the school while Colet, with the help of Erasmus, was working out his plans. The time was soon to come when Thomas More would have to consider how best to educate his own children, and, as we shall see, his ideas tallied with those of Colet and Erasmus. The only direct evidence that connects More with St Paul's School is a fragment of a letter to John Colet which Stapleton has preserved.[11] It is difficult to date it but it was written after the school had been going long enough to rouse opposition; this came, in part, from Richard Fitzjames, Bishop of London. More wrote:

> I am not surprised that your excellent school is arousing envy. For as the Greeks came forth from the Trojan horse and destroyed barbarous Troy, so scholars are seen coming forth from your school to show up and overthrow the ignorance of others.

John Colet preached a sermon before Convocation in February 1512 that sums up his criticism of the state of the Church as he saw it. He emphasized those abuses that could be remedied by the

---

[10]On the history of these Grammars, see C. G. Allen, *Library*, Jan. 1954. Charles Lamb knew the book as "Paul's Accidence" at Christ's Hospital about 1785: *The Old and the New Schoolmaster*.

[11]Stapleton, p. 12.

clergy themselves without any further decrees or canons—the lust
for benefices, the evil lives of some priests, the pride of place and
dignity, and the unjust exaction of tithes and fees. "We are also
nowadays", he said, "grieved of heretics, men mad of marvellous
foolishness. But the heresies of them are not so pestilent and
pernicious unto us and the people as the evil and wicked lives of
priests."[12]

Among his listeners was Thomas Wolsey, Dean of Lincoln,
with his feet firmly placed on a lower rung of the ladder he was to
climb so rapidly. He was deaf to Colet's appeal and in his own
person was to aggravate some of the evils that marred the Church.

How can we picture Thomas More at this period, when, as it
were, he was graduating into public life? The famous Holbein
portrait was not painted until 1527, but, fortunately, we have a
careful description of him written by Erasmus in 1519,[13] largely
based, it may be supposed, on his close association with More
during the years 1509 to 1514. How much of that period they
spent together we do not know. There was a three months' break
in Paris in 1511, and, on his return, Erasmus went to Cambridge
where he taught Greek for two and a half years, but with many
absences on visits to his friends; he remained in England for six
months after leaving Cambridge. It can be assumed that the two
friends must have seen much of each other during those years
even when Erasmus was not actually staying at the Old Barge.
The *Colloquies* and his letters are evidence of the shrewdness with
which Erasmus observed his fellow men who, outside his scholarly
pursuits, were the chief object of his study. We can therefore
accept the fidelity of his account of his greatest friend.

Thomas More was of middle height and well-proportioned
except that his hands seemed all thumbs. His complexion was
clear and neither pale nor florid; his hair was auburn in youth
but darkened in manhood. His eyes were bluish-grey and
flecked. A vivacious expression hinted at his love of fun, fun that
never lapsed into frivolity. He had a clear speaking voice, but

---

[12]The English version of the sermon was at once printed by Berthelet. See Ap. C of
J. H. Lupton, *Life of Dean Colet* (1887).
[13]Allen, 999.

little skill in singing yet he delighted in all kinds of music and
played several instruments. He had no liking for games, and
gambling of any kind he abhorred. He was healthy, but not
robust. His indifference to his appearance distressed his man-
servant who had to watch his master to be sure he was correctly
dressed. He wore his gown carelessly, a mannerism much copied
by the law-students who admired him. He dressed plainly when
not in official garb. Food did not interest him; beef and salt fish
and the coarsest bread met his needs, but he had a liking for milk
dishes and eggs. Like his father, he preferred to drink water or
small beer; wine he rarely touched and when he did it was well
watered. His manners were pleasant but he disliked elaborate
formalities and empty talk. People felt at ease with him at once
and he suited his talk to their understanding, but was a good
listener. To quote Erasmus' revealing words, "He seems born
and created for friendship. . . . Should anyone look for a pattern
of true friendship, he could not do better than seek it in More."

Erasmus particularly praised Thomas More's acuteness of
intellect which was well served by a ready memory and a lively
wit. He added, "John Colet, a man of penetrating and sound
judgment, often observes that in all Britain there is only one
genius—Thomas More".

So much for the man as observed by a friend, but what of his
inner life? We have seen something of the spiritual conflict he
went through as a young man; he emerged with a strong,
unshakable faith that was the mainspring of his life. "He diligently
cultivates true piety", wrote Erasmus, "but is far removed from
all superstitious practices. He prays at set hours, and prays from
the heart."

CHAPTER IX

"Richard III"

ON 19 May 1511 Andrea Ammonio wrote to Erasmus, "Our sweetest More and his gentle wife, who never remembers you without wishing you well, with his children and whole household, are in excellent health".[1] The "gentle wife" died that summer, perhaps in August. Erasmus himself, who had returned to England in June, had been ill with the sweating sickness and it may have been the same disease that carried off Jane More, or she may have died in childbirth.

Twenty years later, Thomas More placed in his chapel in the church at Chelsea, a monument with a long inscribed epitaph.[2] The body of Jane More was removed to the family vault which would be under the chapel. She had probably been buried in St Stephen's, Walbrook, their parish church. The epitaph ends with some lines of verse commemorating the first wife, Jane, and the second, Alice, who was still alive. A literal translation reads:

> Here lies Jane the dear little wife of Thomas More who intends this tomb for Alice and me. The first, united to me in my youthful years, gave me a boy and three girls to call me father. The second—a rare distinction in a step-mother—was as affectionate as if the children were her own. It is hard to say if the first lived with me more beloved than the second does now. O how blessed if fate and religion had permitted us all three to live together! I pray the tomb and heaven may unite us; thus death will give what life could not give.

Jane More's death did not break the connection with the Colt family. Her father, John, left to his son-in-law by will in 1522 the sum of ten marks yearly for the "fynding"[3] of his son Thomas until of age. John Colt also left to More "one of the best colts at

[1]Allen, 221.
[2]The full Latin text is given in Harpsfield, pp. 279-81.
[3]Perhaps "fynding" means "providing for" rather than guardianship. Did he live at the Old Barge?

his own pleasure"—a little jest that would be enjoyed. There is no portrait of Jane More, nor any description of her apart from Ammonio's "gentle wife" and Erasmus' "very young girl". If she was married at sixteen, a not unusual age then, she was only about twenty-two when she died. Her daughters, especially Margaret, may have resembled her in features as they were not as like their father as was their brother John.

The needs of his young children were doubtless foremost in his mind when Thomas More decided to marry a second time, against the advice of his friends, according to Erasmus. It seems to us a cool-headed arrangement but it was according to custom in days when widows and widowers preferred to have partners rather than remain lonely. It proved a wise choice as the epitaph stated, perhaps all the better for its lack of romance. This second marriage took place within a month of the death of Jane More. We learn this from a letter written in 1535 by Father John Bouge,[4] who, before he entered the Charterhouse at Axholme (Epworth, Lincolnshire), had been parish priest at St Stephen's, Walbrook.

> As for Sir Thomas More, he was my parishioner in London. I christened him two goodly children. I buried his first wife, and within a month after, he came to me on a Saturday night late and there brought me a dispensation to be married the next Monday without any banns asking: and as I understand, she is yet living.

The aged monk's fitful memories are worth continuing.

> This Master More was my ghostly [spiritual] child: in his confession so pure, so clean, with great study, deliberation, and devotion, I never heard many such: a gentleman of great learning, both in law, art and divinity, having no man like him now alive a layman. Item, a gentleman of great soberness and gravity, one chief of the King's Council. Item, a gentleman of little refection and marvellous diet.

The wife was Alice, the widow of John Middleton, a prosperous merchant who had died in 1509; she brought with her a sub-stantial dower. She was six or seven years older than Thomas More. Her maiden name is not known but she was presumably

---

[4]John Bouge had been at school and college with John Fisher. L.P. Addenda, I, i. No. 1024.

an Arden as the arms of that family are quartered with those of
More in Chelsea Old Church. In his account of More, Erasmus
wrote:

> Within a few months he married a widow, more for the care of his
> children than for his own pleasure; "neither a pearl nor a girl",
> as he facetiously puts it, but a shrewd and careful housewife. Yet his
> life with her is as pleasant and agreeable as if she had all the charm of
> youth, and with his buoyant gaiety he wins her to more compliance
> than he could by severity. Surely a striking achievement to persuade
> a woman, middle-aged, set in her ways, and much occupied with
> her home, to learn to sing to the cithern or the lute, the monochord
> or the recorder, and to do a daily exercise set by her husband.[5]

The reference to music is supported by More's friend Richard Pace
who noted that she played duets with her husband.[6]

She had a reputation for blunt speech and this may explain the
phrase (if in fact it refers to her) in a letter from Ammonio to
Erasmus of 27 October 1511, where he wrote:

> I have moved at last into St Thomas [of Acon], where I am more
> housed according to my ideas than I was with More. I do not see *the*
> *hooked nose of the harpy*, but there are many other things that offend
> me so I really do not know how I can still go on living in England.

It was a rude comment; perhaps Mistress Alice decided that
Ammonio was a nuisance, as he may have been, and used her
tongue to get him out of the house. The tribute Erasmus paid her
in 1519 carries all the more weight since three years earlier he had
cut short a visit to the Old Barge because he felt that the mistress
had had enough of him.[7] He must have been at the best of times a
pernickety guest and one that spoke only Latin could be a trial to a
housewife with several small children to care for. It may be noted
that her husband did not overrule her.

There are two anecdotes in *A Dialogue of Comfort*[8] that have
been applied to her but without any firm reason for doing so. The
first is of a woman who, after confession, declared that she would
leave off her old shrewdness and "begin afresh", that is, begin her

---

[5] Allen, 999.
[6] *De fructu* (1517), p. 35.
[7] Allen, 451.
[8] *Dialogue of Comfort*, p. 248 and p. 291.

shrewdness afresh. The second story is of a woman who took great pains, in the literal sense, to give herself a slender waist. Such tales may have come to More's ears in many ways, or he may have invented them. Need we assume that every woman he mentions is Mistress Alice?

There were no children by this second marriage, but within two or three years a baby girl, Anne Cresacre, became one of the family. Her father, Edward Cresacre, had considerable estates at Barnbrough in the West Riding of Yorkshire; he died in 1512 shortly after his wife. Anne, the only surviving child, was born in 1511, and, as a minor, she became a ward of the Crown. The purchase of such wardships was a useful investment; the guardian had full control of the estates until an heir reached the age of twenty-one or an heiress sixteen. He had the right to arrange the marriage of his ward. The lower age of the heiress assumed she could marry at sixteen. Thomas More bought the wardship of Anne Cresacre.[9]

Alice Middleton, Mistress Alice's own daughter, also became one of the family. She may have been two or three years older than Margaret More. There were now seven young children at the Old Barge: the son and three daughters of Thomas More, his step-daughter, Alice Middleton, Margaret Giggs, and the baby, Anne Cresacre. One feels almost sorry for little John More among such a bevy of girls!

Each year following More's second marriage saw his increasing absorption in his professional career and in City affairs. With his father John More and his father's friend, John Roper, he was appointed a Commissioner of Sewers for the Thames in 1514.[10] In that year he became a member of the Society of Advocates, which later developed into Doctors' Commons. At that time it was more of a club than a professional body for not all its members were lawyers; they included such non-lawyers as Colet, Grocyn,

---

[9]In 1523 More bought the wardship of Giles Heron, the heir of Sir John Heron, Master of the Jewel House, See below, p. 173n. The system was open to abuse and was abolished under the Protectorate. In 1527 More became guardian of John Moreton, a wealthy landowner who had gone insane.

[10]We now think of Sewers as public drains, but the Commission was concerned with the flooding of the Thames, the Fleet River, etc.

Vergil and Ammonio, and a canon lawyer, Cuthbert Tunstal. Here we meet Tunstal for the first time as an associate, soon to be a close friend, of Thomas More. It has already been noted that Tunstal was at Oxford in 1491; he went on to Cambridge for two or three years and then to Padua where he took his degree in canon law. He returned to England in 1505 and was ordained subdeacon four years later and priest in 1511. He became Chancellor to Archbishop Warham in 1508 and in the following years was actively engaged in day-to-day administrative work. It is not known when he first met Thomas More. They and Erasmus had a common friend in Christopher Urswick who, in his old age, had retired to his living at Hackney, having refused the honours offered him. He was a link with the history of the past forty years, for, as far back as 1482, he had been confessor to the Lady Margaret Beaufort. Few men knew more of the ins and outs of the period. He was at Bosworth Field in 1485 and afterwards carried out a series of missions for Henry VII. More and Erasmus were fond of the old man and sought his company; from him they must have learned much of recent history and of the conduct of public affairs. It was Urswick who gave Erasmus the horse that "thrice carried him safely from and to Basle". Now Tunstal became one of the group. When Urswick died in 1522, he left Tunstal as his executor.

It was about 1513 that Thomas More began to write *Richard III*[11] and he seems to have worked on it intermittently for four or five years and even then left it unfinished. There are two versions, English and Latin. The English text in the folio of 1557 is prefaced by the following note by William Rastell:

> The history of king Richard the thirde (unfinished) writen by Master Thomas More than one of the undersheriffs of London: about the yeare of our Lorde 1513. Which worke hath bene before this tyme printed, in hardynges Cronicle, and in Hallys Cronicle; but very muche corrupte in many places, sometyme having lesse, and some-time having more, and altered in wordes and whole sentences; muche varying fro the copie of his own hand, by which thys is printed.

[11] The Yale edition of *Richard III*, ed. by R. S. Sylvester (1954), is indispensable. The present chapter owes much to this erudite edition.

"Hardynges Cronicle" here means the edition of that metrical history brought out in 1543 by Richard Grafton, who added More's history of Edward IV and Richard III but without the author's name. Edward Hall (as his name is usually now spelt) also used More's history for his Chronicle published in 1542 by Berthelet, and Grafton printed this text in a new edition of his Chronicle; he inserted the following note at the beginning of the account of Edward V: "This kynges tyme wt some part of kyng Richard ye iii as shall apere by a note made at that place was written by syr Thomas More".

This note reads: "From the beginning of Edward the fifte: hetherto is of sir Thomas Mores penning".

It is strange that such precise statements as those made by William Rastell and Richard Grafton should ever have been questioned, yet the suggestion, at one time, was widely accepted that the true author was Cardinal Morton. Thorough examination of this claim has vindicated More's authorship.[12] It is not necessary here to go over the ground again as no responsible scholar now doubts that he was the sole author.

How did Richard Grafton get the copy of *Richard III* which he printed in 1543, a year before the death of Margaret Roper? There is no known connection between him and the Mores; indeed his sympathies were with the reformers for his first printing venture (1539) was Coverdale's translation of the Bible made under Cromwell's patronage. That there was at least one copy of the manuscript of *Richard III* in private hands before 1538 is shown by the reply of George Crofts, Chancellor of Chichester, when he was questioned by the Council on his relations with the Poles: "I have asked him [Sir Geoffrey Pole] if one might without jeopardy have More's books in keeping. He said, 'Yes, for they treated not of the King's matters', and lent me a Chronicle of More's making of Richard III."[13]

This copy may have been one of More's earlier drafts; perhaps

---

[12]See the decisive article by R. W. Chambers in Vol. I of *English Works* (1931). Also the Yale edition, pp. lix-lxiii. The Morton claim will linger as long as the *D.N.B.* (arts. on Thomas More and Cardinal Morton), and the *Cambridge History of English Literature* (Vol. III, p. 17n, and p. 334) are current.

[13]L.P., XIII, ii, 828. Crofts was executed early in 1539 for denying the Supremacy.

he had lent it to his young friend Reginald Pole, the future Cardinal. This may have been seized when his brothers Henry (Lord Montague) and Geoffrey Pole were imprisoned in 1538, or, if Crofts failed to return it, when he, in turn, was put in the Tower. Cromwell may have passed it on to his friend Grafton. The use of such an early draft would explain some, though not all, of the variations to which Rastell objected. This seems a tenable explanation, but we are still left with the problem of how Edward Hall came into possession of a different draft of the book. Here too the answer may be found in the confiscations of papers that were made when those suspected of treason were arrested. Hall as an Under-Sheriff of London would be in a position to know of such papers.

The Latin text was first published in the Louvain edition of the *Opera Latina Omnia* in 1565. The variations between the English and Latin versions show that neither was a close translation of the other, More may have worked at both concurrently. The earlier portion was probably being written while Erasmus was in England, 1509-1514. He could not read the English version and perhaps he suggested a Latin one that could reach a larger public in other countries. Did he include *Richard III* among "experiments of every kind" that he said More made to acquire "a flexible prose style"? Perhaps Stapleton had this in mind when he said More wrote *Richard III* "to practise his pen", and that the English version was written first "with greater fullness of purpose", but Stapleton cannot be regarded as a primary authority on such a point.[14]

The significance of this unfinished work is that it is the first attempt in our language to compose a historical biography or biographical history in which personality and motive are taken into account. Historical writing in England, if we except lives of the saints, had been in the form of annals or chronicles, rather colourless compilations in which the emphasis was on what happened and not on why it happened. For his purpose More had excellent material at hand. As a boy he had lived through the reign of Richard III, and he could draw on the recollections of

[14]Stapleton, p. 31.

D

Cardinal Morton, and, of equal if not greater value, on those of his father and his father's friends. We have already pointed out that the indications are of John More having been in the service of Edward IV. Christopher Urswick would be another informant, and Thomas More could question some who had held office under Richard III and had later made their peace with Henry VII. The reader gets the impression of a contemporary account based on oral information; this comes not so much from direct references, such as, "I have heard by credible report of such as were secret with his chamberers", as by the immediacy of the tone. There is also a personal commitment in More's attitude towards King Richard that surely reflects the antagonism felt by John More and the general public towards the man who betrayed his trust by removing the legitimate King and his brother. We may still argue about the Princes in the Tower, but at the time it was widely and firmly believed that they had been murdered at the orders of their uncle. Thomas More must have shared this horror at a dark deed, and even a boy of five or six can receive impressions that are indelible.

We cannot now know what other sources More used in addition to the recollections of contemporary informants. He may have read the manuscript of Robert Fabyan's Chronicle. Polydore Vergil was at work on his *Anglica Historia* during the period More was writing his *Richard III*. As they were friends they may have exchanged views and they certainly consulted some of the same witnesses, but a comparison between Vergil's comparatively brief account and More's fuller treatment does not suggest close consultation.

When he began his work More would have in mind such classical historians as Sallust, Tacitus and Seutonius, and, with some ingenuity, a number of parallels can be traced, but More's own genius quickly took charge and carried him beyond mere imitation; the result was an original piece of writing, not a pastiche.

The influence of the classical model is early shown by the invented declamation, "The Oration of the King [Edward IV] in his Death-bed". The core of this was perhaps an account by

Cardinal Morton who may have been present, but the speech is developed on classical lines. As More gets into the swing of his narrative, so the classical pattern becomes less discernible. The outstanding quality of the work is its dramatic feeling; the youth who loved interludes is now applying his ability to larger themes. Here it was that More broke new ground in English historical writing; indeed the book may be regarded as a dramatic evocation rather than the kind of systematic inquiry and report that we now expect from historians.

One passage must serve as an example of this dramatic quality; we not only hear the characters speaking but we can visualize their gestures and movements. This is part of the account of the meeting between Queen Elizabeth and Cardinal Bourchier when she resisted as long as she could the proposal that she should allow her younger son, the Duke of York, to leave sanctuary at West-minster to join his brother, the young King. At last she gave way.

> And therewithal she said unto the child: "Farewell, my own sweet son, God send you good keeping. Let me kiss you once ere yet you go, for God knoweth when we shall kiss together again." And therewith she kissed him and blessed him, turned her back and wept and went her way, leaving the child weeping as fast.
>
> When the Cardinal and these other lords with him had received this young Duke, they brought him into the Star Chamber, where the Protector took him in his arms and kissed him with these words: "Now welcome, my lord, even with all my very heart". And he said in that of likelihood as he thought. Thereupon forthwith they brought him to the King his brother, into the Bishop's Palace at Paul's, and from thence through the city honourably into the Tower, out of which after that day, they never came abroad.[15]

More's sense of the comic is shown in such an incident as Dr Shaw's sermon at Paul's Cross. The plan had been that, at the right moment, when enthusiasm had been roused among the populace, Richard should make his entrance. The cue for him was when the preacher cried, "This is the father's own figure", but all was ruined by Richard's failure to be there on time when the words were said; so Shaw had to continue as best he could, and, when at

[15]*Richard III*, p. 42.

last the Protector did arrive, the preacher repeated the cue.

> But the people were so far from crying "King Richard!" that they stood as they had been turned into stones, for wonder of this shameful sermon. After which once ended, the preacher got him home and never after durst look out for shame but keep him out of sight like an owl.[16]

It is perhaps surprising that Shakespeare did not make use of this incident of the missed cue in his play. In Act III, v, 103, Gloucester (Richard) says, "Go, Lovel, with all speed to Doctor Shaw", but that is the only mention of him. He does not appear in the play. Did Shakespeare at first intend using him? What happened at Shaw's sermon is reported by Buckingham in Act III, vii, but the unfortunate duke cannot be blamed for not seeing the funny side of the affair!

More's sense of pity comes out in his treatment of Jane Shore, Edward IV's last mistress:

> I doubt not some shall think this woman too slight a thing to be written of and set among the remembrances of great matters: which they shall specially think, that haply shall esteem her only by that they now see her. But meseemeth the chance so much the more worthy to be remembered, in how much she is now in more beggarly condition, unfriended and worn out of acquaintance, after good substance, after so great favour with the Prince, after as great suit and seeking to with all those that those days had business to speed, so many other men were in their times, which be now famous only for the infamy of their ill deeds. Her doings were not much less, albeit they be much less remembered because they were not so evil. For men use, if they have an evil turn, to write it in marble; and whoso doth us a good turn, we write it in dust: which is not worst proved by her, for at this day she beggeth of many at this day living, that at this day had begged if she had not been.[17]

This account of Jane Shore gives the impression that More was using the witness of someone who knew her well; this may have been John More. As she was the daughter of a Mercer and the wife of a Mercer, it is probable that the family would be known to John More and his son. This was one of the passages that was

[16]*Ibid.*, p. 68.
[17]*Ibid.*, p. 57.

shortened in the Latin version because, presumably, the full details would not have interested a wider public.

More was not only experimenting in a literary form, he was, as Erasmus noted, also trying to gain a flexible prose style. It will be better to postpone a consideration of More's use of our language until we come to his more mature writings which had the advantage of careful revision before printing. One point may be made here as it refers to an element he later toned down. The reader is soon aware of the author's liking for alliteration. Here are a few examples:

Men mused what the matter was.
People diversely divining upon this dealing.
Wise ways to win favours.
Neither none he needeth nor also none to have.
Which whether they sorer thirsted after their own weal, or our woe,
    it were hard I ween to guess.

This alliteration is not obtrusive. The curious point is that there is little alliteration in More's verses though he was writing at a time when alliterative verse was an accepted form. In his poems he followed Chaucer rather than Langland. Yet alliteration was not a characteristic of fifteenth-century prose; it is not to be found, for instance, to any degree, in Caxton's prefaces, nor in Malory, nor in Berners. It is not pronounced in More's later writings.

It would be out of place here to discuss in detail the value of *Richard III* as history;[18] some of More's statements have been questioned and there are gaps and errors in the narrative, yet, as has been well said, "a contemporary's impressions are priceless and they are irreplaceable. A posthumous academic study of the archives can be a supplement to them, but not a substitute for them."[19] Had More finished and revised his work, he would no doubt have checked some of his facts and filled in the gaps; what we have is an incomplete, unrevised draft. He recorded the oral

[18]For the history, see P. M. Kendall, *Richard III* (1956), and E. F. Jacob, *The Fifteenth Century* (1961), Ch. 13. For Shakespeare's use of More, see E. M. W. Tillyard, *Shakespeare's History Plays* (1944). Those who long to whitewash Richard have to malign Henry Tudor; so they argue that he found the two Princes in the Tower and had them murdered. The pro-Richard view is put in Josephine Tey's novel, *The Daughter of Time* (1951), which has had more influence than any academic discussions.

[19]Arnold Toynbee. Foreword to W. Croker, *Nehru* (1966).

tradition while it was still forming. The inclusion of *Richard III* in historical compilations right into the eighteenth century ensured that More's view of Richard III became the commonly accepted one; it was perpetuated by Shakespeare, and no amount of modern research seems able to destroy it.

More hinted that he hoped to carry the story further: ". . . if we hereafter happen to write the time of the late noble prince of famous memory King Henry VII, or percase the history of Perkin [Warbeck] . . .".[20] He may have broken off because of the embarrassment of mentioning living persons, but it is more likely that the time he gave to public affairs left him little leisure for such writing. Whatever the reason, the loss to historical literature is considerable.

Had Thomas More any special reason in writing about Richard III apart from the wish to "practise his pen" and the fact that the material lay at hand? Was it his intention to point a moral, as Hardying had done, and Polydore Vergil, to suggest the working of God's providence in the triumph of Henry Tudor? The theme was again taken up by Edward Hall. More did not declare that he had any such purpose in mind, but the narrative itself, without any gloss, conveys the author's and, it can be added, the popular revulsion at the bloodstained tyranny of Richard. Indeed it would be difficult without special pleading to avoid making the story one of the growth of tyranny and violence leading to more violence and greater tyranny. The few comments More makes arise naturally from his materials. The subject of tyranny was much in the minds of More and Erasmus at this time and finds expression in the epigrams we must study at a later stage.

[20]*Richard III*, p. 82.

CHAPTER X

Hunne and Standish

Two EVENTS, one in 1515 and the other in 1516, call for consideration as each strikingly exemplified the problem that was ultimately
to bring Thomas More to the scaffold—the problem of the relation
between Church and State. They also illustrate the feeling of the
time towards the clergy. More was slightly concerned with the
first, the case of Richard Hunne, but, as far as is known, not
directly with that of Friar Standish, though he would follow
the arguments as they were of importance to a common
lawyer.

Before we deal with these two clashes between Church and
State, it will be necessary to say something about the Statutes of
Praemunire that were to play such a fearful part in Henry VIII's
policy. The word "praemunire" came from the first word of the
writ which was served on anyone charged with a breach of the
statutes. By usage "praemunire" became the name of the statutes
and "a praemunire" the name of the offence. The three Statutes of
Praemunire (1353, 1364 and 1393) with the two Statutes of
Provisors (1351 and 1390) were part of the attempts to regulate
the relations between the King and the Pope chiefly as regards
appointments to benefices or the translation by papal bull of
bishops from one diocese to another. Provision to benefices by
the Pope was, on paper, forbidden and those who accepted such
benefices forfeited their property and goods. Recourse to the
papal courts was forbidden in matters properly the concern of the
Crown. The purpose of these statutes was to limit the power of
Rome to interfere in matters that touched the rights of the English
Crown. Had these statutes been rigidly enforced, the influence
of the papacy would have been considerably reduced; the Pope,
for instance, would have had no voice in the appointments of
bishops or of encumbents to those benefices over which he had

privileges. Edward III and Richard II used the statutes as bargaining counters in their disputes with the papacy; this was made
easier when there were rival Popes from 1378 to 1417. In practice
the appointments of bishops, for instance, were taken away,
except nominally, from the chapters and shared by the King
and the Pope, the King granting the temporalities (the bishops
were his vassals) and the Pope the spiritualities. There were comparatively few disagreements on appointments. It will be noted
that these statutes were primarily concerned with appointments
(provisions) to benefices; they were not abrogated but were
held, as it were, *in terrorem*. Nor was the idea of a breach with
Rome ever seriously considered. The statutes were acts of State
at a time when nations were developing separate political, but not
religious, identities. The somewhat vague terms of the statutes
left many loop-holes, and common lawyers began so to interpret
them in order to restrict the jurisdiction of the ecclesiastical
courts and argued that any attempt to take to an ecclesiastical
court a suit that was cognizable in the king's courts was a breach
of praemunire. As we shall see, praemunire became a terrible
weapon in the hands of Henry VIII and was unscrupulously
applied far beyond the original scope of the statutes.

The Richard Hunne case[1] generated much heat at the time and
can still rouse warm argument, but it remains an insoluble
problem. Such conclusions as we can reach have to be based on
documents that have chanced to survive, and they do not cover
all the issues.

First for the facts as far as they can be stated. Richard Hunne, a
merchant tailor of London, "a fair dealer among his neighbours"
according to More, lost a five-weeks' son in the autumn of 1514;
after the burial the parish priest claimed the child's christening
robe as a mortuary, that is, as the customary gift due to the priest
from the estate of a deceased parishioner. Hunne refused on the
grounds that an infant, in law, could not have any property. The
priest sued him in the ecclesiastical court and won the case.

[1] See A. F. Pollard, *Wolsey* (1929), pp. 31-44, for a clear account. Also the first half of
A. Ogle, *The Tragedy of the Lollards' Tower* (1949) which overstates a reasonable case. The
record of the inquest is given in Hall, Vol. II, pp. 129-40; there is no reason to doubt its
substantial authenticity.

Thereupon Hunne brought an action of praemunire in the King's Bench alleging that the church court had taken cognizance of a matter that rightly came within the jurisdiction of the civil court. This case was not settled at the time of Hunne's death. He was charged with heresy and lodged in the Lollards' Tower at St Paul's. Popular opinion was that this was done out of spite because Hunne had "sued a praemunire". Hunne was found hanged in his cell on 4 December 1514. Was it suicide or murder? On the following day the coroner's court met but its proceedings dragged on until February 1515. Meanwhile the heresy case had been determined. In the presence of the Mayor and Aldermen (the City Magistrates) the trial of the dead man was held at St Paul's and he was condemned as a heretic; his corpse was dug up and burned.[2] To us this seems repulsive but it was accepted as normal at the time. Nor can we in this century afford to criticize when far more gruesome deeds have been done, and are being done, in the name of the civil law. It is important to note the presence of the City magistrates; it was not a hugger-mugger affair behind closed doors. Had they felt the verdict was ill-founded, they would surely have protested, but they did not do so. The City was the last community that could be brow-beaten by anyone from the King downwards. Thomas More was among the City officials at this trial and he was convinced by the evidence produced that Richard Hunne was a heretic. "It was well proved", he wrote, "that he was convict as well of divers other heresies as of misbelief toward the holy sacrament of the altar".[3] Among the exhibits was Hunne's copy of the Wycliffite Bible with its tendentious prologue.[4] This was scored in places that had appealed to him and these, it was argued, proved his heretical leanings. Thomas More further rejected the popular saying quoted by him

[2]The property of a condemned heretic was forfeit to the crown. The wardship of Hunne's two daughters was bought by John Rastell, More's brother-in law. It got him into much litigation, but then many of his affairs ended that way! See, A. W. Reed, *Early Tudor Drama* (1926), pp. 14-16.

[3]For More's comments, see *Dialogue Concerning Heresies*, Book III, Ch. 15; *Supplication of Souls*, E.W., pp. 297-9, and a passing reference in *The Apologye*, p. 142.

[4]A. Ogle believed he had identified the actual copy at Corpus Christi College, Cambridge. See Ch. VII of *The Tragedy of the Lollards' Tower*.
D*

that "Hunne had never been accused of heresy if he had never sued a praemunire".[5]

It was not until late in February (nearly two months after the burning of the corpse) that the coroner's jury brought in a verdict of murder against "William Horsley of London, Chancellor to Richard Bishop of London, and one Charles Joseph, summoner [and gaoler] and John Spalding of London otherwise John Bellringer" who had charge of the keys that fateful night. More's comment was, "And therefore though I cannot think but the jury, which were right honest men, found the verdict as themself thought in their own conscience to be truth; yet, in my own mind for ought that ever I heard in my life, as help me God, I could never think it". He evidently had a better opinion of his fellow citizens than, as we shall see, had the Bishop. At this distance of time it is not possible to reach a definitive judgment on this involved case, but one argument put forward by More has not been given sufficient weight. He asked, in effect, what point was there in Horsley's planning Hunne's murder? Hunne was faced with a charge of heresy, and conviction meant, unless he abjured, a sentence of death by the civil authorities. Suicide, wrote More, "is much more likely to me than the thing whereof I never heard the like before, that the bishop's chancellor should kill in the Lollards' Tower a man so sore suspect and convict of heresy, whereby he might bring himself in business; whereas if he hated the man . . . he might easily bring him to the shame and peradventure to shameful death also".

William Horsley was arrested but, as a cleric, he was not imprisoned; he was placed in the charge of Archbishop Warham. The Bishop of London, Richard Fitzjames, seems to have lost his head for he begged Archbishop Wolsey to have the case dealt with by the Council and not by a common jury. "For assured I am, if my Chancellor be tried by any twelve men in London, they be so maliciously set *in favorem haereticae pravitatis* (in favour of

---

[5]A. F. Pollard accepted More's opinion (*Wolsey*, p. 41n). Dr G. R. Elton, *England under the Tudors* (1955), p. 105, thinks that A. Ogle proved that Hunne was murdered. Could not a case be made out that Charles Joseph murdered Hunne, not at the instigation of Horsley (who had nothing to gain), but at that of Hunne's private enemies? An interesting speculation, but we lack essential documents.

venomous heresy) that they will cast and condemn any cleric though he were as innocent as Abel." The City fathers got wind of this letter (how?) and appointed a deputation to protest to the Bishop at "certain perilous and heinous words as be surmised by him to be spoken of the whole body of the City touching heresy". This seems to have had small effect for, later in the Lords, Fitzjames declared the coroner's jury were "false perjured caitiffs" and added, "I dare not keep mine house for heretics". This cannot be taken as a factual description of the extent of heresy in London, still less in the Bishop's palace at Fulham; there is little to support his outburst which seems almost hysterical. However, the appeal to Wolsey was successful and, with the consent of the King, the case against Horsley was heard. He pleaded "not guilty" and the Attorney-General withdrew the prosecution. Horsley paid the very large fine of £600, which seems a queer way of treating a man who was declared to be innocent. Perhaps it may be regarded as a douceur to Wolsey. William Horsley then disappeared into the West country. Technically that was the end of the Hunne affair, and it would not have been necessary to narrate it here at such length had it been nothing more than a question of the verdict of a coroner's court. It was important, first, as revealing dramatically the anti-clerical (not anti-religious) atmosphere of the times. Secondly, it prompted Parliament to act, and led to official debates on the relations between Church and State in which Hunne's case served as a refrain.

The third Parliament of Henry VIII's reign met on 5 February 1515, and the first session lasted until 5 April; the second session began on 12 November and ended on 22 December. More was not a member. Before the Parliament finally dispersed, Wolsey had become a Cardinal and had succeeded Warham as Lord Chancellor. Parliament was not called again for eight years.

The Commons began by proposing the renewal of an Act of 1512, which ran only until the next Parliament, depriving criminals in minor orders of benefit of clergy. As the Convocation of Canterbury met at the same time, Bishop Fitzjames arranged for Richard Kidderminster, Abbot of Winchcombe, to preach at Paul's Cross a sermon defending the immunity of all clerics and

arguing that the Act was contrary to the law of God and the
liberties of the Church. Pope Leo X had just issued a bull declaring
that civil courts had no jurisdiction over the clergy. The Commons
passed the Bill to renew the Act, but the Lords rejected it. The
fact that the spiritual peers had a majority over the temporal
peers in the Lords roused much bitter comment. The King then
ordered the two Houses with the judges and members of the
Council to meet in the hall at Blackfriars to discuss the question.[6]
The laity found a spokesman in Henry Standish, the warden of the
Greyfriars; he has been called "the last distinguished friar of his
generation".[7] He maintained that the public good must be the
deciding consideration, and that by customary law, criminous
clerks had always been subject to the king's courts. An opponent
(whose name is not recorded) pointed out that the papal bull made
it clear that it was a mortal sin to bring a cleric before a temporal
judge. To which Standish replied that such papal decrees had
never been received in England. He made a shrewd thrust when
he mentioned that there was another papal decree ordaining that
all bishops should be present in their Cathedrals on the great
feasts, a ruling that most bishops ignored. The opposing speaker
then declared that our Lord had said, "Touch not mine anointed
ones". To which Standish replied that those words were said by
the Psalmist David and not by our Lord. So the argument went
on, but it became evident that Standish had the better of it. Some
of the temporal peers thought that the Abbot of Winchcombe
should again preach at Paul's Cross and withdraw his previous
declarations. There is no record of his having done so. The
conference seems to have broken up without reaching any
conclusion.

Parliament and Convocation were adjourned from 5 April
until 12 November. During this interval Thomas More was
absent in Bruges on an embassy. Friar Standish, however, was not
silent. He made his opinions more widely known by his sermons,
and these proved much to the liking of the citizens. It was therefore
not surprising that when Convocation reassembled, he was called

[6]Our knowledge of these debates depends on the reports of Robert Keilway of the
Inner Temple (1496-1581). He became a serjeant-at-law in 1522. His reports were first
published in 1602. See A. Ogle, *The Tragedy of the Lollards' Tower*, pp. 144-54.
[7]D. Knowles, *The Religious Orders in England*, Vol. III, p. 55.

upon to answer a series of pointed objections to his publicly declared views; the chief question was the authority of a temporal court to judge clerics in defiance of a papal decree. Standish wisely refused to answer. As a friar and as provincial of his order, he was in a more independent position than one of the secular clergy. He appealed to the King who had also been approached by the temporal peers, the Commons, and the judges to resolve the dispute. So a second conference was called at Blackfriars. The outcome was startling. The judges declared that Convocation in summoning Standish before it had been guilty of praemunire. Here we can see an attempt to extend the application of the Statutes of Praemunire. As a corollary the judges pointed out that the spiritual peers were in Parliament not by reason of their spiritual functions but as vassals of the Crown, and indeed need not be summoned at all save at the King's pleasure. Here was an explosive situation that called for careful handling. How would the twenty-four-year-old King deal with it?

Henry called a third conference, this time at Baynard's Castle with himself present. According to More the Hunne case was again brought up, but this cannot be confirmed. When the Convocation's dealing with Standish was discussed, Cardinal Wolsey knelt before the King and submitted that the clergy had no intention of encroaching on the royal prerogative but that the summoning of clergy before temporal courts was contrary to divine law; he begged that the dispute should be referred to Rome. So Wolsey began his Cardinalate, as he ended it, on his knees before the King. Henry bluntly declared that Standish had already proved that clerics were not immune from the due process of law. Warham spoke in support of Wolsey's plea. He was answered by Sir John Fineux, Chief Justice of the King's Bench, who claimed that the Early Fathers of the Church had accepted the rulings of the law of the land; the arraignment of felonious clerks before civil courts was a long established practice especially as the church courts had no powers to punish serious crime. At length the King closed the discussion by declaring that, "We intend to maintain the right of our crown and of our temporal jurisdiction, as well in this point as in all other points, in as ample manner as any of our progenitors have done before our time". He was not here claiming any new power; he was re-asserting, correctly, the fact that his predecessors on the throne had never recognized any superior in temporal authority. He was not foreshadowing a fresh quarrel with Rome; he was em-phasizing his prerogative. He was certainly not proposing any limitation on the Pope's spiritual pre-eminence and authority in matters of discipline within the Church. Yet it may have been this critical confrontation of clergy and laity that sowed a seed that was to germinate when another crisis, this time a personal one, brought the issue to a head. Nor was he to forget the part prae-munire had in those tangled proceedings he had abruptly ended. Henry VIII had a long memory.

After the Baynard's Castle conference, the whole matter was dropped. Convocation took no further action against Standish.[8] It was as if everyone drew back from the edge of the precipice when they recognized the dangerous nature of the underlying issues. The time was not yet ripe for a solution.

Thomas More may have been present at the Baynard's Castle conference.[9] In his *Dialogue Concerning Heresies* he referred to it and repeated some amusing, almost farcical, gossip of the time, but he did not state specifically that he was there. He would know many of those present such as Tunstal and perhaps his own father who, through his friend John Roper, would be familiar with the views of his father-in-law, Sir John Fineux.

As we have seen, More gave two extended comments on the Hunne affair, but he did not give an account of the Standish dispute. There is one reference to it in the *Debellation*:

> As for conventing of priests before secular judges, true it is that one time the occasion of a sermon made the matter come in commission before the King's Highness. But neither any time since nor many years afore, I never heard that there was any business about it, and

---

[8]Against Wolsey's wishes, he became Bishop of St Asaph in 1518, and so Erasmus, "Saint Asse" for having criticized the *Novum Instrumentum*. He defended Queen Catherine, but later accepted the King's Supremacy.

[9]Did More confuse this meeting with one of those at Blackfriars? The Hunne case may have been mentioned, but was it discussed at Baynard's Castle?

yet was that matter ceased before any word sprang of this general division [i.e. between the Spirituality and the Temporality].

From this it would seem that he did not regard this problem as of urgent importance, even as late as 1533.

On the question of benefit of clergy, he appealed to his own practice. In *The Apologye* he wrote:

Those that be spiritual persons by profession, and are thereby carnal and wretched in their condition, have never been favoured by me. When I was first of the King's Council, and after his Under-Treasurer and in the time while I was Chancellor of his Duchy of Lancaster, and when I was his Chancellor of this realm, it was meetly [fairly] well known what manner of favour I bare toward the clergy and that as I loved and honoured the good, so was not remiss or slack in providing for the correction of those that were nought, noyous to good people, and slanderous to their own order; which sort of priests and religious running out of religion and falling to theft and murder, had at my hand so little favour, that there was no man that any meddling had with them, into whose hands they were more loath to come. And in this point found I their ordinaries [bishops] so well minded to their amendment and correction that they have me great thanks therefore.[10]

The last sentence seems at variance with the strong opposition of the bishops themselves to the limitation of benefit of clergy as expressed in the Standish dispute, but, when More wrote these lines in 1533, he probably had in mind the period when Tunstal was Bishop of London (1522-30); he was a man of more balanced judgment than his tetchy predecessor, and his successor, the coarse-grained John Stokesley.

Here, although it is leaping ahead chronologically, it will help us to get a glimpse of More's mind, though not of his whole thinking, on the vexed question of the relations between King and Pope, if we quote a statement he made to a committee of the Council in the Nun of Kent case in 1534.[11] The Councillors raised the question of his share in the production of the King's book *Assertio Septem Sacramentorum* published in 1521, six years after the Standish affair. They had charged Thomas More with having

[10]*Apologye*, pp. 53-4.   [11]See below, p. 290.

encouraged the King to give too much weight to the Pope's authority. To this More replied:

> Wherein [the book] I found the Pope's authority highly advanced and with strong arguments mightily defended, I said unto his Grace, "I must put your Highness in remembrance of one thing, and that is this. The Pope as your Grace knoweth, is a prince as you are, and in league with all other Christian princes. It may hereafter so fall out that your Grace and he may vary upon some points of the league, whereupon may grow breach of amity and war between you both. I think it best therefore that that place be amended, and this authority more slenderly touched."
>
> "Nay", quoth his Grace, "that shall it not. We are so much beholden unto the See of Rome that we cannot do too much honour to it."
>
> Then did I further put him in remembrance of the statute of praemunire whereby a good part of the Pope's pastoral cure here was pared away.
>
> To that answered his Highness, "Whatsoever impediment to the contrary, we will set forth that authority to the uttermost. For we received from that See our crown imperial." Which till his Grace with his own mouth told me, I never heard before.[12]

The Hunne and Standish affairs underlined two tendencies in public feeling. The first was the widespread and deeply-felt anti-clericism of the times, and the second was the determination of the common lawyers to resist any encroachment by Rome on the jurisdiction of the Courts of the land. Henry's action had not been taken on the advice of Cardinal Wolsey, but on that of John Veysey, Dean of the Chapel Royal.[13] In the years that followed, Wolsey was able to keep these tendencies in check, but after his fall they found their inevitable outlets.

---

[12]Presumably Henry was referring to the bull (27 March 1487) of Innocent VIII confirming Henry VII as lawful King of England and securing the succession to his children. Henry VII also received the cap and sword of maintenance from Innocent VIII in 1489, from Alexander VI in 1496, and from Julius II in 1505. Henry VIII received them from Leo X in 1514. Roper, p. 67.

[13]See D.N.B., and below, p. 166.

Chapter XI

"Utopia"[1]

UTOPIA
*Woodcut by Ambrosius Holbein. The figures represented are, from the left:
John Clement, Raphael Hythlodaye, Thomas More and Peter Gilles*

In January 1515 Thomas More was orator for the City at the reception of the new Venetian Ambassador, Sebastian Giustinian. They later became good friends as they had much in common, not least an eager interest in the works of Erasmus. The Ambassador reported to Venice that More was "the most linked with me in friendship of any in this kingdom".

Under the date 8 May 1515 we read in the City Records:

It is agreed that Thomas More, Gent., one of the Under-sheriffs of London which shall go on the King's embassy into Flanders shall supply his room and office by his sufficient deputy until his coming home again.

The opening paragraph of *Utopia* reads:

Henry VIII, the invincible King of England, a prince unrivalled in those virtues that grace a great monarch, having some important

[1]See *Utopia* (Yale, 1965), ed. Edward Surtz, S. J., and J. H. Hexter; the Introduction is important. For Ralph Robinson's translation (1551), see J. H. Lupton's edition (1895). There is a lively translation in current English by Paul Turner in the Penguin Classics (1965).

matters in dispute with His Serene Highness, Prince Charles of Castile,[2] sent me to Flanders to discuss these differences. I was joined in commission with Cuthbert Tunstal, a man of distinguished ability, who, much to everyone's satisfaction, has recently been made Master of the Rolls.[3]

It was probably at the suggestion of the City merchants that Thomas More was appointed to this delegation. The "matters in dispute" concerned the trade relations between England and Flanders arising out of the treaties made under Henry VII in 1496 and 1506. A second deputation dealt with political issues; these do not call for consideration here. The wool and cloth trade between England and Flanders was of vital importance to both countries as well as to the Netherlands. The high tide of English raw wool exports had been ebbing for some time but its place was being taken by a flourishing cloth industry. The regulation of these trades called for diplomatic skill. To cope with the practical issues, More must have studied the wool and cloth trades more thoroughly than had been necessary in dealing with local conditions in London. This new interest is reflected in the First Book of *Utopia*. Apparently he was not involved in the full range of negotiations, perhaps only in those of direct concern to the City, for in a letter to Erasmus on his return home, he wrote:

When therefore I saw the business ended for which I myself was sent, and that nevertheless other matters were arising which seemed to be leading to further delay, I wrote at last to the Cardinal and got leave to return.[4]

Erasmus had arrived in England early in May 1515. When he learned that More was about to go Flanders, he at once wrote to his friend Peter Gilles of Antwerp, who was the chief clerk of the magistracy there and a scholar and the friend of scholars.

The two most learned men of England are now at Bruges, Cuthbert Tunstal, the Archbishop of Canterbury's Chancellor, and Thomas More, to whom I dedicated my *Moria*; both great friends of mine.

[2]The Archduke Charles (nephew of Catherine of Aragon) was declared of age in January 1515 shortly before his fifteenth birthday. He made his court at Brussels. He became King of Spain in March 1516, and Emperor, as Charles V, in June 1519.
[3]12 May 1516.   [4]Allen, 388. Rogers (5).

If you should have a chance to offer them any civility, your services will be well bestowed.[5]

When More left England about 12 May, he took with him his young protégé John Clement, one of the earliest pupils of St Paul's School.

The time-table of commercial negotiations has its importance in the study of the composition of *Utopia*, for the writing of that famous book is now the only memorable outcome of More's five months' stay in Flanders. He throws some light on the course of events in the opening passage:

> As we were unable to reach full agreement on some points after one or two meetings, the Prince's commissioners took leave of us and left for Brussels to get his advice. Meanwhile I went straight to Antwerp where I had business. While I was staying there, the most welcome of my visitors was Peter Gilles.[6]

More does not tell us how long these preliminary meetings lasted. On 9 July the English delegation wrote to the Council at Westminster to point out that their funds were exhausted. On the same date Tunstal wrote to Wolsey to report the lack of progress in the negotiations. The full series of letters has not been preserved, but there is a draft of a letter dated 18 July 1515, heavily amended by Wolsey, instructing Tunstal to go to Brussels to consult with the other English delegation.[7] This was crossed by a letter signed by Tunstal, More and Clifford, dated 21 July from Bruges, asking for further instructions. On getting the letter of 18 July Tunstal left his companions at Bruges and went to Brussels.

Erasmus and More had met in Bruges in June when Erasmus was on his way to Basle, and, no doubt, he saw Peter Gilles and again urged him to meet Thomas More. Their first meeting came at some date between 21 July and 1 October during the period in which More seems to have visited Antwerp. In the opening paragraphs of *Utopia*, More said that he had been more than four months away from home when he first met Peter Gilles; this would mean September, but his "four months" need not be taken literally.

[5]Allen, 322.
[6]For More's visit to Antwerp, see *Utopia* (Yale), Ap. I. [7]Herbrüggen, 11a.

The long drawn-out commercial negotiations gave More considerable leisure. His visit to Antwerp may have been used to confer with English merchants there (did Thomas Cromwell give him some introductions?), and he may have renewed his acquaintanceship with the Antwerp officials he had got to know in 1509 when they came to London. He also took the opportunity to visit Jerome Busleyden of Mechlin.[8] He too was a scholar-friend of Erasmus; he was also a diplomatist and a councillor. In a letter to Erasmus from London, February 1516, More recalled this visit with special pleasure:

> During my embassy some things greatly delighted me. First living so long with Tunstal, a man who while he is unsurpassed in culture and regularity of life, is a most pleasant companion. Then too I came to know Busleyden who received me with a magnificence equal to his great fortune, and a kindness in keeping with his goodness of heart. He showed me his house so marvellously built and splendidly furnished and containing so many of those antiquities that, as you know, I find so fascinating. Above all there was his well-stocked library, and a mind even better stocked.[9]

More returned home towards the end of October 1515. On his way to Calais, he met his friend Richard Pace at Gravelines on 24 October. He was being sent by Wolsey to Switzerland to bribe the Swiss mercenaries to attack the French. He probably discussed his mission with More and thereby sowed another seed that was to germinate in *Utopia*.

From the letter just quoted comes the following playful comment on his Flanders experience:

> An Ambassador's position has never had any great charms for me; indeed it does not seem to be so suitable for us laymen as for you clergy who either have no wives or children or find them wherever you go. When I am away I have two households to support, one in England and another abroad. I received a liberal allowance from the King for the persons I took with me, but no account is taken of those whom I left behind, and although you know what a kind husband, what an indulgent father, what a considerate master I am, yet I have

---

[8]He founded the Louvain Collegium Trilingue in which Erasmus took a close interest. Busleyden died in 1517.

[9]Allen, 388. Rogers (5).

never been able to persuade my family to go without food while I am away. Then it is easy for princes to compensate the labours and expenses of the clergy by church preferment without putting themselves to any cost, while we laymen are not provided for so handsomely or so readily. Nevertheless, on my return I had a yearly pension offered me by the King, which whether one looked to for profit or the honour of it was not to be despised. This, however, I have hitherto refused, and shall, I think, continue to do so, because, if I took it, the place I now hold in the City, which I prefer to a higher office, would either have to be given up, or retained much to my regret with some offence to the citizens who, if they had any question with the government, as sometimes happens about their privileges, would have less confidence in me as a paid pensioner of the King.

As we shall see, this problem of whether to enter the King's service or not, became an important theme in the First Book of *Utopia*.

When More left Flanders, he had with him the manuscript, or draft, of what became the Second Book of *Utopia*; he may also have written the introductory pages of the First Book. Erasmus' account reads:

In *Utopia* his purpose was to show whence spring the evils of states, chiefly based on his close study of England. He began with the Second Book, written at leisure, and then, when opportunity came, he added the First rapidly; this accounts for some unevenness in the style.[10]

The "rapidly" does not agree with what we know of the time taken by More to complete the book; perhaps Erasmus meant that the actual writing was done rapidly and not the working out of the ideas. Erasmus was referring to the Latin style of More which was fluent, even colloquial at times, but without the elegance that Erasmus would have preferred. This was probably due to the fact that Latin was a living language for Thomas More as for many of his contemporaries, and he wrote as he spoke. Thus in conversation with Peter Gilles or Busleyden he would speak Latin as they too would do.

There was a local tradition that More completed his *Utopia* at

[10]Allen, 999.

his father's country house of Gobions, North Mimms. It was recorded by Henry Peacham, author of *The Compleat Gentleman* (1622): "Merry John Heywood wrote his Epigrams as also Sir Thomas More his *Utopia* in the parish wherein I was born, where either of them dwelt and had fair possessions".[11]

Peacham's father had held the living of North Mimms, so the story cannot be lightly dismissed; indeed More may have taken refuge there in order to get away from the press of business in the City.

Peter Gilles had evidently expected that the whole book would be ready for the printer early in 1516. In his dedicatory letter, More apologized for the delay. "I am almost ashamed, my dearest Peter," he wrote, "to send you this book about the commonwealth of Utopia after nearly a year when I am sure you expected it within six weeks." He pleaded the claims of his family and the pressure of work. The delay, however, proved an advantage for it gave time for Erasmus, while More's guest for several weeks in July–August 1516, to talk over the book with his host. They no doubt also discussed Erasmus' newly published *Institutio Principis Christiani*. Perhaps other members of the circle, such as John Colet, joined in the talks as they may have done when *Moria* was on the stocks. Nor should it be overlooked that the original conversations in Antwerp may have been shared with others besides Peter Gilles. No doubt John Clement had his say as well, for, as More wrote to Gilles, "I never let him miss any conversation that may improve his mind". Here we may find the origin of some of the details in the polity of Utopia that seem discordant or not closely woven into the texture. One of the friends might have interjected, "Why not make them do so and so?" For the fun of the thing More may have inserted such ideas without bothering to work them into a closely-knit scheme. In a second letter to Gilles, included only in the 1517 (Paris) edition, More noted that some critics had commented on "some of the rather absurd elements" in the account of the commonwealth, and there are undoubtedly some notions that seem inappropriate

---

[11]John Heywood, author of *The Four PP* and other interludes, married Thomas More's niece, Joan Rastell. See A. W. Reed, *Early Tudor Drama.*

or that have not been fully worked out. It is not here implied that anything that seems odd to the reader came from one of More's companions and not from him; all that is suggested is that he used suggestions made by others and did not bother to integrate them.

After Erasmus left London in the middle of August 1516, he went to Rochester to spend ten days with Bishop John Fisher, and while he was there Thomas More "hurried down to have another look at Erasmus whom he seems to fear he will not see again". Perhaps he had hoped to hand over to Erasmus the final copy of *Nusquama* (Nowhere), as *Utopia* was at first called, but he still had some touches to put to the manuscript. On 3 September he at last sent the completed book to Erasmus who was by then in Louvain. "I send you *Nusquama*, nowhere well written, with a prefatory letter to my dear Peter."[12] He wrote again on 20 September to suggest that other preliminary letters of commenda-tion should be obtained; it was as if he feared his little work needed supporting testimonials from scholars and leading personalities. Peter Gilles wrote to Jerome Busleyden whose reply, addressed to More, was also printed in the first edition. Erasmus wrote on 2 October from Antwerp, where he was staying with Peter Gilles, "Every care shall be taken about the island. . . . Peter Gilles is simply in love with you; you are still always with us. He is wonderfully struck with your *Nusquama*."[13] Another month passed before Gerard of Nijmegen, who was corrector to the press of the printer Thierry Martin of Louvain, sent to Erasmus the news that "our Thierry has willingly and joyfully undertaken the printing of *Utopia*. . . . I will take great care that *Utopia* shall be produced in a handsome style so that there may be nothing to interfere with the pleasure of the reader."[14] In the middle of December, More wrote to Erasmus, "I now look forward every day for our *Utopia* with feelings with which a mother awaits the return of her boy from foreign parts".[15] When he wrote "our *Utopia*", he was not suggesting that he and Erasmus were col-laborators; simply that they had talked of the book so much together that it owed something to Erasmus' ideas; in the

[12]Allen, 461.   [13]Allen, 474.
[14]Allen, 487. Note the new title had been adopted.   [15]Allen, 502.

same way either of them could have said "our *Moria*".

Utopia was published in December 1516. It was in Latin so that it could reach as wide a public as possible. English was little known in Europe. The first English translation (would that it had been the author's!) did not appear until 1551; it was by Ralph Robinson who dedicated it, rather apologetically, to William Cecil, later Lord Burghley. On 4 January 1517, Lord Mountjoy, then lieutenant or governor at Tournai, wrote to Erasmus to thank him for "the book on the Island of Utopia"; he added, "as I cannot enjoy the company of More himself, I shall at least find my dear More in *Utopia*".[16]

To what extent is Thomas More to be found in *Utopia*? The First Book reports a conversation and discussion between three speakers: two of them actual persons, More and Gilles, and one, Hythlodaye, a fictitious character. The Second Book is, for the most part, a monologue by Hythlodaye. This would seem to present the same problem of interpretation as that posed by a play by Shakespeare when we try to fathom his own opinions. The parallel, however, does not hold good for *Utopia* is not a drama though it has dramatic elements. We may therefore assume that, by and large, it expresses More's own ideas. Part of the First Book is a discussion on whether a philosopher should serve the State; More is here, as it were, arguing the pros and cons with himself, and no doubt made use of some of the arguments that Erasmus had advanced when they discussed the possibility of More entering the King's service. In the Second Book, Hythlodaye's account of the polity of Utopia gives us More's conception of a well-ordered commonwealth with a running commentary on the contemporary scene. There is, however, More's use of irony and satire and his drollery. As Stapleton wrote, "Even by his most intimate friends, he was thought to be speaking in earnest when he was simply joking".[17] There is a warning in G. K. Chesterton's comment that More "used Utopia as what it really is, a playground. His Utopia was partly a joke, but since his time Utopians have seldom seen the joke." One example of More's leg-pulling is worth giving. It comes from his

[16]Allen, 508.   [17]Stapleton, p. 121.

dedicatory letter to Peter Gilles. This gives us a pleasing impression of Peter Gilles who so far entered the fun of the affair as to devise a Utopian alphabet. In his letter, More, in a matter-of-fact fashion, asked Gilles to get some further information from Hythlodaye about the dimensions of the bridge at Amaurote and about the exact position of the island. Gilles kept up the joke in his letter to Busleyden in which he admits that when Hythlodaye was telling them of the geographical position of Utopia, he himself had a fit of coughing and so missed the details. In his letter More had explained why he wanted this information; it was "because there be with us a certain man, and especially one devout and godly man, a professor of divinity, who is exceedingly desirous to go to Utopia" as a missionary. When Ralph Robinson made his translation thirty-five years later he solemnly added that the "professor of divinity" was "the late famous Vicar of Croyden, Rowland Philips".[18] The translator missed the joke and he was not the last to do so.

Sometimes the irony is unmistakable as in the statement that "in Europe, especially in the Christian countries, treaties are held to be sacred and inviolable, partly on account of the justice and good-ness of princes, and partly on account of the awe and fear of the Supreme Pontiffs". This was written at a period when the manoeuvres of Popes and Princes had little to do with justice or good faith. At no time, perhaps, have treaties and solemn under-takings been more regularly ignored in practice. The reader needs to bring a lively mind and a sense of humour to the appreciation of Utopia, otherwise he may take More's fantasy too literally. This is the objection that must be made to such interpretations as those of Karl Kautsky in Thomas More and his Utopia (1890), who regarded More as an embryo Marxist, or such twentieth-century German scholars as Oncken and Ritter who saw in Utopia the beginnings of British imperial colonialism, a view that amuses a pragmatic Englishman.[19] Those who try to shape a methodical

[18]Philips held two London benefices and was Warden of Merton, Oxford; it is most unlikely that this considerable pluralist read Utopia in manuscript. His first recorded connection with More was on 13 April 1534 at Lambeth. See below, p. 302.

[19]H. Oncken, Die Utopia des Thomas Morus und das Machtproblem (1922). G. Ritter, Machtstaat und Utopia (1940). For an orthodox survey, see H. W. Donner, Introduction to

political philosophy out of *Utopia* are inevitably disconcerted by incongruous elements which they have to sweep under the carpet to avoid spoiling their tidy pattern; such matters as slavery, euthanasia, mercenary warfare, married priests, and queer ways of courtship. The fact is that Thomas More did not plan a watertight and perfect political and social system. Even the title "Utopia" has become a trap. The name quickly acquired the meaning given to it by Sir Thomas Smith in his *De Republica Anglorum* (1583): "feigned commonwealths, such as never were nor never shall be, vain imaginations, phantasies of philosophers to occupy the time, and to exercise their wits". The name had no such meaning originally; it might be said that it had no meaning at all when More or Eramus substituted the Greek "Utopia" for the Latin "Nusquama", both words indicating "Not-place", "Nowhere". The title "Utopia" was not used until 1629 (Cologne edition). The first Latin edition had: "Libellus vere aureus nec minus salutaris quam festiuus de optimo reip. statu, deque noua Insula Vtopia". Robinson's translation of 1551 turned this into, "A fruteful and pleasaunt worke of the beste state of a publyque weale, and of the newe yle called Utopia". The book, however, was usually referred to as "Utopia" long before that became the printed title.

We must keep in mind Erasmus' statement in a letter of February 1517, "If you have not read More's *Utopia*, do look out for it whenever you wish to be amused, or rather I should say, if you ever want to see the sources from which almost all the ills of the body politic arise".[20] Erasmus could not have mistaken the intention of a book he had discussed with its author. We may put the matter in another way; the intention of the book was not so much to give the blue-print of an ideal society, as to censure some aspects of existing society. This criticism is open in the First Book for all to see, but a careful reading of the Second reveals that the same purpose underlies the contrasted picture of Utopia.

The First Book begins with an account of Thomas More and Peter Gilles meeting Raphael Hythlodaye, who is represented as

---

Utopia (1945). For a more stimulating discussion, see J. H. Hexter, *More's Utopia* (1952), E. L. Surtz, *Praise of Wisdom*, and *Praise of Pleasure* (1957) and, of course, the Yale *Utopia*.

[20] Allen, 537.

one of the companions of the Italian Amerigo Vespucci whose *Four Voyages* had been published in 1507. This introductory conversation is closer to ordinary talk between friends than is found in the classical dialogue. After the traveller had given a brief account of his experiences, Gilles commented, "I am surprised you don't enter the service of some prince". For three pages[21] Hythlodaye explained why he had no wish to do so; then the subject was changed and for fifteen pages he examined the problem of why men became wastrels and thieves. This part brings in a lively conversation at Lambeth Palace in the presence of Cardinal Morton. Here More was drawing on his boyhood memories, though the conversation itself was imagined, but he must often have listened as he waited at table to similar exchanges of opinion among the guests. Various causes for thievery and loafing are suggested: discharged soldiers, foot-loose mercenaries, idle retainers, and depopulation caused by enclosures due to the greediness of landowners.[22] This last topic occupies three pages. It contains one of the best-known quotations from the book. "Your sheep that used to be so meek and tame . . . have become such gluttons and so wild that they devour the very men themselves." This statement should not be read in isolation from the rest of the argument; it should be seen as part of the search for root-causes of crime; it echoes a complaint that others voiced besides More. The remedy suggested was the revival of agriculture and of the cloth industry so that more idle hands could be put to work. The point is made, and is indeed one of the themes of the writer, that the pursuit of riches and the spread of luxury are in themselves evil and the cause of evil.

In considering how best to deal with malefactors, Hythlodaye stressed the folly of putting all crimes on the same footing and making the death penalty the common punishment for theft and murder. He advocated penal servitude or hard labour as preferable for smaller crimes. Then he went on to describe how crime was dealt with in the country of the Polylerites in Persia—as

[21]The numbers of pages refer to the Yale edition; they are given to show the proportions allotted to the several topics.

[22]On this contentious subject, see Joan Thirsk in *Agrarian History of England and Wales*, Vol. IV (Cambridge, 1967).

imaginary a state as Utopia. In advocating such a revolutionary change of attitude towards crime, More was ahead of his day when, if a malefactor was not hung he stood a good chance of dying in prison. It could be argued that no part of Utopia showed a greater freshness of thought than is shown in this treatment of crime and punishment. It took several centuries for More's ideas to be accepted. In 1800 in England there were still some 220 offences for which the penalty was hanging.

Hythlodaye returned to the question of whether a philosopher could usefully serve a prince. This was an echo of the remark of Socrates in Plato's *Republic* that "unless either philosophers become kings or those who are now kings become philosophers, there can be no rest from troubles".[23] Hythlodaye showed how unlikely this was by giving an ironic report of a discussion in the council of the French King on his wish to wage war with Italy. This is followed by an equally ironic account of the councillors debating how to raise more money. Hythlodaye maintained that a king should live within his income. He went on to describe the law of another imaginary people, the Macarians, by which they limited the funds at the king's disposal. He reached the conclusion that a philosopher wastes his time in being a prince's councillor. More's reply is important because he set down the principle on which he himself was to act as a councillor:

> If you cannot root out wrong ideas or cure longstanding evils as completely as you would like to do, that is no reason for refusing to take part in public affairs. You must not desert the ship because you cannot control the winds.

We must postpone consideration of the bearing of this discussion on More's personal problem until we come to consider his entry into the King's service. This renewed debate on councillorship fills seven pages, and in the remaining five, Hythlodaye expounds his views of the evil of private property: "I am convinced that you will never get a fair distribution of goods, or a truly happy

---

[23]*Republic*, V, 473. I have not noted other possible sources of ideas in *Utopia*. The sport of source-hunting can be, and has been, carried too far. More was not writing a doctoral thesis where no statement is permissible unless it has already been made by someone else. Works of genius are not written out of "sources", otherwise we could all produce masterpieces. More was writing from a full mind.

life, unless you do away with private property altogether".

So his companions are led to ask for a full account of the polity of Utopia. The Second Book is Hythlodaye's answer to this request.

The Second Book is so packed with details that it cannot be usefully summarized. There are some points that call for comment. The basis of Utopian economy was common ownership in place of private ownership. It is better to avoid the word "communism" as it has now acquired a political connotation that would have been meaningless in More's day. The purpose of this common ownership was not primarily economic; it had a moral basis. Without private ownership the vices of greed and pride would have nothing on which to feed; or, to put it in a positive form, common ownership is the prerequisite for a happy community. A happy life in Utopia was one in which naturally enjoyable pleasures were pursued without injury to others. The introductory letters to *Utopia* from Jerome Busleyden and Guillaume Budé both stressed this moral value. The first commended the state of Utopia because,

> in it all competition for ownership is taken away, and no one has any private property at all. For the rest, all men have things in common with a view to the commonweal itself; so that every matter, every action, however unimportant, whether public or private, instead of being directed to the greed of the many and the caprice of the few, has sole reference to the upholding of one uniform justice, equality and fellowship.

Budé wrote:

> It holds a firm grip on three divine institutions—the absolute equality, or if you like, the community of possessions, of all things good and bad among fellow-citizens—a settled and unwavering love of peace and quietness—and a contempt for gold and silver; three things which overturn, one may say, all fraud, all imposture, cheating, roguery and unprincipled deception. Would that Providence would cause these three principles of Utopian law to be fixed in the minds of men! We should soon see pride, covetousness, insane competition, and almost all the deadly weapons of our adversary the devil, fall powerless.

John Colet had expressed similar views in one of his sermons on the Epistle to the Romans:

> This law of corrupted nature is the same as that Law of Nations resorted to by nations all over the world; a law which brought *meum* and *tuum*—of property, that is to say, and deprivation; ideas clean contrary to a good and unsophisticated nature, for that would have a community in all things.

Erasmus was not so forthcoming on the subject; his own experience of community-living had been unfortunate as he had no vocation for such a life, and Utopia seemed to make no allowance for those who felt as he did. He doubted if common ownership was a practical policy and noted that the experiment in the Apostolic Church had broken down. The notion of common ownership was not so alien to public opinion in More's day as it is in ours; we know that a number of attempts to form such communities have failed. For the sixteenth-century man, the monastic life was an example of community-living; although there were recognized defections from the ideal, the ideal was still there. Large-scale monastic ownership of land often proved the agent of decline even though, technically, the property was that of the whole community. The Rule of St Benedict (*c.* 55) speaks of "this evil of private ownership" for monks.

Most of us would find the kind of life described in *Utopia* as both dull and too restrictive. All such ideal states, from Plato's *Republic* onwards, are too regimented, leaving the individual little scope for his own personality. The Utopians even had to have passports to visit neighbouring cities within their own island, and they were always "under the eyes of all". There was no place for the idler, nor presumably for those who believe

> A poor life this if, full of care,
> We have no time to stand and stare.[24]

The Utopian would retort that life for him was not "full of care". Yet there is no mention of poets and artists among them.

The family was the basic unit of the community, but patriarchal rather than parental. But when one comes to work out the actual time-table there seems to have been little intimate family life as

[24]W. H. Davies, "Leisure".

we think of it. There were no family meals save on rare occasions, nor did the children sit with their parents at the communal table. There are many gaps in More's scheme and it is not clear what the kids did while Mum and Dad were at lectures, or were spending a riotous evening with friends playing Vices-and-Virtues; let us hope that was just a bit of More's fun!

The reader will soon note the part played by slaves in the economy of Utopia. They served families on the farms; they acted as butchers; they were the coachmen, and they did all the heavy and dirty work in the communal halls. Some of these unfortunates, and there seem to have been many of them, were Utopian offenders; others were bought from foreign countries; both groups worked in chain-gangs, and though the chains were of gold, they were chains nonetheless. Anyone who rebelled was put to death.[25]

Considerable space is given to the question of warfare. There is a curiously modern flavour about this section. The Utopians loathed war, as we all do, but waged it "to liberate people from dictators", or "to protect the rights of traders". If a Utopian was ill-treated in a foreign country "they declare war right away". No wonder German commentators (taking it all heavily and seriously) have seen here the germ of British Imperialism! Agents were sent into an enemy country to wage propaganda and weave conspiracies; traitors and even assassins were bribed and rewarded. Most of the fighting was done by mercenaries, but if the Utopians fought, then their priests encouraged them on the field. Mechanical weapons were invented and used in surprise attacks. Finally, reparations were exacted from the defeated. The Utopians considered that an offensive war was justifiable if they needed *lebensraum*, and the natives refused to give ground.

The whole of this section was an ironic comment on the contemporary scene; it is also prophetic. More shared the views of Erasmus and Colet on war. As Erasmus wrote:

Because one prince offends another in some trifle, and that a private

[25]It may be noted that the Parliament of 1547 under the Protector Somerset condemned vagabonds to two years' slavery, or, if contumacious, to slavery for life. They wore rings of iron round their necks, but there were no chains of gold! Was this an echo of *Utopia*? The Act proved unworkable and was repealed by the next Parliament.

matter, such as a relationship by marriage, what is this to the people as a whole? The good prince measures all things by the benefit they bring to the people, otherwise he would not be a good prince. . . . But if some dissensions arise between princes, why not rather resort to arbitrators? There are so many bishops, abbots, scholars, serious magistrates by whose judgment such a matter might be far more decently composed than by so much murder, pillage and misery.[26]

In John Colet's Good Friday sermon of 1513, as reported by Erasmus, we read:

They who through hatred and ambition were fighting and slaughtering one another by turns, were warring under the banner, not of Christ, but of the Devil. At the same time, he pointed out to them how hard a thing it was to die a Christian death; how few entered on a war unsullied by hatred or by love of gain; how incompatible a thing it was that a man should have a brotherly love without which no one could see God, and yet bury his sword in his brother's heart.

More's own opinion is surely expressed in a passage in *Utopia* that immediately precedes his account of their military organization. The Utopians, according to Hythlodaye,

judge that no man is to be esteemed our enemy that has never injured us, and that the partnership of human nature takes the place of a political league, and that kindness and good-nature unite men more effectively and with greater strength than any agreements whatsoever, since thereby the engagements of men's hearts become stronger than the bond and obligation of words.

It would be possible to draw other parallels between the thought of Thomas More and that of Erasmus and, to a lesser degree, with that of John Colet. The three friends shared ideas and ideals but each made his distinctive contribution to the common fund.

The religion of Utopia had an ethical basis and happiness was the test applied to their beliefs and practices; they held that reason alone could not suffice to guide men's lives, but must be strengthened by certain religious principles which included the immortality of the soul which a beneficent God has designed for happiness; vice and virtue would receive their punishment or reward in the after-life. Thus to deprive oneself of an immediate personal pleasure in order to promote the happiness of a neighbour

[26] *Institutio Principis Christiani.*

would merit an eternal reward. Human reason, they believed, could not go further, and unless they were granted some divine revelation, nothing better could be devised than their own system for the promotion of human happiness. A Utopian was left to formulate his own beliefs and to discuss them rationally with his fellows, always provided he did not indulge in personal abuse or provoke violence. Should anyone become too trouble-making in controversy, he was either exiled or enslaved. Hythlodaye mentioned the case of one of his converts to Christianity—a religion the Utopians welcomed—who outran discretion by violently denouncing the beliefs of his neighbours. For this he was exiled.

These ideas of toleration (a notion alien to the sixteenth century) have been seized upon by critics of Thomas More who contrast the Utopian attitude with his own practice in dealing with heretics. This aspect of his thought must be considered in greater detail at a later stage; here it must suffice to point out that even in Utopia there were limits to the forbearance permitted. It should be remembered that when More wrote his *Utopia*, there was no threat of serious heresy in England, nor indeed, as yet, in Germany. Luther was still an unknown Austin friar in a remote monastery on the far eastern frontier of the Empire. In later years, More expressed regrets for some of his earlier writings and said that he would gladly burn such books "rather than folk should take harm from them". Presumably he included *Utopia* among such writings. When times were settled, some liberty of speculation was permissible, but when the Church itself was threatened with disruption, then a stricter discipline on speculation was required.

It has been pointed out above that More's account of Utopian attitude to war was an ironic comment on his own times. This Second Book includes other censures; a few may be mentioned. There were hordes of idle folk—nobles and their retainers, blustering ex-soldiers and beggars (131);[27] the dullest man could command the service, or servitude, of more intelligent people than himself if he had enough money (157); Utopians did not

[27]The numbers in brackets refer to pages in the Yale edition.

E

bother themselves with the nice distinctions made by the logicians in the schools (159); contemporary nobility was based on inherited wealth and land (165); Utopian laws were few and simple so no over-subtle lawyers were needed (195); their priests were holy men and therefore few in number (227). So one could go on extracting a sentence here and another there that throws into relief the contrast between Utopia and the early sixteenth century in England. If, after he has read the Second Book, the reader will turn again to the First, he will see how closely linked they are in purpose and thought.

The last four pages are of particular importance; these give Hythlodaye's final reflections; here he shows the evils that flow from an economy based on private property; once again the emphasis is on the moral effects; the greatest evil is pride, and here surely Hythlodaye is the mouthpiece of Thomas More.

> And I've no doubt that either self-interest, or the authority of our Saviour Christ—Who was far too wise not to know what was best for us, and far too kind to recommend anything else—would have led the whole world to adopt the Utopian system long ago, if it weren't for that beastly root of all evils, pride. For pride's criterion of prosperity is not what you've got yourself, but what other people haven't got. Pride would refuse to set foot in paradise if she thought there'd be no under-privileged classes there to gloat over and order about—nobody whose misery could serve as a foil to her own happiness, or whose poverty she could make harder to bear, by flaunting her own riches. Pride, like a hellish serpent gliding through human hearts—or shall we say, like a sucking-fish that clings to the ship of state?—is always dragging us back, and obstructing our progress towards a better way of life.[28]

The curse of pride is a theme that runs through More's works; it is the subject of one section of the unfinished *Four Last Things* (1522), and among his last writings he returned to it: "For surely this sin of pride, as it is the first of all sins, began among the angels in heaven, so it is the head and root of all other sins and of them all the most pestilent".

Finally, it may be asked, why has this small book retained its

[28]Penguin Classics translation of *Utopia*, p. 131—a fair specimen of this most readable version.

hold through more than four centuries? There is a pleasure in speculating on how we would rebuild society if the slate could be wiped clean—a harmless business provided we remember that the slate cannot be cleaned. Our dreams are reflections of our own personal tastes and inclinations, and *Utopia* is no exception to this rule for it tells us a lot of things about Thomas More's likings and dislikings. His *Utopia* is a good jumping-off place for such fantasies and it is so packed with ideas, some obviously puckish, that it remains a stimulus to thought. Later ideal states, whether projected by William Morris or H. G. Wells, seem insubstantial in comparison—but as equally uninviting! It is this provocativeness that gives the book its perennial value and appeal; it makes us reflect on issues that are still with us. We are still arguing about the treatment of criminals, and there is a general complaint that those best qualified are reluctant to enter the service of the State whether in local or in central government, and we have not yet banished war.

*   *   *

NOTES

1. The woodcut at the head of this chapter, probably cut by Ambrosius, brother of Hans, Holbein, was for the Basle (1518) edition of *Utopia*. The representations are imaginary. Underneath are the names: Io. Clemens. Hythlodaeus. Tho. Morus. Pet. Aegid.

2. The only successful application of the communal and cultural economy of *Utopia* would appear to be the kibbutzim of modern Israel.

CHAPTER XII

The King's Servant

FEW YEARS have brought two such influential books as those published in 1516—the *Novum Instrumentum* of Erasmus and Thomas More's *Utopia*. The edition of the Greek New Testament produced by Erasmus has been superseded, but *Utopia* is still read. The title *Novum Instrumentum* stressed Erasmus' intention; it was to give scholars a new tool in their search for an understanding of Christ's teaching. The text was faulty, but this pioneer work remained the basis of subsequent editions of the Greek New Testament until well into the nineteenth century. Successive editors were content to make revisions and the book was not finally replaced until the principles of textual criticism had been established.

Even the rumour that Erasmus was proposing to publish a "corrected" text roused opposition. In September 1514 Martin Dorp put forward the objections made by the theologians of Louvain. Erasmus wrote a good-natured reply, but sixteenth-century controversialists were always reluctant to let go, so Dorp published another letter in August 1515. Thomas More, then in Antwerp and cogitating *Utopia*, sprang to the defence of Erasmus and replied to Dorp in a letter of some eighteen thousand words.[1] This was dated 21 October from Bruges just before More left for home. He must have had considerable leisure and have been able to work quickly to have written both this long letter and the Second Book of *Utopia*.

Part of Dorp's first letter had referred to *The Praise of Folly*, and More's reply to this has already been mentioned.[2] He also dealt with the main attack on the proposed new edition of the Greek New Testament. He pointed out that Erasmus objected to

---

[1] It was not printed until 1563 in More's *Lucubrationes*. A manuscript of the letter now in the Bibliothèque Nationale in Paris may be the original. Rogers, 15 (4).

[2] See above, p. 68.

those theologians who were content to go on repeating their text-book knowledge and the notes they had taken down in their student days, those "who read nothing of the Fathers or of the Scriptures except in the Sentences and the commentators on the Sentences".[3] He respected those theologians who had studied the Scriptures at first hand as well as reading the works of St Jerome and St Augustine and of the other Fathers instead of spending their time quibbling about trifles. To illustrate the limitations of some of these miscalled theologians, More gave an account of an incident that probably occurred at the table of his friend Antonio Bonvisi.

I was once dining with an Italian merchant as learned as he is rich indeed, very rich. There was at table a monk who was a theologian and a notable disputant. . . . At the dinner nothing was said by anyone, however well weighed and carefully expressed, that this man did not, before the speaker had finished, seek to refute with a syllogism though the matter belonged neither to theology nor philosophy and was altogether foreign to his profession. But I am wrong; his profession was to dispute. . . . By degrees our host turned the conversation to theological subjects, such as usury, tithes, or confession to friars outside the penitent's parish. The merchant soon saw that the monk was not so well acquainted with the Bible as he was ready with his syllogisms, so he began to draw his arguments more from authority than from reasoning. He invented on the spur of the moment certain quotations in favour of his own side of the question, taking one from an Epistle of St Paul, another from St Peter, a third from the Gospels, and affecting to do this with the precision, naming the chapter, but so that if a book was divided into sixteen chapters, he would quote from the twentieth. What did our theologian do now? He had to dodge from side to side to escape these fictitious texts. He managed it, however. He had no notion that the passages he quoted were spurious. "Yes, sir," he would say, "your quotation is good, but I understand the text in this way." And, when he was contradicted, he declared he was speaking on the authority of Nicholas of Lyra.

That, More pointed out, was the kind of pseudo-theological

[3] A collection of the opinions of the Fathers on points of doctrine, compiled by Peter Lombard (twelfth century) who was called "The Master of the Sentences". This was the standard text-book.

discussion to which Erasmus objected; hence the need for a reliable text of the Greek New Testament on which all discussion of our Lord's teaching could be securely based. More also dealt with Dorp's contention that any doubt thrown on the integrity of the text of the Vulgate must undermine the authority of the Scriptures. He noted that exactly the same charge had been brought against St Jerome, and that there must be many revisions of the original text before a perfect translation into Latin could be made. Some of the contemporaries of More and Erasmus were deeply and sincerely troubled at what seemed to them an almost sacrilegious tampering with Holy Writ. Fortunately Erasmus did his work when humanistic studies had created a favourable atmosphere, and the printing press was waiting for him.

It is pleasant to record that Dorp withdrew his objections after the publication of the *Novum Testamentum*, and he did so publicly in a lecture at Louvain much to the annoyance of some of his older colleagues. To him Thomas More wrote in December 1516:

> Believe me, my dear Dorp, what you have done with such great humility, it is impossible to demand even from those whom the world nowadays considers as most humble. . . . For that letter of mine was verbose rather than convincing, and, when I compare it with your lecture which is so eloquent and so full of cogent arguments, I feel quite ashamed, my dear Dorp, to see what little power my words could have had to win your consent, although your modesty or your courtesy leads you now to ascribe such power to them.[4]

Thomas More was an enthusiastic agent for the *Novum Testamentum* in England. He composed some Latin verses to the reader in which he pointed out how the inaccuracies of early translators, and still more of copyists, had been corrected; he declared that there was no greater nor more helpful work for the Christian. In sending a copy to Wolsey, he added a verse commendation and suggested that the Cardinal should cherish the author; but this produced no result. The copy presented to Warham contained verses that rightly praised the Archbishop's

[4]Rogers, 82 (25).

generosity to Erasmus. "He provided the labour; you, good bishop, provided the means."

Warham was among the most constant of Erasmus' patrons. In 1512 he arranged for him to have a pension of £20 a year from the living of Aldington in Kent.[5] One of More's minor tasks was to see that this was transmitted to Erasmus with fair regularity. Erasmus was still largely dependent on such financial support and his friends did not grumble when he occasionally became exigent; they knew he would repay the world of learning a hundredfold.

One unexpected outcome of the *Novum Testamentum* was that both John Colet and Bishop John Fisher decided to learn Greek. Colet took lessons from an early pupil of his school, John Clement, More's "boy". John Fisher had Erasmus as his first tutor in August 1516. Both More and Erasmus tried to persuade William Latimer to continue the Bishop's instruction, but that rather shy scholar pleaded other engagements. Fisher speeded up the teaching of Greek at Cambridge where Erasmus' earlier tuition had had only meagre, though important, results.

Thomas More had good reason to be pleased at the welcome given to *Utopia*. He valued most the praise from his scholar friends. When they were both in Brussels, Erasmus probably gave Tunstal a copy. His letter to More has not survived but More's acknowledgement shows that Tunstal was an appreciative reader. More thanked him

for having so carefully read through *Utopia*, for having undertaken so heavy a labour for friendship's sake. I owe you the deepest gratitude, and my gratitude is not less deep for your having found pleasure in the work. For this, too, I attribute to your friendship which has obviously influenced your judgment more than the strict rules of criticism demand. However that may be, I cannot express my delight that your judgment is so favourable, for I have almost succeeded in convincing myself that you say what you think, for I know that all deceit is hateful to you, whilst you gain no advantage by flattering me, and you love me too much to play a trick upon me. So that if you have seen the truth without any distortion, I am over-joyed at your verdict; or, if in reading you were blinded by your

[5] According to the *Valor Ecclesiasticus* of 1535, this was worth £15 1s. 2d. after tax had been deducted. There is a modern ring about that!

affection for me, I am no less delighted with your love, for vehement indeed must that love be if it can deprive a Tunstal of his judgement.[6]

More again mentioned Tunstal's letter in writing to Erasmus at the end of 1516:

Tunstal has lately written to me in the warmest terms; his opinion of our commonwealth, so frank, so complimentary, has given me more pleasure than an Attic silver talent! You cannot imagine how I leap for joy, how tall I have grown, how I hold up my head, when a vision comes before me of my Utopians making me their perpetual sovereign. I see myself in procession, crowned with a diadem of wheat, conspicuous in a grey cloak, and carrying a sceptre of a few ears of corn, surrounded by a noble company of Amaurotians; then, with this numerous retinue meeting the ambassadors and princes of other nations—poor creatures in comparison with us since they take pride in their appearance—loaded with childish ornaments and feminine frippery, bound with chains of that detested gold, and ridiculous with their purple robes and gems and other trivial baubles. But I would not have either you or Tunstal form an estimate of me from the character of others whose behaviour changes with their fortune. Even though it has pleased heaven to raise me from my humble position to this pinnacle of fortune, with which no kingdom in my opinion can be compared, you shall never find me unmindful of that old friendship which has joined us while I was only a private citizen, and if you take the trouble to make so short a journey as to visit me in my Utopia, I will ensure that all the subjects under my kindly rule, will show the honour they owe to those whom they know to be dearest to their sovereign. I was proceeding further with this most beguiling dream, when the break of day dissolved the vision, deposing poor me from my sovereignty and recalling me to prison, I mean, my legal tasks. Nevertheless I console myself with the thought that real kingdoms are not much more lasting.

Farewell, dearest Erasmus.[7]

The year 1517 was a calamitous one for London; it saw the outbreak of lawlessness known as Ill or Evil May Day, and, in addition, the recurrent plague of sweating sickness raged for six months.

The privileges and protection enjoyed by foreign merchants

[6]Rogers, 28 (10).   [7]Allen, 499. Rogers 29 (11).

and their employees were a constant irritant to the populace. In times of bad trade or poor harvests this discontent was turned against anyone who was not English. Some of the foreigners were at times overbearing and insolent, relying as they did on the protection of their ambassadors. The cavalier treatment by a Lombard of a citizen's wife brought matters to a head about Easter 1517. A Dr Beale was persuaded to voice the grievances of the commons in a sermon and this emboldened some agitators to organize the opposition to foreign traders. Rumours that some kind of demonstration was being planned for May Day reached Wolsey; the Council sent a warning to the Mayor through the Recorder and Thomas More that householders should remain indoors with their servants and apprentices from the Eve of May Day until seven the next morning. This would have hampered the usual early May Day junketings that were a traditional part of the City's year. There seems to have been a muddle in making the prohibition known, and some apprentices were arrested for breaking the curfew of which they may not have been informed. At once the dreaded cry was raised of "'Prentices and Clubs!'". Edward Hall tells the story of what he himself in part witnessed.

> Then out at every door came clubs and weapons. . . . Then more people arose out of every quarter, and out came serving men and watermen. . . . There [at St Martin-le-Grand] met with them Sir Thomas More and others, desiring them to go to their lodgings. And as they were entreating, and had almost brought them to a stay, the people of St Martin's threw out stones and bats [bricks], and hurt diverse honest persons that were persuading the riotous people to cease, and they bade them hold their hands, but still they threw out bricks and hot water. Then a sergeant-at-arms called Nicholas Downe, which was there with Master More, entreating them, being sore hurt, in a frenzy cried "Down with them!" Then all the misruled persons ran to the doors and windows of St Martin's and spoiled all that they found, and cast it into the street.[8]

The rioting was dying down by the time forces of order had been gathered for its suppression; several hundreds of rioters were arrested, and thirteen were hung on gallows erected at various

[8]Hall, Vol. I, p. 159.

E*

points in the City; the others remained in custody; there were
so many that the City compters could not hold them, and churches
and other buildings were used as temporary prisons.

On 12 May, Thomas More was one of a deputation from the
City to ask when the Mayor and Aldermen could wait upon the
King and pray his pardon for the riot. At the audience the
petitioners wore black gowns. The King told them that the
Cardinal would declare his will and pleasure. Ten days later,
four hundred wretched apprentices and other culprits, each in his
shirt and with a halter round his neck, came before the King in
Westminster Hall. They were pardoned and the London tradition
was that Queen Catherine had interceded for them in spite of
Wolsey's anger.

Another tradition is preserved in the unacted Elizabeth play
known as *The Booke of Sir Thomas More*.[9] This exists in manuscript
in the British Museum and bears the censor's comments who
objected to the representation of an anti-alien riot on the stage;
that kind of trouble was still a source of worry to the authorities.
The censor may also have felt it imprudent to praise Sir Thomas
More while Anne Boleyn's daughter was on the throne. In the
play More is shown as succeeding in his efforts to pacify the
rioters; for this he was knighted then and there and declared to be
a member of the Council.

> Sir Thomas More, humbly upon his knee,
> Did beg the lives of all, since on his word
> They did so gently yield. The king hath granted it,
> And made him Lord High Chancellor of England.

And one of the reprieved declared:

> More's name may live for this right noble part.
> And whenso'er we talk of Ill May Day,
> Praise More.

Like the tales of the first meeting of More and Erasmus, history
goes haywire in this play. Its interest lies in the belief of the play-

[9]One special interest of this play is that some scholars believe that three pages of the
manuscript are in Shakespeare's hand; these pages include a speech by More on "degree".
See *Shakespeare's Hand in the Play of Sir Thomas More* (1923), A. W. Pollard, *et al.* Also
the Malone Society's 1961 edition of the play.

wrights that the name of Sir Thomas More would make a popular appeal.

When More came to write his *Apologye* in 1533,[10] he recalled that he "was appointed among others to search out and inquire by diligent examination, in what wise and by what persons, that privy confederacy began". It was discovered, he said, that it all began "by the conspiracy of two young lads that were 'prentices in Cheap". They persuaded others that hundreds of apprentices, journeymen and serving-men were in the plot, and, having prepared the ground, they "fled away themselves and never came again after".

One of these two lads made himself a nuisance to More's brother-in-law, John Rastell, when he set off in the summer of 1517 for a voyage of discovery to the New Found Lands. (Was he inspired by Utopia?) When his ship the *Barbara* put into Falmouth, the purser insisted on taking on board a youth named Coo: "and because the said Rastell heard say that the said Coo should be one of the 'prentices that made the insurrection in London, he warned the purser that he should not suffer him to go with him".[11]

The expedition got no further than Waterford in Ireland owing to a mutiny. So Coo, the stirrer-up of trouble, passes out of history.

One of the victims of the outbreak of sweating sickness in 1517 was Andrea Ammonio. More broke the news to Erasmus. His letter gives us a glimpse of a recurrent threat during Tudor times.

We are in greater distress and danger than ever; deaths are frequent all around us, almost everybody at Oxford, at Cambridge and here in London, having been laid up during the last few days, and very many of our best and most honoured friends being lost. Among these—I am distressed to think how it will distress you—has been our friend Andrew Ammonio, in whom both good letters and all good men have suffered a grievous loss. He thought himself protected against contagion by his temperate habits and attributed it to this that, whereas he scarcely met any person whose family had not been sick, the malady had not attacked any one of his. This boast he made

[10]*Apologye*, p. 177.   [11]A. W. Reed, *Early Tudor Drama* (1926), p. 198.

to me and others not many hours before his death. For in sweating sickness, as they call it, no one dies but on the first day. I with my wife and children am as yet untouched; the rest of my family have recovered. I can assure you that there is less danger upon a field of battle than in this town. It is now, I hear, raging in Calais, just when we are being forced there ourselves to undertake a diplomatic mission—as if it were not enough to have been living in contagion here without following it elsewhere. But what is one to do? What our lot brings us must be borne, and I have composed my mind for every event.

Farewell.

London, in haste, the 19th day of August.[12]

This mission to Calais was again concerned with trade disputes; the English negotiators were Sir Richard Wingfield,[13] Dr William Knight,[14] and Thomas More. They left London late in August; the discussions proved tedious and prolonged; this was in part due to the fact that Wolsey used these commercial disputes as a cover for his own manoeuvres in foreign policy. It was not until December that More returned to Bucklersbury to find his family in good health. He brought back with him portraits of Erasmus and Peter Gilles painted by Quentin Metsys. The first news of the project was given in a letter from Erasmus to More in May 1517 from Antwerp.[15]

Peter Gilles and I are being painted in one picture which we intend to send you as a present before long. But it unluckily happened that on my return I found that Peter had been attacked by a serious illness from which he has even now not fully recovered. I was myself fairly well, but somehow or other it occurred to my doctor to order me some pills for the purging of bile, and what he was fool enough to prescribe, I was idiot enough to take. The portrait was already begun, but when I returned to the painter after taking the physic, he said it was not the same face; so the painting was put off for some days till I could look more cheerful.

Shortly before leaving Calais, More wrote:

The picture which represents your likeness with that of our Peter

[12]Allen, 623.   [13]Deputy of Calais; see D.N.B.
[14]He succeeded John Clerk as Bishop of Bath and Wells in 1541.
[15]For letters about the portraits, see Allen, 584, 601, 654, 706.

is expected greedily by me. I have no patience with that illness which delays my satisfaction for so long.

It was not until early September that Erasmus was able to send the diptych to More at Calais.[16]

I send you the portraits so that we may in some way still be with you if anything should take us off. Peter pays half and I half—not that we should, either of us, have been unwilling to pay the whole, but that the present may be common to us both.

The portrait of Erasmus shows him in his prime; the more familiar Holbein portraits were painted some years later when sickness had already made its mark. At the same time, Metsys made a fine medallion portrait of Erasmus. In his portrait, Peter Gilles is holding a letter from More with his handwriting skilfully copied. This led More to write:

My dear Peter, our Quentin has not only marvellously imitated all the objects he has depicted, but has also shown his ability to be, if he so desired, a most skilful forger, having copied the address of my letter to you in such a way that I could not write it myself so like again. Therefore, unless he wants to keep the letter for some purpose of his own, or you for any purpose of yours, please send it back to me; it will double the marvel when it is put against the picture.

He enclosed some Latin verses with the letter. The first six lines read in translation:

> As Castor was to Pollux, so are here
> Gilles and Erasmus—each to other dear.
> More, joined to both in love, regrets that he
> Is severed from them in locality.
> To soothe his longing heart, their mental graces
> A loving scroll recalls, and I their faces.

These verses were soon in circulation as was the manner of the day. Such compositions and even letters were not regarded as things to be kept to oneself but to be shared with friends and the lettered public. The possibility that a letter might be published (or go astray) must have put some restraint on the writer especially in

---

[16]The portraits have long been separated; that of Peter Gilles is in Rome, and that of Erasmus at Longford Castle in Derbyshire. See Plates 2 and 3.

referring to public affairs. Some criticism of his verses came back to
More and he wrote to Erasmus:

> I am glad you liked my verses about the picture. Tunstal praised the
> eleven-syllable lines more than enough; the piece in six lines moder-
> ately. A friar has ventured to find fault with the latter because I
> compared you to Castor and Pollux, whereas I ought to have likened
> you to Theseus and Pirithous, or Pylades and Orestes, who, like
> you were friends not brothers. I could not stomach this friar though
> there is some truth in what he says, so I followed up his good sugges-
> tion with a bad epigram.

> > The warmest friendship to express
> > Castor, I said, loved Pollux less,
> > On this a friar disputed whether
> > Friendship and brothers matched together,
> > Why not? said I, can any other
> > Love a man better than a brother?
> > The friar laughed to hear a saying
> > Such childish ignorance betraying.
> > Our house is large and full, said he,
> > More than two hundred brothers we;
> > But hang me if in all you find
> > A pair of brothers of one mind.

In a letter to Erasmus from Calais in October 1517, Thomas
More expressed his dislike of the kind of mission on which he was
then engaged.

> I approve of your plans in not wishing to be involved in the busy
> trifles of princes; and you show your love for me by desiring that
> I may be disentangled from such matters in which you can scarcely
> imagine how unwillingly I am engaged. Nothing indeed can be more
> harmful to me than my present mission. I am sent to stay at a little
> seaport, with a disagreeable soil and climate; and whereas at home I
> have naturally the greatest abhorrence of litigation, even when it
> brings me profit, you may imagine what annoyance it must cause
> me here when it comes accompanied by loss. But my Lord [Wolsey]
> kindly promises that the King shall reimburse the whole; when I
> receive it, I will let you know.[17]

That last sentence suggests that he would be pleasantly surprised

[17]Allen, 688.

if his expenses were met; it was only too true that ambassadors and lesser representatives, especially if laymen, were more often out of pocket than not.

Once again Thomas More had shown his skill in negotiations; it was therefore almost inevitable that, on his return to England, another effort would be made to enlist him for the royal service. Roper tells us that the immediate occasion was his successful advocacy in a cause concerning "a great ship" that was in dispute between the Pope and the King.[18] We have seen how, in Utopia, he discussed with Raphael Hythlodaye whether a philosopher could render any useful service in a prince's council. Hythlodaye had argued that such a man's wisdom would be wasted as he could not hope to affect decisions taken on empirical grounds and not on philosophical principles. More in reply had contended that the man of wisdom should serve the prince provided that he gave the best advice he could and did not sulk if it were not taken; no man can expect to win everyone to his opinion, but he should nevertheless take his share in State affairs.

When he wrote Utopia he was considering an invitation to give up his private practice as a lawyer and devote his legal knowledge and ability to the King's service. This would not be an immediate appointment to the Council; he would be a King's Counsel (to use our modern term) and not a King's Councillor. This explains his reluctance to accept lest he should find himself obliged to argue against his beloved City in some cause. More refused that first invitation, but on his return from Calais towards the end of 1517, when the invitation was renewed, he decided to accept. What was the compulsive reason for his change of mind? It may be that he did not regard himself as one of Hythlodaye's category of philosophers, but as an experienced lawyer and negotiator. It has been argued[19] that the vigour of Wolsey's administration of the law in favour of under-privileged people and his apparent commitment to a peace policy, convinced Thomas More that he could render useful service and his own good relations with Wolsey may have strengthened his hopes. No one, at that time,

[18]Research has failed to trace this case.
[19]J. H. Hexter, More's "Utopia" (1952), p. 138.

could have predicted the rapid decline in Wolsey's early good intentions. This is an attractive conjecture, but there is no clear evidence in its support. Thus it is doubtful if Wolsey would discuss his policies with a man like More who had little influence in public affairs. He had, however, a strong sense of the duty every man owed to his prince, a sense that was reinforced when he chose to live an active life in the world instead of a contemplative life in the cloister. Moreover, his renewed experience of official negotiations, however tiresome they may have proved, could not but make him aware of his abilities in that kind of public work, and a man likes to exercise the powers he finds he possesses. An invitation to enter the King's service in those times was little short of a command though a refusal would not have led to consequences more serious than the loss of the King's good will, but that was not to be lightly risked. Thomas More must also have considered that a number of those whom he highly respected had given themselves to the public service. Of the older generation there were Cardinal Morton and Christopher Urswick. Of his own contemporaries there were Archbishop Warham, Peter Gilles, Jerome Busleyden, Cuthbert Tunstal and Richard Pace. Erasmus had himself become a councillor to the future Emperor Charles V, though this did not entail regular duties. It may have been Tunstal who finally persuaded More to consent.

Yet, in saying all this, we must not forget that the mainspring of Thomas More's life was his religious faith; that must always be kept in mind as we follow his temporal career. He may have hesitated about entering the King's service for fear that its exigencies might tempt him to compromise his faith. He seems to have discussed this problem with the King himself, a fact he revealed when he wrote to his daughter Margaret from his prison cell in 1535: "I had always from the beginning used myself to looking *first upon God and next upon the King*, according to the lesson his Highness taught me at my first coming to his noble service".[20]

To the end of his life, Thomas More held the King to that word. Erasmus was far from happy when he learned of his

[20]Rogers, 216 (64).

friend's decision. In a letter to Tunstal, 24 April 1518, he wrote:

I should deplore the fortune of More in being enticed to court if it were not that under such a King and with so many learned men for companions and colleagues, it may seem not a court but a temple of the Muses. But meanwhile there is nothing brought us from Utopia to amuse us, and he, I am quite sure, would rather have his laugh than be borne aloft in a curule chair.[21]

Erasmus' opinion of Henry VIII was not well founded, but there were, as we shall see, several scholars at the court with whom More could have happy relations.

Perhaps Thomas More too wondered at first if he had made a mistake for he wrote to Bishop John Fisher about this time:

It was with the greatest unwillingness that I came to court, as everyone knows, and as the King himself in a joke often throws up in my face. I am as uncomfortable there as a bad rider is in the saddle. I am far from enjoying the special favour of the King, but he is so courteous and kindly to all that anyone who is in any way hopeful, finds a ground for imagining that he is in the King's good graces, like the London wives who, as they pray before the image of the Virgin Mother of God which stands near the Tower, gaze upon it so fixedly that they imagine she smiles upon them. But I am not so happy as to perceive signs of favour or so hopeful to imagine them.[22]

It may be noted that this letter is additional evidence that More had had a frank discussion with the King before entering his service. The letter also hints at some reservation in More's attitude towards Henry.

We may ask, "What kind of man was Henry at this time?" He was twenty-six years old in 1517. The enormous vitality of his youth had not yet declined and he spent long days hunting and in all kinds of sports. It is, however, a mistake to think of him as a royal play-boy. His considerable intelligence and his sense of his high office ensured that he would be King in fact as well as in title. We have already seen how, in the previous year, he had taken his own line in the Standish affair and had brought the newly-created Cardinal to his knees. Wolsey, it is true, was allowed a large measure of liberty in framing policy and the King was con-

[21]Allen, 832.   [22]Rogers, 57 (18).

tent to have it so as long as it suited him. We shall refer in detail later to a series of letters written to Wolsey by More on behalf of the King during the period 1522 to 1526 when More was in attendance on the King away from Westminster; these show that Henry expected to be kept informed and that he had his own ideas on what should be done. This impression is, of course, amply confirmed by the State papers. His attention to affairs may have been intermittent at this time, but it was never entirely withdrawn.

Whatever Thomas More's initial duties may have been, he seems to have been quickly brought into the King's Council. The first payment of a councillor's annual fee of £100 was made on 21 June 1518 and backdated to Michaelmas 1517, perhaps to cover his expenses at Calais. His father was apparently made a judge in the Common Pleas and knighted about the same time.

The King's Council had not yet taken a regular form with defined functions. The councillors were chosen by the King and they were his personal advisers. They numbered just over a hundred but did not all meet as one body. Some would be away on special missions, but the general work was done by committees or commissions. When, at rare intervals, a whole council was called the numbers attending ranged from fifteen to twenty. The regular attenders were the Treasurer, the Lord Chancellor, the Lord Privy Seal and the two Chief Justices (King's Bench and Common Pleas). At the time of More's appointment Wolsey was Chancellor; the Earl of Surrey (who became Duke of Norfolk in 1524) was Treasurer, and Privy Seal was Thomas Ruthall, Bishop of Durham, who had been one of the King's secretaries until 1516 when he was succeeded by Richard Pace. The position of King's secretary was still ill-defined and carried no special influence. A very small number of councillors formed the "Council attendant upon his Majesty's Honourable Person". They went with him as he moved from palace to palace or from manor to manor. Small commissions of councillors were appointed to deal with petitions and other matters outside the scope of the regular courts. Nine councillors formed a commission to hear poor men's causes. This became the Court of Requests. When Roper said that Thomas

More was made "Master of Requests" he was using a term of later date. Roper was mistaken if he implied that "Master" was a kind of president; all it meant was that, for a time, More was a regular member of that commission. He would also serve his turn in the Star Chamber where petitions were heard; that name, too, had not yet gained its later, and sinister, meaning. The point to note is that no rigid system had yet been evolved and a councillor might "in his time play many parts". Occasionally the term "Privy Council" was used but it was still loosely applied and did not have the precise meaning it was given later in the reign.

All this was typical of a period when government was in a state of flux; it was still very much the personal concern of the King; the increase in the work to be done necessitated a more orderly system which developed as new needs arose. Wolsey was no friend of the Council; while he did something to stabilize the legal work in his early years as Chancellor, he was opposed to any strengthening of the influence of the councillors as advisers to the King; he preferred to be the sole adviser.[23] It was not therefore surprising that, at his fall, he found himself without supporters and friends.

[23]The Ordnance of Eltham (1526) proposed a reorganization of the administration that would have established a cabinet (as we should call it) of councillors with defined functions. Wolsey saw to it that this sensible proposal was pigeon-holed. Improvements in administration had to wait until Thomas Cromwell took charge.

CHAPTER XIII

In Defence of the New Learning

THE THIRD EDITION of *Utopia*, printed by Froben at Basle, was published in March 1518; the volume included the *Epigrammata* of Thomas More and Erasmus. The original plan had been to produce a large volume containing a number of pieces by Erasmus, such as *Querela Pacis*, with the Lucian translations made by him and More, and also *Utopia* and *Epigrammata*. By the time page 643 had been set up, Froben decided that the book was long enough to be issued as one volume, so *Utopia* and the *Epigrammata* appeared together in March 1518 as a separate volume which was reprinted in December without any corrections. Then another edition of More's *Epigrammata* alone with his corrections was issued in December 1520.[1]

The earlier section consists of the parallel Latin versions of Greek epigrams made by More and Lily in friendly rivalry about 1508. Some of the other pieces, such as the verses on the coronation of Henry VIII and Queen Catherine, can be dated, but many may have been composed at any time within the decade 1508 to 1518.[2] Fourteen of More's epigrams are on kings and tyrants; such as:[3]

> To you, the king, who ravaged the world, they set up a statue of iron, far cheaper than bronze. This economy was the result of starvation and slaughter, the clash of arms and destitution. These are the instruments by which your lust for wealth brought all to ruin.

Among the later verses in this collection were several against German De Brie (Germanus Brixius), a French scholar who became a Canon of Notre-Dame in Paris. These would not call for special notice were they not part of a paper quarrel that also involved Erasmus. The trouble began in 1514 when De Brie published some verses in praise of the French commander in a

---

[1]Gibson, 3, 4, 57.
[2]*The Latin Epigrams of Thomas More*, trans. and ed. by L. Bradner and C. A. Lynch (1953). See also, H. A. Mason, *Humanism and Poetry in the Early Tudor Period* (1954).
[3]See above, p. 57.

recent naval engagement.[4] On 12 August 1512, during the war between France and England, an English ship, the *Regent*, grappled a French ship, *La Cordelière*; both were blown up when the magazine of the latter caught fire. De Brie took the high patriotic line and lauded the courage of the French commander; More was annoyed and maintained the accuracy of the English version of the affair in which the praise was given to the English commander. It was a puerile argument since the facts could not be known, but we may note that Thomas More was not exempt from an attack of chauvinism. He wrote some pointed epigrams which were soon circulating in manuscript. When the contents of *Epigrammata* were being considered, More asked Erasmus not to include those against De Brie. There may have been a failure in communications, a not unusual happening in those times, or perhaps Froben had other views and went on with the printing. De Brie was annoyed and let it be known that he would give as good as he had been given, if not better. Erasmus did his best to persuade him to refrain as he disliked seeing two friends at logger-heads, but *Antimorus* duly appeared in Paris in 1519.[5] It was a satirical poem with an appendix on the metrical and grammatical errors De Brie claimed to have found in More's verses. More penned what Erasmus regarded as a "mordaunt" reply; he urged More not to print it as De Brie could do him no harm and it would be more dignified to keep silent. Before this appeal was received by More, his *Epistola ad Germanum Brixium* (1520)[6] had been printed by Pynson. More tried to suppress it, but a number of copies are extant. Among other points made by Brixius was that in his coronation verses to Henry VIII, More had disparaged the new King's father. Both More and Erasmus were disquieted at this; perhaps they thought that Henry VIII would be annoyed, but there was no sign of this. More frankly recognized that some of De Brie's criticisms of his verses were justified and he made some corrections in the final versions. He ended his letter by wishing that he himself would have sound feet in his verses and that De Brie would have a sound head on his body.

[4]Gibson, 209. *Chordigerae nauis conflagratio.*
[5]Gibson, 208.   [6]Gibson, 60; Rogers, 86.

One amusing aspect of the More-De Brie wrangle is that Erasmus, having tried to stop his two friends from quarrelling, was himself soon involved in a quarrel with one of More's friends, and this time it was More's turn to be the pacifier. Before we come to this episode, something should be said of a long letter written by More to an unnamed monk in defence of Erasmus.[7] The story of the Coventry friar has already been extracted from it.[8] The monk was probably John Batmanson who died as Prior of the London Charterhouse in 1531.[9] He was ordained in 1510 so at the time of the letter he would probably be in his early thirties. His letter is not extant but the drift of it can be inferred from More's reply; this was included in 1520 in a miscellany entitled *Epistolae aliquot eruditorum* published at Antwerp.[10] The monk had been concerned lest More should be led through his attachment to Erasmus to adopt false doctrines and even to believe that the Early Fathers could have made mistakes. He brought up again the well-worn objections to *Moria* and also referred to *Julius Exclusus* as the work of Erasmus. More did not go further than to say that he had heard conflicting opinions on the authorship of the latter satire. As to *Moria*, the criticisms originally made by Dorp had been fully answered. The monk had called in question some readings in the *Novum Instrumentum*, such as "sermo" for "verbo", which were the stock-in-trade of Erasmus' opponents. More defended the readings in some detail. He pointed out that the book had won the approval of the Pope and of such English scholars as Colet, Fisher, Warham and Tunstal. It was therefore temerarious for a "self-taught young fellow" to go against such weighty opinion. As to the Early Fathers: "Do you deny that they ever made mistakes? I put it to you, when Augustine thought that Jerome had mistranslated a passage, and Jerome defended what he had done, was not one of them mistaken?"

The monk had expressed his resentment at the attacks Erasmus had made on monks and friars. More did not shirk the issue.

Into what factions, into how many sects, are they not divided! Then

---

[7]Rogers, 83 (26).   [8]See above, p. 60.
[9]See Dom David Knowles, *The Religious Orders in England*, Vol. III (1959), Ap. 1.
[10]Gibson, 152.

what tumults, what tragedies arise about little differences in the
colour and mode of girding the monastic habit, or some matter of
ceremony, which, if not altogether despicable, is at all events not so
important as to warrant the banishing of all charity. . . . They make
more of things that appertain especially to the religious orders than
of those very humble things that are in no way peculiar to them
but shared by all Christian people, such as the common virtues—
faith, hope, charity, the fear of God, humility. . . . From reflections
such as these you should not grow proud of your own order,
nothing could be more fatal, nor trust in private observances, and
that you should place your hopes rather in the Christian faith than
in your own, and not trust in those things that you can do for yourself, but in those that you cannot do without God's help.

That might be a quotation from Erasmus, but More was not
content to leave the matter there; he went on to express his deep
love for the life of the cloister from which he had felt obliged,
for want of a true vocation, to draw back. He did not, however,
make any reference to his earlier association with the Charterhouse.

I have no doubt that there is no good man to be found anywhere to
whom all religious orders are not extremely dear and cherished. Not
only have I ever loved them, but intensely venerated them; for I
have been wont to honour the poorest person commended by his
virtues more than anyone else who is merely ennobled by his riches
or illustrious by his birth. I desire, indeed, all men to honour you
and your order, and to regard you with the deepest charity, for your
merits deserve it, and I know that by your prayers the misery of
the world itself is somewhat diminished. If the assiduous prayer
of the just man is of so much value, what must be that of the un-
wearied prayers of so many thousands? Yet, on the other hand, I
would wish that you would not with false zeal be so partial to
yourselves, that if anyone ventures to touch on what regards you,
you should try, by your way of relating it, to give an evil turn
to what he has said well, or that what he at least intended well,
you should misinterpret and pervert.

The letter ends, "Farewell, and if you do not wish to be cloistered
in vain, give yourself to the life of the spirit rather than to these
squabbles".

We can now return to the efforts made by Thomas More to prevent a quarrel between one of his own friends and Erasmus, who had returned to Louvain from Basle in September 1518. He found that some of the theologians there were highly critical of his work. By this time his earlier resilience had given way to resentment at any doubts expressed about his scholarship. To him his opponents were barbarians and obscurantists who were the enemies of sound learning. Among the younger critics was an Englishman, Edward Lee. He was the brother of the Joyeuce Lee (or Leigh) to whom More had dedicated his *Picus*. Edward had been to Oxford and Cambridge and had been ordained deacon in 1504; he was a good scholar and it was in search of further learning that he went to Louvain in 1517. He was very critical of the *Novum Instrumentum* and made some notes which he submitted to More, Fisher and Latimer as well as to theologians at Louvain. Lee was also in touch with John Batmanson of the London Charterhouse. There may be a link here with the letter written by Batmanson (assuming he was the "Monk") to More. Did Lee prime Batmanson with material against the *Novum Testamentum*? Lee wrote to More in April 1519 and asked for his encouragement in what he regarded as the sacred task of refuting Erasmus. Stapleton has preserved the following passage from More's reply.

> You ask me, my dear Lee, not to lessen my affection for you in any way. Trust me, my good Lee, I shall not. Although in this case my sympathies are with the party you are attacking, yet I trust you will withdraw your troops from the siege with perfect safety. I shall ever love you, and I am proud to find that my love is so highly valued by you. . . . So that if ever you bring out a book of your own, and Erasmus, casting a critical eye on it, should write a pamphlet to refute it, though it would be much more seemly that he should not retaliate, I, although my talents are poor, will stand by you to defend you with all the energy of which I am capable. Farewell, my dearest friend.[11]

Thomas More was to find it difficult to "stand by" Edward Lee. He wrote again to urge Lee not to publish his criticisms. We are

[11]Stapleton, p. 43.

reminded of how Erasmus had tried to persuade More not to publish his epigrams against De Brie. Erasmus was rightly annoyed that Lee had not discussed the points of difference with him although they met several times when he could have done so; as a friend of More, Lee would have had every consideration from Erasmus. Lee's *Annotationes*, dedicated to the theologians of Louvain, was published in February 1520. In a prefatory letter to Erasmus, Lee said that he would have published his book months earlier but for the restraining hand of Thomas More. Erasmus at once replied with his *Apologia* and followed this up with a *Responsio*. In the same month appeared the volume to which reference has already been made, *Epistolae aliquot eruditorum*. This contained letters against Lee from More, Pace, Lupset and others, for Erasmus did not lack defenders. More had found it impossible to "stand by" Lee when he read the extreme opinions expressed in the *Annotationes*. Nor did Erasmus restrain his language; he called Lee a "viper" and "monster", but such terms were common change between controversialists in those days.

Meantime More had been engaged in another defence of the New Learning. A fierce debate had broken out at Oxford on the subject of Greek. Cambridge had been more fortunate in having had the foundations of the teaching of Greek laid by Erasmus himself with the continued encouragement of Bishop John Fisher, the University Chancellor. Oxford was still dominated by men who kept to the old ways; to them Greek smacked of heresy. The students gaily joined the battle, ranging themselves in the ranks of the Greeks or the Trojans. The quarrel may appear trivial to us as the issues no longer seem important; indeed we are now busily ridding ourselves of both Latin and Greek. But in those days it was a momentous question that inflamed men's passions. Thus John Skelton objected to the teaching of Greek on the grounds that it was a dead language while Latin was a living one. His argument may seem quixotic to us but it had substance. Latin was indeed a living language, and anyone who had had some schooling could make himself understood throughout Europe. Latin was the diplomatic language; hence the importance of having a Latin scholar in the administration. Scholars of different countries conversed in Latin.[12] Books of any claim to importance were written in Latin. Erasmus and More spoke and wrote to one another in Latin, as did their friends Peter Gilles, Busleyden, Budé, and other scholars. Indeed by this time Erasmus probably thought in Latin and he confessed that he could no longer write correctly his native Dutch.

We owe to Erasmus our knowledge of an incident at Henry VIII's court, when it was at the royal manor of Abingdon, that led to More's intervention in the Oxford controversy. Richard Pace was also at the court at that time and he may have passed the story on to Erasmus. A theologian who was preaching before the King seized the opportunity to decry the learning of Greek. Afterwards More spoke eloquently in favour of the new study. The theologian tried to excuse himself by declaring that he had been inspired to speak as he did. Let Erasmus give the sequel.

"The spirit that inspired you", said the King, "was certainly not that of Christ, but rather the spirit of Folly." Then he asked him if he had read any of the writings of Erasmus, since the King perceived that he had been girding at me. He said he had not. "Then you clearly proved your folly," said the King, "since you condemn what you have not read." "Well, I have read one thing called *Moria*", replied the theologian. "May it please your Highness", interposed Pace, "his argument well befits the book." Meanwhile the theologian hits on an excuse for his blunder. "I am not altogether opposed to Greek", says he, "since it is derived from the Hebrew." The King, astonished at the man's folly, dismissed him and forbade him ever to preach at court again.[13]

Probably at the suggestion of the King, Thomas More wrote a letter to the University[14] to urge the importance of Greek studies. One passage gives the main argument:

Although no one denies that a man can be saved without a know-ledge of Latin and Greek or any literature at all, yet learning, yea even worldly learning, as he [the preacher] calls it, prepares the mind for virtue. . . . And as regards theology itself, which alone he seems to approve, if indeed he approved even that, I do not see how he

[12]An interesting modern example was the use of Latin at the Second Vatican Council.
[13]Allen, 948.
[14]Rogers, 60.

can attain it without knowledge of Hebrew, Greek, or Latin, unless, indeed, this frivolous fellow thinks that sufficient books on the subject have been written in English. Or perhaps he thinks that the whole of theology is contained within the limits of those "Sentences" on which such as he are always disputing, for the knowledge of which I confess that little enough Latin is wanted. But to confine theology, the august Queen of Heaven, within such narrow limits would not only be iniquitous but impious. For does not theology also dwell in the Sacred Scriptures, and did it not thence make its way to the cells of all the ancient holy Fathers, I mean Augustine, Jerome, Ambrose, Cyprian, Chrysostom, Cyril, Gregory, and the others like them, with whom the study of theology made its abode for more than a thousand years after the Passion of Christ before these trivial questions arose? And if any ignorant man boasts that he understands the works of those Fathers without a thorough knowledge of the language in which each wrote, he will have to boast a long time before scholars will believe him.

Soon after writing this letter, More received one from Erasmus (5 March 1518) enclosing, without comment, two pamphlets by Martin Luther; here was the sign of a movement that was to drive the Greek-Latin controversy into the background.[15]

It must have been a great satisfaction to Thomas More when his protégé John Clement was appointed in 1518 by Wolsey to be reader in rhetoric and later in Greek at Bishop Richard Fox's new college of Corpus Christi at Oxford which had been founded as a school of the New Learning. Clement's name had probably been put forward by More and it would have the support of John Colet. The University wrote to Wolsey on 9 November 1518, "The plague which raged at Oxford for three months has abated. The students have returned, all the more eagerly as John Clement has announced his lectures." About the same time More wrote to Erasmus:

My Clement has a larger audience for his lectures at Oxford than any other lecturer. The approbation and the affection he has won among all is astonishing. Even those who detested classical letters are his supporters and attend his lectures; their attitude is slowly

[15]Allen, 785. A month earlier Luther had said he was eager to get a copy of *Utopia* (*Briefwechsel*, I, p. 147).

changing. Linacre, who, you know, never lavishes praise on anyone, cannot admire his learning too highly, so that, much as I love Clement, I almost envy the high praise he has had heaped on him.[16]

This letter may give the impression that Thomas Linacre was living at Oxford; no doubt he visited the university from time to time, but normally he lived in London where he had a high reputation as a physician, having not only the King but also such leading men as Wolsey and Warham among his patients, as well as his old friends, Colet, Lily and More.

John Clement did not hold his appointment at Oxford for more than a year or so; he had decided to study medicine. His successor was Thomas Lupset, another old pupil of St Paul's School. He came to Oxford from Paris where he had seen the 1517 edition of *Utopia* through the press. As this edition alone gives More's second letter to Peter Gilles, Lupset must have had the author's collaboration; unfortunately the press work was inferior. At the same time Lupset had seen to the printing of Linacre's Latin version of Galen's *De Sanitate Tuenda*.

Reginald Pole,[17] with whom Lupset was to have close relations in later years, was also at Oxford at this period previous to his leaving for Italy in 1521. The King still favoured his young kinsman and provided for his maintenance. A letter from More to Pole and Clement can probably be dated about 1518. It refers to another epidemic of sweating sickness.

I thank you, my dear Clement, for being so keenly solicitous about the health of my family and myself that although you are absent you are careful to warn us what food to avoid. I thank you, my dear Pole, doubly for deigning to procure for me the advice of so skilful a physician and no less for obtaining from your mother[18]— noblest and best of women, and fully worthy of such a son—the remedy prescribed and for getting it made up. Not only do you

[16]Allen, 907.

[17]He was the grandson of George, Duke of Clarence, the brother of Edward IV and Richard III. This near-relationship to the throne was a sword of Damocles, but, in these early days, Henry VIII was certainly on the best of terms with Reginald Pole.

[18]Margaret, daughter of Clarence, was created Countess of Salisbury by Henry VIII in 1513. She was the beloved governess of the Princess Mary. Notwithstanding his declaration that the Countess was the most saintly woman in England, Henry had her beheaded at the age of seventy-eight.

willingly procure us advice, but equally evident is your willingness to obtain for us the remedy itself. I love and praise you both for your bounty and fidelity.[19]

A further example of More's interest in the younger generation is shown in a letter from him to Richard Croke, who became professor of Greek at Cambridge in 1518. He had been one of Erasmus' early pupils. Croke seems to have apologized for not writing more frequently as he feared such a master of Latin would "nose out" faults in his style. To this More replied, "There is no reason why you should fear my nose like an elephant's trunk. Your letters are not so poor that they need fear any man's criticism nor am I so long-nosed as to put any man in fear of my criticism."[20]

[19]Stapleton, p. 42.   [20]Stapleton, p. 40.

CHAPTER XIV

Affairs of State

WE HAVE JUST SEEN how Thomas More's letter to the University of Oxford in March 1518 was written from Abingdon. He would then be one of the councillors attendant on the King. Official letters show that More moved with the court from manor to manor; it was only by an annual itinerary of this kind that it was possible to feed the royal household; when the supplies at one manor were exhausted, the court moved to the next. The extant documents do not allow us to follow Thomas More month by month but the evidence is sufficient to indicate that for four or five years he was kept in close attendance except when absent on special missions. He could not therefore have carried out regular legal duties at Westminster, but, wherever the King might be, his attendant councillors, one of whom at least would need to be a lawyer, acted as a court of poor men's causes and dealt with local petitions.

Roper tells us that both the King and the Queen liked to have Thomas More with them. The King sought his company and liked to discuss not only State affairs but more general subjects such as divinity and astronomy. After supper they welcomed his conversation and wit. More found this constant demand on his company somewhat irksome as he could seldom get away to his family, so, according to Roper, he began "to dissemble his nature and so by little and little from his former mirth to disuse himself" that the royal couple no longer called for him so frequently.[1]

Twenty-one official letters written on behalf of the King to Wolsey by More have been preserved; this must be a small part of the whole. No fewer than six letters, for instance, were written during a fortnight in September 1523. Letters were addressed from Woking, Guildford, Newhall, Easthamstead, Abingdon, Woodstock, Hertford, Stony Stratford and Windsor.[2]

[1]Roper, p. 11.
[2]Rogers, 77-9, 109-11, 115-27, 136, 145, 161; from Wolsey, 137, 141, 144, 146.

As in all service at court, there must have been long empty
periods of waiting on the King's pleasure. Fortunately More had
congenial companions in such scholars as Richard Pace and John
Clerk. An occasional glimpse is given of these vacant hours.
While they were at Abingdon in March 1518, Richard Pace
wrote to Wolsey that "carding and dicing were turned into
pitching arrows over the screen in the hall";[3] the card-players
and dicers would probably not include More for he abhorred both
pastimes, but it is pleasant to think of him and the other learned
councillors passing the time trying to fling arrows over the screen.
Pace wrote again a month later to complain:

> Dr Clerk and Master More desire your Grace to write to my Lord
> Steward that they may have their daily allowance of meat which was
> granted them by the King. Here is such bribery that they be com-
> pelled to buy meat in the town for their servants, which is to
> them intolerable and, to the King's Grace, dishonourable.[4]

Pace and Clerk could be called Wolsey's men, but, although
More had a high regard for the Cardinal, they would not seem to
have been intimate, nor could More be regarded as one of the
watch-dogs Wolsey liked to have in attendance on the King.
According to Cavendish, the itinerant court was "slenderly
furnished" or manned, as Wolsey preferred to have the councillors under his eye at Westminster. Indeed, the King at length
complained at the small number in attendance on him.

From Abingdon, the court moved to Woodstock,[5] and while
there More was engaged in seeing that precautions were taken to
prevent the plague from spreading from Oxford which was so
afflicted that the students were dispersed. Later the court reached
Woking. Three of the letters from More to Wolsey are dated
from there in July 1519 and, as they came within a period of five
days, they show how closely the King kept in touch with his
Chancellor, and, what is often overlooked, how carefully
Wolsey kept the King informed and noted his comments on his
reports. One of the letters instructs Wolsey to congratulate the

[3]L.P., II, 4043.   [4]L.P., II, 4055.
[5]The royal manor of Woodstock was given by Queen Anne in 1704 to the Duke of
Marlborough. Blenheim Palace was the result.

King of Castile on his election as Emperor. Richard Pace had been sent to Frankfurt in May 1519 to see that King Henry's name was put before the Electors when they met to choose a new Emperor after the death of Maximilian. The suggestion could hardly have been taken seriously, but perhaps Henry and Wolsey thought there was no harm in trying! So Henry had to congratulate his wife's nephew Charles.

Another of these letters ends on a personal note:

> His Grace was very joyful that, notwithstanding your continual labours in his matters, your Grace is so well in health, as he heareth by divers and saith that ye may thank his counsel thereof, by which ye leave the oft taking of medicines that ye are wont to use, and while ye do so, he saith ye shall not fail of health, which Our Lord long preserve.

In June 1520 Thomas More accompanied the King to the Field of Cloth of Gold, a pretentious farce that was like a stage presentation of a medieval pageant. More's brother-in-law, John Rastell, had the task of decorating the temporary palace. These meetings of princes might have been designed to give point to the comments in *Utopia* on the fatuity of leagues and treaties that were not based on honest intention. After Henry of England and Francis of France had vowed eternal friendship, the English moved on to Gravelines to greet the new Emperor who was the declared enemy of France. Among the counsellors with the Emperor was Erasmus who thus had the delight of greeting such old friends as Thomas More, John Fisher, Warham, Tunstal and Mountjoy. Erasmus took the opportunity to introduce Francis Cranevelt, pensionary of Bruges, to Thomas More, who thus added another scholar to his growing list of correspondents. More later gave Cranevelt two Roman coins and a ring for his wife. Such personal reunions must have been some consolation for the tediousness of a very royal occasion. In a sermon on his return, John Fisher described the colourful and costly scene. "But yet doubtless many were full weary of them at length and had a loathesomeness of them, and some of them had much rather be at home."

During the Emperor's stay in England two months earlier, More had been concerned with Bishop Ruthall, Tunstal and Pace in negotiating a commercial treaty.[6] This was followed after the Field of Cloth of Gold by an Anglo-Hanse Conference at Bruges which opened on 21 July; no agreement was reached at this first meeting. The discussions were resumed more than a year later and lasted from the middle of September until nearly the end of November. On his return from the Conference, the King "considering the good and faithful counsel and the good services that our counsellor Thomas More on many an occasion has hitherto exerted and still is exerting" granted to him and George Ardeson jointly to be keeper "of the change and foreign exchange in England towards foreign parts and Calais".[7] George Ardeson, like Antonio Bonvisi, was an Italian banker and merchant domiciled in London. This kind of grant was the usual way of remunerating a layman engaged in the royal service.

Cuthbert Tunstal was not concerned with the Anglo-Hanse negotiations; he was accredited ambassador to the Emperor Charles V in September 1520. Shortly afterwards Luther published his explosive pamphlet *De Captivitate Babylonica Ecclesiae* (The Babylonish Captivity of the Church). Tunstal sent a copy of this to Wolsey on 29 January 1521 with another, probably *De Libertate Hominis Christiani* (The Liberty of a Christian Man); it was the day of the opening of the Diet of Worms, but Tunstal left before Luther arrived. Tunstal was greatly perturbed at these publications and urged that they should be kept out of England.

In the following year, 1521, Thomas More was advanced to the position of Under-Treasurer following the death of Sir John Cutte in April.[8] The Treasurer was the Duke of Norfolk but the Under-Treasurer did the work. He had a salary of £173 6s. 8d.; the first payment to More gives the date of his appointment as 2 May, and he was no doubt knighted at the same time. Among those who congratulated him was Bishop John Fisher who wrote to ask More's good offices on behalf of a young priest at Cambridge.

[6]Rogers, 89, 8 April 1520. Pace is described in the instructions as "our first secretary"; Ruthall and Tunstal by their official positions. Thomas More's name had no distinction attached; he had not yet been knighted.
[7]Herbrüggen, 98A.
[8]Roper was mistaken in naming More as Treasurer and his predecessor as Sir Richard Weston; it was the other way round, for Weston followed More.

F

We rejoice that you are raised to the dignity of knighthood and become so intimate with the King and we offer you our heartiest congratulations for we know that you will continue to show us the same favour. Please now, give your help to this young man who is well versed in theology and a zealous preacher to the people.[9]

From this we may infer that Cambridge University had already had reason to be grateful to the new Under-Treasurer. More replied:

As to this priest, Reverend Father, of whom you write that he will soon obtain a prebend if he can find a powerful advocate with the King, I think I have so wrought that our Prince will raise no obstacle. Whatever influence I have with the King—it is very little, but such as it is—is as freely at your disposal for yourself or your scholar as a house is to its owner. I owe your students constant gratitude for the heart-felt affection of which their letters to me are the token.

These two letters indicate that More must have had friendly relations with the University, friendly enough for the students to write to him; unfortunately no particulars have been recorded.

It was not only the students of Cambridge who had him in high regard. A quotation from Robert Whittinton's *Vulgaria* is evidence of a wider recognition.[10] The author was an Oxford grammarian and his book was published in 1520.

More is a man of angel's wit and singular learning. I know not his fellow. For where is the man of that gentleness, lowliness and affability? And, as time requireth, a man of marvellous mirth and pastimes, and sometime of a sad gravity. A man for all seasons.

That reads like the opinion of a man who knew Thomas More personally. They seem to have been about the same age; the link may have been Oxford where Whittinton went to school and later to college. In the previous year he had published two indifferent poems praising More and his *Utopia*.

Thomas More was in the vast retinue that accompanied Cardinal Wolsey at the beginning of August 1521 to Calais on a mission of arbitration between the Emperor Charles V and Francis

[9]Stapleton, pp. 43-4.
[10]*Vulgaria* (E.E.T.S.), p. 69. The last phrase gave the title to Robert Bolt's play of 1960. Gibson, 593, 594.

of France. The King's instruction to Wolsey included the following passage:

> The King signifieth your Grace, that, whereas old men do decay greatly in this realm, his mind is to acquaint other young men with his great affairs, and, therefore, he desireth your Grace to make Sir William Sandys and Sir Thomas More privy to all such matters as your Grace shall treat at Calais.[11]

The King may not have been referring to Wolsey's own age (he was then just on fifty), but he may have been hinting that Wolsey kept things in his own hands too tightly.

This meeting at Calais was a specious business that, like most foreign negotiations of the times, meant that someone was double-crossing someone else, unless they were double-crossing one another. Later in the year, a treaty of alliance between Henry and Charles V was directed against Francis. Thomas More was at Calais or Bruges for over two months. During his weeks at Calais he must have been thrown into the company of Lord Berners,[12] the Deputy, who was then translating Froissart's *Chronicles* at the suggestion of the King.

A story told by Stapleton may refer to this embassy. A learned but conceited lawyer of the imperial court declared that he could solve any problem in the law of any nation. More took up the challenge and asked "Whether cattle taken in Withernam be irrepleviable?" The challenger had to admit that the term "withernam" defeated him.[13] To this stay in Bruges may perhaps be assigned an amusing incident told by More of his jester-servant Henry Patenson who was jeered at in the streets and was amazed to find that these foreigners could not understand plain English.[14]

It was during this visit that Thomas More was able to meet Erasmus, as it was to prove, for the last time. Erasmus took the opportunity to introduce the young Spanish scholar Juan Luis Vives who wished to go to England. He was then working on a

[11]S.P., I, p. 19. Sir William Sandys was favoured by Henry VIII; a solid but unenterprising courtier who did good service. His retirement from court in 1536 may have been due to religious scruples.

[12]Hall spells the name "Barnes" thus giving the contemporary pronunciation.

[13]Stapleton, p. 127; see J. D. M. Derrett's explanation in *Catholic Lawyer* (Brooklyn), Spring, 1963.

[14]*Confutation*, E.W., p. 768.

commentary done at Erasmus' suggestion on St Augustine's *De Civitate Dei*; this alone must have commended him to More. When Erasmus was admitted to an audience with Wolsey, the Cardinal promised to send him a copy of the *Assertio Septem Sacramentorum* in which King Henry controverted Luther's opinions on the sacraments.

Richard Pace had written to Wolsey on 16 April 1521 apologizing for a delay in sending him some newsletters from Germany as the King had only just read them; "he commanded me to write to your Grace declaring he was otherwise occupied, i.e. in scribendo contra Lutherum, as I do conjecture".[15] A few days later he found the King reading a new pamphlet by Luther; this must have been *The Babylonish Captivity*, in which Luther argued that only three sacraments—baptism, penance and the eucharist—were authorized in the Gospels; the other four— confirmation, marriage, ordination, and extreme unction—he regarded as usages introduced by the Church and not essential to salvation. It seems that as early as 1518 Henry had begun to write against Luther, a project encouraged by Wolsey, and it may be that the *Assertio* developed out of this preliminary essay. Henry must have worked quickly for on 21 May 1521 he informed the Pope of this evidence of "the resources of my mind".[16] A few days earlier Wolsey had staged at St Paul's Cross a solemn burning of Luther's writings which seem to have been coming into the country in some quantity, presumably through the Steelyard merchants. Bishop John Fisher preached the sermon. It was not an angry diatribe but an exposition of the promise that the spirit of truth would ever safeguard the faith. He referred briefly to the King's book:

> But touching these sacraments, the King's Grace, our sovereign Lord in his own person, hath with his pen substantially foughten against Martin Luther that I doubt not every true Christian man that shall read this book shall see those blessed sacraments cleared and delivered from all the slanderous mouth and cruel teeth that Martin Luther hath set upon them.

He went on to make a reference to Plato that takes the mind back

[15]L.P., III, 1233.   [16]L.P., III, 1659, 1772.

to *Utopia*: "Plato saith, then shall commonwealths be blessed when either those that be philosophers govern, or else those that govern give them to philosophy".[17]

The implication was that England was blessed with a philosopher-king.

Doubts were expressed at the time, and have been since, as to Henry's authorship of the *Assertio*. Some said Bishop Fisher had written it; others that Erasmus was the author, but he was later blamed for various contributions on both sides of the controversy! The clearest statement about the authorship was made by Thomas More when he was questioned on his relations with the Nun of Kent in March 1534.[18] That part of his reply concerning the Pope's primacy has already been quoted.[19] On this further matter More declared, "I never was procurer nor counsellor of his Majesty thereunto, but after it was finished, by his Grace's appointment and consent of the makers of the same, only a sorter out and placer of the principal matters therein contained". How are we to interpret this statement? More denied that he had anything to do with the conception or actual writing. The word "makers" seems a difficulty. Did they write the book? Perhaps they did in the same way in which the speeches of a President of the United States are written for him; the writers have his ideas to guide them and he revises and changes at will. More might be called the sub-editor. The book, however, is not a profound theological treatise; it sets down clearly the teaching of the Church as understood by an informed and intelligent layman, as Henry undoubtedly was; only his name has kept the book alive.

The *Assertio* was printed by Richard Pynson in July 1521 and a sumptuously bound and autographed copy was presented to Leo X by Dr John Clerk at the beginning of October; on the 11th of that month the Pope conferred on Henry VIII the title of *Fidei Defensor*.[20] He was thus able to take his place with the "Catholic" King of Castile and the "Most Christian" King of France.

When Martin Luther read the book, he expressed the opinion

[17]*English Works* (E.E.T.S.), p. 327.   [18]Roper, p. 64.   [19]See above, p. 96.
[20]This became part of the royal style by statute (35 Hen. VIII, c. 3.).

that it was the work of Edward Lee. Luther's reply was published in July 1522, first in German and then in a longer Latin version, *Contra Henricum Regem Angliae*. The book was notable even in those days, when no holds were barred, for its scurrility; among the least indecent epithets hurled at the King were—brigand, ass, king of lies, buffoon, Thomist pig, dolt. It is said that Henry declared that the author was fit only to be the fool at the Lord Mayor's banquet. It would have been beneath the dignity of a king to have answered such a vilification, but Luther's reply contained arguments of substance. Bishop John Fisher wrote the theologian's reply in his *Defensio Regiae Assertionis contra Babylonicam Captivitatem* published in Cologne in 1525 in the same month as his other anti-Lutheran book, *Sacri Sacerdotii Defensio contra Lutherum*. Fisher had postponed publication of the first book for two years in the hope that Luther might even yet see the light and recant. Meanwhile, no doubt at the suggestion of the King, Thomas More also wrote a reply to this attack on Henry's book. It is probable that More had read Fisher's *Defensio* in manuscript and had taken counsel with the Bishop. The book was published by Pynson in 1523 with an involved Latin title attributing the work to Guilielmus Rosseus.[21] How long the identity of Thomas More with William Ross was concealed is not known, but in his sermon on 12 February 1526 at St Paul's Cross at the abjuration of Robert Barnes and four Steelyard merchants, Bishop Fisher referred to "the book of Master More" against Luther.[22] This must have been the book ascribed to William Ross.

It must be admitted that, while More did not sink to Luther's scurrility, he went some way towards doing so. A modern comment may be quoted. "More had certainly for once forgotten his manners, and Luther never had any. We must excuse Luther because of the provocation he had received, and we must excuse More for the same reason. Nearly all controversies in the sixteenth century are in many respects deplorable. More's book, however,

---

[21]A cancelled title-page of a first edition used the pseudonym of Ferdinand Baravell. This was soon withdrawn and the second edition, rather longer, had the name of William Ross. Apparently there was such a person who had fled from England and died abroad. The reason for the substitution is not known. Gibson 62, 63.

[22]*English Works* (E.E.T.S.), p. 454.

is certainly not deficient in reasoning and humour. He wrote in his best forensic style and much of his raillery is inspired by wit."[23] It would be little to our purpose to summarize the arguments and counter-arguments of the two books; they were to be repeated *ad nauseam* for a generation or more. We may note, however, the emphasis More put on Luther's suggestion that princes should free themselves from the yoke of the Papacy.

> The people in their turn will throw off the yoke of the princes, and deprive them of their possessions. And when they shall come to this, dumb with the blood of princes, and exalting in the slaughter of the nobles, they will not submit to plebian governors, but, following the teaching of Luther, and trampling the law under foot, then, at last without government and without law, without rein and without understanding, they will turn their hands against each other.[24]

Erasmus voiced the same fears. Writing to Pope Adrian VI in September 1522, he said, "I foresee more danger than I could wish, that the end may be slaughter and bloodshed". The extravagances of such extremists as Carlstadt and Münzer and the Peasants' War of 1524 were a grim commentary on these warnings.

There are two letters[25] extant written by More from the court at Newhall in September 1522. From these and later letters, it seems that Wolsey sent his letters for the King to Thomas More who then read them to Henry, usually after supper, sometimes with the Queen present. He then gave More instructions for the replies, and on one occasion summoned him again after ten at night, a late hour in days when men got up at dawn. More tried to get the King to deal with his papers earlier in the day, but not with much success. For instance when asked to sign, among others letters, one to the Emperor, "his Grace laughed and said, 'Nay, by my soul, that will not be. I will read the remainder at night'."[26]

The war with France that came in 1522 was a futile business; it was Wolsey's choice for the council favoured neutrality because the war could bring no advantage to England and because the Treasury, as the Under-Treasurer well knew, was empty. When

---

[23]H. Maynard Smith, *Pre-Reformation England* (1930), p. 514.
[24]Bridgett, pp. 210-20, gives other passages.
[25]Rogers, 109,110.   [26]Rogers, 110.

he was in the Tower, More told his daughter Margaret of their failure to prevent this war.

> For of truth in times past when variance began to fall between the Emperor and the French King, in such wise that they were likely, and did indeed, fall together at war, and that there were in the Council here sometime sundry opinions, in which some were of the mind that they thought it wisdom that we should sit still and let them alone; but evermore against that way, my Lord [Wolsey] used this fable of those wise men, that because they would not be washed with the rain that should make all the people fools, went themselves into the caves and hid them under the ground. But when the rain had once made all the remnant fools and that they came out of their caves and would utter their wisdom, the fools agreed together against them and there all to beat them. And so said his Grace that if we would be wise that we should sit in peace while the fools fought, they would not fail after to make peace and agree and fall at length all upon us. I will not dispute upon his Grace's counsel, but I trust we never made war but as reason would. But yet this fable for his part did in his days help the King and the realm to spend many a fair penny. But that gear is past, and his Grace is gone; Our Lord assoil his soul.[27]

The war did indeed prove a costly business and all Wolsey's skill was unable to avoid additional, heavy taxation. A Parliament was inevitable, and it met on 15 April 1523. This was the first for eight years and the only one during Wolsey's chancellorship. There are no journals of the House of Commons for this period but fortunately there is a full account in Hall's *Chronicle*.[28]

Sir Thomas More was made Speaker; the "election" of a Speaker was little more than the acceptance of the member already designated by the King or Chancellor. The Parliament met at Blackfriars and after Mass of the Holy Ghost had been sung "the King came into the Parliament Chamber and there sat down in the seat royal or throne". Before him were the lords, spiritual and temporal, and the judges, and, beyond the bar, the Commons with their Speaker. There is a contemporary drawing of the

---

[27]Rogers, p. 518. It is possible that this story refers to 1528 and not 1522, but there is no indication of the year.
[28]Hall (ed. Whibley), I, pp. 278-9, 284-8.

scene; the original has deteriorated but a careful engraving[29] was made more than two hundred years ago and this enables us to visualize the opening of the Parliament, when Sir Thomas More, as Speaker, stood with the Commons to listen to the oration made by Bishop Tunstal who stood behind the bench on which sat Wolsey and Warham. Normally the Chancellor made this oration; perhaps Wolsey felt that as Cardinal-Legate it was better to have a deputy. The subject of the speech was "the office of a king" and not a declaration of policy.

When the Commons presented Sir Thomas More as their Speaker, he "according to the old usage, disabled himself both in wit, learning and discretion, to speak before the King", but, also according to old usage, the Cardinal-Chancellor replied that "the King knew his wit, learning, and discretion by long experience in his service". Sir Thomas then made a speech of some constitutional importance. He asked first, that he himself should be regarded as the mouthpiece of the Commons and not as speaking for himself, and secondly, to quote Roper:

> It may therefore like your most abundant Grace, our most benign and godly King, to give all your Commons here assembled your most gracious license and pardon, freely, without doubt of your dreadful displeasure, every man to discharge his conscience, and boldly in every thing incident among us to declare his advice; and whatsoever happen any man to say, that it may like your noble majesty of your inestimable goodness, to take all in good part.[30]

The wording may seem to us fulsome, but we shall not sense the temper of the age unless we see that it expressed the common attitude towards kingship. This request for freedom of discussion did not imply a desire to discuss anything they liked, for the Commons had not yet gained the right to originate subjects for legislation. Proposals that were before them came from the King and Council, or, for this Parliament, from Wolsey. There was no Front nor Opposition Bench; those councillors who were Members represented the "government". The records do show,

[29]See Plate 5.
[30]Roper, p. 16. For the significance of More's speech, see Sir John Neale, "The Commons Privilege of Free Speech" in *Tudor Studies* (1924).

F*

however, that the Commons debated matters of policy put before them very fully with greater freedom, indeed, than was allowed in later years.

Wolsey demanded a tax of four shillings in the pound on lands and goods in order to raise the sum of £800,000, an enormous figure for those days if not for ours. The Commons, in spite of Sir Thomas More's support for the proposal, were by no means willing to make the grant. They pleaded the poverty of the realm and said they hoped the King would be content with a smaller sum. As the debate went on, it was clear that the Commons were determined to resist this exorbitant demand. This angered the Cardinal and, ignoring custom, he entered the chamber. He was told that it was customary for the Commons to debate in private. Then, according to Roper, the Cardinal began to ask each member for his opinion. No one would reply. Finally he appealed to the Speaker,

> who first reverently upon his knees excusing the silence of the House, abashed at the presence of so noble a personage, able to amaze the wisest and best learned of the realm, and after by many probable arguments proving that for them to make answer was it neither expedient nor agreeable with the ancient liberty of the House. In conclusion for himself showed that though they had all with their voices trusted him, yet except every one of them could put into his one head all their several wits, he alone in so weighty a matter was unmeet to make his Grace answer.[31]

So the debate went on, and it was not until July that at last it was proposed to offer a tax of two shillings in the pound over a period of two years, one shilling each year. Sir Thomas persuaded them to raise this to three shillings, so the final offer was three-quarters of what Wolsey had demanded, but on the instalment system.

Roper's account must be read with some reservation. For instance, he said that Sir Thomas made the following remarks when the Commons were informed that the Cardinal was on his way:

It shall not in my mind be amiss with all his pomp to receive him,

[31]Roper, p. 18.

with his maces, his pillars, his pollaxes, his crosses, his hat, and the great seal too.[32]

One may doubt if More would speak in this sarcastic style to the Commons; perhaps he may have said something of the kind to his family. Roper further says that Wolsey was angry with More:

And after the Parliament ended, in his gallery at Whitehall in Westminster, he [the Cardinal] uttered unto him his griefs, saying, "Would to God you had been at Rome, Master More, when I made you Speaker". "Your Grace not offended, so would I too." And to wind such quarrels out of the Cardinal's head, he began to talk of that gallery, and said, "I like this gallery of yours my lord much better than your gallery at Hampton Court."[33]

There is no other evidence for such animosity as the story suggests. More had, in fact, actually got better terms from the Commons than seemed likely, and this was achieved in spite of their difficult mood. There is, however, evidence to show that the two were still on good terms. On 4 August, Wolsey wrote to the King:

And, Sire, whereas it hath been accustomed for the Speakers of the Parliaments in consideration of their diligence and pains taken, have had, though the Parliament hath been right soon finished, above the £100 ordinary, a reward of £100 for the better maintenance of their household and other charges sustained in the same, I suppose, Sir, that the faithful diligence of the said Sir Thomas More in all your causes treated in this your late Parliament, as well as for your subsidy, right honourably passed, as otherwise considered, no man could better deserve the same than he hath done. . . . I am the rather moved to put your Highness in remembrance thereof because he is not the most ready to speak and solicit his own cause.[34]

More acknowledged Wolsey's good offices in this matter in a letter from the court at Easthamstead on 26 August.

Furthermore it may like your Grace to understand that at the contemplation of your Grace's letters, the King's Highness is graciously content that beside the £100 for my fee for office of Speaker of his Parliament . . . I shall have one other hundred pounds out of his coffers by the hands of the Treasurer of his Chamber, whereof in most humble wise I beseech your good Grace that as your gracious

[32]Roper, p. 17. [33]Roper, p. 19. [34]L.P., III, 3267.

favour hath obtained it for me so it may like the same to write to Master Wyatt[35] that he may deliver it to such as I shall send for it, whereby I and all mine, as the manifold goodness of your Grace hath already bound us, shall be daily more and more bounden to pray for your Grace, whom Our Lord long preserve in honour and health.[36]

Roper has a story that Wolsey, in his annoyance, proposed sending More on an embassy to Spain in the hope that it would "send him to his grave".[37] This too must be doubted. The recurring attacks of sweating sickness and plague in London made the chances of a fatal illness as likely in England as in Spain. This embassy of 1525 was led by Tunstal (recently appointed Bishop of London). The business was connected with the imprisonment in Spain of King Francis of France after his defeat at Pavia in the previous February. Wolsey thought it a favourable opportunity to make a joint attack on kingless France by Henry and the Emperor; Tunstal soon found that he was wasting his time. Charles V had other ideas. He may even have thought Wolsey's proposal dishonourable. While it is true that Tunstal's companion, Sir Richard Wingfield, died in Spain (22 July 1515), there is no reason to see anything sinister in that misfortune.

Sir Richard had been Chancellor of the Duchy of Lancaster and High Steward of the University of Cambridge. Sir Thomas More was appointed to both offices towards the end of 1525. The High Stewardship was not an academic appointment; the holder was the official intermediary for legal matters. In the previous year Sir Thomas had been made High Steward of the University of Oxford; this association with both Universities must have given him great satisfaction. Some of his correspondence with Oxford is extant, but nothing from or to Cambridge; we have seen, however, that some of the students had been in touch with him before he had any official link with the University. Roper tells us that this connection with both Universities brought many scholars and students to his house, and he took particular pleasure in their conversation.

---

[35]Sir Henry Wyatt (d. 1537), father of the poet. Sir Henry's portrait by Holbein in the Louvre was long described as one of Sir Thomas More.
[36]Rogers, 115.   [37]Roper, p. 19.

CHAPTER XV

The School

THE DEATH of William Lily at the end of 1522 was a grievous loss to Thomas More; their friendship had been cemented in the days when they studied and translated Greek together, and Lily's all too short high-mastership of St Paul's School had strengthened their common interest in education. Christopher Urswick had died some months earlier; he was of the older generation and was a link with the cultured circle of the Lady Margaret Beaufort; he had been a wise counsellor to his young friends. Both William Grocyn and John Colet had died in 1519. The death of Linacre in 1524 may be said to mark the dissolution of the first generation of English humanists.[1]

John Colet had hoped to pass his last years in a "nest", as he called it, in retreat with the Carthusians at Sheen, but he died before he could carry out his plan. On Colet's death, More wrote, "For generations we have not had among us any man more learned or holy". And Erasmus wrote to Bishop Fisher, "Thus far have I written, grieving for the death of Colet; a death so bitter to me that the loss of no one for the last thirty years has afflicted me more. . . . I cannot but lament the loss of so rare a pattern of Christian piety, so unique a preacher of Christian doctrine."[2]

The year before his death, Colet had made the final Statutes for his school and amply endowed it from his inherited wealth. Both Erasmus and More had taken a close interest in the project. More himself was concerned as he was planning the education of his own children.

In Utopia learning was open to all without distinction of sex. "A large part of the people, men and women alike, throughout their lives, devote to learning the hours which we said were free from manual labour."[3] More made no distinction in his own

[1]Tunstal and Stokesley were his executors and the trustees of his estate for the foundation of a lectureship in medicine at Oxford.
[2]Allen, 1030.   [3]Utopia, p. 159.

household in the training given to boys and girls. His own four children, Margaret, Elizabeth, Cecily and John, were fortunate in having his personal care and guidance in their early years, but from about 1516, when Margaret was eleven years of age, the time he could give to them was limited as he was called away so much for public service at Westminster and the court. This was a matter of great concern to him. His children had as their companions his step-daughter, Alice Alington, and his wards Margaret Giggs and Anne Cresacre; later others were entrusted to his care just as he himself had been to that of Cardinal Morton. Giles Heron, another ward, was one of them; then there were his nephews and nieces, such as Joan and William Rastell and Frances Staverton. Stapleton wrote, "More's own four children and eleven of his grandchildren were instructed in his school during his lifetime".[4] And Erasmus wrote, "His house was a school for knowledge and for the practice of the Christian faith".[5] There seem to have been other children in the "school"; for instance, Margaret à Barrow, who afterwards married Thomas Elyot, is mentioned as having been educated with the More children.[6]

Thomas More took great care in selecting tutors for his school; we know the names of some of them. The first was John Clement, who, as we have seen, was with More during the planning of *Utopia*, and later, in 1518, entered the household of Cardinal Wolsey, and from thence passed to Oxford as a lecturer in Greek. Later he went abroad to study medicine and on his return became one of the King's physicians and was sent to attend the fallen Wolsey at Esher in his illness. Clement married Margaret Giggs about 1526.

The next house tutor of whom we know was William Gonell, who was recommended by Erasmus. Gonell was a native of Landbeach, some five miles out of Cambridge; he did copying work for Erasmus and also looked after his horse. Gonell was given the living of Conington in Cambridgeshire in 1517, but did not then take up residence. In an undated letter to a friend, he

---

[4]Stapleton, p. 93.   [5]Allen, 2750.
[6]There are portraits of Sir Thomas and Lady Elyot among the Holbein drawings at Windsor.

mentioned that "Clement is well and so is More's family", and he went on to ask if he could borrow Cicero's Letters for More's use.[7]

In a letter to his children which may be dated 1521, More referred to two other tutors:

> I am glad that Master Drew has returned safely, for, as you know, I was anxious about him. Did I not love you so warmly, I should really envy your good fortune in that so many and such excellent tutors have fallen to your lot. But I think you no longer need Master Nicholas as you have learned whatever he had to teach you in astronomy.[8]

Nothing certain is known of Master Drew; he may have been the Roger Drew who became a Fellow of All Souls, Oxford, in 1512. Master Nicholas Kratzer was a German scholar—we should say, scientist—who in 1519 became astronomer to Henry VIII; there is a fine portrait of him by Holbein in the Louvre. Kratzer was one of the visiting tutors and, though his formal engagement may have ended about 1512, he remained a friend of the family.

The last of the tutors of whom there is any record was Richard Hyrde, who may have been educated at More's expense for in a dedicatory epistle to his translation of Vives' *Instruction of a Christian Woman* he referred to More as "my singular good master and bringer-up". Hyrde took his degree at Oxford in 1519; nine years later he accompanied Stephen Gardiner and Edward Foxe as Wolsey's emissaries to the Pope. Gardiner described him as "a young man learned in physic, Greek and Latin". He died in Italy.

These and other young men may have owed their later advancement to the recommendation of Thomas More.

Doubtless there were some tutors whose names have not been recorded. There must surely have been music teachers; More himself was devoted to music and played the viol and other instruments. According to Erasmus, More had "no natural gift for singing" but that did not prevent him from singing in the parish choir and at home. Perhaps Erasmus' standard was high as he himself had been trained as a choir boy. No doubt John Heywood, who was to marry Joan Rastell, was among those who

---

[7]L.P., II, ii, Ap. 17.   [8]Rogers, 101 (29); Stapleton, p. 97.

made music with the Mores. It is probable that he was introduced
to the court by More where Heywood had a successful career.[9]
His later skill in writing Interludes may have owed something to
More's love of acting, and we can be sure that the household
took part in home-made plays with the example of More to
encourage them. Erasmus also tells us that Mistress Alice did her
part in seeing that the children carried out their tasks when their
father was absent.

He planned their education on carefully thought-out principles.
Fortunately Stapleton preserved for us a letter More wrote to
William Gonell setting out his ideas. It is difficult to date the
letter, but, assuming that Gonell did not take up his benefice in
1517, the letter may come within the next year or so. Thomas
More emphasized the importance of training for virtue and the
good life.

> Though I prefer learning joined with virtue to all the treasures of
> kings, yet renown for learning, when it is not united with the good
> life, is nothing else than a splendid and notorious disgrace especially
> in a woman. Since erudition in women is a new thing and a reproach
> to the sloth of man, many will gladly assail it, and impute to letters
> what is really the fault of nature, thinking from the vices of the
> learned to get their ignorance esteemed as a virtue. On the other
> hand, if a woman (and this I desire and hope with you as their teacher
> with all my daughters) to eminent virtue should build an outwork
> of even moderate skill in letters, I think she will have more real
> benefit than if she had obtained the riches of Croesus or the beauty
> of Helen. I do not say this because of the glory that will be hers,
> though glory follows virtue as a shadow follows a body, but because
> the reward of wisdom is too solid to be lost like riches or to decay
> like beauty, since it depends on the intimate conscience of what is
> right, not on the talk of men, than which nothing is more foolish or
> mischievous.

He then urged the need

> to warn my children to avoid the precipices of pride and haughtiness
> and to walk in the pleasant meadows of modesty; not to be dazzled
> at the sight of gold; not to lament that they do not possess what they
> erroneously admire in others; not to think more of themselves for

[9] A. W. Reed. *Early Tudor Drama* (1926), p. 47.

Iudge More Sr Tho: Mores Father.

9. SIR JOHN MORE

10.   SIR THOMAS MORE

Tho: Moor Ld Chancelour

11. SIR THOMAS MORE

Iohn More Sʳ Thomas Mores Son.

12. JOHN MORE

13.   ELIZABETH MORE (DAUNCE)

14. CECILY MORE (HERON)

15. MARGARET GIGGS (CLEMENT)

16.   ANN CRESACRE (MORE)

gaudy trappings, nor less for want of them; neither to deform the beauty nature has given them by neglect, nor to try to heighten it by artifice; to put virtue in the first place, learning in the second; and in their studies to esteem most whatever may teach them piety towards God, charity to all, and Christian humility in themselves.

He advised Gonell to introduce his pupils to the works of St Augustine and St Jerome:

From them they will learn in particular what end they should propose to themselves in their studies and what is the fruit of their endeavours, namely the testimony of God and a good conscience. Thus peace and calm will abide in their hearts and they will be disturbed neither by fulsome flattery nor by the stupidity of those illiterate men who despise learning.[10]

The Latin letters Thomas More wrote to his children[11] are among his most characteristic familiar writings. Stapleton tells us that when he copied them (about 1588) they were "almost worn pieces". We owe it to him that the text of them has been preserved for the originals have been lost. He does not give the years when they were written but the period between 1517 and 1523 seems probable. The first to be quoted is addressed to "Margaret, Elizabeth and Cecily his dearest children and to Margaret Giggs whom he regards as his child".

I cannot express, my dearest children, the deep pleasure your eloquent letters gave me, especially as I see that although travelling and frequently changing your abode you have not allowed your customary studies to be interfered with, but have continued your exercises in logic, rhetoric and poetry.

There is no hint of why the family was moving about so much— perhaps to and from Gobions. The letter continues:

When I return, you shall see that I am not ungrateful for the delight your loving affection has given me. I assure you that I have no greater solace in all the vexatious business in which I am immersed than to read your letters.

A later passage suggests that he may have had his son John with him; his name is not in the heading:

I am longing to return home so that I may place my pupil by your

[10]Rogers, 63 (20); Stapleton, pp. 94-7.
[11]Rogers, 69, 70, 76, 101, 106-8 (22-3, 29, 31-3); Stapleton, pp. 97-102.

side and compare his progress with yours. He is, I fear, a little lazy, but he cannot help hoping that you are not really so advanced as your teacher's praise would imply.

Margaret showed the most ability of the children and she became a learned woman. Her father wrote to her:

I was delighted to receive your letter, my dearest Margaret, informing me of Shaa's[12] condition. I should have been still more delighted if you had told me of the studies you and your brother are engaged in, of your daily reading, your pleasant discussions, your essays. ... I assure you that rather than allow my children to be idle and slothful, I would make a sacrifice of wealth, and bid adieu to other cares and business, to attend to my children and my family, among whom none is more dear to me than yourself, my beloved daughter.

The last of this series of letters to the school is worth quoting in full:

The Bristol merchant brought me your letters the day after he left you, with which I was extremely delighted. Nothing can come from your workshop, however rude and unfinished, that will not give me more pleasure than the most accurate writings of anyone else. So much does my affection for you recommend whatever you write to me. Indeed without any recommendation your letters are capable of pleasing by their own merits, their wit and pure Latinity. There was not one of your letters that did not greatly please me, but, to confess frankly what I feel, the letter of my son John pleased me best, both because it was longer than the others, and because he seems to have given it more labour and study. For he not only put his matter neatly and composed in fairly polished language, but he plays with me both pleasantly and cleverly, and turns my jokes on myself wittily enough. And this he does not only merrily, but with due moderation, showing that he does not forget that he is joking with his father, and that he is cautious not to give offence at the same time that he is eager to give delight.

Now I expect from each of you a letter almost every day. I will not admit excuses; John makes none, such as want of time, sudden departure of the letter-carrier, or want of something to write about. No one hinders you from writing, but, on the contrary, all are urging you to do it. And that you may not keep the letter-carrier waiting,

[12]Probably a servant.

why not anticipate his coming and have your letters written and
sealed for anyone to take? How can a subject be wanting when you
write to me since I am glad to hear of your studies or your games,
and you will please me most if, when there is nothing to write about,
you write about that nothing at some length. Nothing can be easier
for, since you are girls, chatterboxes by nature, you have always a
world to say about nothing at all. One thing, however, I admonish
you, whether you write serious matters or the merest trifles, it is
my wish that you write everything diligently and thoughtfully. It
will be no harm if you first write the whole in English for then you
will have much less trouble in turning it into Latin, not having to
look for the matter, your mind will be intent only on the language.
That, however, I leave to your choice, whereas I strictly enjoin you
that whatever you have composed, you carefully examine it before
writing the fair copy, and in this examination first scrutinise the
whole sentence and then every part of it. Thus, if any grammatical
errors have escaped you, you will easily detect them. Correct these,
write out the whole letter again and even then examine it once more,
for sometimes in rewriting faults slip in again that one had removed.
By this diligence your little trifles will become serious matters, for
while there is nothing so neat and witty that will not be made insipid
by silly and inconsiderate wordiness, so also there is nothing in
itself so insipid that you cannot season it with grace and wit if you
give a little thought to it.

Farewell, my dear children.

From the Court, the 3rd September.

This letter gives us a pleasant impression of John More and it
should dispose of the legend that he was dimwitted.[13] The fact
that he did not, as far as we know, go to a university nor to
an Inn of Court suggests that his inclinations were not intellectual, though, as we shall see, he had his share of the family
Latinity.[14]

Among the letters from Thomas More to his school is one in
Latin verse, in elegaic couplets. This can be dated with some
confidence as it was first printed in the 1520 edition of the
Epigrammata and not in the 1518 edition. There is no hint in the
poem of his whereabouts and the reference to foul roads could

[13]The earliest suggestion seems to come in Francis Bacon's *Apophthegms* (1625).
[14]See below, pp. 261-2.

apply equally to England or the Low Countries. The poem opens by telling his children that it was composed on horseback when he was soaked with rain and his small horse was often stuck in the mud. He tells them of his love and reminds them that he could not bear to see them weep but gave them cakes and apples and pears, and that, on rare occasions when he whipped them, he used a birch of peacock's feathers.

> Scitis enim quam crebra dedi oscula, verbera rara,
> Flagrum pavonis non nisi cauda fuit.

He praised their manners, pleasant way of speaking and their nicety in the choice of words.

The dialectical disputation which had such a large place in medieval universities was a method favoured by More and Erasmus. In 1505-6, each of them translated Lucian's *Tyrannicida* and then wrote a declamation on the same theme. Erasmus wrote, "I very much wish this sort of exercise to be introduced into our schools, where it would be of the greatest utility". J. L. Vives gives us an instance of this method being used in the "school":

> More had told the story of Quintilian's first declamation to his little boy John and to his daughters, the worthy offspring of their father. He had discoursed in such a way as to lead them all by his eloquence the more easily to the study of wisdom. He then begged me to write an answer to the declamation which he had expounded so that the art of writing might be disclosed more openly by contradiction and, as it were, by conflict.[15]

Vives paid tribute to the encouragement Thomas More gave to the education of women. The following passage comes from *The Instruction of a Christian Woman*[16] in Richard Hyrde's translation which was made at More's suggestion:

> Now if a man may be suffered among queens to speak of more mean folks, I reckon among this sort the daughters of Sir Thomas More, whom their father, not content only to have them good and chaste, would also they should be well learned, supposing that by that means they should be more truly and surely chaste. Wherein neither that great, wise man is deceived, nor none other that are of the same opinion.

[15]Foster Watson, *Vives and the Renaissance Education of Women* (1912), p. 17.
[16]Published in 1524. Hyrde's translation, 1529. Gibson, 580.

Vives had written his book at the request of Queen Catherine who was concerned with the best way of educating the Princess Mary. Among the books to be read, Vives suggested *Utopia*.

Here it will be appropriate to give the eulogy of Thomas More that Vives wrote in his notes to St Augustine's *De Civitate* (1523). Vives had just been quoting from Lucian's *Necromantia;* he went on:

> Thus far Lucian. We have rehearsed it in the words of Thomas More, whom to praise negligently, or as if we were otherwise employed, were grossness. His due commendations are sufficient to exceed great volumes. For what is he that can worthily limn forth his sharpness of wit, his depth of judgement, his excellence and variety of learning, his eloquence of phrase, his plausibility [agreeableness] and integrity of manners, his judicious foresight, his exact execution, his gentle modesty and uprightness, and his unmoved loyalty, unless he will call them (as they are indeed) the patterns and lustres, each of his kind? I speak much, and many that have not known More will wonder at me, but such as have will know I speak the truth. So will such as shall either read his works, or but hear or look upon his actions. But another time shall be more fit to spread our sails in this man's praises, as in a spacious ocean, wherein we will take this full and prosperous wind, and write much in substance and much in value of his worthy honours.[17]

The impression of these letters to his children may be that Latin was almost the sole subject taught to them. That it was the main subject cannot be questioned, but there are references to Greek, Logic, Philosophy, Theology, Mathematics and Astronomy—a formidable list it is true! Mathematics at that period meant geometry; we should now expect arithmetic to be the first step but the working of sums was then regarded as the business of tradesmen and merchants—a plebeian task. Perhaps the More children had this subject added to their curriculum through the influence of Cuthbert Tunstal. When he and their father were on embassy in Flanders in 1515, they had difficulty in checking the transactions of the money-changers and they suspected they were being swindled, but neither scholar knew any arithmetic. On their return, Tunstal decided to study the subject, and, as a result,

[17]Healey's translation of 1610. Everyman's Library ed., Vol. 2, p. 412.

wrote in Latin the first book on arithmetic to be published in England. *De arte supputandi*, published in 1522, was dedicated to Thomas More.[18] Part of the dedicatory epistle reads: "you, who can pass the book on to your children for them to read—children whom you take care to train in liberal studies".

Tunstal also hoped that his friend would find the book useful in his duties as Under-Treasurer. Whether the More children profited or not is unrecorded, but it is interesting to note that with the last letter he wrote to Margaret from the Tower, More returned to Margaret Giggs "her algorism stone"—a slate on which calculations were made.

It may be felt that this scheme of education was a heavy one to impose on the children, but probably some of the subjects mentioned did not go much beyond the elements. Nor should we forget the cakes and apples and pears—nor the peacock's feathers!

How successful the system was with Margaret may be judged from the following letter her father wrote to her not later than February 1521. This was the month in which Reginald Pole, at the age of twenty-one, left England for Italy.

I cannot put down on paper, indeed I can hardly express in my own mind the deepest pleasure that I received from your very well-expressed letter, my dearest Margaret. As I read it there was with me a young man of the noblest rank and of the widest attainments in letters, one, too, who is as conspicuous for his piety as he is for learning, Reginald Pole. He thought your letter nothing short of miraculous, even before he understood how you were pressed for time and distracted by ill-health. I could scarce make him believe that you had not been helped by a master until I told him in all good faith that there was no such master at our house.[19]

It was probably about the same time that More was able to report a second compliment:

I happened this evening to be in the company of his lordship John Veysey [Bishop of Exeter], a man of deep learning and of a wide reputation for holiness. Whilst we were talking I took out from my desk a paper that bore on our business and, by accident, your letter appeared. Delighted by the handwriting, he began to look closely at

[18]Rogers, III. Gibson, 157.   [19]Stapleton, p. 43.

it. When he saw the signature that it was the letter of a lady, he read it the more eagerly because it was such a novelty to him. When he had finished he said he would never have believed it to have been your work unless I had assured him of the fact, and he began to praise it in the highest terms (why should I hide what he said?) for its Latinity, its correctness, its erudition, and its expressions of tender affection. Seeing how delighted he was, I showed him your declamation. He read it and your poems as well, with a pleasure so far beyond what he had hoped that although he praised you most affusively, yet his expression showed that his words were all too poor to express what he felt. He took out at once from his pocket a gold coin which you will find enclosed in this letter. I tried in every possible way to decline it, but was unable to refuse to send it to you as a pledge and token of his goodwill towards you. This hindered me from showing him the letters of your sisters, for I feared it would seem as though I had shown them to obtain for the others too a gift which it annoyed me to have to accept for you. But, as I have said, he is so good that it is a happiness to be able to please him. Write to thank him with the greatest care and delicacy. You will one day be glad to have given pleasure to such a man.[20]

Here we see the proud father passing on the praise his eldest daughter had gained; what effect this may have had upon Margaret's character is not known, but a girl of sixteen would have been less than human if she had not been tempted to fall into that sin of pride on which her father had so much to say in his letter to William Gonell.

She did not see another tribute, this time from Erasmus. In a letter to Guillaume Budé in September 1521 he wrote:

A year ago it occurred to More to send me a specimen of their progress in learning. He told them all to write to me, each without any help, nor did he suggest the subject nor make any corrections. When they offered their papers to their father for him to correct, he affected to be displeased with the bad handwriting and made them copy their letters out more neatly and accurately. When they had done so, he sealed the letters and sent them to me without changing a syllable. Believe me, my dear Budé, I never was more surprised; there was nothing whatever silly or girlish in what they said, and the style was such that you could feel they were making daily progress.[21]

[20]Stapleton, p. 106.   [21]Allen, 1233.

Erasmus referred to More's "school" in his *De Pueris* . . .
Instituendis in 1529. "He, although deeply occupied in affairs of
state, devoted his leisure to the instruction of his wife, his sons
and his daughters, both in the uprightness of life and in the
liberal studies of Greek and Latin." Here again, "uprightness of
life" is conjoined with "liberal studies".

CHAPTER XVI

The Ropers

IN 1521 the Bishop of London (Fitzjames) issued a licence for the marriage on 2 July of "William Roper of St Andrew, Holborn,[1] and Margaret More of St Stephen's, Walbrook". She was then in her sixteenth year. According to two miniatures painted by Holbein,[2] William Roper was twelve years older than his wife; this would give the date of his birth about 1493. This does not agree with other information. His epitaph (no longer extant) in St Dunstan's, Canterbury, stated that he was eighty-two at the time of his death on 4 January 1578; this would give 1496 as the year of his birth. Further confusion is caused by a Chancery deposition of 14 May 1562, which gave his age as sixty-four, making the year of his birth 1498. We can take our choice! The exact year is not important; the fact that matters is that he was about ten years older than Margaret More.

The Mores and the Ropers had been associated in the law at Lincoln's Inn and at Westminster for a quarter of a century or more. John Roper, William's father, and Sir John More were old friends and they often served on commissions together. "You come of a worthy pedigree", wrote Harpsfield of William Roper, "both by the father's and the mother's side; by the father's side of ancient gentlemen of long continuance, and by the mother's side of Apulderfields, one of the chiefest and ancient families of Kent."[3] John Roper's house was Well Hall, near Eltham, and he also had lands in St Dunstan's parish, Canterbury. The Roper Chantry there is now the Chapel of St Nicholas. He was sheriff of Kent in 1521, the year of his eldest son's marriage; he was appointed Attorney-General at the same time. For many years he was Protonotary, or Clerk of the Pleas of the King's Bench Court, an office to which William succeeded, and his son after him. John Roper died in 1524, but his will being so badly drawn (he being

---

[1]Lincoln's Inn was in this parish.   [2]See Plates 20, 21.   [3]Harpsfield, p. 5.

a lawyer!) it took an Act of Parliament in 1529 to sort it out. After his father's death, William was a man of considerable means.

In the opening paragraph of his memoir of his father-in-law, Roper stated that "I was continually resident in his house by the space of sixteen years or more". This takes us back three or four years before his marriage to Margaret. It was without doubt a marriage of deep affection on both sides. It is sometimes overlooked that Roper's little book on Sir Thomas More is as much a tribute to his wife as it is to his father-in-law. It is not without significance, if we consider the customs of the age, that William Roper remained a widower for thirty-four years after Margaret's death.

From the Black Books of Lincoln's Inn we learn that on Christmas Day, 1518, "William Roper, son of Master John Roper, was admitted to the Society by George Treheyon, then the Marshal and Feb. 26 1520, he was pardoned all vacations, past and future; he may be at repasts at his pleasure".

He was called to the Bar in 1525. The year of his admission to the Inn would seem a convenient time for the young law student to lodge with the Mores at the Old Barge.

Harpsfield recorded that "the said Master William Roper, at what time he married with Mistress Margaret More, was a marvellous zealous Protestant".[4] The particulars of this lapse into heresy must have been told to Harpsfield by Roper, but the fact was well known in the More circle and beyond it for "neither was he content to whisper it in hugger mugger, but thirsted very sore to publish his new doctrine". The use of the term "Protestant" is here an anachronism; so too was Harpsfield's later statement that Roper "gat to him a Lutheran Bible". Perhaps this means a copy of the Wycliffite version, unless, which is doubtful, Roper could read German. He had absorbed Luther's two pamphlets of 1520, *The Babylonish Captivity* and *The Liberty of a Christian Man*, copies of which (in Latin) were brought into the country by merchants of the Steelyard and through other channels. Was Roper one of the secret society of Christian Brethren who arranged for the distribution and discussion of Luther's writings?

There were sympathetic English merchants in the City such as Humphrey Monmouth, a leading draper and patron of William Tyndale. Roper got himself into trouble by his outspoken opinions; as Harpsfield wrote:

> who, for his open talk and companying with divers of his own sect, of the Steelyard and other merchants, was with them before Cardinal Wolsey convented of heresy, which merchants for their opinions were openly for heresy at Paul's Cross abjured; yet he, for love borne by the Cardinal to Sir Thomas More, was with a friendly warning discharged.[4]

This seems to point to 12 February 1526 when Robert Barnes and four Steelyard merchants made their abjurations at Paul's Cross when Bishop John Fisher preached. The four merchants appear to have been arrested when, three weeks earlier, More had given orders for a search to be made of the Steelyard for Lutheran books and for Bibles and unorthodox prayer books. The year 1526 seems rather late for Roper's discharge, but Harpsfield said that he clung to his heretical opinions "a long time".

Thomas More tried to reason William Roper out of his new fangled ideas, but failed to convince him. Indeed, at that period, according to Harpsfield, Roper had come to dislike his father-in-law, "Whom then of all the world he did, during that time, most abhor, though he was a man of most mildness and notable patience". At length Thomas More gave up argument, saying to Margaret, "And therefore, Meg, I will no longer argue and dispute with him, but will clean give him over, and get me another while to God and pray for him". Soon afterwards, Roper "perceived his ignorance and returned to the Catholic faith". This close association and argument with a heretic in his own family gave More an understanding of the problems of Lutheranism that was to stand him in good stead when he himself was called to defend the faith.

A letter Margaret wrote to her father about 1522 seems to have been an apology for having neglected her studies; this may have been due to her preoccupation with her new duties as a wife. Her father replied: "I am therefore delighted to read that you have

⁴Harpsfield, pp. 84-9.

now made up your mind to give yourself diligently to philosophy, and to make up by your earnestness in future for what you have lost in the past by neglect".[5]

He then passed on to refer to the study of medicine in which he evidently had a strong interest. Utopia was notable for its health services. It will be recalled that two of the tutors, John Clement and Richard Hyrde, had taken up the subject, perhaps at More's instigation. To this may be added the fact that Margaret Giggs was skilled in medical lore. The letter continues:

> Though I earnestly hope that you will devote the rest of your life to medical science and sacred literature, so that you may be well furnished for the whole range of human life, which is to have a healthy mind in a healthy body, and though I know that you have already laid the foundations of these studies, and that there will always be opportunity to continue the building, yet I am of opinion that you may with great advantage give some years of your yet flourishing youth to humane letters and liberal studies.

The final paragraph of this letter reads:

> Farewell, my dearest child, and salute for me my most gentle son your husband. I am most delighted that he is following the same course of study as yourself. I have been accustomed to urge you to yield in everything to your husband, now, on the contrary, I give you full leave to strive to get before him in the knowledge of the celestial system.

That does not sound as if More was then at odds with his son-in-law, yet, if Harpsfield was right in saying that Roper's bout of Lutheranism lasted "a long time", 1522 seems too early for his recovery. It is hard to believe that More would have allowed Margaret to marry a heretic, or that she would have accepted one as a suitor. This suggests that the lapse came later; if so, the St Paul's Cross abjurations of 1526 may have been those that Roper escaped by the leniency of Wolsey.

The Ropers spent much of their time at the Old Barge after their marriage as he had his duties at Westminster during term time. When Margaret's two sisters were married in 1525, they too seem to have spent much of their time at their old home.

Elizabeth married William Daunce,[6] or Dauntsey, and Cecily married Giles Heron[7] the same day, 29 September. The licence of the new Bishop of London, Cuthbert Tunstal, allowed both marriages to be celebrated in the chapel of Giles Alington at Willesden.[8] He was the second husband of More's step-daughter, Alice Middleton; her first husband, Thomas Elrington of Hitchen, had died in September 1523.

The three daughters had married into landed families. William Roper came into his share of his father's estates in Kent and elsewhere in 1529; Giles Heron had lands in Essex, and William Daunce in Hertfordshire. Giles Alington had estates in Suffolk and Cambridgeshire. They all seem to have divided their time between their manors and the Old Barge and, later, Chelsea. Thomas More had a patriarchal conception of family life and he loved to have his children, and, in due course, his grandchildren, about him.

On the day of this double wedding, Thomas More took up his appointment as Chancellor of the Duchy of Lancaster. Today this is not a position entailing many duties, but it is useful for a member of the government unencumbered with departmental work. In Tudor times the Chancellor had a close association with the King. Since 1399 the very extensive Lancaster estates had provided a substantial part of the royal income; the Duchy was administered as a distinct unit, and, in the Court of the Duchy Chamber, the Chancellor exercised executive and judicial powers of wide scope.

A letter from Thomas More to Margaret of 1522 or 1523 tells us of her approaching confinement:

In your letter you speak of your approaching confinement. We pray most earnestly that all may go happily and successfully with you. May God and our Blessed Lady grant you happily and safely a little one like to his mother in everything except sex. Yet let it by all

[6]Son of Sir John Daunce, a member of the Council.

[7]More's ward; son of Sir John Heron, Treasurer of the Chamber.

[8]Research has not revealed any trace of Alingtons in Willesden. The manor belonged to the Elrington family, and in 1577 Thomas Elrington left the manor by will to Thomas More of Barnburgh, grandson of Sir Thomas and son of John More. An interesting puzzle!

means be a girl, if she will make up for the inferiority of her sex by her zeal to imitate her mother's virtue and learning. Such a girl I would prefer to three boys.[9]

More certainly held the Pauline view of the respective positions of man and woman; this was, of course, the accepted attitude of his day, but, as we have seen, this did not mean an inferior education for a girl. On marriage, he wrote:

This holy sacrament of matrimony was begun by God in Paradise and he there instituted it to signify the conjunction between himself and man's soul, and the conjunction between Christ and his Church. Yet in that coupling of matrimony (if they couple him) he coupleth himself also to their souls, with grace, according to the sign, that is to say the which he hath set to signify that grace, and with that grace, if they apply to work therewith, he helpeth them to make their marriage honourable and their bed undefiled. And with that grace also he helpeth them toward the good education and bringing up of such children as shall come between them.[10]

In 1524 Erasmus published in one volume a commentary on the poem *Nux*, attributed to Ovid, and another on two hymns by Prudentius.[11] The first was dedicated to John More and the second to his sister Margaret. To her, Erasmus wrote:

William Roper, who is gifted with such nobility and gentleness of character that, were he not your husband, he might seem to be your brother, has given you (or, if you prefer it, you have given him) the most fortunate first-fruits of your union, or to put it better, each has given the other a child—to whom a kiss is sent; I send you another child. . . . Thank you for your letters; even without a signature, they would be recognised as from Thomas More's children.

The "child" he sent was the work dedicated to her. The letter ends, "A warm farewell to you who are not a lesser light of the age and of Britain. Greet also for me the whole of your choir." By "choir" we may understand the family and the school. By the time the book was published the baby was dead.

It was during the early years of her marriage that Margaret Roper made a translation of Erasmus' *Precatio dominica*, published

[9]Rogers, 128 (35); Stapleton, p. 105.
[10]E.W., p. 378.   [11]Gibson, 133; Allen, 1402, 1404.

in Basle in 1523. Margaret's translation was printed by Berthelet in 1526.[12] Richard Hyrde wrote an introduction to one of his pupils, "the studious and virtuous young maid, Frances S." This was Frances Staverton, Margaret's cousin. There is a reference to the "school".

> Howbeit, I have no doubt in you, whom I see naturally born into virtue, and having so good bringing up of a babe, not only among your honourable uncle's children, of whose conversation and company they that were right evil, might take occasion of goodness and amendment. . . .

We can assign to this 1520 to 1525 period an unfinished treatise by More on *The Four Last Things*, a commentary on the text, "Remember the last things, and thou shalt never sin".[13] He did not complete the work, but dealt only with the first, Death, and even that part was unfinished; he did not treat of Judgment, Heaven and Hell. He suggested to Margaret that she should take the same subject and deal with it independently. His pleasure at the result is recorded, but, though she preserved his manuscript, her own has not survived.[14]

In this grim fragment we see the Thomas More of Holbein's portrait, for here is the stern thinker with his mind and spirit intent on the profound mysteries of death and judgment. The early reference to the "Dance of Death pictured in St Paul's"[15] sets the tone, for the treatment is medieval in its stark realism.

> For those pictures express only the loathly figure of our dead, bony bodies, bitten away the flesh; which, though it be ugly to behold, yet neither the sight thereof, nor the sight of all the dead heads in the charnel house, nor the apparition of a very ghost, is half so grisly as the deep conceived fantasy of death in his nature, by the lively imagination graven in thine own heart. For there seest thou, not one plain grievous sight of the bare bones hanging by the sinews, but thou seest (if thou fancy thine own death, for so art thou by this counsel advised), thou seest, I say, thyself, if thou die no worse

[12]Gibson, 487. The original text and Margaret Roper's translation will be found in *Moreana*, 7 (1965).
[13]Ecclus. 7, 40.   [14]Stapleton, p. 103.
[15]On the walls of the cloister of Pardon Church Haugh (cemetery) on the north side near the west end. John Lydgate (d. 1450) provided the verses. The Charnel House was near Paul's Cross.

death, yet at the leastwise lying in thy bed, thy head shooting, thy back aching, thy veins beating, thine heart panting, thy throat rattling, thy flesh trembling, thy mouth gaping, thy nose sharpening, thy legs cooling, thy fingers fumbling, thy breath shortening, all thy strength fainting, thy life vanishing, and thy death drawing on.[16]

Thomas More could not use his pen for long without giving play to his imagination.

Have ye not ere this, in a sore sickness, felt it very grievous to have folk babble to you, and namely such things as ye should make answer to, when it was pain to speak? Think ye not now that it will be a great pleasure, when ye lie dying, all our body in pain, all our mind walketh awayward, while our death draweth toward, while the devil is busy about us, while we lack stomach and strength to bear any one of so manifold heinous troubles, will it not be, as I was about to say, a pleasant thing to see before thine eyes and hear at thine ear a rabble of fleshly friends, or rather of flesh flies, skipping about thy bed and thy sick body, like ravens about thy corpse, now almost carrion, crying to thee on every side, "What shall I have? What shall I have?" Then shall come thy children and cry for their parts; then shall come thy sweet wife, and where in thy health she spake thee not one sweet word in six weeks, now shall she call thee sweet husband and weep with much work and ask thee what shall she have; then shall thine executors ask for the keys and ask what money is owing thee, ask what substance thou hast, and ask where thy money lieth. And while thou liest in that case, their words shall be so tedious that thou wilt wish all that they ask for upon a red fire, so thou mightest lie one half-hour in rest.[17]

Then the devil's ways of tempting us at death are described:

And instead of sorrow for our sins and care of heaven, he [the devil] putteth us in mind of provision for some honourable burying,—so many torches, so many tapers, so many black gowns, so many merry mourners laughing under black hoods, and a gay hearse, with the delight of goodly and honourable funerals: in which the foolish sick man is sometimes occupied as though he thought that he should stand in a window and see how worshipfully he shall be brought to church.[18]

We must accept this satirical strain as an element in a personality that was far from simple.

[16]E.W., p. 77.   [17]E.W., p. 78.   [18]E.W., p. 79.

So the writer turned to consider the deadly sins of pride, envy, wrath, covetousness, gluttony and sloth. He used familiar instances; thus vainglory is illustrated from the stage.

If thou shouldst perceive that one were earnestly proud of the wearing of the gay golden gown, while the lorel [rogue] playeth the lord in a stage play, wouldst thou not laugh at his folly, considering that thou art very sure that when the play is done he shall go walk a knave in his old coat? Now thou thinkest thyself wise enough while thou art proud in thy player's garment, and forgettest that when thy play is done, thou shalt go forth as poor as he. Nor thou remembrest not that thy pageant may happen to be done as soon as his.[19]

One passage in this unfinished treatise refers to the judicia murder of Edward, Duke of Buckingham in May 1521. As he was a direct descendant of Thomas of Woodstock, the youngest son of Edward III, he stood dangerously near the throne and this was probably the root cause of his destruction. His own foolishness did the rest. This arbitrary act, for there was no evidence of actual treason, was an early example of that ruthlessness that was to grow upon the King. The people at the time blamed Wolsey. John Skelton in his *Colin Clout* (1522) could write of Wolsey:

Men say how ye appal
The noble blood royal.

So More could write:

If it so were that thou knewest a great Duke, keeping so great estate and princely port in his house that thou, being a right mean man hadst in thine heart a great envy thereat, and specially at some special day in which he keepeth for the marriage of his child a great honourable court above other times; if thou being thereat, and at the sight of the royalty and honour shown him of all the country about resorting to him, while they kneel and crouch to him and at every word barehead begrace him, if thou shouldst suddenly be surely advertised, that for secret treason, lately detected to the King, he should undoubtedly be taken the morrow, his court all broken up, his goods seized, his wife put out, his children disinherited, himself cast into prison, brought forth and arraigned, the matter out of question, and he should be condemned, his coat armour reversed, his

[19]E.W., p. 84.
G

gilt spurs hewn off at his heels, himself hanged, drawn and quartered, how thinkest thou, by thy faith, amid thine envy shouldst thou not suddenly change into pity?[20]

We can connect this passage with a story told by Stapleton. According to this, Wolsey wanted to become "Supreme Constable", as the personal representative of the King. This probably means the position of Lord High Constable that Buckingham had held. More, according to the story, was the only councillor to object and he argued so persuasively that the Council took no further action.

The Cardinal was angry and thus addressed More: "Are you not ashamed Master More, being the lowest of all in place and dignity, to dissent from so many noble and prudent men? You show yourself to be a stupid and foolish councillor." "Thanks be to God", replied More instantly, "that the King's Majesty has but one fool in his Council."[21]

Stapleton placed this incident "soon after More's entry into the Council"; at that time Wolsey was not yet the power he had become in 1521. The execution of the Lord High Constable seems a more likely occasion.

[20]E.W., p. 86. Buckingham was beheaded on Tower Hill.
[21]Stapleton, p. 125.   No appointment was made.

CHAPTER XVII

Chelsea

THE INCREASING NUMBER in the household with the marriages of his three daughters may have been the reason for More's decision to leave the City for the country up river. Before doing so he may have thought of moving to Crosby's Place, a group of tenements and buildings with the Hall as its main feature in Bishopsgate. This had been Richard III's headquarters before he usurped the throne. More bought the lease in June 1523, but in the January 1524 he resold it to his old friend Antonio Bonvisi and instead bought land at Chelsea on the banks of the river.[1] This was an enormous change for More who had lived in the heart of the City for over forty-five years. The property was of some thirty-four acres. The date of the removal is not certain, but Richard Hyrde's Introduction to Margaret Roper's little book on the Paternoster is dated "At Chelcheth, the year of our Lord God, a thousand five hundred xxiii, the first day of October". If that means the family was already settled there, then the building of the mansion must have been carried out with speed unless More had bought some land at an earlier date than has been recorded. It seems that the King may have lent him money to buy land and build the mansion.[2]

The northern end of Battersea Bridge occupies the position of the landing stage or quay of More's grounds. No remains of the house exist; it was pulled down by Sir Hans Sloane after 1737 when he bought the estate.[3] There is a carefully drawn ground

[1]It has been suggested (Yale, *Richard III*, p. 213) that from the beginning More was acting for Bonvisi, but, as he was a freeman, there was no legal difficulty in 1523 that did not also operate in 1524. It may be that Sir Thomas and Dame Alice changed their minds and decided for a country residence, and Bonvisi took Crosby's Place off his hands.

[2]See below, p. 332.

[3]The walls of the Moravian Burial Ground contain some Tudor brickwork. See Randall Davies, *The Greatest House at Chelsey* (1914). Also, L.C.C. *Survey of London*, Vol. IV, Chelsea, Pt. II, for the house and Thorpe's plans, etc.; Vol. VII, Chelsea, Pt. III, for the Old Church before the blitz.

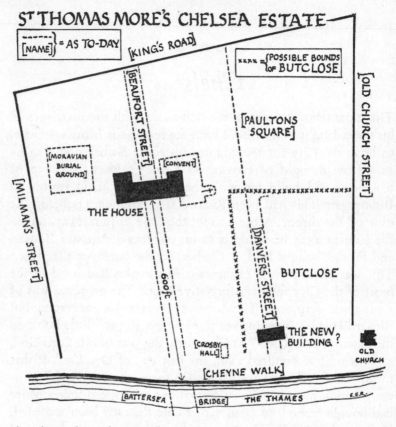

plan by John Thorpe (d. 1610) in the Soane Museum which probably follows the original plan though with some later additions. There is also an engraving by Johannes Kipp, dated 1699, of Beaufort House, as it came to be named, which gives an impression of what the exterior may have looked like, but, again, allowance has to be made for rebuilding and refronting. The house was six hundred feet from the river bank and had a frontage of two hundred and fifty feet. The Beaufort Street of today passes over the centre of the site which is now, in part, occupied by the convent of the Congregation of Adoration Réparatice.

Holbein's sketch for the family portrait shows the interior of the hall and this suggests a house suited to a man of position of the period but without the extravagances that some liked to lavish on their buildings. This is borne out by the description given by Dame Alice More when she visited her husband in the Tower. "A right fair house, your library, your books, your gallery, your garden, your orchard, and all other necessaries so handsome about you."[4] The present King's Road, Old Church Street, and Milman's Street mark approximately the boundaries of the property. More also bought or leased some farm land in Chelsea and Battersea. The parish church (the Old Church, as it is known) was off the south-east corner. More added a chapel, or rebuilt an old one, in 1528 with a vault as a family mausoleum.[5] Four years later he placed a wall-tablet in the chapel (it is now in the main church) with an inscribed epitaph. At the same time he moved the body of his first wife, Jane, from St Stephen's, Walbrook, to the new vault.

It must have been difficult for Thomas More to have had much solitude with such a large and lively household and with so many visitors coming and going. So, as Roper noted, "A good distance from his mansion builded he a place called the New Building, wherein was a chapel, a library and a gallery".[6] After More's execution, this building seems to have been adapted as the home of the Ropers and known as Butclose. The exact position cannot be determined. The present Danvers Street probably passes over the site.

In a letter written in 1532 to his friend John Faber, Bishop of Vienna, Erasmus told him of More's house:

More has built for himself on the banks of the Thames not far from London, a country house that is dignified without being so magnificent as to excite envy. Here he lives happily with his family, consisting of his wife, his son and daughter-in-law, three daughters and

[4] Roper, p. 82.

[5] The More Chapel survived the blitz of 16–17 April 1941; "yet, rising out of all this ruin there, almost incredibly, stood the More Chapel, the pillars with the Holbein capitals, supporting the arch, intact, unscathed" (Official record). The epitaph tablet was shattered but has been skilfully pieced together. There was no tower in More's day. See Plate 22.

[6] Roper, p. 26.

their husbands and already eleven grandchildren. It would be difficult to find a man more fond of children than he.[7]

Stapleton, and others after him, have assumed that Erasmus had visited Thomas More at Chelsea. He did not come again to England after 1517 and the two friends met for the last time, as far as is known, in Bruges in July 1521. Erasmus was using information given him by Hans Holbein (of whose visit more will be said), or by one of the scholar's pupil-secretaries who went to Chelsea in the course of tours of his many friends to give and gather news and letters and books.

Nothing further need be added to what has already been said about the regular studies that were part of the life of the More household. As the grandchildren grew up, the mothers and aunts no doubt acted as their first tutors, but the children must have been impressed by the fact that their grown-up relatives went on learning.

The religious life of the household was the primary concern of the master. There is no reference to a resident chaplain; William Gonell was a priest but he was engaged as a tutor and had left before the move to Chelsea; the other tutors were not, it seems, priests. The Mores went to Mass at their parish church whose priest was their confessor. The first was Robert Dandie, of whom nothing further is known. It was in 1530 that Sir Thomas presented John Larke, the future martyr, to the living. He had been rector of St Ethelburga (St Elburga) in Bishopsgate. Besides attendance at Mass on Sundays and Feasts, the whole household went to midnight Mass at Christmas and Easter. Morning prayers at the house consisted of the seven Penitential Psalms, followed by the Litanies of the Saints; night prayers were Psalms 24, 61 and 50 (Vulgate), followed by the *Salve Regina* and the *De profundis*.

At meals John More or one of his sisters or Margaret Giggs read a passage from Scripture; this was followed by some comments on what had been read. Then More turned the conversation to lighter topics and Henry Patenson would be expected to do his duty as domestic fool or entertainer.

Each member of the family had some special charitable work;

[7] Allen, 2750.

thus Margaret Giggs would help the sick, and Margaret Roper had the care of an almshouse her father maintained in Chelsea. She also undertook the washing of the hair shirt he wore for penance.[8]

The Thames became the highway for the Mores and their visitors. When Sir Thomas More's barge, manned by his watermen in his livery, bore him to Westminster, to the City, or perhaps as far as Greenwich down the river or to Hampton Court up the river, the family gathered at the quay to see him off. As Chancellor of the Duchy of Lancaster and later as Lord High Chancellor, it was necessary for him to keep state in accordance with his office. His personal servant found this a difficult task for his master was negigent of his dress and was apt, for instance, to set off to court wearing his old comfortable slippers. There were many visitors to Chelsea. Some were scholars bearing introductions from his friends, or students from the universities, or foreign visitors commended by Erasmus and other friends; there were ecclesiastics or councillors who sought his advice or simply enjoyed his company. The Duke of Norfolk was an occasional visitor; it was he who rebuked More for singing in the choir of his parish church. "God's body, my Lord Chancellor, a parish clerk!" he exclaimed.

King Henry "for the pleasure he took in his company, would suddenly sometimes come home to his house at Chelsea to be merry with him. Whither on a time, unlooked for, he came to dinner to him, and after dinner, in a fair garden of his, walked with him by the space of an hour, holding his arm about his neck." More appreciated the honour but this did not blind him to the character of the King. After this visit, he said to Roper, "If my head could win him a castle in France, it should not fail to go".[9] The reference to France suggests that this royal visit to Chelsea took place before the battle of Pavia, February 1525. It must have been about the same time that the three daughters of Sir Thomas were engaged in a formal disputation before the King. We learn

[8]See below, pp. 267-8.
[9]Roper, p. 20.

this from a letter to More from John Palsgrave,[10] who, about 1525, was appointed tutor to the six-year-old Duke of Richmond, the King's natural son by Elizabeth Blount. Palsgrave wrote to enlist More's support in favour of giving the boy-duke a more thorough classical education than others thought necessary. The last sentence reads, "and when your daughters disputed in philosophy before the King's Grace, I would it had been my fortune to be present". One of the King's visits to Chelsea would have been an appropriate occasion.

There was another side of life at Chelsea much less formal or severe. In 1520 Thomas More engaged as his personal servant Walter Smyth, who remained with his master for nine years; then, at the personal recommendation of More, he was appointed Sword-Bearer to the Lord Mayor. John Rastell published in 1525 *Twelve Merry Jests of one called Edyth, the lying widow that still liveth*.[11] This was the work of Walter Smyth, but it is safe to suggest that Thomas More himself had a hand in it; it is much in the vein of his early verses. Not that Walter Smyth was illiterate. In his will dated 1538 he left his copies of Chaucer and Boccaccio "to John More his master's only son". He left other books to no less than three widows of his acquaintance. It would seem that he was not only a man of books but that he had a weakness for widows.

It is impossible to say how far the story of the Widow Edyth is based on fact, but as several important persons of the day are named with members of their households, it would seem that the story had substance. We need not concern ourselves with eleven of the pseudo-widow's adventures. She left her husband in Exeter and made her way to Andover in Hampshire where her series of deceptions began. Her tale was that she was a woman of property in temporary difficulties owing to the machinations of her enemies; on the strength of this tale, she obtained lodging and money from her dupes. At the first sign of disclosure, she disappeared and resumed her Odyssey. This took her all over the

---

[10]Rogers, 168. When Palsgrave went to Louvain in 1516, More gave him an introduction to Erasmus (Allen, 499, 597). See D.N.B.

[11]Gibson, 530. Reprinted in *Shakespeare's Jest Books*, III, ed. W. C. Hazlitt (1864).

home counties and, as she passed, she left a trail of disillusioned
and angry victims who had hoped to marry her and share her
faerie money.

The ninth jest ends:

> And when she saw her time, on an holy day,
> She walked to a thorp called Battersea;
> And, on the next day after, she took a wherry,
> And over the Thames was rowed full merry.

The tenth jest begins:

> At Chelsea was her arrival,
> Where she had best cheer of all,
> In the house of Sir Thomas More.

She was welcomed with the kindness that any other wayfarer
would receive in that hospitable household. Her story this time
was that she had substantial property at Eltham in Kent with
fifteen men employed on her farm and in her mills as well as
seven women servants. Her adoption of Eltham as her supposed
domicile was maladroit as the Ropers had property there.

> She recounted her family and household so great
> That three young men she cast in a heat,
> Which servants were in the same place,
> And all they wooed her a good pace.

> One of them had to name Thomas Croxton,
> And servant he was to Master Alington.

> And of the second wooer I shall you tell,
> Which had to name Thomas Arthur,
> And servant he was to Master Roper.

There was much merrymaking and horseplay in the servants'
quarters as the pursuit of the widow became a household jest.

> There was the revel and the gossiping,
> The general bumming, as Margaret Giggs said;
> Everybody laughed, and was well a-paid.

The widow decided to go on foot to the Benedictine Convent at
Clerkenwell, a walk of some four miles; perhaps she hoped to
G*

impress the Mores with her piety. The third pretender thought this a favourable opportunity to advance his suit.

> She roamed in the cloister to and fro,
> Till a young man saw where she did go,
> And Walter Smyth was this young man's name,
> One of her lovers, and I might tell for shame.

Meantime Thomas Arthur, Roper's man, had been making inquiries, no doubt at Eltham, so that by the return of the widow and Walter, the fraud had been discovered.

> To Chelsea she came the same night,
> But all that world was changed; all was come to light;
> Her substance was known and herself also,
> For Thomas Arthur that day had rid to and fro,
> And tried her not worth the sleeve lace of a gown
> In all England, in city nor yet in town.

In revenge the servants doctored her beer with a powerful purgative. Did Sir Thomas now step in as local magistrate? Perhaps so, for she was sent to gaol for three weeks. Walter Smyth plaintively ended his verses with the line:

> God save the Widow, wherever she wend!

It is tempting to think that this doggerel was a family production, and, as it was printed by John Rastell, it would probably have had More's imprimatur. Its interest, however, is the glimpse it gives us of the Chelsea household and of the high spirits that were as characteristic as its piety.

We are given a glimpse of another side of life at Chelsea in an incident that occurred in the autumn of 1529 when Thomas More was with the court at Woodstock. His son-in-law, Giles Heron, came to tell him that there had been a disastrous fire which had destroyed the barns in which More allowed his poorer neighbours to store their corn. He at once wrote to his wife.

I pray you to make some good search what my poor neighbours have lost and bid them take no thought therefor, for and I should not leave myself a spoon there shall no poor neighbour of mine bear no loss by any chance happened in my house. I pray you be with my children and your household merry in God and devise somewhat

with your friends what way were best to take for provision to be
made for corn for our household and for seed this year coming, if
ye think it good that we keep the ground still in our hands, and
whether ye think it good that we so shall do or not, yet I think it
were not best suddenly thus to leave it all up and to put away our
folk off our farm, till we have somewhat advised us thereon, howbeit if we have more now than we shall need and which can get them
other masters ye may then discharge us of them but I would not
that any man were suddenly sent away he wot never whither. At my
coming hither I perceived none other but I should tarry still with the
King's Grace but now I shall, I think, by cause of this chance get
leave this week to come home and see you, and then shall we further
devise together upon all things what order shall be best to take.[12]

A very different kind of visitor to the "lying widow" came to
Chelsea in October 1526—the twenty-nine-year-old Hans
Holbein, called the Younger, of Basle.[13] He had already painted
at least three portraits of Erasmus who gave him, when he left to
seek fortune elsewhere, introductions to friends in the Low
Countries and in England. One of these letters, to Peter Gilles,
included the sentence, "Here the arts are coldly treated, so he
makes for England (Angliam) in the hope of collecting some
golden angels (Angelatos)". The English gold coin, the angel-
noble, gave the scholar the chance to make his little pun.

Thomas More wrote to Erasmus on 18 December, "Your
painter, my dearest Erasmus, is a wonderful artist, but I fear he
will not find in England the rich and fertile field he had hoped;
however, lest he find it quite barren, I will do what I can".[14] So
he commissioned Holbein to paint the family portraits and a large
family group. It was an unusual proposal at that period for this
was to be a conversation piece and not linked with any devotional
purpose, such as may be seen in many Renaissance religious
pictures with the donors kneeling in adoration.

Eight drawings at Windsor Castle were studies either for

[12]Rogers, 174 (42).
[13]For expert studies of the More portraits and drawings, see Stanley Morison and
Nicolas Barker, *The Likeness of Thomas More* (1963), and K. T. Parker, *The Drawings of
Hans Holbein at Windsor Castle* (1945).
[14]Allen, 1770.

separate portraits or for the large group. A sketch for the family group is now at Basle and was probably taken to Erasmus by Holbein on his return in the summer of 1528. It was not until a year later that Erasmus referred to it in a letter to Margaret Roper.

> I cannot find words to express the joy I felt when the painter Holbein gave me the picture of your whole family which is so completely successful that I should scarcely be able to see you better if I were with you. I often hope that at least once before my last day, I may look upon that dear society to which I owe a great part of whatever little fortune or glory I possess, and to none could I be more willingly indebted. I recognise you all, but no one better than yourself. I seem to behold through all your beautiful household a soul shining forth still more beautiful. I felicitate you all on that family happiness, but most of all your excellent father.[15]

Holbein's final painting, in watercolour or tempera on cloth, was destroyed in a fire at Kremsier, Moravia, in 1752; fortunately there are copies in oils, the best of which is at Nostell Priory. This was painted by Rowland Locky about 1590 for the Ropers.[16] But these copies are a long way from Holbein's mastery.

The Basle sketch (Plate 7) gives us a better idea of the hall at Chelsea than the later painting (Plate 8) where Locky used drapings and coverings unlike the tapestries that Holbein loved to paint in detail. In the right-hand corner at the back is an interior porch with a fleur-de-lis cresting; on the left, against the wall, is a buffet; the back is of linen-fold or wavy woodwork and the canopy repeats the cresting of the porch. Some plate and a vase of flowers are on the buffet. The painting adds a lute or viol in accordance with a note written by Holbein on the sketch against a viol hanging on the wall: *Klafikordi und ander seyte spill uf den bank* (clavichord and other instruments on the shelf). There are three books on the buffet in the painting, one is the *De consolatione* of Boethius, and, in the painting, Margaret Roper holds a copy of Seneca's *Oedipus*. In front of a wall-hanging (green in the painting)

---

[15] Allen, 2212.
[16] For Rowland Locky, see E. Auerbach, *Nicholas Hillyard* (1962); this contains a reproduction of his miniature copy of the family group.

is a weight-driven chamber clock[17] suspended from the ceiling which is of wood with moulded beams. On the right is a window with clear diamond glazing, and on the ledge, more plate, a candlestick and two books. The sketch suggests that the floor was covered with rushes.

Two aspects of the sketch must impress even the casual observer. The room and its furnishings show that the Chelsea house was designed in a style that was new-fashioned. Only forty years had passed since Bosworth Field, yet here is a domestic interior that, at first glance, might be described as Elizabethan. The second impression is that the family was cultured; the musical instruments and the books (there are a dozen in the sketch) indicate this.

The Basle sketch is a more satisfactory representation of the family than the existing derivative paintings; the original must have been a remarkable work. A critic has written of the sketch: "The brilliant characterization in the drawing of each individual is, even today, among the most outstanding achievements of Holbein's art".[18] A small reproduction cannot bring out the finish of the drawing; every line is firm and unhesitating.

In the centre of the group is Sir Thomas More. There are two drawings of him at Windsor; the first of these, marked in a contemporary hand, *Sier Thomas Moore*, was made for the group picture, but it lacks life. The second, and better known, was later inscribed *Tho: Moor Ld Chancelour* and was for the separate painted portrait. The hair is tinted brownish-red and the eyes blue-grey. The drawing had been pricked for transfer to the panel. In the sketch for the family group, Sir Thomas is wearing the ordinary cap and furred robe of the period and carries a muff on his left arm.[19] He wears the knight's collar of SS and portcullis with the Tudor rose as a pendant. The separate painted portrait by Holbein does not give the impression that More was, as

[17]Now in possession of the Waterton family, the best-known member of which was Charles Waterton, the naturalist. He was a direct descendant through Cresacre More of Sir Thomas. It is impossible to say how much of the clock is now original. See T. Raworth, "St Thomas More's Clock", in *The Month*, June 1952.

[18]P. Ganz, *Hans Holbein* (1950), p. 284. The original measures 17 x 12 in.

[19]I am aware that experts state that the muff did not come into use until the end of the sixteenth century, but what else is the object? Sir John also has one on his arm. Perhaps it was part of legal robes.

Erasmus wrote, "always pleasant and friendly and cheerful".
Here we see the "sad gravity" noted by Robert Whittinton. A
stranger to his life and reputation might be excused if he thought
this the portrait of a stern man of powerful intellect. Perhaps
Holbein was unable to depict lighter moods; in the whole gallery
of his portraits there is not one really cheerful face. The grimness
of the period was doubtless reflected in the countenances of the
men whose fortunes were precarious, but in 1527 the clouds were
distant.

There is a brief note written against each figure in the Basle
sketch. The writer was probably Nicholas Kratzer, the astronomer.[20] If only we knew whether the sketch was made in 1526 or
1527, problems of dates of birth would be solved. More's painted
portrait has the date 1527 on the edge of the table; the sketch has
the note *Thomas Morus anno 50*.

The first figure on the left is inscribed *Elizabeta Dancia Thome*[21]
Mori filia anno 21. In the sketch she is shown as pregnant. Next to
her stands Margaret Giggs: *Margareta Giga Clementis uxor Thome
Mori filiabus condiscipula et cognata anno 22*. The word *cognata*
normally means "related by birth" and Kratzer may have thought
they were so related. "Foster-sister" is more likely to be correct.
In the painting the positions of these two figures have been inter-
changed. Margaret Giggs is shown with a simpler head-dress than
in the sketch. The Windsor drawing of her (incorrectly labelled
by a later hand "Mother Jack", the nurse of Prince Edward)
shows her wearing the plain head-dress of the painting. This
changed position indicates that the alteration was Holbein's, but
it is not an improvement in the composition; in the sketch she
is seen bending down towards Sir John and is pointing to an open
book in her hand, though he does not seem interested! The effect
is more intimate than that made by the rather two stiff figures in
the derivative paintings.

Next to Margaret Giggs is Sir John More: *Johannes Morus
pater anno 76*. In the paintings his red robes make an agreeable
splash of colour. Standing at the back is the diminutive figure of

[20]See Otto Pächt, *Burlington Magazine*, 1944, p. 138.
[21]In the sketch the ending -e is given for -ae as was usual in Vulgar Latin.

Anne Cresacre: *Anna Grisacria Johanni Mori sponsa anno 15*. She married John More in 1529. He is standing at his father's side: *Johannes Morus Thome filius anno 19*. He is bareheaded and holds a book. Holbein noted on the drawing *lipfarb brun* (brown complexion). Next to John More is Henry Patenson, the domestic fool: *Henricus Patensonus Thome Mori morio anno 40*.

More's other daughters, Margaret and Cecily, are seated on the floor in the foreground. *Cecilia Herona Thome Mori filia anno 20*, and, *Margareta Ropera Thome filia anno 22*. Cecily has a rosary in her hand but this is not included in the paintings. Locky did his copy during the reign of Elizabeth when "papist baubles" were frowned upon. Dame Alice More is on the extreme right; she is kneeling at a prie-dieu on which is a book of devotion; a pet monkey is clawing at her skirt. The inscription reads, *Alicia Thome Mori uxor anno 57*. At the edge is a note by Holbein *dise soll sitzen* (this one shall sit), and she is accordingly seated in the paintings in which a dog, of indeterminate breed, has been added and placed at More's feet. An additional figure in the paintings is John Harris, More's secretary, who married Dorothy Colley, one of Margaret Roper's maids; he stands in the doorway.

The drawings and paintings show that the family, especially the women folk, were richly dressed in the highest fashion of the day. Indeed the total impression we get is that Thomas More in 1527 was a prosperous man.

The National Portrait Gallery in London now possesses the version of the family group as re-painted in 1593 for Thomas More, the grandson of Sir Thomas. The left half is a copy of the Holbein painting but omitting Dame Alice, Margaret Giggs and Henry Patenson. Elizabeth Daunce stands behind her two sisters. The right-hand portion shows Thomas More II with his grim-looking wife, his eldest son John and his youngest Cresacre. One oddity is that a portrait of Anne Cresacre (mother of Thomas More II) looks down on herself as a girl of fifteen with her future husband beside her.

There are several versions of Holbein's great portrait of Thomas More. Two are of outstanding merit; the one in the Frick Museum, New York, and the other in the National Portrait

Gallery, London, known as the Bedford version. The history of
these is far from complete, but the Frick version may be the
original, yet the Bedford version runs it so closely that even
experts have confused it with the Frick version.[22]

More may have presented this portrait to Henry VIII, or been
asked to do so. This is suggested by the story that after More's
execution Anne Boleyn was so conscience-stricken or irritated at
seeing More's portrait day after day that she threw it out of the
window of Whitehall and a lucky passer-by picked it up and
walked off with it. Another version of the story says it was the
King who threw the portrait away.

What is the relationship between the Windsor drawings, the
existing portraits and the Basle sketch? The opinion of experts is
best given.

If, then, any guess about the order of the earliest portraits of More is
admissible, it might be this. First of all, Holbein did a head and
shoulders sketch from life in which, perhaps because More moved
during the sitting, there are some inaccuracies (Plate 10). He then
executed a half-length portrait in oils, in which the inaccuracies were
put right (the Frick version). Next, there is the family group portrait,
for which the first Windsor drawing may have been a secondary
study (Plate 11) and for which other studies exist, and of which the
Basle sketch represents a report of work in progress, possibly at the
point when Holbein was transferring a full-scale composite cartoon
to the surface of the group portrait. The Bedford version and the
Locky copies of the family group are a subsequent stage. . . . It is,
however, possible to say that in all these versions the authority of
Holbein can be traced, an authority which lasted through centuries
when the originals were lost to view, to be vindicated three hundred
years later when the revival of interest in More demanded an
authentic likeness.[23]

[22]Both Paul Ganz, *Hans Holbein* (1950), Plate 71, and H. A. Schmid, *Hans Holbein der
Jungere* (1945), Plate 47, reproduce the Bedford version in mistake for the Frick version.
[23]*Likeness*, p. 28. The inaccuracies referred to concern the second of the Windsor
drawings (Plate 11); "there is a disparity in the angle of vision from which the right and
left sides of the face are seen which gives the impression the right eye is incorrectly sited
. . . caused perhaps by a movement of the sitter".

CHAPTER XVIII

The Conscience of the King

As THOMAS MORE advanced in responsibility so he received from the King those material rewards that were the customary way of recognizing State service when salaries were often nominal and pensions almost unknown. In May 1522 he was granted the manor of South in Kent (now swallowed up in Southborough) out of the confiscated lands of the Duke of Buckingham.[1] Three years later, he received the manors of Doglington (now Duckington) and Fringeford in Oxfordshire with the advowson of Barley in Hertfordshire. These were small properties; his revenue from his lands was assessed at £340 in 1527.

He was concerned as a councillor in decisions affecting war and peace during the period 1526 to 1529; perhaps it would be more true to say that, like his fellow councillors, he had to accept the policy of Wolsey; the Council, as such, had little control over foreign policy and Parliament could exert influence, when it met, only through voting or not voting supplies. Foreign policy was the prerogative of the King, as it was to remain for a long time. It is impossible, and would be fruitless, here to follow the involutions of Wolsey's foreign policy; he veered first this way then that in trying to assert England's influence with the Emperor, the French King and the Pope, each of whom used England as it suited his immediate needs, but, in effect, having gained some temporary advantage, each went his own way regardless of Wolsey's pretentious diplomacy. After Pavia (1525), as we have seen, Wolsey tried to take advantage of the French King's imprisonment to organize an attack on France. That did not fall in with the Emperor's plans, so had to be dropped. Then Wolsey negotiated a treaty with the French. This was signed at the Moor, Wolsey's Hertfordshire palace, at the end of August 1525. Thomas More was one of the signatories and, in accordance with custom, he received a pension from the French of a hundred and

[1] L.P., III, ii, No. 2239.

fifty crowns in contrast with Wolsey's of twenty-five thousand. It would have been remarkable had this been paid regularly, if at all.

In the following year, the Pope tried to re-establish a league against the Emperor; Pavia had smashed an earlier one, but again the Emperor acted before his opponents could come to terms with one another. His troops took Rome and partially sacked it in the September and forced the Pope to negotiate. What help could the Defender of the Faith give the Pope? Henry played the usual gambit by promising to go to his aid if other princes would do the same. The following letter from Wolsey to More is here of interest as an example of contemporary diplomacy. It was written in the autumn of 1526.

Master More,
Forasmuch as in this my letter be contained matters of great importance, requisite to be maturely considered and pondered, I therefor pray you heartily so to take your time that ye may distinctly read the same to the King's Highness. And as to the letters of consolation to the Pope's Holiness [on the first sack of Rome], I trust I have so couched and qualified them that they shall be to the satisfaction of the Pope's Holiness and such other as shall hear and read the same, without binding the King to anything that might redowned to his charge or pardon other. And thus heartily fare ye well.[2]

The second sacking of Rome came in May 1527 when the unpaid mercenary troops of the Emperor went berserk. According to Hall, "the commonalty little mourned for it, and said the Pope was a ruffian and was not meet for his room [his position], wherefore, they said, that he began the mischief and so he was well served".[3] Even allowing for Hall's anti-papal bias, his report is an indication of the mood of the times. Once more the Pope was a prisoner and now in close confinement. Thomas More and Stephen Gardiner (Wolsey's secretary) were commissioned to treat with the French delegates; an agreement was signed by which Henry undertook to support a French expedition to Italy with men and money. Plans were also made for Wolsey to meet the French King, who had been freed in February 1526,

[2]Rogers, 146.   [3]Hall, II, p. 95.

having made, needless to say, all kinds of promises to the Emperor, none of which were kept. Wolsey had hoped to snatch some advantage to himself out of the situation; he had a notion of getting himself appointed as a kind of deputy-pope, but the support he got was minimal. His war policy was unpopular and the murmurings against him grew more strident; general feeling was on the side of the Emperor and the City merchants were opposed to a war that would sever trade with the Low Countries. How far Henry was aware of the rising opposition to Wolsey is not known, but the Tudors had their ears to the ground.

On 3 July 1527 Cardinal Wolsey set out with a train of nine hundred to meet the French King at Amiens to negotiate yet another "perpetual peace". Cavendish has left us a rapturous account of Wolsey's progress through London to Rochester and Canterbury down to Dover, "having all his accustomed and glorious furniture[4] carried before him". Wolsey was given plenipotentiary powers and, as if to emphasize his all-but regal state, he took the Great Seal with him. It was the zenith of his great power, yet he must have been far from easy in his mind for the King had posed a problem that called for all the Cardinal's skill in solving, and he knew that either it must be solved to the King's satisfaction, or he himself would lose his influence.

A bizarre transaction had been staged in May 1527 at York Place, Wolsey's Westminster palace.[5] No less a person than the King was there to answer a complaint brought against him that, for the past eighteen years, he had been living in sin with his brother's widow. The assessors were Cardinal Wolsey as legate a latere, and Archbishop Warham; the case was stated and argued. Catherine was not there, nor was she represented; she was not even aware of what was happening. This secretly convened court reached no conclusion; its purpose had been, presumably, to enable the legate to pronounce a decision that could later be confirmed by the Pope. There is no reason to think that such a procedure would have succeeded; the one-sided investigation

[4]That is, "his two great crosses of silver, two great pillars of silver, the great seal of England, his cardinal's hat".

[5]17, 20, 31 May. L.P., IV, 3140. York Place became Whitehall when taken over by the King.

was cut short by the news that the Pope was a prisoner in Rome. In view of this unprecedented situation, it seems to have been decided that Wolsey should deal with the papal problem and also collect the opinions of the bishops. Henry had the delicate task of informing Catherine of his intentions; it took him three weeks to summon up enough courage; the abrupt announcement momentarily unnerved the Queen.

She had come to England in 1501 to be the bride of Arthur, Prince of Wales. Six months after her marriage, her fifteen-year old husband died. Catherine's parents, Ferdinand of Aragon and Isabella of Castile, negotiated with Henry VII for their daughter to marry the King's second son, Henry, Duke of York. Owing to the affinity between Henry and his brother's widow, it was necessary to get a papal dispensation for the marriage; this was, after some difficulty, granted. It is true that, at the time, some doubts were expressed, by Warham for instance, as to the power of the Pope to grant such a dispensation, and Henry himself, at the age of fourteen, had made a protest, but this had obviously been a move in the intricate dealings of the two fathers, partly political but mainly financial. Within seven weeks of his accession, Henry VIII, of his own volition, married Catherine of Aragon.

By 1527 the only surviving child of this marriage was the Princess Mary, born in 1516. A succession of miscarriages, still-births and infant deaths destroyed Henry's hope of an heir. We must not underestimate the King's anxiety to ensure the security of the throne; it was an anxiety shared by all those who peered into the future. A queen-regnant was not an attractive prospect; the long years of near-anarchy before 1485 haunted the national memory. When in 1525 Henry made his bastard son Duke of Richmond, it seemed a first step towards his recognition as heir-apparent. The alternative was the annulment (usually called the divorce) of the marriage with Catherine on the grounds that she had been the wife of Henry's brother.[6] We cannot now know when it was, or at whose instigation, Henry first became aware of the words in Leviticus, "He that marrieth his brother's wife

[6]The best account of the unhappy affair will be found in *Henry VIII* by J. J. Scarisbrick (1968).

doth an unlawful thing . . . they shall be without children.⁷"
Here was a divine law that even the Pope could not set aside.
Nor is it possible to determine to what degree Henry was moved
by reasons of State, or by his passion for Anne Boleyn. It soon
became apparent that events were to be dominated by Henry's
assumption that what he wanted must be right and just and that
any hint of opposition was a form of treason. He made his
conscience the servant of his appetites.

The argument was that the Pope had exceeded his authority in
granting the dispensation of 1504, and therefore that the marriage
could be annulled. At first there must have seemed no special
difficulty. Even while Henry's case was under consideration, his
immoral sister, Queen Margaret of Scotland, and the Earl of
Angus were divorced in 1527, and his still more immoral or
amoral brother-in-law the Duke of Suffolk got his own doubtful
divorce confirmed in 1528. The King's problem, however, was
far from simple. The Queen's popularity had to be taken into
account. Had her marriage with Prince Arthur been consum-
mated? She firmly maintained that it had not been. Then, could
one Pope declare that a dispensation granted by a predecessor was
invalid? To these were added two difficulties of considerable
moment. The Pope was under the control of Catherine's nephew
the Emperor, and if it suited his policy, he could impose his ban
on a decision in favour of Henry. Secondly, and it may be
decisively, Henry had fallen in love with one of his wife's maids-
of-honour, Anne Boleyn, whose sister, Mary, had earlier been
his mistress. It seems to have been the one selfless love of his life
even if it was threadbare within a few years. Anne Boleyn was
not willing to be another mistress, but, urged on no doubt by her
relatives, including her uncle, the Duke of Norfolk, she aimed
higher. They were more intent on bringing down the Cardinal
than on elevating her. It was wheels within wheels. Popular
opinion, and indeed Catherine herself, blamed the Cardinal, a
view perpetuated by Shakespeare in his *Henry VIII*.

Norfolk.　　　　　What's the cause?

⁷He preferred the injunction in Leviticus 20, 21, to that in Deuteronomy 25, 5: "his
brother shall take her and raise up seed for his brother".

Lord Chamberlain. It seems the marriage with his brother's wife
                    Has crept too near his conscience.
Suffolk.   No, his conscience
                    Has crept too near another lady.
Norfolk.   'Tis so:
                    This is the Cardinal's doing, the king-cardinal.[8]

The weight of informed opinion today is against this popular
view. Certainly Wolsey would not have raised a finger to make
Anne Boleyn a queen, though he was on the alert to see how he
could profit by the King's difficulties, but he was outmanoeuvred
for it was while he was playing the viceroy in France that the
Boleyn faction was able to gather force, and Henry took advantage of his absence to send his own emissaries to the Pope.

Wolsey's cavalcade had halted at Rochester; it must have
severely strained the resources of that small city to house such an
array even for one night. Wolsey stayed with Bishop John Fisher
and probably Thomas More, who was one of the accompanying
councillors, was also his old friend's guest but he did not share in
the important discussion that was held. The Cardinal did not break
his progress for love of the Bishop, but for a reason of State. He
wanted to get Fisher's opinion on the King's problem.

The possibility of a royal divorce was now a matter of common
speculation, so much so that Henry summoned the Lord Mayor
of London and bade him stifle such rumours.[9] The King may have
hoped that it could all be arranged quietly, within the family so
to speak, but circumstances, and Queen Catherine, defeated that
prospect. What was whispered at court one day, would be
discussed in the streets the next. So far Henry had not broached the
question to More, whose first reaction is given in a passage to be
quoted presently. Both King and Cardinal realized how influential would be Fisher's attitude not only in England but on the
Continent where he had high prestige as a theologian. Wolsey
put the problem before his host and asked for his opinion. A full
report, no doubt coloured a little in the Cardinal's favour, went
to the King from Canterbury the next day. Fisher "would not
reason the matter, but noted the great difficulty in it". He refused

[8] II, ii, 17-20.   [9] Hall, II, p. 96.

to pronounce on the problem until he had examined it more fully. With that non-committal attitude Wolsey had to be content. Fisher did study the question thoroughly and later he told the King that the marriage was valid and that he could set his conscience at rest. This was not the advice Henry wanted and "from that date forward never looked on him with merry countenance as the bishop did well perceive for that his grudge daily increased towards him."[10] Not that Henry had ever favoured Fisher who remained bishop of the poorest diocese for thirty years. At the opening of the reign, as has been noted, they had clashed; Fisher had tried to prevent the King from diverting to his own uses the funds intended by his grandmother, the Lady Margaret, for the foundation of St John's College at Cambridge. Henry had a long memory and nursed his grudges.

John Fisher had done nothing to ease Wolsey of his worries; indeed this refusal to fall into line warned the Cardinal that the King's Proceedings would not have a smooth passage.

We need not follow the Cardinal's French negotiations. Edward Hall, who loved a good show, gives detailed accounts of the pageants, processions and public occasions that marked the visit.[11] Nor do we know what part Thomas More played in it all. Only one letter of his can be dated at this period; it was a polite note to Francis Crenevelt from Calais.[12] During the three months of the French affair, he may have been able to meet some of his scholar friends; that would be some consolation during the kind of proceedings the Utopians found so ridiculous.

It was on the return of this embassy at the end of September that Henry first asked for More's opinion on the marriage problem. His account is to be found in a letter to Thomas Cromwell dated 5 March 1534.[13] The King, he wrote, while walking in the gallery at Hampton Court,

> showed me that it was now perceived that his marriage was not only against the positive laws of the Church and the written laws of God, but also in such wise against the law of nature, that it could in no wise by the Church be dispensable. Now so was it that before my

[10]*Life of Fisher* (E.E.T.S.), p. 53.   [11]Hall, II, pp. 99-105.
[12]Rogers, 155.   [13]Rogers, 199 (53).

going over the sea, I had heard certain things moved against the bull of the dispensation concerning the words of the Law Levitical and the Law Deuteronomical to prove the prohibition to be *de iure divino*, but yet perceived I not at that time but that the greater hope of the matter stood in certain faults that were founden in the bull, whereby the bull should by the law not be sufficient.

The King then opened the Bible and pointed out the text in Leviticus,

and asked me further what myself thought thereon. At which time not presuming to look that his Highness should anything take that point for the more proved or unproved for my poor mind in so great a matter, I showed nevertheless as my duty was at his commandment what thing I thought upon the words which I there read. Whereupon his Highness accepting benignly my sudden unadvised answer commanded me to commune further with Master Foxe, now his Grace's Almoner, and to read a book with him that was in making for that matter.

How thoroughly Thomas More studied this problem is shown in his letter to his fellow prisoner in the Tower, Dr Nicholas Wilson,[14] who had been the King's confessor, and was one of those whom More consulted. More first recounted the opening up of the question to him by the King as in the above extract, and he added that the King repeated what he had said "what time I first came into his noble service", namely "that I should look therein first unto God and after God unto him". The letter proceeds:

I remember well also by your often conference in the matter that by all the time in which I studied about it, you and I were in every point both twain of one opinion and remember well that the laws and councils and the words of Saint Augustine *De civitate Dei* and the epistle of Saint Ambrose *Ad paternum* and the epistle of Saint Basil translated out of the Greek and the writing of Saint Gregory you and I read together and over that the places of the Scripture self both in Leviticus and in the Deuteronomy and in the Gospel and in Saint Paul's epistles and over this in that other place

[14]Rogers, 208 (59). Like Fisher and More, Wilson had refused to take the oath; after three years in the Tower he submitted; a few years later he was back in the Tower for having maintained the Pope's authority; again he gave way and was later appointed to a prebend in St Paul's.

of Saint Augustine that you remember now and beside that other places of his, wherein he properly toucheth the matter expressly with the words of Saint Jerome and of Saint Chrysostom too, and I cannot now remember of how many more.

He also pointed out in this letter that he had always refrained from giving any opinion on the validity of the bull of dispensation. "Now concerning those points, I never meddled. For I neither understand the doctors of the law nor well can turn their books."

As a result of these intensive studies, Thomas More informed the King that, in his view, the marriage was valid. The King took this in good part; for the present he refrained from further pressure.

War was declared on the Emperor in January 1528, but there was little the English could do to help the French. English merchants in Spain and the Low Countries were arrested, but a truce limited to Flanders allowed some trade to be resumed. The following year saw the collapse of all Wolsey's elaborate schemes; the French were again defeated; the Pope and the Emperor were reconciled and Francis was compelled to treat with Charles. They had both tricked Henry before, so why not again? Bishop Tunstal, Dr William Knight and Sir Thomas More went to Cambrai for the negotiations.[15] Wolsey wanted to lead the embassy himself but the King's Great Matter had to take precedence and he remained in London. The trial of Henry's marriage suit had been opened on 31 May at Blackfriars before Cardinal Campeggio, and it was still on when Tunstal and his colleagues left London on 1 July.

There was little they could do to modify the political terms of the subsequent treaty. Henry was insistent that someone, either Charles or Francis, should recoup his expenditure and repay his loans, but the accounts between the three princes were by this time so confused that it was a simple matter to evade responsibility.

[15]Rogers, 169–173. Herbrüggen, 169B–F. The King may have wished to get Tunstal out of the way; the Bishop had prepared a "book" or "libel" defending the Queen; he was thus unable to present it in the court and Campeggio's wish for it to be read in Tunstal's absence was ignored. See Life of Fisher (E.E.T.S.), p. 64; also C. Sturge, Cuthbert Tunstal (1938), p. 175.

The English envoys did, however, achieve one gain—a trade agreement re-established full relations with the Low Countries and Spain. Hall noted that the peace "was solemnly proclaimed by Heralds with trumpets of the City of London, which Proclamation much rejoiced the English merchants repairing into Spain, Flanders, Brabant, Zeeland and other the Emperor's dominions, for during the wars the merchants were evil handled on both parties".[16] As a true son of the City, Thomas More was glad to have had a share in this commercial success. Wolsey was far from pleased; he, no doubt, felt that, had he been there, better terms could have been gained.

Peace lasted fourteen years and might have begun fourteen years earlier to the benefit of England for all the profit Wolsey's adventures had brought. Sir Thomas More's own feelings about the Peace of Cambrai were expressed in his epitaph in Chelsea Church:

> . . . last of all to Cambrai, being associated with Cuthbert Tunstal, the chief of that embassy, then Bishop of London and since of Durham, a man than whom the world can scarely boast of one more learned, wiser or better. There he had the pleasure to see and negotiate the renewal of leagues between the chief princes of Christendom and the restoration to the world of longed-for peace, which peace, may Heaven confirm and long preserve.

In his own mind, Thomas More certainly overestimated the part played by the English embassy in the settlement reached in what is sometimes called The Ladies' Peace, since it was negotiated between Margaret of Savoy, aunt of Charles V, and her sister-in-law Louise, the mother of Francis I. The two princes were not on speaking terms so they left the matter to their two relatives.

The period of peace for England was due not so much to Henry's concern with European politics as to his preoccupation with the personal problem that was proving unexpectedly intractable. At the same time, there was a growing tension between Church and State resulting from the spread of anti-clerical and heretical teaching.

16Hall, II, p. 160.

CHAPTER XIX

Heresy

WHEN TUNSTAL and More returned to England from Cambrai in the last week of August 1529, the legatine court at Blackfriars under Cardinal Campeggio had been prorogued; the ostensible reason was that the court must go into vacation at the same time as the Roman court of which it was part. There was, however, a new factor. The Queen had appealed to the Pope. The prorogation and the Queen's appeal fell in line with the Pope's anxiety to play for time rather than run the risk of further trouble with the Emperor by granting Henry his annulment, and time might bring its own solution, as it might have done had Catherine died. At one stage Henry himself caused delay by trying to prevent the case being heard in Rome. Time did bring its solution but it was Henry's, not the Pope's. This Fabian policy brought irreparable harm to the Church in England. If Clement VII was lacking in will-power, Henry had a superabundance of it, and, once he had set his mind on something, he would allow no one to stand in his way. This is not to repeat the misinterpretation of events that long was part of the accepted presentation of history—that the Reformation in this country was caused by the divorce. The quarrel with the Pope did precipitate the breach with Rome, but Lutheran and other Protestant teachings would undoubtedly have gained ground steadily. The political problem—that is the relation between the papacy and the nation-state—might have been resolved by something akin to the Gallicanism of France. Thomas More had warned the King of these political implications but events were to turn on Henry's personal problem. Had he been less vindictive, he could have ignored those who thought he was wrong in his Levitical predilections. It was his determination to compel everyone to agree with him, and at the same time to give three cheers, that led to the tragedy of More and Fisher and their fellows victims.

There are no indications that Tunstal and More were greatly

disturbed about the marriage proceedings on their return from Cambrai. More seems to have decided that, as he could not agree with the King, he would not take any active part in the matter, but leave the question of the papal dispensation to the canon lawyers. While it is true that Tunstal was one of the counsellors of the Queen, his later actions suggest that he did not feel strongly one way or the other, an attitude he shared with most of the bishops and councillors. As an expert on canon law, he was one of six advisers to write statements on behalf of Catherine, but his "book" or "libel" is not extant.[1] On the other hand he was one of the commissioners who saw her at Buckden and demanded that she should take the oath to the 1534 Act of Succession.

While they may have disagreed in some respects on the marriage case, More and Tunstal were in full agreement in their opposition to Lutheranism. On their way to Cambrai they had asked Stephen Vaughan, Thomas Cromwell's agent in Antwerp, to keep them informed of the movements of known English heretics.[2]

After John Eck, the theologian of Ingoldstadt, had been in England in 1525, he wrote,[3] "When last summer I passed over to England to visit the King and the Bishop of Rochester, though tumults and seditions were raging in Germany, I never once heard the name of Luther mentioned except in malediction". It may be doubted if a foreign visitor could give a reliable report on the religious attitude of a people whose language he could not speak. Yet, even five years later, Bishop Nix of Norwich could write to Archbishop Warham, "the gentlemen and commonalty be not greatly infect with Lutheranism but merchants and such that have their abiding not far from the sea".[4] The ordinary folk could not read Luther's Latin or German, but ideas derived from him slowly percolated down in distorted forms. This was also the history of Lollard ideas. We can follow the transition from what may be called vulgarized Lollardism to vulgarized Lutheranism[5]

---

[1] L. P., IV, iii, 5768. Part of Fisher's "book" has survived. See my *Saint John Fisher*, pp. 155–6. "Book" here means, not a printed volume, but a statement of a case.

[2] L, P., IV, iii, 5823.   [3] Strype, *Cranmer*, I, p. 695.   [4] L.P., IV, iii, 6385.

[5] The terms "Lollardism" and "Lutheranism" are used rather loosely here to indicate tendencies.

in the registers of Bishop Fisher. Thus a John More was accused in 1525 of expressing "divers doubts concerning Scripture", and, in particular, that "Christ did not die in perfect charity on Good Friday because he did not die to redeem Lucifer as well as Adam and Eve". He further declared that our Lady "is but a sack" and the Son of God desired the Father to come to "middle earth" to take a sack upon his back. It is impossible to make sense of the last statement, or to trace the ancestry of such muddled notions.

Lutheran ideas were being discussed in the universities in the 1520's; the meetings at the White Horse Inn at Cambridge are part of the religious history of England. Not all who met there were "reformers". Some went about preaching and a few were burned as heretics. Others rose to high positions in the Church in its "reformed" state. London was the centre from which much of the literature from abroad was disseminated. As Bishop Nix noted, the traders were often the agents; this influence was of limited scope as it could reach only the literate. The picture is of the passing on by word of mouth of ideas that were often ill-digested; such notions would link up with the widespread anti-clericism that was becoming more vocal in the second decade of the century. The aftermath of Lollardism provided the favourable soil for the planting of Lutheranism, but it is safe to say that it was not until William Tyndale's translation of the New Testament became available from 1526, followed by his writings, that the new teachings began to reach a wider public. In this the reading of the New Testament, privately or aloud to a listening circle, had an important, perhaps decisive, part.

As we have seen, when Tunstal was in the Low Countries and at the Diet of Worms in 1521, he came into touch with Lutheranism and he was alarmed at the possibility of such ideas gaining ground in London. As Bishop of London from 1522 he was directly responsible for the suppression of heresy in his diocese. William Tyndale applied to him for a post in his household in 1523; there is no reason to think that Tunstal's refusal to employ him was based on personal grounds; his household, he said, was already greater than he needed, but Tyndale never forgave Tunstal.

When Tyndale's New Testaments began to circulate, Warham

asked his suffragans to search for and seize copies they could find. Tunstal was active in this and on 26 October 1526 he preached at Paul's Cross at the burning of the confiscated books. His scheme, or perhaps Warham's, to buy up copies in Antwerp misfired, for, as Hall noted, the Testaments "came thick and threefold into England".[6] Tunstal had been warned by More that by this extravagant scheme he was only providing funds for further printings. The trade was well organized by such merchants as Humphrey Monmouth. The demand was steady but it would be misleading to picture the commonalty as clamouring for English New Testaments which so many of them could not read or afford to buy. Tunstal and others, including More, as we shall see, pointed out errors of translation, but their legitimate criticism was, to quote Tunstal, "intermeddling therewith many heretical articles and erroneous opinions" in the prefaces and glosses. He was determined to prevent this "pestiferous and pernicious poison" from spreading further. He came to see that burning copies of the new translation was ineffective; it might be regarded, in fact, as an advertisement. The heretics must be met on their own ground.

Criticism of Luther's teaching had hitherto been made by learned theologians, and some not-so-learned, who had written in Latin and had their works printed abroad. All this was on too high a level to have any real influence among ordinary folk. Erasmus too, though reluctantly, had at the urgent request of his friends, written against Luther. Tunstal had begged him in a letter of June 1523 to "come to grips with this Proteus, this veritable monster".[7] Erasmus was sceptical of how far all this flood of controversial writing could help men to the truth of Christ's teaching. He wrote, "There is a danger lest in the words of the apostle, we should have zeal but not according to knowledge, lest we not merely pluck up the wheat with the tares but pluck up wheat instead of tares". He had sympathized with Luther's attack on ecclesiastical abuses, and indeed More as well recognized that some of Luther's complaints were just, but an entirely different threat to the faith came when Luther went further and questioned the validity of the sacraments and later

---

[6]Hall, II, p. 161.   [7]Allen, 1367.

developed his doctrine of justification by faith alone. Luther had become a heresiarch. Erasmus would have preferred to calm the waters, not stir them more vigorously, but at length he yielded to his friends' importunities as well as to appeals from Rome and wrote his *De Libero Arbitrio* (On Free Will); this was published in 1525. He argued against Luther's teaching that man of himself had no freedom of will by stressing that each of us is constantly having to choose between good and evil. Various opinions have been expressed on the effectiveness of Erasmus' argument, but Luther himself said, "You alone . . . have attacked the real thing, that is the essential issue", and in reply he wrote a major exposition of his teaching, *De Servo Arbitrio* (On the Bondage of the Will). Erasmus replied with his *Hyperaspistes*[8] (1526). More wrote to Erasmus in December 1526[9] begging him to continue the argument, and a year later Erasmus published a second volume of his *Hyperaspistes*, "since you and Tunstal are so anxious for me to do so". In this he attacked Luther's conception of God as a terrible judge who condemned the "non-elect" however persevering they were in virtuous living. Here he showed a fervour and conviction that rarely found expression in his writings. His opposition to Luther had become absolute. Luther did not carry the controversy further, but in conversation he could refer to "that enraged viper, Erasmus of Rotterdam, the vainest creature in the world", and "this barefaced scoundrel to whom God is merely funny".

Thomas More did not immediately follow up his Rosseus book with further controversial writings, but in 1526, or more probably 1527, he wrote a Latin letter of some fifteen-thousand words in reply to the *Epistola ad Anglos*, by John Bugenhagen (Pomeranus), a pastor of Wittenberg who became the organizer of the Lutheran congregations. This letter had been published in 1525 both in German and Latin; an English translation was published ten years later. It was comparatively short for those days. Bugenhagen expressed his regret that few in England had yet heard the new Gospel; he went on to correct some wrong impressions about Luther's teaching, especially on free will and the sacraments. More did not have his reply printed and it was not published until

[8]The Champion, or Protector.   [9]Allen, 1770.

1568.[10] He evidently had Erasmus' *De Libero Arbitrio* freshly in mind for he echoed some of his friend's arguments.

Why should you try to persuade anyone to do good if there is no freedom of the will? You should simply pray God that he would achieve all things in me, but not urge me to try for myself. If all things come from faith, if nothing is truly free for man, as you Lutherans obstinately insist, you have assuredly left no reason why you should urge anyone to be virtuous or punish anyone who is vicious. Nor can you have any complaint against your opponents if they do nothing freely but are in everything forced by fate, unless perhaps you reply that even the things which you yourself write, you write not of your own impulse but by the prompting of fate.

As we have seen, More, as Rosseus had three or four years earlier, predicted that Luther's teaching must result in a disruption of the Church and in civil tumults. He could now point to the Peasants' War as proof of his fears and to the schisms among Luther's followers on the nature of the Eucharist. Here it will not be out of place to quote a modern comment. Dietrich Bonhoeffer[11] wrote:

One wonders how it was Luther's action led to consequences which were the direct opposite of what he intended, and which over-shadowed the last years of his life and work so that he doubted the value of everything he had achieved. He desired a real unity for the Church and for Western Christendom, but the consequence was the ruin of both. He sought the "Freedom of Christian Man", and the consequence was apathy and barbarism. He hoped to see the estab-lishment of a genuine social order free from clerical privilege and the outcome was the Peasants' War, and soon afterwards the gradual dissolution of all cohesion and order in society.[12]

Thomas More may have shown the manuscript of his letter to Tunstal, who would have this in mind when, in March 1528, he made an official request to his old friend that he should write in English against the new and heretical teachings. It will be noted that the Bishop linked Wycliffe with Luther.

Since now of late the Church of God throughout Germany has been

[10]Rogers, 160. It was printed at Louvain by John Fowler, son-in-law to John Harris, More's former secretary, who provided the copy. Gibson, 61.
[11]He was a Lutheran pastor who was shot in a Nazi prison-camp.
[12]*Letters from Prison* (1953), p. 54.

infested with heretics, there have been found certain children of iniquity who are endeavouring to bring over into our land the old and accursed Wycliffian heresy and along with it the Lutheran heresy, foster-daughter of Wycliffe's. . . . And since you, dearest brother, can play the Demosthenes in our native tongue just as well as in Latin, and are wont in every fight to be a most keen champion of Catholic truth, you could in no wise better occupy your leisure hours—if you can steal any from your duties—than in putting forth some writings in English which will reveal to the simple and uneducated the crafty malice of the heretics and render such folk better equipped against such impious supplanters of the Church.

With his letter, he sent More some of Luther's books with permission to read and study them.

Thomas More's aim in carrying out Tunstal's wishes was to appeal to the literate but unlearned public that had proved so receptive of Tyndale's New Testament with its propagandist prefaces and notes which were based on Luther's interpretation of the text.

The first of these English controversial books was entitled *A dyaloge of syr Thomas More knyghte: one of the counsayll of oure souerayne lorde the kyng and chauncellour of hys duchy of Lancaster. Wherein be treatyd dyuers maters/as the veneration and Worship of ymagys & relyques/prayng to sayntys/ & goyng on pylgrymage. Wyth many other thyngys touchyng the pestylent sect of Luther and Tyndale/by the tone bygone in Saxony/and by the tother laboryd to be brought in to Englond.*[13] It was printed by More's brother-in-law, John Rastell, "at London at the synge of the meremayd at Powlys gate next to chepe syde". The date was June 1529. A second edition was called for,[14] but this was printed by More's nephew, William Rastell; he began setting it in 1530 and published it in 1531. It is not known why this second printing went to the nephew; it may have been to start him in his printing venture. On the new title page More was now described as "chauncellour of England". For this second edition, More was able to add a long passage referring

[13]Gibson, 53, 54. This long title is usually reduced to *Dialogue Concerning Heresies.*
[14]We have no knowledge of how many were printed; the earliest indication is a ruling of the Stationers' Company in 1586 that no more than 1,250 copies of a book could be printed from one setting.

H

to *Image of Love*, by an Observant Friar, John Ryckes, alleged to contain heresy. A shorter addition notices Tyndale's *Answer to Sir Thomas More's Dialogue* published in the spring of 1531, too late for more extended comment.

While Thomas More was at work on his first edition, William Tyndale published two books; the first came out in May 1528 and was entitled *Parable of the Wicked Mammon;* this was an exposition, based on Luther's exegesis of the parable of the unjust steward (Luke 16, 1-8); it was in part concerned with the social obligations of owners of property, but mainly with the doctrine of justification by faith alone. More described it as "a very treasury and well-spring of wickedness". The second book, *The Obedience of a Christian Man*, appeared five months later. In this Tyndale emphasized that it was the duty of a subject to obey the king without question. "The king is in the room of God: and his law is God's law." It is said that when Henry, at the request of Anne Boleyn, read this book, he exclaimed, "This is the book for me and all kings to read". More's comment was that it was "able to make a Christian man that would believe it, leave off all Christian virtues and lose the verity of Christendom". In saying this he was not controverting the injunction on subjects to obey authority, a duty he himself accepted, but he was objecting to the many attacks on the Church and on the Catholic faith that Tyndale insinuated into his argument. Neither book was as innocent as it seemed at first glance.

The *Dialogue Concerning Heresies* is not a learned theological treatise; to have added yet another such book to the growing controversy would have defeated Tunstal's purpose, so More produced a readable argument; indeed, it remains the most readable of his books in this field. He supposed that a friend had sent a young man (the Messenger) to him to discuss some of the notions that were being widely talked about. The frequent use of "quoth he" and "quoth I" led Tyndale to refer to the book as "Quoth I, and quoth he, and quoth your friend". Indeed, the phrases do become tedious by repetition, but it will be better to postpone a consideration of More's style to the next chapter.

The setting of the discussion is not unlike that of *Utopia*—a garden, but this time at Chelsea. At one point the Messenger said he had a fresh problem to raise, but it would be better to postpone it until after dinner.

> Nay, quoth he, it were better ye dine first. My lady will, I wene, be angry with me that I keep you so long therefrom. For I hold it now well toward twelve. And yet more angry would she wax with me if I should make you sit and muse at your meat—as ye would, I wote well, muse on the matter [i.e. the next question], if ye wist what it were.

> If I were, quoth I, like my wife, I should muse thereon now and eat no meat for longing to know. But come on then and let us dine first and ye shall tell after.

> After dinner, we walked into the garden, and there shortly sitting in an arbour began to go forth to our matter.[15]

It is not proposed to attempt here a summary of this book, nor of any of More's later controversial writings; the orthodox arguments put forward are supported by frequent references to the Gospels and to the Epistles of St Paul and to the writings of the early Fathers, especially to his beloved St Austin. It will give a better idea of his approach if we see how he dealt with one specific topic.

One subject recurs—the Bible, its authority, its interpretation, its relation to the tradition of the Church, its translation and its dissemination.[16] First More emphasized that the Church was established before the Gospels were written and it was the Church that fixed the canon of the Scriptures.

> And therefore sayeth holy Saint Austin, "I should not believe the Gospel, but if it were for the Church". And he sayeth good reason. For were it not for the spirit of God keeping the truth thereof in his church, who could be sure which were the very gospels? There were many that wrote that gospel. And yet hath the church, by secret instruction of God, rejected the remnant and chosen out these four for the sure undoubted truth.

The Messenger accepted this but suggested that once the canon of Scripture was decided, then we can take the gospels for our guide and prefer what they say to any man's word, even if he claims to be speaking for the Church. To this More replied:

[15]E.W., p. 177.   [16]E.W., pp. 175-6.

But the church biddeth you not to believe the contrary of that the scripture sayeth. But he telleth you that in such places as ye would better believe the scripture than the church, there ye understand not the scripture. For whatsoever words it speaketh, yet it meaneth not the contrary of that the church teacheth you. And the church cannot be deceived in any such weighty point.

More was fearful of the private interpretations that the unlearned would read into the Bible; he saw the dangers of a "pot Parliament", as he termed it, in which Tom, Dick and Harry disputed about the meaning of a text when not one of them had a sufficient basis of learning on which to build. "For it is a thing that requireth good help, and long time, and an whole mind given greatly thereto." Nor was that fear baseless. The seventeenth century, and indeed our own, has seen some eccentric meanings read into the Bible, particularly into the Old Testament; strange sects have arisen as a result of ignoring the traditional teaching of the Church.

The Messenger went on to ask why Tyndale's translation had been banned and burned.

It is, quoth I, to me a great marvel that any good Christian man having any drop of wit in his head, would anything marvel or complain of the burning of that book, if he know the matter. Which also calleth the New Testament calleth it by a wrong name, except they call it Tyndale's Testament or Luther's Testament. For so had Tyndale, after Luther's counsel, corrupted and changed if from the good and wholesome doctrine of Christ to the devilish heresies of their own, that it was a clean and contrary thing.

That were marvel, quoth your friend, that it should be so clean contrary. For to some that read it, it seemed very like.

It is, quoth I, nevertheless contrary; and yet the more perilous. For like as to a silver groat as a false copper groat is, never the less contrary is it, though it be quick silvered all over; but so much the more false in how much it is counterfeited the more like to truth, in how much it was craftily devised like; so much the more perilous, in how much it was to folk unlearned more hard to be discerned.

The Messenger asked for instances of the errors made by Tyndale. More selected three words; Tyndale used "seniors" for "priests", "congregation" for "church", and "love" for "charity".

We need not here discuss the validity of these and similar criticisms; the first two certainly showed Tyndale's bias, but on the third, translators have varied.

The Messenger went on to object that by a provincial ruling of the Church, no English translation of the Bible was permitted. More pointed out that the ruling, made by Archbishop Arundel in 1408, had been misunderstood. It enacted that only translations that had been approved by the bishops were permissible.

But never meant they, as I suppose, forbidding of the Bible to be read in any vulgar tongue. Nor I never yet heard any reason laid why it were not convenient to have the Bible translated into the English tongue.[17]

The failure of the bishops to provide a translation of the Bible left a vacuum which Tyndale filled, nor did they see the urgent need for providing an authorized version as a substitute for his.[18] Increased literacy and printing made it inevitable that a translation would come sooner or later.

More went on to say that all readers can find spiritual nourishment in the Scriptures. "Every man may take good thereby and no man harm but he that will study thereof *lean proudly to the folly of his own wit*." His charge against the Lutherans and Tyndalists was that in their pride of intellect they had discarded the traditional teaching and interpretation of the Church and had coloured their translations to support their own new-fangled doctrines.

The *Dialogue* ends with a prayer that God may

send these seditious sects the grace to cease, and the favourers of those factions to amend, and us the grace, that stopping our ears from the false enchantments of all these heretics, we may, by the very faith of Christ's Catholic Church, so walk with charity in the way of good works in this wretched world, that we may be partners of the heavenly bliss, which the blood of God's own son hath brought us unto.

And this prayer, quoth I, serving us for grace, let us now sit

[17]E.W., p. 243.
[18]Credit must be given to Thomas Cromwell, who, probably with the support of Anne Boleyn, forced the pace, so to speak, and licensed the printing of Coverdale's version of the Bible in 1535.

down to dinner, which we did. And after dinner, departed he home toward you, and I to the court.

No sooner had More written the *Dialogue* than he turned his attention to an explosive pamphlet of fourteen pages entitled *A Supplication for the Beggars*. This came out, anonymously, towards the end of 1528. It was the work of Simon Fish, a Gray's Inn lawyer, who fled abroad where his pamphlet was printed. He had been a colporteur for Tyndale's Testament. If John Foxe is to be believed, the King, to whom the *Supplication* was addressed, did not discourage its circulation. The demand for it called for further printings; this suggests that here again the merchant patrons had been active in making it available.

Fish imagined that the beggars of England complained that they could not get alms for their relief because the clergy took most of the wealth of the country for their own support. Then followed a series of wild statements, which probably reflect much popular gossip, about the extortionate demands of these "wolves". As an example Fish declared that the friars alone gathered in £43,333 6s. 8d. a year! When the commissioners toured the country before the dissolution, it was found that the friars were so poor that they could not pay the visitation fees. The attack made by Fish on the wealth of the clergy would have been justified had he concentrated on such pluralists as Cardinal Wolsey who, besides being Archbishop of York, abbot of St Albans (though not a monk) and Bishop of Durham, became in 1528, on the death of Richard Fox, Bishop of Winchester—all this in addition to many other rich pickings. Most of the parish priests were poor men. Fish also referred to the Hunne case, the celibacy of the clergy, their vices and dissipations, their fees for prayers for the souls in purgatory, the withholding of the English New Testament, the statute of mortmain, and so on. His solution was to take away the property of the clergy and set them to work for a living. Such a hotchpotch of abuse could not be answered briefly and More took ten times the length for his reply.

The Supplication of Souls must have been written with speed for it was ready for the printer, William Rastell, when More left for France in 1529. The book was published, and reprinted,

before he became Lord Chancellor in October 1529. In his reply
More imagined the souls in purgatory pleading that they should
not be deprived of the prayers of the living. He dealt with the
charges Fish made as to the evil-living of the clergy, Tyndale's
New Testament, and the Hunne case. He saw, however, that
the root of this scurrilous attack was opposition to the faith and to
the authority of the Church. He therefore devoted much space to
an exposition of the doctrine of purgatory. He lightened the
discussion with touches of humour. Thus he told the story of "a
lewd gallant and a friar":

> Whom when the gallant saw going barefoot in a great frost and
> snow, he asked him why he did take such pain. And he answered
> that it was very little pain if a man would remember hell. "Yea,
> friar", quoth the gallant, "but what an there be none hell, then art
> thou a great fool." "Yea, master", quoth the friar, "but what an
> there be hell, then is your mastership a much more fool."[19]

There is true pathos in the final passage:

> If any point of your old favour, any piece of your old love, any
> kindness of kindred, any care of acquaintance, any favour of old
> friendship, any spark of charity, any respect of Christendom, be
> left in your hearts, let never the malice of a few fond fellows, a few
> pestilent persons borne towards priesthood, religion, and your
> Christian faith, rase out of your hearts the care of your kindred, all
> force of your old friends, and all remembrance of all Christian souls.
> Remember our thirst while ye sit and drink; our hunger while you
> be feasting; our restless watch while ye be sleeping; our sore and
> grievous pain while ye be playing; our hot burning fire while ye be
> in pleasure and sporting; so mote God make your offspring after
> remember you; so God keep you hence or not here, but bring you
> shortly to that bliss, to which for our Lord's love help you to bring
> us, and we shall set hand to help you thither to us.

This *Supplication* was Thomas More's last publication before he
was called to yet greater service to the State.

[19]E.W., p. 329.

CHAPTER XX

The Writer

WITH HIS *Dialogue Concerning Heresies,* Thomas More established his prose style.[1] The period of experiment of which Erasmus spoke was over and More now had an instrument at his command that he could use for the many tasks that lay ahead. Most of them, it is true, were of a controversial character, and that can mean hasty writing. The *Dialogue,* however, has all the marks of a carefully planned and thoughtfully written book. Bishop Tunstal had made his appeal to his old friend in March 1528; the first fruits did not appear in print until June 1529, so More took about a year in the composition. Moreover, it was a time before anxieties began to disturb his peace of mind, and before greater duties left him less leisure.

The form, a dialogue, was the one that More found most congenial. His translations from Lucian and his reading of Plato familiarized him with its possibilities. In this *Dialogue* he was so successful that a modern critic has said, "it is a great Platonic dialogue; perhaps the best specimen of that form ever produced in England".[2] The word "dialogue" can be misleading today; it does not mean the kind of free conversation we expect in a novel; it is a device for setting out in an attractive, dramatic way the author's opinions in a managed argument with an opponent. In this *Dialogue,* as in More's final work, the *Dialogue of Comfort,* the exchange is of a friendly character. It would be straining the term too far to describe the *Confutation of Tyndale* as a dialogue; in it More comments on the quoted words of Tyndale, but there is no question and answer, only statement and answer. In the classical dialogue form, the argument is on more formal and less discursive lines than would occur in actual conversation. The

---

[1]See R. W. Chambers, *The Continuity of English Prose,* prefaced to Harpsfield, and also separately published. Also J. Delcourt, *Essai sur la langue de Sir Thomas More* (Paris, 1914).
[2]C. S. Lewis, *English Literature in the Sixteenth Century* (1954), p. 172.

main arguments are displayed at greater length than would be considered well-mannered in ordinary life. This does not mean that there is not a true interchange of opinion, though inevitably the author has the best of it.

The doubts put before him by the visiting Messenger are fairly stated. It may be that More was recalling the discussions he had had with Son Roper. At times the Messenger voices complaints and criticisms that are as much More's as his companion's. Take such a passage as this:

> For what reverent honour is there daily done, under the name and opinion of a saint's relic, to some old rotten bone that was haply sometime, as Chaucer saith, a bone of some holy Jew's sheep. See we not that some saint's head is shewed in three places; and some one whole saint's body lieth in divers countries, if we believe the lies of people. And in both places is the one body worshipped where the one or the other is false and one body mistaken for another, an evil man haply for good. And yet will the priests of both places take offerings and toll men thither with miracles too.[3]

If not More speaking, that is surely Erasmus!

It is this frankness of discussion, this evident desire to meet serious criticism with serious argument, that gives this *Dialogue* its special flavour.

The style meets the need for clear expression. It is less convoluted than in some of More's later controversial writings, but occasionally, as in the concluding passages of the *Dialogue*, he launches out into an involved sentence that is not easy reading though modern punctuation can help to disentangle the thought. Such passages are, however, exceptional in this book. The extracts given in the previous chapter are more typical. It was noted in discussing *Richard III* that More had a liking for alliteration; this had lessened by the time he came to write the *Dialogue*. One rare instance seems like a burlesque of the device. "But since he would while he lived mistrust that halting priest for his halting horse, if I find a holy horeson halt in hypocrisy, I shall not fail while I live to trust all his fellows the worse."[4]

Nor is the classical influence so noticeable; his style became

[3]E.W., p. 139.   [4]E.W., p. 136.
H*

simpler perhaps because he kept in mind Tunstal's plea for something suited "to unlearned men".

This book shows More's range of treatment. His lucidity in marshalling his arguments was the result of his early schooling in dialectic and his subsequent training in the moots at Lincoln's Inn. To this must be added his study of such classical masters as Lucian and Plato and his wide reading in the Early Fathers. Occasionally the lawyer seems to be uppermost. The use of the expression "I put case" brings out this tendency, and the Messenger is at times submitted to cross-examination.

Here is a good example of this form of argument; the passage also illustrate's More's facility in inventing conversation within the convention of the dialogue.

For I now put case that there came ten divers honest men of good substance out of ten divers parts of the realm, each of them with an offering at one pilgrimage, as for ensample at our Lady of Ipswich, each one of them affirming on their oath a miracle done upon themself, in some great sudden help well appearing to pass the power of craft or nature, would ye not believe that among them all, at the leastwise twain of those ten said true?

No, by our lady, quod he, not and there were ten and twenty.

Why so? quod I.

Mary, quod he, for were they never so many, having none other witness but each man telling his tale for himself, they be but single all, and less than single. For every miracle hath but one record, and yet he not credible in his own cause. And so never a miracle well proved.

Well, said I, I like well your wisdom, that ye be so circumspect that ye will nothing believe without good, sufficient and full proof.

I put you then, quod I, another case, that ten young women not very specially knowen for good, but taken out at adventure, dwelling all in one town, would report and tell that a friar of good fame, hearing their confessions at a pardon, would have given them all in a penance to let him lie with them, on your faith, would ye not believe that among so many some of them said true.

Yes, that I would, quod he, by the Mary mass believe they said true all ten; and durst well swear for them and they were but two.

Why so, quod I, they be as single witness as the other of whom I told you before. For none of them can tell what was said to another, and yet they be unsworn also, and therewith be they but women which be more light and less to be regarded, dwelling all in one town also, and thereby might the more easily conspire a false tale.

They be, quod he, witness enough for such a matter, the thing is so likely of itself that a friar will be womanish, look the holy horeson never so saintly.

Ye deny not, quod I, but God may as easily do a good turn by a miracle, as any man may do an evil by nature.

That is true, quod he, and he list.

Well, quod I, see now what a good way ye be in, that are of your own good godly mind more ready to believe two simple women that a man will do nought,[5] than ten or twenty men that God will do good.[6]

This passage also serves as an example of More's dramatic ability which comes out not only in this kind of argument but even more so in the anecdotes with which he lightens his pages. "A merry fable," quod I, "cometh never amiss to me." Two have already been given in these pages[7] that tell us something of his father who comes also in the following tale.

Nor though the Jews were many so noughty that they put Christ to death, yet be wiser I wot well than the gentlewoman was, which in talking once with my father, when she heard say that our lady was a Jew, first could not believe it; but said, "What ye mock I wis; I pray you tell truth". And when it was so fully affirmed that she at last believed it: "And was she a Jew", quod she, "so help me God and halidom, I shall love her the worse while I live".[8]

In one "merry tale" he tried to reproduce a local dialect. A Commission had been sent down to Sandwich Haven in Kent to find out why the sea was receding and leaving the harbour without sufficient depth of water.

There started up one good old father and said, Ye masters say every man what he will, cha marked this matter well as some other. And, by God, I wot how it waxed nought well enough. For I knew it good, and have marked so chaue when it began to wax worse. And what hath hurt it, good father? quod the gentlemen. By my faith, masters, quod he, yonder same Tenterden steeple, and nothing else, that, by the mass, cholde t'were a fair fish pole. Why hath the steeple hurt the haven, good father? quod they. Nay, by our Lady, masters, quod he, yche cannot tell you well, why, but chote well it hath. For, by God, I knew it a good haven till that steeple was builded, and by the Mary mass, cha marked it well, it never throve since.[9]

These brief stories show More's skill in narrative; they are a reflection of his love of "a merry tale" in conversation with his friends. He had a dramatic instinct that, as we have seen, displayed itself in his boyhood and in devising in his youth, according to Erasmus, "little comedies". *Utopia* has its dramatic side. It is not too fanciful to suggest that, in Elizabethan times, Thomas More might have been a dramatist.

We may note also his love of popular sayings; these add to the salty flavour of some passages; a sentence put into the mouth of the Messenger will give us an example. "And a tale that fleeth through many mouths catcheth many new feathers: which, when they be pulled away again, leave him as bald as a coot, and sometimes as bare as a bird's arse."[10]

These tales and the homely expressions and the author's bantering humour make for pleasant reading without blunting the force of the argument. They hint how delightful a talker he must have been. This is the tone of the greater part of the book; here More is dealing with current objections to prayers to saints, to the worshipping of images, the abuse of pilgrimages and the belief in miracles. These he could treat with some sympathy for both he and Erasmus, particularly Erasmus, had echoed such criticisms. When, however, we come to the last third of the book, there is a hardening of tone. More's attitude towards heresy will call for considered treatment later in these pages; here we are concerned with the effect his righteous anger had on his manner. We may take his treatment of Luther's marriage in 1525 to the former nun, Katherine von Bora. To Catholics it was a double

[9]cha, chaue = I have; cholde = I would; yche = I; chote = I wote. No record of such a Commission has been traced. Hugh Latimer, in a sermon of March 1550 before Edward VI, retold the story but assumed that "Maister More" was a member of the Commission; perhaps he was. E.W., pp. 277-8.
[10]E.W., p. 238.

apostasy and Thomas More was horrified; so he wrote:

> Whereas Luther not only teacheth monks, friars and nuns to marriage
> but also, being a friar, hath married a nun himself, and with her
> liveth under the name of wedlock in open incestuous lechery
> without care or shame, because he hath procured and gotten so
> many shameful and shameless companions.[11]

This acerbity was to increase as he got more and more entangled
in the coils of controversy; he did not regain his full serenity until
he was a prisoner in the Tower and wrote his *Dialogue of Comfort*.

Another element in his style should be noted. Perhaps it is not
surprising that the author of *Epigrammata* should have a flair for
turning an aphorism. The following examples are taken from
several books.

> For God is as mighty in the stable as in the temple.

> The devil is ready to put out men's eyes that are content willingly
> to become blind.

> And let us fence as with faith and comfort us with hope, and
> smite the devil in the face with a firebrand of charity.

> For better is yet of truth a conscience a little too strait than a little
> too large.

> I counsel him that cannot be sad for his sin, to be sorry at the least
> that he cannot be sorry.

> A few doting dames make not the people.

> If faith were gone, all were gone, and then hath God here no church
> at all.

> Let every man fear and think in this world that all the good that he
> doth, or can do, is a great deal too little.

No one can read many pages of Thomas More's writings
without sensing his close knowledge of the Scriptures. In the
Dialogue there are two hundred and sixteen biblical references, a
hundred and sixty of which are from the New Testament. St
Matthew's Gospel seems to have been his favourite book. So too
we see fruits of his study of the Early Fathers, above all of his

[11]E.W., p. 260.

beloved St Augustine, but he also draws upon St Ambrose, St Basil, St Cyprian, St Gregory, and St Jerome, who comes second to St Augustine.

Large claims have been made for Sir Thomas More's position as a formative writer of English prose. Thus Sir James Mackintosh declared that More was "the father of English prose".[12] This was an extravagant estimate, particularly in view of the fact that only his early *Richard III* was easily available to readers. More's contemporaries shared with him the task of establishing a prose that would become the standard for later writers who developed it to meet new demands. We may compare his style with that of three writers of his own day. The first is from Bishop John Fisher's *Spiritual Consolation*.

> What life is more painful and laborious of itself than is the life of the hunters which most early in the morning break their sleep and rise when other do take their rest and ease, and in his labour he may use no plain highways and soft grass, but he must tread upon the fallows, run over the hedges, and creep through the thick bushes, and cry all the long day upon his dogs, and so continue without meat or drink until the very night drive him home, these labours be unto him pleasant and joyous, for the desire and love that he hath to see the poor hare chased with dogs. Verily, verily, if he were compelled to take upon him such labours, and not for this cause, he would soon be weary of them, thinking them full tedious unto him: neither would he rise out of his bed so soon, ne fast so long, ne endure these other labours unless he had a very love therein. For the earnest desire of his mind is so fixed upon his game, that all these pains be thought to him but very pleasures. And therefore I may say that love is the principal thing that maketh any work easy, though the work be right painful of itself, and that without love no labour can be comfortable to the doer.[13]

The second passage is from Lord Berner's translation of Froissart published in 1523. We have noted that Sir Thomas More must have seen much of Lord Berners when they were both in Calais in 1520; indeed, Berners may have shown More some of the translation.

---

[12] *Misc. Works*, I, p. 412.   [13] *English Works* (E.E.T.S.), p. 365.

And as the king and the earl of Derby talked together in the court, the greyhound, who was wont to leap upon the king, left the king and came to the earl of Derby, duke of Lancaster, and made to him the same friendly countenance and cheer as he was wont to do to the king. The duke, who knew not the greyhound, demanded of the king what the greyhound would do. "Cousin," quoth the king, "it is a great good token to you and an evil sign to me." "Sir, how know you that?" quoth the duke. "I know it well", quoth the king; "the greyhound maketh you cheer this day as king of England, as ye shall be, and I shall be deposed. The greyhound hath this knowledge naturally: therefore take him to you; he will follow you and forsake me." The duke understood well those words and cherished the greyhound, who would never after follow king Richard, but followed the duke of Lancaster.[14]

The minor point may be made that More's use of "quoth" was evidently not peculiar to him.

Our last passage comes from the writings of More's adversary, William Tyndale. Both Berners and Tyndale had far more influence on our prose than Thomas More or John Fisher; indeed, through his New Testament and later by its being largely incorporated in the King James version of the Bible, Tyndale was to prove a major influence in our language. This passage comes from his *Obedience of a Christian Man*.

The most despised person in the realm ought to be treated as if he were the king's brother and fellow-member with him in the kingdom of God and of Christ. Let the King, therefore, not think himself too good to do service to such humble people nor seek any other thing in them than a father seeketh, yea than Christ sought in us. Though that the king, in temporal regiment, be in the room of God, and representeth God Himself, and is without comparison better than his subjects; yet let him put off that, and become a brother, doing and leaving undone all things in respect of his commonwealth, that all men may see that he seeketh nothing but the profit of his subjects.[15]

Dr Johnson, in the "History of the English Language" prefaced to his Dictionary (1755), gave over eight folio pages out of twenty-seven to extracts from More; three of these pages were from

[14]Froissart, ch. 238.   [15]*Works*, II, p. 203.

Richard III, but five were from the poems. Johnson justified this proportion on the grounds of vocabulary rather than of style. When, however, he stated that "it appears from Ben Jo(h)nson, that his [More's] works were considered as models of pure and elegant style", he was going beyond his book, for Jonson made no such statement in his *English Grammar* nor elsewhere. He drew examples of construction from More but to no greater a degree than from such writers as Ascham, Jewel, Cheke and Foxe (of the Martyrs) among others.

It was a misfortune that Thomas More's English writings dropped out of circulation (apart from *Richard III*) for nearly three centuries. Even now there is, for example, no popular edition of the *Dialogue Concerning Heresies* in print. The 1557 folio was little known outside the circles of those studying Tudor prose. The rediscovery, as it may be called, of his writings early in this century led to an overestimation of his position as a prose writer. Thus J. S. Phillimore wrote in 1913, "whatever the language was when More found it, where he left it, there it remained until Dryden definitely civilized it".[16] One hesitates to say that such a distinguished scholar could come perilously near talking nonsense; such a pronouncement ignores the range and development of our prose during the century that followed More's death—a period that included the Elizabethans, the Jacobeans and the early Carolines. In their exuberance, some of the writers left the main stream, but the stream flowed on and deepened itself.

Thomas More has an important place among those who moulded our printed language; that others had greater influence because their books could be come at more easily, has to be accepted as mischance. His prose at its best was of fine quality; the *Dialogue Concerning Heresies* shows what he could achieve when he was unhurried and unharried; those conditions were not to return and his later works, sometimes written against time and without peace of mind, are not such notable pieces of writing.[17]

---

[16]*Dublin Review*, July 1913. The thesis is effectively answered in D. Bush, "Tudor Humanism and Henry VIII" (*University of Toronto Quarterly*, 1938).

[17]For an excellent example (too long to quote here) of his later style at its best, the reader should turn to Book III, Ch. 10, of the *Dialogue of Comfort*.

Even so, they contain many fine passages touched with that sense of humour that never left him for long. It is a vain regret to wish he could have spent more time and thought on their construction and composition.

CHAPTER XXI

Lord Chancellor

WHEN TUNSTAL and More returned to England at the end of August 1529, they could have had no suspicion of the sudden turn about to take place in State affairs. Wolsey's power had been shaken as he had proved unable to get the King what he wanted; moreover, the Peace of Cambrai was another blow to his prestige. He took a very different view of the Peace from that of Thomas More. Charles V and Francis I had reached agreement, thus leaving the Emperor free to exert pressure on the Pope, and England no longer had the support of France. The prospects of a papal decision favourable to Henry VIII were more remote than ever. Wolsey's method of handling the problem had failed completely and, in his anger, the King turned on his Lord Chancellor. Only the bare facts need be recalled here; at no stage was Sir Thomas More directly involved, for he was certainly not among those—mostly of the Duke of Norfolk's following—that were intent on ruining Wolsey. The issue of the summons on 9 August 1529 for a new Parliament was an indication of how the King was beginning to view Wolsey. Henry evaded consultations with him and the court soon sensed the changing atmosphere. When, on 9 October, Wolsey went in full state to Westminster as Chancellor he found himself deserted; all the rats had left. Even as he sat in the Chancery, the attorney-general, Sir Christopher Hales, was indicting him for praemunire in the King's Bench. He was accused of using his legatine powers contrary to the law; the fact that the King had acquiesced did not count. Wolsey submitted himself to the King's mercy. On 18 October he was deprived of the great seal, and his riches and possessions were forfeited. The King allowed his former Chancellor to retain some of his wealth and the Archbishopric of York. The story is well known of his illness when he was attended by John Clement and other physicians, of his fluctuating hopes, his reluctant progress towards York, his arrest on 4 November and his death at Leicester on 29 November 1530.

Who was to be the new Lord Chancellor? Among the peers Norfolk and Suffolk were possible choices, but neither had shown much statesmanship; among the bishops, Tunstal and Gardiner had claims, but they were not whole-hearted king's men. According to Hall—

> The King came to his manor at Greenwich, and there much consulted with his Council for a meet man to be his Chancellor, so that in no wise he were no man of the Spirituality, and so after long debate the King resoluted himself upon Sir Thomas More, Knight, a man well learned in the tongues, and also in the Common Law, whose wit was fine, and full of imaginations, by reason whereof he was much given to mocking, which was to his gravity a great blemish.[1]

The Great Seal was handed to Sir Thomas on 25 October 1529. He was installed the following day in the Chancery at Westminster; the Duke of Norfolk presented the new Lord Chancellor to the assembled councillors and other notables in a conventional speech, to which Sir Thomas More replied as conventionally.

Roper was of the opinion that More had been chosen by the King "the rather to move him to incline to his side" in the matrimonial problem. This may have been a contributory but hardly the decisive reason. At that time the King, exasperated as he was by Rome's delays, probably thought that he must succeed in the long run, and his immediate policy was to threaten the Pope and bring all the pressure possible to exact a decision, one that would be, needless to say, in his favour. The accession of More as a supporter at that stage would have been welcome but it was not a pressing need.

It is best to give More's own account of what happened. He refers to his return from the negotiations at Cambrai.

> After my coming home his Highness of his only goodness (as far unworthy as I was thereto) made me, as you well know, his Chancellor of this realm, soon after which time his Grace moved me again

---

[1]Hall, II, p. 158. More was not, as has been said, the first layman to be Lord Chancellor. Between 1341 and 1455 there had been six laymen, but their tenure of office was usually brief.

yet eftsoons, to look and consider his great matter, and well and indifferently to ponder such things as I should find therein. And if it so were that thereupon it should hap me to see such things as should persuade me to that part, he would gladly use me among other of his councillors in that matter, and nevertheless he graciously declared unto me that he would in no wise that I should other thing do or say therein, than upon that that I should perceive mine own conscience would serve me, and that I should first look unto God and after God unto him, which most gracious words was the first lesson also that ever his Grace gave me at my first coming into his noble service.

After consulting those whom the King named, More still felt unable to support the case for an annulment of the marriage. His account continued:

His Highness graciously taking in good part my good mind in that behalf used of his blessed disposition in the prosecuting of his great matter only those (of whom his Grace had good number) whose conscience his Grace perceived well and fully persuaded upon that part, and as well myself as any other to whom his Highness thought the thing to seem otherwise, he used in his other business, abiding (of his abundant goodness) nevertheless gracious lord unto any man, nor never was willing to put any man in ruffle or trouble of his conscience.[2]

It is worth noting that there were others besides More who were not willing to support the King in this matter. We need not doubt that at the time Henry meant what he said; he had a vast capacity for believing and dramatizing his own sentiments, but he had an equal capacity for changing his opinion when it suited him.

More's position was unusual. As a commoner he could not be a member of the House of Lords, but, as Lord Chancellor, he presided over it as the King's voice. No doubt had he remained Lord Chancellor for a while longer he would have been ennobled.

Parliament met on 3 November 1529 at Blackfriars. It has been said that the Commons House was packed by royal nominees.[3] It was originally no more packed than previous Parliaments; the influence of the Crown had always been used, and for several

[2]Rogers, 199, (53). To Thomas Cromwell, 5 March 1534.
[3]The probable numbers were: County Members, 74: Borough Members, 236.

more centuries continued to be used, to bring in members likely to be favourable to the sovereign's wishes; that influence was never absolute and free speech was not a figment of theory. The length of the 1529 Parliament (it was not dismissed until April 1536) meant that an increase in the number of royal nominees could be arranged, and as soon as Thomas Cromwell was in effective control, the business of using Crown influence was carried out more systematically. Deaths and withdrawals (it was not a popular service) gave Cromwell opportunities to exercise pressure on the patrons of constituencies; thus in January 1534 there were as many as forty seats to be filled out of some three hundred. The creation of new boroughs was another way of using influence. Even so the Commons were never completely sub-servient and had to be as "managed" as is done today by the leaders of political parties. The managers then were the King and Council, but they knew just how far they could go. Among the members were several of More's relatives. His brother-in-law, John Rastell, sat for Dunheved (Launceston), Cornwall; three sons-in-law, William Roper, Giles Heron and William Daunce, were elected, the first for Bramber, Sussex, and the other two for Thetford; Sir Giles Alington, husband of More's step-daughter, sat for Cambridgeshire.

When the Lords and Commons were assembled in the royal presence at Blackfriars, Sir Thomas More delivered what we should call the King's Speech. It is reported at some length in Hall;[4] some have doubted his accuracy, but the substance is also given in the briefer account sent to the Emperor by his new ambassador, Eustace Chapuys.[5] Objection has been taken to More's attack on his predecessor, and the excuse has been put forward that the words were not his but the King's. The words were as follow:

So the great wether which is of late fallen as you all know, so craftilty, so scabbedly, yea and so untruly juggled with the King, that all men must needs guess and think that he thought in himself, that they had no wit to perceive his crafty doing, or else that he pre-sumed that the King would not see nor know his fraudulent juggling

4Hall, II, p. 164.   5Span. Cal. I, pp. 323-4.

and attempts; but he was deceived, for his Grace's sight was so quick and penetrable, that he saw him, yea and saw through him, both within and without, so that all thing to him was open, and according to his desert he hath had a gentle correction.[6]

At that time Wolsey had been allowed to retain his Archbishopric and some of his wealth instead of being, as his enemies no doubt hoped, sent to the Tower. There seems no valid reason for supposing that More's speech was in the King's own words; even Henry could hardly have referred to himself in such glowing terms. Present-day susceptibilities are against ungracious attacks on a man when he is down, though that does not prevent them being made! Such a feeling would have been incomprehensible in an age when men felt, spoke and acted violently, and More was not out of step with his fellows as his controversial writings demonstrate. We know that he had a regard for Wolsey in the early stages of the Cardinal's career, and there was much to applaud, but it would be surprising if that opinion survived the lavish display and utter selfishness of Wolsey's full-blown ambitions. More, it will be recalled, accompanied the Cardinal on that all-but regal progress to Calais and Amiens in 1527. It must have scandalized the author of *Utopia*. One of More's later references to Wolsey has already been quoted. A more extended criticism comes in the *Dialogue of Comfort:*

It happed me to be somewhat favoured with a great man of the church, and a great state,[7] one of the greatest in all that country there. And indeed, whosoever might spend as much as he might in one thing and other were a right great estate in any country of Christendom. But glorious was he very far above all measure, and that was great pity, for it did harm and made him abuse many great gifts that God had given him. Never was he satiate of hearing his own praise.

More went on to narrate two instances of Wolsey's pride and desire for praise. The passage ends with a typical quip:

But out of question, he that putteth his pleasure in the praise of the people hath but a fond fantasy. For if his finger do but ache of an hot blain, a great many men's mouths blowing out his praise will

[6]Hall, II, p. 164.
[7]state, estate = status, especially high dignity; glorious = eager for glory.

scantly do him among them all half so much ease as to have one little boy blow upon his finger.[8]

At the end of his speech to the new Parliament, the Chancellor instructed the Commons to resort "to the nether house" and elect their Speaker. As plague had just broken out in the City, the Commons met next day in the Chapter House at Westminster where they continued to meet until 1547.[9]

As far as the records go (there are none for the Council) Thomas More did not have the policy-making influence that Wolsey had come to exercise. This may have been because Henry had decided to limit the powers of the Lord Chancellor; certainly Thomas Audley, who eventually succeeded More, was little better than a cipher. With Thomas Cromwell's appointment as King's Secretary in 1533, the centre of policy-making began to shift. It seems that the King kept his word in not involving More in his "great matter". There is some support for this view in an apologia written by Sir George Throgmorton of Coughton, who, early in 1540, was imprisoned when Cromwell accused him of denying the Supremacy.[10] Sir George had been one of the Commons who had spoken against the Annates Bill in the 1532 session. (In his statement he speaks of the Bill of Appeals but this did not come before the House until a year after More's resignation; there may have been an earlier proposal of which there is no record.) Sir George wrote:

After I had reasoned to the Bill of Appeals (sic), Sir Thomas More, then being Chancellor, sent for me to come and speak with him in the Parliament Chamber. And when I came to him, he was in a little chamber within the Parliament Chamber, where, as I remember, stood an altar, or a thing like unto an altar, whereupon he did lean and, as I do think, the same time the Bishop of Bath [Clerk] was talking with him. And then he said this to me, "I am very glad to

---

[8]*Dialogue of Comfort*, pp. 331-6.

[9]The Parliament Chamber was the Upper Frater of the Priory; the Commons met in the lower (nether) chamber. This seems the origin of the terms "Upper" and "Lower" House. After 1547 the Commons met in St Stephen's Chapel in the Palace of Westminster. The Chapter House remains Crown property.

[10]L.P. XII, ii, No. 952. The document is not dated, but is calendered under 1537. It would seem to fit in better with Throgmorton's imprisonment in 1540. There is no superscription; it was probably addressed to the King.

hear the good report that goeth of you, and that ye be so good a Catholic man as ye be. And if ye do continue in the same way that ye begin, and be not afraid to say your conscience, ye shall deserve great reward of God, and thanks of the King's Grace at length, and much worship to yourself."

The inference is that Sir Thomas had not been taken into the full confidence of the King who must have approved of both the Annates and Appeals Bills, otherwise they would not have been brought forward.

It may be added that Throgmorton was soon released as Cromwell's influence was on the wane, and Sir George was one of the witnesses (the other was Sir Richard Rich) against the fallen minister a few months later.

As we shall see, Sir Thomas could not be kept completely out of transactions connected with the King's Matter. It was no doubt in accordance with More's own inclinations that he was able to concentrate on his duties as head of the judiciary.

What knowledge we have of Thomas More as judge comes from William Roper who had a professional interest in the subject and as Clerk of the Pleas must have had frequent occasion to know what was happening in the Chancery. He noted the different ways in which his two brothers-in-law regarded their family connection with the Lord Chancellor. Giles Heron expected favourable treatment in any case of his that came before his father-in-law, but William Daunce knew that this was foolish. He once pointed out to Sir Thomas that this meant a loss of the gifts that Wolsey's entourage found so profitable. To this Sir Thomas replied:

You say well, son; I do not mislike that you are of conscience so scrupulous, but many other ways be there, son, that I may both do yourself good and pleasure your friend also. For sometime may I by my word stand your friend in stead [of benefit], and sometime may I by my letter help him; or if he have cause depending before me, at your request I may hear him before another. Or, if his cause be not of the best, yet may I move the parties to fall to some reasonable end by arbitrament. Howbeit this one thing, son, I assure thee on my faith, that if the parties will at my hands call for justice, then, all were my father stood on one side, and the Devil on the other, his cause being good, the Devil should have right.[11]

Giles Heron, a determined litigant, had a case before More and hoped for a favourable treatment, so much so that he refused the friendly settlement suggested by the Chancellor. So, Roper tells us, "then made he in conclusion a flat decree against him".[12]

Sir John More must have been a proud man when his son became Lord Chancellor; this did not lessen Thomas More's deference to him, for, as William Roper tells us,

> Whensoever he passed through Westminster Hall to his place in the Chancery by the court of the King's Bench, if his father, one of the judges thereof had been sat ere he came, he would go into the same court, and there reverently kneeling down in the sight of them all, duly ask his father's blessing. And if it fortuned that his father and he at readings in Lincoln's Inn met together, as they sometime did, notwithstanding his high office, he would offer in argument the pre-eminence to his father, though he, for his office sake, would refuse to take it.[13]

Sir John died within the first twelve months of his son's Chancellorship. His will was proved on 5 December 1530. Roper tells us that during Sir John's last illness his son frequently visited him and spoke "comfortable words".[14]

It is hazardous for a layman to write on legal matters, so it is safer to quote the words of a distinguished lawyer and judge:

> More's custom was to hear and adjudicate upon causes in the morning, and in the afternoon to place himself at the disposal of petitioners for the purpose of examining their cases and giving redress where possible. Under the old regime writs had been issued without any examination whether any probable cause of action existed. This had led to vexatious litigation and heavy arrears of causes for adjudication. More changed all this. Before a suit could be commenced a bill had to be filed, signed by an attorney. After

[11]Roper, pp. 41-2.

[12]It is suggested in Harpsfield, p. 326, that this was the case of *Heron v. Millisante* (interestingly a case in "withernam"—see above, p. 147). Heron was involved in a number of other cases which await expert assessment.

[13]John More is first mentioned as a judge in 1518. He may have been knighted at the same time as he already bore a coat of arms. Roper, p.43. The two courts were contiguous; see Plate 9.

[14]Roper, p. 44.

perusing the bill, the Chancellor, if he thought it a fitting case, would grant his fiat for the commencement of the suit. That put an end to the involving of innocent persons in vexatious litigation. The arrears of causes unheard were cleared off by unremitting attention to the discharge of his judicial duties, with the result that the lists actually ran dry.

Those were the days when equity was beginning to insist on softening the rigours of the Common Law; and it was often necessary for the Chancellor to issue injunctions to this end. More was firmly of opinion that Law and equity might be beneficially administered by the same tribunal, anticipating in this respect the Judicature Act 1873. He endeavoured, accordingly, to induce the Common Law judges to relax the rigour of their rules. Failing in this, he had to grant injunctions. The judges, or some of them, complained; but More, summoning them to dine with him, convinced them of the propriety of his proceedings.

While it is not possible to describe More as a great chancellor from a lawyer's point of view, for his name is associated with no leading judgment or recorded display of legal reasoning, nevertheless this may be truly said: that if to discharge judicial duties conscientiously, speedily and without favour, to make the machinery of justice work smoothly and efficiently, and to soften the rigours of the law so as to meet the rights of particular cases, are marks of a great chancellor, then Sir Thomas More must be so described.[15]

A rhyme of the times summed up popular opinion:

> When More some time had Chancellor been,
>   No more suits did remain;
> The like will never more be seen
>   Till More be there again.

[15]Lord Russell of Kilowen (1867-1946) in *The Fame of Blessed Thomas More*, pp. 71-2. He was a Chancery judge and a lord of appeal. In the Public Record office (see *Early Chancery Proceedings*) there are between four and five thousand bills addressed to More as Chancellor. These await expert assessment, but it is unlikely that they will add anything significant to our knowledge of him.

CHAPTER XXII

Tyndale

THE BUSY LIFE of a Lord Chancellor engaged not only on his work
as head of Chancery but as a member of the Council, could not
have left Sir Thomas More much leisure, yet he found time to
continue his task of refuting heresy. His *Dialogue Concerning
Heresies* had called a reply from William Tyndale in 1530 entitled
An answere unto sir T Mores dialogue,[1] printed in Antwerp. The
sub-title reads: 'Wherein he [Tyndale] declareth what the church
is, and giveth a reason of certain words in the translation of the
New Testament. After that he answereth particularly unto every
chapter which seemeth to have any appearance of truth through
his four books."

As we have seen, More was able to refer briefly to Tyndale's
book in the second printing of the *Dialogue*, but a full reply was
necessary. The first part of *The confutacyon of Tyndales answere
made by syr Thomas More knight lord chancellour of Englonde*[2] was
published in the spring of 1532; this contained three books; a
second part, of five books, appeared in 1533. Both were printed
by William Rastell. When the work was included in the English
Works of 1557, part of a ninth book was included though this
broke off with the words, "These things hath (I say) . . .",
followed by a note, "There can no more be found of this ix book
written by Sir Thomas More."

Five hundred folio pages of black letter in double column are a
deterrent to a modern reader, and his first impression is of the
contrast between the lengths to which the two controversialists
wrote. Tyndale's book contains some ninety thousand words;
More's unfinished reply runs to ten times that length. This
prolixity must have limited the effect of the book; a shorter, less
expensive, book would have had a wider circulation and the

¹Gibson, 563.   ²Gibson, 48.

discipline thus imposed on the author would have made the arguments more pointed. One gets the feeling that More did not plan the book as a whole but just went on and on. There are, of course, passages that capture the attention and repay the laborious reading, but these become rarer as the pages are turned. It may have been that the cares of State and the strain of reconciling conflicting loyalties made concentration of mind all but impossible. It is certainly true that when the tension was over, and, as he put it, the field was won, More regained his ease of writing and his cheerfulness of spirit.

The most readable part of the *Confutation* is the "Preface to the Christian Reader". More here dealt with a number of erroneous and heretical opinions on, for instance, the nature of the Church, the relation between faith and good works, prayers to the saints, and the Blessed Sacrament. A digression on "the devil's stinking martyr", Thomas Hilton, is not to our modern taste; it showed the increasing exasperation that seized More as he wrestled with the hydra-headed foe of heresy.

He again stated clearly his attitude towards heresy which he likened to a carbuncle:

> Towards the help whereof, if it haply be incurable, then to the clean cutting out that part for infection of the remnant am I by mine office by virtue of mine oath, and every officer of justice through the realm for his rate, right especially bounden, not in reason only and good congruence, but also by plain ordinance and statute.

He was here referring to the Act of 1489 which reminded justices of the peace of their duty (dating back to Henry V's time) of arresting suspected heretics and delating them to the Ordinary. As late as March 1529, Wolsey had reminded justices of this duty.

The Preface ended with some good counsel:

> For surely the best way were neither to read this book nor theirs [heretics'] but rather the people unlearned to occupy themself beside their other business in prayer, good meditation, and reading such English books as most may nourish and increase devotion. Of which kind is Bonaventure of the life of Christ, Gerson of the following of Christ, and the devout contemplative book *Scala*

Perfectionis with such other like, than in learning what may well be answered unto heretics.[3]

The three books he mentions may not be recognized by the names and titles he uses. "Bonaventure of the life of Christ" was the free translation of his *Meditationes* made by Prior Nicholas Love of Mount Grace (Carthusian) under the title *The Mirrour of the blessed lyf of Jesu Christ*, which was printed by Caxton in 1487. Thomas à Kempis' *Imitatio Christi* was long ascribed to the French theologian, Jean Gerson, Chancellor of the University of Paris. A translation into English of the first three books only was made by William Atkinson, Canon of Windsor, at the request of the Lady Margaret Beaufort; this was printed in 1502 by Wynkyn de Worde. It was to be superseded by the complete and fine translation of the whole work by Richard Whitford, the close friend of Erasmus and More; in this form it was a beloved book for many generations. Walter Hilton's *Scala Perfectionis* was widely circulated in manuscript copies for many years before being printed by Wynkyn de Worde in 1494.

Thomas More would not have recommended these books unless he himself, and probably his family, had proved their value. The many editions that were published showed that there was a need for devotional guidance. Those who used such books, however, would not form a substantial part of the population; certainly not large enough to exert a determinative influence on popular attitudes towards the clergy.

He reassured those who felt unable to ignore the controversies of the day by saying:

> Yet have I not so slightly seen unto mine own [book] nor shoffled it up so hastily, nor let it so pass unlooked over by better men and better learned than myself, but that I trust in God it may among the better stand yet in some good stead.[4]

Later in the book he referred to his own writings and to those of Erasmus:

> In these days in which men, by their own default, misconstrue and take harm of the very Scripture of God, until men better amend, if any man would now translate *Moria* into English, or some works

[3]E.W., p. 357.   [4]E.W., p. 357.

either that I myself have written ere this, albeit there be none harm therein, folk yet being (as they be) given to harm of that that is good, I would not only my "darling's" books, but mine also, help to burn them both with mine own hands, rather than folk should (through their own fault) take any harm of them, seeing that I see them likely in these days so to do.[5]

That is not one of More's clearest sentences! Tyndale in his *Answer* had referred to Erasmus as More's "darling" and had claimed that on some points of vocabulary in the New Testament the two friends disagreed. More must here have been thinking of his *Utopia* and have feared that some of its light-hearted notions might be taken too seriously.[6] He was more alive to the dangers that were threatening the faith than Erasmus proved to be. The difference in their sense of urgency was not so much one of personality, though that was a factor, but of circumstances. Thomas More had heresy, so to speak, on his door-step; one might say literally so in William Roper's lapse into Lutheranism. The great and immediate problem was the continued circulation of Tyndale's New Testament and his writings. Quite apart from his devotion to the Church and the faith, More had his duties as a magistrate, duties that he would not take lightly. He had responsibilities that Erasmus escaped. The time had gone by for wit and satire; the very faith was in peril. He put this point of view to Erasmus in a letter in June 1532:

Your opponents cannot be unaware of how you confess candidly that, before these pestiferous heresies arose, which have since spread everywhere and subverted everything, you dealt with such matters in a way you would not have treated them had you been able to foresee that such enemies of religion and such traitors would ever arise. You would then have expressed what you had to say less provocatively and more moderately. You wrote strongly then because you were indignant at seeing how some cherished their vices as if they were virtues.[7]

Erasmus did not entirely give up his mocking; some of his later *Colloquies* keep up the strain.

[5] E.W., p. 422.
[6] He would have been shocked to know that some Anabaptists found *Utopia* congenial.
[7] Allen, 2659.

Let us return to the *Confutation*. Beginning with Tyndale's Preface, More dealt with the *Answer* chapter by chapter, almost paragraph by paragraph, until he had reprinted nearly three-quarters of Tyndale's book, and always with scrupulous accuracy. To us it seems an odd way of handling an opponent by disseminating his very words! It was the accepted method of the times. Near the end of the century, St Robert Bellarmine was criticized for the lavish quotations he gave from heretical books. His defence was: "If that objection were sound, it would be necessary to prohibit the book of the holy bishop and martyr of Rochester in which he quotes verbatim the complete text of one of Luther's works". He was referring either to John Fisher's *Confutatio* (1523), a reply to Luther's *Assertio* (against the Bull of Leo X), or to his *Sacri Sacerdoti Defensio* (1525), an answer to Luther's *De abroganda missa privata*. Both of Fisher's books were in Latin and added to his European reputation as a theologian.

As an example of the method one of the shorter exchanges in More's *Confutatio* will serve.

Tyndale
Finally, I say not, charity God, or charity your neighbour, but love God, and love your neighbour.[8]

More
This is a pretty point of juggling, by which he would make the reader look aside that himself might play a false cast the while, and men should see wherein the question standeth. For he maketh as though I reproved that he hath this word love in his translation in any place at all, where I neither so said, nor so thought. But the fault I found, as in my dialogue I said plainly enough, was that he rather chose to use this word love, than this word charity, in such places as he might well have used this word charity, and where the Latin text was *charitas* and where this holy word charity was more proper for the matter than this indifferent word love. This was the fault that I found. And therefore whereof serveth this trifling between the noun and the verb. I let him not say, love thy neighbour, nor I bid him not say charity thy neighbour, nor good affection thy neighbour, nor good mind thy neighbour, nor more than drink thy neighbour. And yet as he may say there, give thy neighbour drink, so may he if

[8] *Tyndale's Works*, III, p. 21.

it please him, say, bear thy neighbour good mind, bear thy neighbour charity.⁹

This is a good specimen of More's style at its least involved; it will be noted that he takes eight times the space to answer Tyndale's point, and that he tends to repeat or vary the same idea at some length. If we leave aside the validity of the argument, we can see how Tyndale's more direct style would make a greater impact on his readers especially if they were not accustomed to following, as More was, a drawn-out exposition of a case.

The argument is occasionally eased by a flight of imagination that recalls a lighter-hearted More. He is discussing the relations between the tradition of the Church and the Gospels as against the Lutheran position that all truth is to be found in the New Testament. In his *Obedience of a Christian Man*, Tyndale had referred to Origen as "the greatest of heretics".¹⁰

But divers things were by God to them [the Apostles] and by them to other taught by mouth, and by tradition from hand to hand delivered, and from age to age hitherto continued in Christ's Church. And that I say truth in this point, I have divers good and honest witnesses to bring forth when time requireth, Saint Austin, Saint Jerome, Saint Cyprian, Saint Chrysostom and a great many more, which have also testified for my part in this matter more than a thousand year ago. Yet have I another ancient sad [serious] father also, one that they call Origen. And when I desired him to take the pain to come and bear witness with me in this matter, he seemed at first content. But, when I told him that he should meet with Tyndale, he blessed himself and shrank back and said, he had liever go some other way many a mile than once meddle with him. For I shall tell you, sir, quoth he, before this time a right honourable man very cunning [clever] and yet more virtuous, the good Bishop of Rochester, in a great audience brought me in for a witness against Luther and Tyndale, even in this same matter, about the time of the burning of Tyndale's evil translated Testament. But Tyndale as soon as he heard of my name, without any respect of honesty, fell in a rage with me and all too rated me, and called me stark heretic and that the starkest that ever was. This tale Origen told me and swore by Saint Simkin that he was never so said unto of such a lewd fellow since he

⁹E.W., p. 434.   ¹⁰*Tyndale's Works*, I, p. 220.

was first born of his mother, and therefore he would never meddle with Tyndale more.[11]

Bishop John Fisher's sermon in 1521 at the burning of Lutheran books contained a quotation from Origen and then continued: "Of the which words of Origen it clearly doth appear that many such traditions were left unto Christian people by Christ and his Apostles, the which we must follow notwithstanding they be not written in Scripture."[12]

There is no record of Fisher having preached at a burning of Tyndale's Testament which would not be before 1526, but he may have done so. Perhaps More had forgotten the circumstances of this 1521 sermon.

The *Confutation* increases in dryness as More plods his way across the dreary waste-land of controversy. At the Eighth Book, he left Tyndale to deal with a tract *What the Church is and who be thereof* by Robert Barnes, one of the most unhappy of the reformers. He fled abroad in 1528 from imprisonment as a heretic although he had publicly recanted; in 1531 he was back in England under a safe-conduct from the King or Thomas Cromwell. More was of the opinion that Barnes had forfeited his safe-conduct by continuing to advocate heretical opinions. "But let him go this once, for God shall find his time full well." After enjoying the passing favour of Henry and Cromwell on account of their negotiations with the German Reformers, Barnes was discarded; he had served their purpose. He took part in the condemnation in 1538 of John Lambert who was burned as a heretic. Barnes shared the same fate two years later, a day or so after the execution of Thomas Cromwell. In the argument against Barnes, More covered familar ground and there is no point in following him.

[11]E.W., p. 410.   [12]Fisher, *English Works*, p. 334.

J

Chapter XXIII

Resignation

WHEN THE COMMONS met in November 1529 they passed a number of Bills affecting the clergy; these regulated fees for probate, mortuary dues, pluralities, chantry priests, sanctuary, and benefit of clergy. It was a formidable assault on established usages but it was only a beginning. None of these affected the faith of the Church. Each dealt with a recognized and long-standing grievance. The significance of all this was that the secular power was invading a province that, hitherto, had been under the control of the ecclesiastical authorities. Convocation could, and indeed should, have dealt with such matters, but it acted too leisurely to meet the rising feeling of the populace. At that time, under the guidance of the aged Warham, the Convocation of Canterbury was considering how to improve the training of priests; this was a fundamental need on which both More and Erasmus, and especially Fisher, placed considerable stress, but it was not the kind of problem to excite popular support.

There is no record of More's opinions on these Bills; he shared the desire, so strongly expressed by Colet, for a remedy of acknowledged abuses, but he probably did not think that this was the business of the Commons. As he listened to the subsequent debate in the Lords, his sympathies may well have been with the view expressed by Bishop John Fisher:

> These men now among us seem to reprove the life and doings of the clergy, but after such a sort as they endeavour to bring them into contempt and hatred of the laity and so finding fault with other men's manners whom they have no authority to correct, omit and forget their own, which is far worse and much more out of order than the other. But if the truth were known, ye shall find that they rather hunger and thirst after riches and possessions of the clergy than after amendment of their faults and abuses. . . . Wherefore I will tell you, my lords, plainly what I think; except you resist manfully by your authority this violent heap of mischief offered by the

Commons, ye shall shortly see all obedience withdrawn, first from the clergy, and after yourselves, whereupon will ensure the utter ruin and danger of the Christian faith; and in place of it, that which is likely to follow, the most wicked and tyrannical government of the Turk; for ye shall find that all these mischiefs among them ariseth through lack of faith.[1]

Fisher's reference to "the Turk" may seem far-fetched and rhetorical, but the advance into Europe under Suleiman the Magnificent was a grave menace to Christendom. Belgrade had been taken in 1521, and the battle of Mohacs in 1526 broke the power of Hungary; three years later the Turks camped outside Vienna but later withdrew. The appeals of the Popes for a new crusade fell on deaf ears though lavish promises were made, only to be forgotten. The Christian Princes were too busy fighting one another; Lutheranism had split the Germans into two factions. Francis of France went so far after his defeat at Pavia in 1525 as to try to enlist the active support of Suleiman. The Turkish peril was part of the background of the period.

The Commons resented Bishop Fisher's attack on their motives and complained to the King, who was content to ask the Bishop to moderate his language; the Commons would have liked some more drastic rebuke.

Meanwhile the King's Matter was unresolved and Henry was seeking new ways of reaching his objective. The opinions of the theologians of Oxford and Cambridge and of foreign universities were sought and bought.[2] Early in 1530 the King sent an embassy to the Pope; it was an unpropitious moment as the Pope was then crowning Charles as Emperor at Bologna, and the tactless inclusion in the embassy of the Earl of Wiltshire, Anne Boleyn's father, did not increase the chances of success. Then the peers and prelates were persuaded to send a memorial to the Pope urging him to grant Henry's wishes. Neither Sir Thomas More nor Bishop John Fisher signed this petition and they thereby incurred the King's displeasure. Chapuys reported to the Emperor that for a time it looked as if the Great Seal would be taken from Sir

[1] *The Life of Fisher* (E.E.T.S.), p. 69.
[2] For Cranmer's part in this, see Chapter 2 of Jasper Ridley, *Thomas Cranmer* (1962).

Thomas More,[3] but he was not to have such an acceptable release from a burden that was becoming increasingly irksome.

Only a few weeks after the death of Wolsey in November 1530, the clergy as a body were accused in the King's Bench of having violated the statutes of provisors and praemunire; at first it was proposed to indict selected bishops (including Fisher), but a wholesale proceeding was felt more effective. The ground of the charge was that the clergy had recognized the Cardinal's authority as *legatus a latere*, a dignity that had been granted him at Henry's request and with his approval; to this was added the claim that the operation of the ecclesiastical courts was in itself a breach of praemunire—an even more ridiculous charge. Many were to find how easy it was to "fall within the compass of a *praemunire*" now that Henry had found this unexpected means to bring the clergy under control. It was a perversion of justice to apply these statutes collectively to men who had acted in good faith and with the tacit approval of the King. As a way out of the difficulty, it was proposed that the Canterbury Convocation should purchase the pardon of the clergy by a fine of £40,000, but this was considered too small by the King, so, after some bargaining, the fine was raised to the enormous figure of £100,000; but even this was not enough; the clergy must also accept the King as Supreme Head of the Church of England. In spite of Bishop Fisher's opposition, the clergy gave way but added the qualifying clause, "as far as the law of Christ allows". That was in February 1531; it was not until May that the York Convocation reached a decision; this was largely due to Tunstal who had succeeded Wolsey as Bishop of Durham, and, in the absence of an Archbishop, presided over the Convocation. He wrote to the King to express his objections to the title as it seemed to encroach on the spiritual functions of the clergy; he suggested as an alternative, "Only and Supreme Lord, after Christ, in Temporal Matters". The King's reply was a skilful and reassuring answer with which Tunstal seems to have been satisfied.[4] When Parliament passed an Act of Pardon for the clergy, the Commons added a second

[3]Span. Cal., pp. 599, 727, 762.
[4]See C. Sturge, *Cuthbert Tunstal* (1938), pp. 191-3.

Act pardoning the laity, but free of charge. They were taking no chances![5]

Chapuys again reported to the Emperor that Sir Thomas More was so distressed at these happenings that he wished to resign; he added that Bishop Fisher had fallen very ill, no doubt through anxiety.[6] The Emperor's ambassador would have liked to have close relations with the Lord Chancellor especially to get his views on the marriage question. More, however, was not talking with anyone on this dangerous topic; in return for the King's promise not to press him on the matter, he kept his own counsel. He not only asked Chapuys not to visit him, but refused to receive a letter from the Emperor. Such a letter, he said, he must in duty show to the King, and any suggestion that he was in communication with the Queen's nephew "might deprive him of the liberty he had always used in speaking boldly to King Henry in those matters which concerned Charles and Queen Catherine of Aragon".[7]

Public opinion was still in favour of the Queen, so the King decided to put his case again before Parliament for the information of its members. On 30 March 1531, Sir Brian Tuke, the clerk of the Parliament, delivered a message to the Lords from the King. Once more Henry explained how troubled he had been in conscience as to the validity of his marriage; then the opinions so far received from the universities were read aloud. Bishop Fisher was ill at the time, and both Warham and Tunstal were absent. Two bishops, Bath (John Clerk) and St Asaph's (Henry Standish), spoke in favour of Catherine, as did the Earl of Shrewsbury. When More was asked his opinion, he stated that his views were known to the King; that in itself told his listeners how he stood. The same message was then delivered to the Commons, but this time, according to Hall, the Chancellor opened the proceedings. Edward Hall represented Wenlock in this Parliament, so his report has first-hand value:

The Lord Chancellor said, you of this worshipful House I am sure be

[5]22 Hen. VIII, c. 15 (clergy), c. 16 (temporal subjects), c. 19 (York clergy).
[6]Span. Cal. IV, 2, i, p. 71.
[7]L.P., V, 148, 171. See Herbrüggen, 183A.

not so ignorant but you know well that the King our sovereign lord hath married his brother's wife, for she was both wedded and bedded with his brother Prince Arthur, and therefore you may surely say that he hath married his brother's wife, if this marriage be good or no, many clerks do doubt. Wherefore the King, like a virtuous prince, willing to be satisfied in his conscience, and also for the surety of his realm, hath with great deliberation consulted with great clerks, and hath sent my Lord of London here present [Stokesley] to the chief Universities of all Christendom to know their opinion and judgment in that behalf. And although that the Universities of Cambridge and Oxford had been sufficient to discuss the cause, yet because they be of this realm and to avoid all suspicion of partiality he sent into the realm of France, Italy the Pope's dominions, and Venetians to know their judgment in that behalf, which have concluded, written and sealed their determinations according as you shall hear read. [*Here the opinions of seven were read aloud by Sir Brian Tuke.*[8]] Now you of this Common House may report to your countries [counties] what you have seen and heard and then all men shall openly perceive that the King hath not attempted this matter of will or pleasure, as some strangers report, but only for the discharge of his conscience and surety of the succession of his realm. This is the cause of our repair hither to you, and now we will depart.[9]

The duty of making this report to the Commons could not have been a welcome one, but it may be noted that More was not voicing his own opinion; it seems certain that he himself was quite sincere at that time in believing that the King was acting "for the discharge of his conscience and surety of the succession". More's opposition to the divorce was that he was convinced that the dispensation for the marriage of Henry and Catherine was valid and could not be set aside.

Nonetheless More was finding himself, willy-nilly, involved in the King's policy. In Chancery he was, so to speak, his own master, but in Parliament he was the King's servant and he must have grown increasingly uneasy at being carried along in a direction that he was sure was wrong. His continued refusal to

[8]Hall, II, pp. 185-195. The opinions are printed in full.

[9]The Latin text of the opinions was printed by Berthelet in April 1531: *Gravissimae Academiarum Censurae.* Meanwhile Thomas Cranmer was preparing an English report which appeared in November with the title, *The Determination of the most excellent Universities.*

express his own opinions on the King's Matter must have proved disturbing and annoying to the King, who may still have hoped that his Chancellor would come to agree with him, but, for the present, Henry was unwilling to allow More to resign. It was useful to have as Chancellor, while the issue was still not clear, a man whose known integrity would quieten opponents with the hope that wiser counsel might prevail.

In his preoccupation with State affairs and with his legal duties, Thomas More could still find time to welcome scholars to his Chelsea house. Among them at this time was Simon Grynaeus who came with a letter of introduction from Erasmus. He was a lecturer in Greek at Basle and a supporter of the reforming party. Earlier he had followed Luther but had come to accept the opinions of Zwingli. He came to England in the spring of 1531 to study Greek manuscripts. More welcomed him for the sake of Erasmus, but as he was aware of his guest's Zwinglian views, he took precautions to prevent any proselytism. They had discussions together and these no doubt gave More a closer knowledge of how opinion was moving on the continent. He kept an eye on his visitor either personally or by arranging for his secretary, John Harris, to accompany Grynaeus. This is told us in the Preface to an edition of Plato which Grynaeus dedicated to John More in March 1534.

Your father at that time held the highest rank, but apart from that, by his many excellent qualities, he was clearly marked out as the chief man of the realm, whilst I was obscure and unknown. Yet for the love of learning, he found time to converse much with me even in the midst of public and private business: he, the Chancellor of the Kingdom, made me sit at his table: going to and from the Court, he took me with him and kept me ever at his side. He had no difficulty in seeing that my religious opinions were on many points different from his own, but his goodness and courtesy were unchanged. Though he differed so much from my views, yet he helped me in word and deed and carried through my business at his own expense. He gave us a young man, of considerable literary attainments, John Harris, as a companion on my journey, and to the authorities of the University of Oxford he sent a letter couched in such terms that at once not only were the libraries of all the Colleges thrown open to us but the students showed us the greatest favour. . . . Accordingly I returned to my country overjoyed at the treasures I had discovered, laden with your father's generous gifts and almost overwhelmed by his kindness.[10]

Grynaeus does not seem to have sensed the significance of the attention Thomas More gave to him and his inquiries. The courtesy was part of his nature, but he was not going to allow this visitor to spread his Zwinglism. In a letter dated 14 June 1531 More referred to this visit in writing to Erasmus. "Concerning the person you recommended to me for scholarly not for religious purposes, my friends have prudently put me on my guard so as not to be deceived by him."[11]

Among the members of the 1529 Parliament was Thomas Cromwell; at its first meeting he was still in the difficult period between the fall of Wolsey and his own rise to influence. It was not until early in 1531 that he became a member of the Council. It will be of interest here to consider his relations with Thomas More. Cromwell was only seven or eight years the younger. He came of the tradesman class and so had to make his way by his own ability and not by patronage. As a young man he spent two or three years in Italy, not as a scholar but in the rather rough everyday life of a country of quarrelsome princes and noblemen. He gained some knowledge of business affairs in Florence before going north to Antwerp, where the English merchants were quick to make use of his commercial acumen. He seems to have settled in London about 1512; he gained sufficient legal knowledge to strengthen his position in the world of trade and general affairs. He was a member of the 1523 Parliament of which Thomas More was Speaker. How he came to the notice of Wolsey is not known—in fact his whole early career is obscure—but he was soon acting as Wolsey's trusted business agent, nor was he one of the rats who left as soon as the Cardinal fell from power.

Cromwell had learned to keep his own counsel in a society where it was easier for a commoner to fail than to succeed in the struggle for the prizes of public life. He and Thomas More must

[10]Allen, 2502.   [11]Allen, 2659; Rogers, (44).

soon have come to know each other; they moved in the same official circle and they were neighbours in the City until More moved to Chelsea. The few indications we have suggest they were on friendly though not intimate terms. It is noticeable, for instance, that the tone of Roper's references to Cromwell is never resentful. Cromwell was of a social disposition and though he liked to entertain his friends, he carefully kept his social and his public life in separate compartments. Perhaps a hard experience of the world had made it difficult for him to be prodigal in friendship; he had always had to calculate the chances. The few glimpses we get of his unofficial life are tantalizing. Harpsfield, for instance, refers to conversations between More's old friend Antonio Bonvisi and Thomas Cromwell, but fails to give details with the remark "whereof there is no place to talk".[12] Did the three men come together? Both Bonvisi and Cromwell were actively interested in trade, and perhaps More's negotiations in Flanders would be a link. Then there is the intriguing letter from the Austin Friar Miles Coverdale to Thomas Cromwell. It is undated but as it is signed "Frere Myles Cov'dale", it must have been written before 1527 when Coverdale threw off his friar's habit. In this letter, Coverdale recalled to Cromwell's memory "the godly communication with your Mastership . . . in Master More's house". There were other Thomas Mores, but it may be this was our Thomas More. Finally, More's close official connection with Wolsey must have meant contacts with the Cardinal's business agent.

Let it be admitted that much of this is speculative; the fact remains that More and Cromwell must have known one another fairly well. Their views on some matters, for example the divorce and Church policy, were divergent, but it was not until about 1530 or even later that Cromwell let these views be known as far as was prudent. There is no evidence of any clash between the

---

[12]R. W. Chambers commented, "I sometimes think that Archdeacon Harpsfield deserved his sixteen years in the Fleet, for having left untold these anecdotes of Bonvisi". And what is one to think of Stapleton who failed to give us all the More letters he had on his desk with the excuse, "These letters and *all the others*, I will omit for already my account has become longer than I expected"? Perhaps it is churlish to wish for more when both writers gave us so much.
J*

two. We are, however, dealing with a stage in Cromwell's career when he had to watch his step on what was at best, for a commoner, a slippery slope and he would be careful not to antagonize one of More's reputation. Indeed, it was not until after More's resignation that Thomas Cromwell moved to the front of the political stage.[13]

According to Roper it was this obligation to present the university opinions to the Commons that decided Thomas More that he could not go on much longer; to quote Roper:

> Nevertheless, doubting lest further attempts after should follow, which, contrary to his conscience, by reason of his office, he was likely to be put unto, he made suit unto the Duke of Norfolk, his singular dear friend, to be a mean to the King that he might, with his Grace's favour, be discharged of that chargeable room of the Chancellorship, wherein, for certain infirmities of his body, he pretended himself unable any longer to serve.[14]

We must not interpret the word "pretended" in our modern sense of feigning but in the older meaning of putting forward a true statement about oneself. "Chargeable" here means "burdensome". It was certainly not a diplomatic illness. A year later, More told Erasmus that "a disorder of I know not what nature has attacked my chest. . . . For when it had plagued me without abatement for some months the physicians whom I consulted gave their opinion that the long continuance of it was dangerous."[15] He was warned that his long hours of stooping over his writing desk were making his cure uncertain; we must remember that he was still working on his controversial books.

On 11 July 1531 King Henry saw Queen Catherine for the last time; she did not realize that it was so; he had gone off hunting without even saying goodbye.

In March 1532 the Commons presented to the King a Petition or Supplication against the Ordinaries (Bishops) setting out their grievances against the clergy; this was a summary of complaints

[13]Thomas Cromwell is one of the more enigmatic Tudor characters. John Foxe in his *Acts and Monuments* regarded him as one of the Early Fathers of the Reformation; present-day historians regard him as one of the Early Fathers of the Civil Service. See A. G. Dickens, *Thomas Cromwell and the English Reformation* (1959).
[14]Roper, p. 51.   [15]Allen, 2659; Rogers (44).

that had become almost commonplace, but it is interesting to note that earlier drafts, going back to 1529, contain corrections and alterations in the handwriting of Thomas Cromwell, but the exact history of the documents is not now discernible. The Commons do not seem to have regarded it as a matter of urgency, for, at the time of presenting the final Supplication, they begged the King to consider the "pain, charge and cost his humble subjects of the nether House had sustained" and to discharge them so that they could go home. Henry shrewdly pointed out that, having started such a hare, they could not give up the chase: "therefore if you will profit of your complaint, you must tarry the time". The Supplication was submitted to the Canterbury Convocation; the reply was a spirited defence by the bishops, which the King handed to the Speaker (Audley) with the comment, "We think their answer will smally please you, for it seemeth to us very slender; you be a great sort of wisemen, I doubt not but you will look circumspectly on the matter, and we will be indifferent between you". He went on to complain of a speech made in the Commons by "one Temse" in which he had dared to urge that the King should "take the Queen again into his company". Once more Henry told the Commons how sorely he had been "vexed in conscience".[16]

While Convocation was discussing the Supplication, the Lords were occupied with a Bill to abolish the payment of Annates (the first year's revenues paid by bishops to the Pope). This roused some opposition in the Commons but the reason is obscure; perhaps this reflects the general confusion in men's minds as to the King's intentions. The application of the subsequent Act was postponed so that it could be used as a threat to Rome.[17]

Hall recorded the last appearance of the Chancellor before the Commons:

When the Parliament was begun again after Easter [1532] there came down to the Common House the Lord Chancellor, the Dukes of Norfolk and Suffolk, the Earls of Arundel, Oxford, Northumber-

---

[16]Hall, II, 203, 209.

[17]Hen. VIII, c. 20 (1532). Finally applied, 25 Hen. VIII, c. 20 (1534). The bishops did not profit; annates were paid to the King instead of to the Pope. In 1704 these became Queen Anne's Bounty.

land, Rutland, Wiltshire and Sussex, and after they were set, the Lord Chancellor declared how the King was advertised by his Council and in especial by the Duke of Norfolk, how on the Marches between England and Scotland was very little habitation on the English side, but on the Scottish side was great habitation. . . . Wherefore the King intended to make dwelling houses there.[18]

For this purpose he asked for a "reasonable aid toward his charges". This was granted but there seems to be no further information about this early housing scheme.

The negotiations on the Supplication resulted in a number of demands being made on Convocation; their effect was to cripple the powers of that body, but Henry was still not content. On 11 May 1532 he announced a great discovery, all the more astonishing in that he was now in the twenty-fifth year of his reign. Hall recalled the incident:

> The King sent for the Speaker and twelve of the Common House, having with him eight lords, and said to them, "Well-beloved subjects, we thought that the clergy of our realm had been our subjects wholly, but now we have well perceived that they be but half our subjects, yea, and scarce our subjects: for all the Prelates at their consecration make an oath to the Pope clean contrary to the oath they make to us, so that they seem to be his subjects and not ours; the copy of both the oaths I deliver here to you requiring you to invent some order, that we be not this deluded of our spiritual subjects".[19]

Had the Lord Chancellor been present, Hall would probably have said so.

Meanwhile yet another matter was agitating Convocation. The King had expressed his opinion that the bishops should no longer have the power to seize heretics, saying, "it is not their duty to meddle with bodies and they are only doctors of the soul". Chapuys reported to the Emperor that "The Chancellor and the Bishops oppose him. The King is very angry, especially with the Chancellor and the Bishop of Winchester [Gardiner], and is determined to carry the matter." Convocation at length gave up the struggle and agreed to all the King's demands; they submitted

[18]Hall, II, p. 204.   [19]Hall, II, p. 210.

on 15 May 1532. On the following day Sir Thomas More surrendered the Great Seal to the King. Roper tells us how they parted:

> Then, at a time convenient, by his Highness's appointment, repaired he to his Grace, to yield up unto him the Great Seal. Which, as his Grace, with thanks and praise for his worthy service in that office, courteously at his hands received, so pleased it his Highness further to say unto him, that for the service that he before had done him, in any suit which he should after have unto him, that either should concern his honour (for that word it liked his Highness to use unto him) or that should appertain unto his profit, he should find his Highness good and gracious lord unto him.[20]

It has been usual to see a direct connection between the submission of the clergy in Convocation and More's resignation, but in those days resignation of high office was not such a simple process as today; ill-health and old age were legitimate reasons, but voluntary withdrawal from the King's service implied opposition to his policy and that could be a dangerous proceeding. As we have seen, Roper tells us that Sir Thomas had, for some time, been urging his resignation through the good offices of the Duke of Norfolk, on the grounds of ill-health.

However great the sense of relief may have been, Thomas More must have given up his office with a heavy heart. It was true that he had been able to effect some improvements in the administration of the law, but he had seen the separation of the King and Queen, and the increasing pressure on the clergy. The future was full of menace. He tried to pass on to the coming man, Thomas Cromwell, what he had learned by bitter experience. As Roper tells us:

> Now upon his resignment of his office, came Master Thomas Cromwell, then in the King's high favour, to Chelsea to him, with a message from the King; wherein, when they had thoroughly communed together: "Master Cromwell," quoth he, "you are now entered into the service of a most noble, wise and liberal prince. If you will follow my poor advice, you shall, in your counsel giving unto his Grace, ever tell him what he ought to do, but never what

[20]Roper, p. 52.

he is able to do. So shall you show yourself a true faithful servant and a right worthy councillor. For if a lion knew his own strength, hard were it for any man to rule him."[21]

Did Cromwell know what the dying Wolsey had said to Sir William Kingston, Constable of the Tower?

He is sure a prince of a royal courage, and hath a princely heart; and rather than he will either miss or want any part of his will or appetite, he will put the loss of one half of his realm in danger. . . . I warn you to be well advised and assured what matter ye put in his head, for ye shall never put it out again.

It was a hazardous service in which Thomas Cromwell was now engaged.

[21]Roper, p. 56.

CHAPTER XXIV

Interregnum

WHEN HE GAVE UP the Great Seal, Sir Thomas More lost the greater part of his income. As Lord Chancellor he had £142 15s a year and an additional £200 as a judge of the Star Chamber Court; his perquisites included £64 a year for twelve tuns of wine, and £16 for wax. It is not known how much he received in fees but it was probably less than the £2,000 year that Wolsey is said to have had. The manors he possessed (South in Kent, Doglington and Fringeford in Oxfordshire) were small and together did not bring him in substantial rents. His salary as a councillor (£100) was continued until Easter 1534 when the King stopped it. He had not feathered his own nest and many of his contemporaries must have thought him foolish not to have done so. He faced the situation with his usual good humour and took counsel with his family, which meant not only his children but his sons-in-law. William Roper has given us an account of the occasion:

> calling us all that were his children unto him, and asking our advice how we might now, in this decay of his ability (by the surrender of his office so impaired that he could not, as he was wont, and gladly would, *bear out the whole charges of them all himself*) from thence forth be able to live and continue together, as he wished we should.

They were silent, so in his bantering way he put the case to them for economy.

> "Then will I", said he, "show my poor mind to you. I have been brought up", quoth he, "at Oxford, at an Inn of Chancery, at Lincoln's Inn, and also in the King's Court, and so forth from the lowest degree to the highest, and yet have I in yearly revenues at this present little above an hundred pounds by the year, so that now must we hereafter, if we like to live together, be contented to become contributaries together. But, by my counsel, it shall not be best for us to fall to the lowest fare first; we will not therefore descend to

Oxford fare, nor to the fare of New Inn, but we will begin with Lincoln's Inn diet, where many right worshipful and of good years do live full well; which, if we find not ourselves the first year able to maintain, then will we next year go one step down to New Inn fare, wherewith many an honest man is well contented. If that exceed our ability too, then will we the next year after descend to Oxford fare, where many grave, learned and ancient fathers be continually conversant; which, if our power stretch not to maintain neither, then may we yet, with bags and wallets, go a-begging together and hoping that for pity some good folk will give us their charity, at every man's door to sing *Salve Regina*, and so still keep company and be merry together."[1]

This playful speech has been taken too literally. More was saying pleasantly to his married children that they must now become "contributaries" to the upkeep of the household instead of being his guests whenever they stayed at Chelsea. His banter covered his own chagrin at having to make such a request, but it was part of the price he had to pay for his freedom of action. Fortunately his four children were comfortably off. John More's wife, Alice Cresacre, brought him her Yorkshire estate. Each of the three sons-in-law was a landed man; indeed William Roper may already have been on the way to wealth. More had a second purpose in mind; it seems that Dame Alice found it difficult to grasp all the implications in her husband's loss of place; so he gently intimated that the housekeeping would have to be on a greatly reduced scale. A story told by Roper illustrates how slow she was to adjust herself to the new situation:

And whereas upon the holidays during his high Chancellorship, one of his gentlemen, when the service at the church was done, ordinarily used to come to my lady his wife's pew, and say unto her, "Madam, my lord is gone", the next holiday after the surrender of his office and departure of his gentlemen, he came unto my lady his wife's pew himself, and making a low courtesy, said unto her, "Madam, my lord is gone".

The staff at Chelsea had to be severely cut down; this may have upset Sir Thomas as much as any of the material consequences

[1]Roper, pp. 52-55.

17. FAMILY GROUP

18. DAME ALICE MORE

19. MARGARET ROPER

20. WILLIAM ROPER

21.   MARGARET ROPER

22.

THE
MORE
MONUMENT
AND CHAPEL
IN CHELSEA
OLD CHURCH

23. SAINT JOHN FISHER

24.
WESTMINSTER
HALL

of his resignation. He was parting with faithful men and women
who would go with regret. We get a glimpse of some of them
in *The Widow Edyth*. Roper noted that he "placed all his gentlemen and yeomen with bishops and noblemen, and his eight
watermen with the Lord Audley that in the same office followed
him, to whom he also gave his great barge".

Cresacre More tells us: "Wherefore his children went to their
own livings, all but my uncle Roper and my aunt, who lived in
the house next to him". The household was now reduced to
Thomas More and his wife and a servant or two, except when
their children visited them.[2]

While this sudden change meant a careful economy, it did not
mean hardship;[3] that was to come later when all his property was
forfeited to the King. There is no doubt that he knew that sooner
or later he would have to face a crisis of decision; Wolsey's fate
was a warning of what might come. So he gave a hint to his
family.

> He showed unto them afore what trouble might after fall unto him;
> wherewith and like virtuous talk, he had so long before his trouble
> encouraged them, that when he after fell into trouble indeed, his
> trouble to them was a great deal less: *Quia spicula previsa minus
> laedunt* [because troubles foreseen hurt less].

As he had once told his family, "We may not look at our pleasure to
go to heaven in feather beds".[4]

Had it not been for his family responsibilities, More would
have welcomed his release from State affairs. Some years earlier,
in sending a copy of *Utopia* to Warham with a letter congratulat-
ing the Archbishop on his resignation of the Chancellorship, he
had said:

> I ever judged your paternity happy in the way you exercised your
> office of Chancellor, but I esteem you much happier now that you
> have laid it down and entered that most desirable leisure in which

[2]Cresacre More, p. 205.

[3]Harpsfield (p. 145), unsupported by Roper, Stapleton or Cresacre More, says that the
household were so reduced in circumstances that they warmed themselves at a fire of 'a
great burden of fern'. This is incredible, because (1) it is impracticable, and (2) the sons-in-
law would not have allowed things to come to such a pass.

[4]Roper, p. 26.

you can live for yourself and God. Such leisure, in my opinion, is not only more pleasant than the labour you have forsaken, but more honourable than all your honours.[5]

Warham was not to have that "desirable leisure" for the cares of the Church increased with the years; in the last months of a long life he protested against the usurpation of the authority of the Church by Parliament and dared to remind Henry VIII of the outcome of the struggle between Henry II and St Thomas of Canterbury. Had he been a younger man he might well have been more active in Convocation against the encroachments of King and Parliament. He is believed to have been over eighty years of age when he died, three months after the resignation of Sir Thomas More.[6]

More expressed the same sentiments about retirement in a letter to Erasmus in June 1532:

From the time I was a boy I have longed, dear Desiderius, that what I rejoice in you having always enjoyed, I myself might one day enjoy too—that is, that being freed from public business, I might have some time to devote to God and myself, and that, by the grace of a great and good God, and by the favour of an indulgent prince, I have at last obtained.[7]

He went on to lament the fact that his poor health might rob his leisure of some of its ease.

A year later he wrote again to Erasmus and this time sent him a copy of an epitaph he had composed for "my tomb"[8] in Chelsea Old Church. He explained his reasons for doing this:

Some gossips here have been spreading it about that I had resigned against my will, though I pretend it was not so. So when I set up my tomb, I determined to state the matter as it is in my epitaph, that anyone might refute it who could. As soon as they had taken note of it, as they could not show it to be false, they found fault with it as

[5]Rogers, 31.
[6]He died 22 August 1532. "Sat est viatici", he said on his death-bed when they told him he had only £30 in ready money. Shade of Wolsey!
[7]Allen, 2659; Rogers (44).
[8]Strictly speaking it was not a tomb but a memorial tablet in an architectural setting. The family vault is under the More Chapel. The simplicity of the memorial is in pleasing contrast to the later pretentious monuments that encumber the church. The history of the tablet is not clear; it has possibly been twice re-cut. It was moved to its present position in 1666.

boastful. I preferred this to allowing the other rumour to gain ground, not indeed for my own sake, for I do not care very much what men say of me, provided that God approves of me; but since I had written in our own tongue some little books against some of our defenders of contentious doctrines, I considered that I ought to defend the integrity of my name; and that you may know how boastfully I have written you shall receive my epitaph, by which you will see that in my security of conscience I by no means flatter them, to prevent them from saying about me whatever they please. I have waited now till the meeting of Parliament[9] since I exercised and resigned my office, but as yet no one has come forward to attack me. Either I have been so innocent or else so cautious, that my opponents must let me boast of one or other of these qualities.

More then went on to refer to the tributes he received from the King on his resignation:

The King has spoken many times privately, and twice in public. For in words that I blush to repeat, when my illustrious successor [Audley] was installed, the King by the mouth of the Duke of Norfolk, Lord High Treasurer of England, ordered him to testify with what difficulty he had yielded to my request to retire. And not contented with this, the King out of his singular goodness to me, had the same tribute repeated by my successor in his own presence at the opening of Parliament.

The expressions Thomas More here used when speaking of Henry VIII may puzzle us since we know what was to come. The epitaph speaks of the "incomparable kindness of his most indulgent King", and, in the last two letters he wrote to Erasmus, More spoke of "the favour of an indulgent prince", and of "his singular goodness to me". There is no reason to think that he used such phrases—and others of later date could be given— without meaning what he said. It must be remembered that to him, and to his contemporaries, the office of a prince was of divine sanction, and he could never write of the holder of that office without full deference. This attitude—so hard for us to share— makes it all the more significant that, ultimately, he felt compelled

---

[9]Parliament was adjourned on 14 May 1532; this may have determined the date of More's resignation. It reassembled on 4 Feb. 1533. So this letter was written soon after that date and not as late as June as suggested in Rogers (46); Allen, 2831; this is the last extant letter from More to Erasmus.

in conscience to oppose that prince outside the Council. We have noted two comments More made that imply a shrewd estimate of the King's character, one to Roper and the other to Cromwell,[10] but these defects or weaknesses in the man who held the office in no way lessened the duty that More, as a subject, owed to the King. Where he disagreed with the King, he kept silence in public; his arguments were stated in the Council or to the King himself. His duty, as he saw it, was to give the best counsel he could and to do the work entrusted to him with integrity. More's expressions of gratitude were not conventional; he had indeed received many marks of royal favour, not the least being his exceptional choice to be Chancellor. Even to the bitter end, his attitude towards Henry was deeply influenced by the memory of those years when Thomas More was the councillor the King most liked to have at his side. More could not forget those halcyon days of their early friendship. There is no record of a broken friendship in More's life; there is no record of an unbroken friendship in Henry's life.

The opening lines of the epitaph[11] briefly record the official positions Thomas More had held in the City and the State. His share in the making of the Peace of Cambrai clearly gave him special satisfaction, and this led him to pay a tribute to Cuthbert Tunstal, "than whom no one could be more learned, wiser, or more virtuous". More then turned to his own position and claimed that neither the King, nor the nobility, nor the people could find fault with him though "he had been relentless to thieves, murderers and heretics". Then followed the praise of his father already quoted.[12] Thomas More next justified his own retirement. The passing of the years and the presence of eleven grandchildren made him feel that he was growing old. This was shown also by the distressing complaint he had in his chest. Ever since boyhood he had looked forward to a period of retirement from public life so that he could make his peace with God. "By the incomparable kindness of his most indulgent King" he had been allowed to

[10]See above, p. 75, and p. 202.
[11]Harpsfield, pp. 279-81, gives the full Latin text.
[12]See above, p. 19.

resign his offices. He begged the prayers of the reader. Finally came the verses to Jane and Alice More that have been quoted.[13]

There is something macabre or morbid to our minds in arranging one's own tomb and composing the epitaph, but in those days men were concerned to preserve their reputations for future generations, and, those who could afford it, made careful provision for their family tombs. Cardinal Wolsey had his sarcophagus prepared and so did Bishop Fisher.[14] The More monument was of a plain design compared with contemporary styles. No one at that period would regard such self-obituaries as egoistic; it was something a man owed his family. Thomas More did, however, as he wrote to Erasmus, expect to be accused of taking pride in his achievements. No one seems to have done so, nor is that surprising for his references to himself were factual. He gave a list of the public offices he had filled but made no claims for exceptional virtue or piety, such as he ascribed to his father and to Cuthbert Tunstal. His emphasis was on the voluntary nature of his withdrawal from public life—an indication of how unusual such a course was in those days. This point seems to have been much on his mind. It is worth noting what he did not say. He made no comment on his integrity as a lawyer and judge, nor did he refer to his classical and patristic learning; he made no mention of *Utopia* nor of his controversial writings. The plea with which he ended the main epitaph gave a glimpse of the deeper motives of life:

> That he may not have erected this monument in vain while he yet lived, that he dread not the approach of death, but meet it cheerfully from the love of Christ, and that he find death not the end of all things but the entrance to a happier life, do thou, reader, help him with thy pious prayers as well now while he lives as after his death.

During this period of waiting, Thomas More must have found great pleasure when his son John made a translation of a sermon by Frederick Nausea on the words "Do this in remembrance of

---

[13]See above, p. 75.

[14]Wolsey's was eventually used for the entombment of Nelson in St Paul's; Fisher's was put aside after his execution and the materials were found in the eighteenth century under piles of rubbish.

me". John was anxious to get it printed before Easter 1533 as good reading for Lent. His next translation was of a very different book; this was an account of the land of Prester John by the Portuguese writer, Damiao de Goes. Both these small books were printed by John's cousin, William Rastell, in 1533.[15]

[15]Nausea, born in 1480, became Bishop of Vienna and died at the Council of Trent in 1552. The Nausea sermon is printed in *Moreana*, No. 2 (1964), and Prester John in facsimiles of both the original and the translation, in *Moreana*, No. 14 (1967).

CHAPTER XXV

"*The Apologye*"

IT WAS NOT only ill-health and family cares that prevented Thomas More from enjoying the full fruits of his retirement. His duty, for such he regarded it, was to continue the fight against heresy. The second part of his *Confutation* was on the stocks; this was published in 1533. At the end of 1532 he wrote *A Letter . . . impugning the erroneous writing of John Frith against the Blessed Sacrament of the Altar*.[1] Frith, then about thirty years of age, was a prisoner in the Tower on a charge of heresy. He had gone abroad in 1528 and had associated with the German reformers. It was while he was on a private visit to England that he was arrested, not, as has been said, by More's instructions. Frith was not in England while More was Lord Chancellor but arrived two months after the resignation. He wrote a pamphlet on the Holy Eucharist putting forward the views that are now set out in the XXVIIIth Article of the Church of England, which declares that "the Body of Christ is given, taken, and eaten, in the Supper, only after an heavenly and spiritual manner". Three copies of this pamphlet in manuscript came into More's hands, and his answer took the form of a *Letter* which he sent to various sympathizers with Frith. It was printed in 1533.

The Blessed Sacrament meant so much to Thomas More that any tampering with the teaching of the Church on the Eucharist hurt him more deeply than attacks on any other dogma. Indeed it would be true to say that the Eucharist became the centre of More's theology. Yet the tone of his letter is not harsh; it may be that he hoped that "this young man", as he called Frith, was still open to conviction of his error. He even delayed printing for this reason, but it became clear that Frith was not likely to change his views. One passage will show the manner of the argument. Frith maintained that an allegorical and not a literal meaning should be

[1]Gibson, 45; Rogers, 190.

given to the words, "This is my body", "This is my blood".
More replied:

> And over this, the very circumstances of the places in the Gospel in
> which our Saviour speaketh of that sacrament, may make open
> difference of his speech in this matter and of all those other, and that
> as he spake all those but in allegory, so spake he this plainly meaning
> that he spoke of his very body and his very blood besides [aside]
> from all allegories. For neither when Our Lord said he was a very
> vine, nor when he said he was the door, there was none that heard
> him that anything marvelled thereof. And why? For because they
> perceived well that he meant not that he was a material vine indeed,
> nor a material door neither. But when he said that his flesh was very
> meat, and his blood was very drink, and that they should not be
> saved but if they did eat his flesh and drink his blood, then were
> they all in such wonder thereof that they could not abide. And
> wherefore? But because they perceived well by his words and
> manner of circumstances used in the speaking of them, that Christ
> spake of his very flesh and his very blood indeed. For else the
> strangeness of his words would have made them to have taken it as
> well for an allegory, as either his words or the vine or of the door.
> And then would they have no more marvelled at the one than they
> did at the other. But now whereas at the vine and the door they
> marvelled nothing, yet at the eating of his flesh and drinking of his
> blood, they so sore marvelled, and were so sore moved, and thought
> the matter so hard, and the wonder so great, that they asked how
> could that be, and went almost all their way whereby we may well
> see that he spake these words in such wise as the hearers perceived
> that he meant it not in a parable nor an allegory, but spake of his
> very flesh and his very blood indeed.[2]

The year of the Supplication of the Commons saw the publication of *A Treatise concerning the Division between the Spirituality
and the Temporality*. This was published anonymously, but the
author was the septuagenarian Christopher Saint-German, whose
Doctor and Student, printed by John Rastell in 1523, had become a
standard handbook for legal students. There may have been some
connection between the Supplication of the Commons and "The
Book of the Division" as Thomas More called Saint-German's

---

[2]Rogers, 190, p. 447. More's reference is to John 6, 41-58. See below, p. 273. John
Rastell joined in the controversy with Frith and seems to have been converted to his views.

book; but this cannot be established beyond noting that they covered much the same ground. More did not know the author's name. Saint-German regretted that the clergy and the laity were at loggerheads, but he concentrated his criticism on what he considered to be the faults of the clergy at whose doors he laid the blame for "the division"; he had nothing to say on the faults of the laity. His list of grievances ranged widely over those complaints that were commonly being made; some were fair; others were little better than gossip of the street. He did not attempt to support his assertions by evidence but introduced them with the words "some say". His inference was that the powers of the Church courts should be curtailed and that the common law should be given full scope. He looked to the bishops to put their house in order.

This short book was the occasion for the writing of *The Apologye*, printed in 1533, but More's criticism of Saint-German is part of a more general defence of the clergy and himself. Some of the accusations against the Church were well founded as More must have admitted, and indeed were of the kind that Colet and Erasmus and himself had made. One has only to refer to Colet's Convocation sermon to find similar, but not such exaggerated or irresponsible, complaints. More was rightly sceptical of Saint-German's sincerity in setting himself up as "the Pacifier" of these discords. A less biased arbitrator was needed.

In a later work Thomas More explained that

> mine *Apologye* is an answer and a defence not only for my former books, wherein the new brethren[3] began to find certain faults, but over that in the selfsame part wherein I touch the "Book of Division" it is an answer and a defence of many good, worshipful folk against the malicious slander and obloquy so generally set forth with so many some-says in that seditious book. The selfsame piece is also an answer and a defence of the very good, old, and long-approved laws of the realm and of the whole corpse of Christendom; which laws this Pacifier in his "Book of Division", to the encouragement of heretics and peril of the Catholic faith, with warm words and cold reasons oppugneth.[4]

[3]For an account of such names as "the known men", "the brethren", etc., applied to early Protestants, see E. G. Rupp, *The English Protestant Tradition* (1949), ch. I.
[4]E.W., p. 931.

More was faced with a dilemma. On the one hand he recognized that there were abuses within the Church that urgently called for reform; on the other he saw clearly that the intervention of the civil power combined with the spread of heresy would undermine men's faith and foster a spirit of discontent that could ultimately disrupt the unity of both Church and State. He decided that the paramount need was to preserve the faith and unity of "Christ's Catholic known Church".

The Apologye is not solely concerned with "The Book of the Division", but with a number of criticisms made of More's earlier controversial works; here he reinforced his previous arguments against points made by Tyndale, Barnes and Frith. The second half of the book criticizes only a portion of "The Book of the Division"; More deals with complaints against the clergy and with the treatment of heretics. *The Apologye* is of interest now chiefly for its autobiographical passages.

The charge had been made against him that he had defended the clergy for personal profit. Tyndale declared that "covetousness blinded the eyes of that gleering fox". To this More replied:

> And for as all the lands and fees that I have in all England, beside such lands and fees as I have of the gift of the King's most noble grace is not at this day nor shall be while my mother-in-law [stepmother] (whose life and good health I pray God keep and continue) worth yearly to my living the sum of full fifty pounds. And thereof I have some of my wife, and some by my father (whose soul our Lord assoil) and some have I also purchased myself and some fees have I of some temporal men. . . . I have not had one groat granted me since I first wrote, or went about to write my *Dialogue*, and that was, ye wot well, the first work that I wrote in these matters.[5]

His step-mother, another Lady Alice More, had Gobions as her jointure after Sir John More's death. She survived Sir Thomas for some years; her death occurred in 1545 and she was buried at Northaw. More went on to deal with the specific charge that he had received money from the clergy. He admitted that he had been offered such a gift but had refused it saying, "as I plainly told them, I would rather have cast their money into the Thames than

[5] *Apologye*, p. 51.

take it". Roper adds to our knowledge of this proffered gift. A sum of four or five thousand pounds had been subscribed by the bishops and others and a deputation of Tunstal of Durham, Clerk of Bath and Wells, and Veysey of Exeter, waited upon the ex-Chancellor and asked him to accept this gift in recognition of the valuable work he had done, and was doing, in combating heresy. They would realize that More had lost the greater part of his income. Tunstal may have felt especially responsible as he had urged More to undertake the work. More refused the gift saying:

> For though your offer, my lords, be indeed very friendly and honourable, yet set I so much by my pleasure and so little by my profit, that I would not, in good faith, for so much and much more too, have lost the rest of so many nights' sleep as was spent upon the same. And yet wish would I, for all that, upon condition that all heresies were suppressed, that all my books were burned and my labour utterly lost.[6]

Roper added, "Thus departing were they fain to restore unto every man his own again."

We can link one passage in *The Apologye* with More's personal life.

> Then preacheth this Pacifier yet farther that the clergy should wear hair. He is surely somewhat sore if he bind all thereto, but among them I think that many do already and some whole religion [religious] doth. But yet saith this Pacifier that it doth not appear that they do so. Ah, well said! But now if all the lack stand in that point, that such holiness is hid, so that men may not see it, it shall be from henceforth well done for them, and so they will do if they be wise, upon this advertisement and preaching of this good Pacifier, come out of their cloisters every man into the market place, and there kneel down in the kennel and make their prayers in the open streets and wear their shirts of hair in sight upon their cowls and then shall it appear, and men shall see it. And surely for their shirts of hair in this way were there none hypocrisy and yet were there also good policy, for then should it not prick them.[7]

This recalls the following passage in Roper's book.

> And albeit outwardly he appeared honourable like one of his calling yet inwardly he no such vanities esteeming, secretly next his body

[6]Roper, p. 48.   [7]*Apologye*, p. 119.

wore a shirt of hair; which my sister More a young gentlewoman, in the summer, as he sat at supper, singly in his doublet and hose, wearing thereupon a plain shirt without ruff or collar, chancing to spy, began to laugh at it. My wife, not ignorant of his manner, perceiving the same, privily told him of it; and he, being sorry that she saw it, presently amended it.[8]

"My sister More" was Anne Cresacre who was married to John More in 1529. She evidently did not hold her father-in-law in great awe; the scene is a glimpse of their easy family relations. Dame Alice was of course aware that her husband wore a shirt of hair. Father Bouge, in the letter from which a quotation has been made, wrote:

This mistress his wife desired me to counsel him to put off that hard and rough shirt of hair: and yet is very long, almost a twelvemonth, ere she knew of this habergeon of hair; it tamed his flesh till the blood was seen on his clothes.[9]

An important autobiographical section of *The Apologye* deals with the accusation made by Saint-German that the clergy were too hasty and often unjust in their treatment of heretics. More replied that he could recall only seven cases during the previous four or five years of heretics being condemned in the Bishops' Courts and handed over to the sheriffs for the penalty of burning prescribed by the civil law. Only three of these were in the London diocese. He challenged the Pacifier to appear before "the King's Grace and his Council, or in what place he list, and there prove, calling me thereto, that any one of all these had wrong".[10]

The period he gave covered his own Chancellorship and possibly during the year before his appointment as Chancellor when a Thomas More was on the Commission of the Peace for Middlesex; this was probably our Sir Thomas as he was then living in Middlesex. Thus he could have had authority to investigate possible cases of heresy during a period of three years at most. A recent estimate is that, *during the seven years 1527-33, only five heretics were burned in London* and More was not necessarily involved with each of these; there are no records of any in Middlesex.[11] The magistrate carried out a preliminary inquiry to

[8]Roper, p. 48.   [9]See above, p. 76.   [10]*Apologye*, p. 105.
[11]Philip Hughes, *The Reformation in England*, I, p. 131.

see if there was a *prima facie* case; if he decided that there was, then he delated the man to the Bishop; after that the magistrate had no further standing in the case. These facts make it clear that some of the references to Thomas More's dealings with heretics are wide of the mark. John Foxe in his *Acts and Monuments* (*Book of Martyrs*)[12] accused More of brutality towards the heretics he examined. J. A. Froude swallowed Foxe's stories hook, line and sinker, and wrote of "the merciless bigot" who "fed the stake with heretics". Once a reputation of that kind is given, it is difficult to eradicate it. For instance, the author of a popular history of Tudor England published in 1950 and frequently reprinted, writes of "the More who committed Protestants to the Fires".[13] The reader is given the impression that Thomas More was personally and frequently responsible for condemning heretics to the stake. He had no such powers. After his preliminary examination, the matter was judged, not by him nor by any other magistrate, but by the Bishop's Court. If the heretic proved obdurate—the vast majority abjured—he was handed over to the Sheriff for the dread penalty prescribed by law. There was no civil trial after the Bishop's verdict.

There are indications that Thomas More would invite suspected heretics to come to him at Chelsea and discuss their "new-fangled" doctrines with them in the hope of bringing them back to the true faith. This, however, was not a judicial process but a charitable attempt to argue his visitors out of their mistaken ideas.

This is not to claim that Thomas More was more lenient to heretics than in fact he was, for in his own epitaph he declared that he was "relentless towards thieves, murderers and heretics".[14] The juxtaposition is significant. To him and to his orthodox contemporaries and to those who set up new orthodoxes of their own, a heretic was not only an enemy of the truth, seducing souls

[12]John Foxe's partisanship led him to exaggerations and to build up some cases on shaky foundations. In spite of this, his remarkable book contains valuable material, but it needs careful sifting. A scholarly edition is much to be desired.

[13]S. T. Bindoff, *Tudor England* (Penguin History), p. 104.

[14]At some later date, perhaps under Edward VI or Elizabeth, the word "haereticisque" was deleted; the gap remains.

to their damnation, but a threat to the civil order. To Erasmus he wrote:

> As to my declaration that I gave trouble to heretics, I did this deliberately. For I so entirely detest that race of men, that there is none to which I would be more hostile, unless they amend. For every day more and more, I find them to be of such a kind that I greatly dread what they are bringing on the world.[15]

The fullest exposition of his attitude towards heretics is found in the last six chapters of his *Dialogue Concerning Heresies*. The summary of the thirteenth chapter of Book IV reads:

> The author sheweth his opinion concerning the burning of heretics and that it is lawful, necessary and well done, and sheweth also that the clergy doth not procure it, but only the good and politic provision of the temporality.

To us it seems a quibble to say that the clergy, that is the bishop, was not responsible for the burning but only for handing over the heretic to the civil authorities. More's point was that the clergy were not acting under canon law but under statute law, a law that had been made in 1401, *De heretico comburendo*, for dealing with the Lollards, and had proved effective in their suppression; it could prove equally effective, men thought, in dealing with Lutheranism.

It has been objected that More's attitude towards heretics was at variance with the toleration shown in Utopia. This view is based on a superficial reading. More narrated, for instance, how a convert to Christianity had been over-zealous (a not uncommon trait in converts) and had been banished "for inflaming the people to sedition". Those who "mixed reproaches or violence" in advocating their religious opinions were "condemned to banishment or slavery". Those who were guilty of impiety and did not repent were "seized by the Senate and punished". Those were the notions More ascribed to his imagined island in 1516. The events in Europe during the following decade—the rise of Luther, the sack of Rome, the Peasants' War—sharpened men's opposition to those who would disrupt both Church and State in the name of new religious doctrines.

---

[15] Allen, 2831; Rogers (46).

More's abhorrence of heresy must have been influenced by his knowledge of St Augustine's dealings with the Donatists. For years he had used his pen to convince the Donatists that they were in schism, but argument failed to bring them into the One Church. Then their more fanatical adherents began a reign of terror against the Catholics. At length St Augustine was forced to see that an appeal to the civil authorities was inevitable; he believed that the Church had a right to make use of the powers of this world to safeguard the faith; that too was Thomas More's opinion.

Toleration between religions and sects was inconceivable to the sixteenth-century mind; two centuries of blood and tears had to pass before men realized the futility of the use of force in matters of belief. The same idea of toleration in political philosophies and in national pretensions will have to be accepted before there is peace in the world.

In *The Apologye*, Thomas More did not object to those who questioned his attitude towards heresy. Such objectors were the new sectaries who were not themselves prepared to tolerate Catholicism. He did refute charges that he had exceeded his legal powers and had been guilty of cruelty. It was said that he put heretics in the stocks and flogged them; both punishments were commonplace in those days and excited little compassion. More declared that he had had only two offenders flogged. The first was a boy, Dick Purser, in his employ, who had spoken slightingly of the Blessed Sacrament to another boy in the household. "I caused a servant of mine", wrote More, "to stripe him like a child before my household for amendment of himself and en-sample of such other." The second offender had been flogged after the local parishioners had complained that he had several times at Mass sneaked behind a kneeling woman, flung her skirts over her head and revealed her nakedness. More ordered the constables to flog him.

Then there was the case of George Constantine, a colporteur of Tyndale's New Testament. More put him in the stocks but so insecurely that Constantine managed to free himself. More's comment was, "Never will I for my part be so unreasonable as to be angry with any man that riseth if he can, when he findeth himself that he sitteth not at ease".[16] Hall records a conversation between More and Constantine that has its amusing side. More asked him how it was that so many of the New Testaments could be printed. Constantine declared that when the Bishop of London (Tunstal) began buying up the New Testaments to burn them, this provided additional funds for further printings. "Now by my troth", quoth More, "I think even the same, and I said so much to the Bishop when he went about to buy them." Hall says nothing about ill-treatment.[17] Constantine outlived More to become eventually Archdeacon of Brecon.

Another case was that of Segar, a bookseller of Cambridge, of whom nothing more is known, even by Foxe. He spread a tale about that he was kept in More's house and had been bound to a tree and beaten; a cord had been twisted round his head until he fainted, and while he was in a swoon, More had robbed him of his purse, "and put it in my bosom, and that Segar never saw it after and therein I trow he said true, for no more did I neither nor before neither, nor I trow did Segar himself himself neither in good faith". More did not bother even to deny such an unconvincing yarn.

The libel on his friend's reputation came to the knowledge of Erasmus. In a letter to Bishop John Faber of Vienna he commented:

> But what is it that these scatterers of false tales purpose? Is it to convince the sects, and favourers of sects, that a safe retreat is at hand for them in England? Why, from letters that have reached me from most trustworthy men, it appears that the King is even less tolerant of the new doctrines than the Bishops and priests. There is no man of any piety who would not wish to see a reform of morals in the Church, but no one of any prudence considers it right to tolerate universal confusion.[18]

Saint-German did not accept More's challenge to produce his evidence but in his reply, also anonymous, he repeated his vague accusations against the harsh and, as he maintained, unjust treatment of heretics by the Church. The title was, *A Dialogue*

[16]*Apologye*, p. 133.   [17]Hall, II, p. 162.   [18]Allen, 2750.

between two Englishmen, whereof one was called Salem and the other Bizance (1533). More answered with *The Debellation* [Conquest] *of Salem and Bizance.*[19] Saint-German's book appeared early in September and More's reply late in October. More twitted his opponent for avoiding specific statements.

> Thereto, ye wot well, he will bring forth for the plain proof of his plain truth in the matter his old three worshipful witnesses—which yet all stand unsworn—that is to wit, Some-say, and They-say, and Folk-say.[20]

The *Debellation* need not detain us; it is in the main a defence of the existing laws and of their enforcement against heretics. More's lighter mood occasionally finds expression:

> And as for the railing fashion—if I durst be bold to tell so sad a man a merry tale, I would tell him of the friar that, as he was preaching in the country, spied a poor wife of the parish whispering to her pew-fellow; and he, falling angry thereto, cried out unto her aloud, "Hold thy babble, I bid thee, thou wife in the red hood". Which when the housewife heard, she waxed as angry again, and suddenly she start up and cried out unto the friar again, that all the church rang thereon, "Marry, sir, I beshrew his heart that babbleth most of us both. For I do but whisper a word with my neighbour here, and thou hast babbled there all this hour."[21]

The last of More's controversial writings was *The Answer to the first part of the poisoned book which a nameless heretic hath named the Supper of the Lord* (1533).[22] The "nameless heretic" was almost certainly William Tyndale, who wrote in defence of John Frith's doctrine of the Blessed Sacrament. More's *Answer* contains his own translation of St John's Gospel, chapter six, verses 41-58. It will be of interest to set it out here parallel with Tyndale's translation of the same passage.

More	*Tyndale*
The Jews murmured therefore of that that he had said, I am the living bread, that am descended from heaven. And they said, Is not this man the son of Joseph	The Jews murmured at it because he said, I am that bread which is come down from heaven. And they said, Is not this Jesus the son of Joseph whose father and

[19]Gibson, 50.   [20]E.W., p. 963.   [21]E.W., p. 948.
[22]Gibson, 45, where it is incorrectly described as an answer to Frith.

K

whose father and mother we have known. How saith he therefore I am descended from heaven. Jesus therefore answered and said unto them, Murmur not among yourself. There can no man come to me, but if the father that sent me draw him, and I shall raise him again in the last day. It is written in the prophets: And they shall be all taught of God. Everyman that hath heard of the father and hath learned, cometh to me, not because any man hath seen the father, but he that is of God hath seen the father. Verily, verily I tell you, he that believeth in me hath life everlasting. I am the bread of life. Your fathers have eaten manna in the desert and be dead. This is the bread descending from heaven, that if any man eat thereof, he should not die. I am the living bread that am descended from the heaven. If a man eat of this bread, he shall live forever, and the bread which I shall give, is my flesh, which I shall give for the life of the world. The Jews therefore strove amongst themselves saying, How can this man give us his flesh to eat. Then said Jesus to them, Verily, verily, I say to you, but if ye eat the flesh of the son of man and drink his blood, ye shall not have life in you. He that eateth my flesh and drinketh my blood, hath life everlasting,

mother we know. How is it then that he saith I am come down from heaven. Jesus answered and said unto them. Murmur not between yourselves. No man can come to me except my father which hath sent me draw him. And I will raise him up at the last day. It is written in the prophets, And they shall all be taught of God. Every man which hath heard and learned of the father cometh unto me, not that any man hath seen the father save he which is of God. The same hath seen the father. Verily, verily, I say unto you, he that believeth me hath everlasting life. I am that bread of life. Your fathers did eat manna in the wilderness and are dead. This is the bread which cometh from heaven that he which of it eateth should also not die. I am that living bread which came down from heaven. If any man eat of this bread he shall live forever. And the bread that I will give is my flesh which I will give for the life of the world. The Jews strove among them saying, How can this fellow give us his flesh to eat? Jesus said unto them, Verily, verily I say unto you except ye eat the flesh of the son of man and drink his blood, ye shall not have life in you. Whosoever eateth my flesh and drinketh my blood, the same hath eternal life.

and I shall raise him in the last day. My flesh is verily meat and my blood is verily drink. He that eateth my flesh and drinketh my blood, dwelleth in me and I in him. As the living father sent me, I also live for the father. And he that eateth me, he shall also live for me. This is the bread descended from heaven, not as your fathers have eaten manna and are dead. He that eateth this bread, shall live for ever.[23]

And I will raise him up at the last day. For my flesh is meat indeed, and my blood is drink indeed. He that eateth my flesh and drinketh my blood, dwelleth in me and I in him. As my living father hath sent me even so live I by my father, and he that eateth me shall live by me. This is the bread which came from heaven, not as your fathers have eaten manna and are dead. He that eateth of this bread, shall live forever.

Thomas More expounded this Gospel in the first book of the *Answer*, and then went on to examine the teaching of the "nameless heretic", or "Master Masker", as he called him.

The concluding words of this book expressed the hope that these heretics may yet renounce their errors and return to the Church:

From which [heresy] our Lord give them grace truly to turn in time, so that we and they together in one Catholic Church, knit unto God in one catholic faith, faith I say, not faith alone as they do, but accompanied with good hope and her chief sister well working charity, may so receive Christ's Blessed Sacrament here, and specially that we may so receive himself, his very blessed body, very flesh and blood, in the Blessed Sacrament, our holy blessed housel, that we may here be with him incorporate so by grace, that after the short course of this transitory life, with his tender pity poured upon us in purgatory, at the prayer of good people, and intercession of holy saints, we may be with them in their holy fellowship, incorporate in Christ in his eternal glory. Amen.[24]

His hopes of reconciliation between the Church and the dissident sects could not have been strong. With his experience of men and affairs and his prescience he must have felt how slender were the chances of recapturing those who had defected from the teaching of the Church. Roper records two occasions

[23]E.W., p. 1043. [24]E.W., p. 1138.

when Thomas More expressed his feelings on this problem. The earlier occasion, though it comes second in Roper's order, was "before the matter of the said matrimony [was] brought into question", perhaps about 1525. He then said:

> I pray God that some of us, as high as we seem to sit upon the mountains, treading heretics under our feet like ants, live not the day that we gladly would wish to be at a league and composition with them, to let them have their churches quietly to themselves, so that they would be content to let us have ours quietly to ourselves.[25]

The second conversation came somethat later as the question of the "matrimony" was under active discussion.

> So on a time, walking with me along the Thames side at Chelsea, in talking of others things he said unto me: "Now would to our Lord, son Roper, upon condition that three things were well established in Christendom, I were put in a sack, and here presently cast into the Thames".
>
> "What great things be those, sir," quoth I, "that should move you so to wish?"
>
> "Wouldst thou know what they be, son Roper?" quoth he.
>
> "Yea, marry, with good will, sir, if it please you", quoth I.
>
> "In faith, son, they be these", said he. "The first is that where the most part of Christian princes be at mortal war, they were all at an universal peace. The second, that where the Church of Christ is at this present sore afflicted with many errors and heresies, it were settled in a perfect uniformity of religion. The third, that where the King's matter of his marriage is now come in question, it were to the glory of God and quietness of all parts brought to a good conclusion."[26]

The hope never left him, even if at times it seemed slender. In his last completed book, *The Dialogue of Comfort*, written in the Tower, he used the Turkish threat as a kind of allegory of the war against heresy. The mention of "some communications" suggests that he had heard of the exploratory, but, as it proved, sterile, approaches Henry and Cromwell had been making to the Lutheran princes of Germany. Though there was the appearance of a desire for doctrinal understanding, the underlying intention was political.

[25]Roper, p. 35.   [26]Roper, p. 24.

And albeit that is a right heavy thing to see such variances in our belief rise and grow among ourself to the great encouragement of the common enemies of us all, whereby they have our faith in derision and catch hope to overwhelm us all, yet do there three things not a little comfort my mind.

The first is, that in some communications had of late together, hath appeared good likelihood of some good agreement to grow together in one accord of our faith.

The second, that in the meanwhile, till this may come to pass, contentions, dispicions, and uncharitable behaviour, is prohibited and forbidden in effect upon all parts: all such parts, I mean, as fell before to fight for it.

The third is, that all Germany, for all their divers opinions, yet as they agree together in profession of Christ's name, so agree they now together in preparation of a common power in defence of Christendom against our common enemy the Turk. And I trust in God that this shall not only help us here to strength us in this war, but also that as God hath caused them to agree together in defence of His name so shall He graciously bring them to agree together in the truth of His faith. Therefore will I let God work and leave off contention; and nothing shall I now say, but that with which they that are themself of the contrary mind shall in reason have no cause to be discontented.[27]

This longing for the restoration of unity in the Church grew upon him until it became the dominant element in Thomas More's thought.

[27]*Dialogue of Comfort*, p. 174.

Chapter XXVI

The Nun of Kent

Thomas More so completely avoided being involved in the King's Matter that there is no trace of any action, or of any opinion expressed, by him during the period of waiting for the problem to be resolved. We have seen how he refused to receive a letter from the Emperor brought by his ambassador Eustace Chapuys. A draft of what may have been the letter has been discovered.[1] It was written in French from Brussels and dated 11 March 1531. It did not refer, as More may have feared, to the affairs of the Emperor's aunt, Queen Catherine, but was a general expression of thanks for the English Chancellor's courtesies to the Emperor's subjects and in their relations with King Henry, "mon très chère oncle, cousin et bon frère". The letter was by implication an invitation to confide in Chapuys. The guarded expressions could be interpreted as thanks for support given to Queen Catherine.

John Fisher was not so prudent. He was the most persistent supporter of Queen Catherine and in his writings and sermons did his utmost to promote her cause. He discussed the question with Chapuys, who, in three despatches during 1533 (April, September and October), informed Charles V that the Bishop urged armed intervention.[2] These despatches are the only evidence that Fisher took this view, but there is no reason to think that Chapuys was inventing. In one of his despatches Chapuys had pointed out that Henry had no standing army. The people, he claimed, supported the Queen; the Scots would invade, and the French would not stir. "The Pope", he declared, "should invoke the secular arm."[3]

Fisher, too, may have thought of the Emperor of the Holy Roman Empire as the sword-arm of the Pope; this seems archaic

[1]See above, p. 245. Herbrüggen, 183A.   [2]Span. Cal. IV, ii, 592, 1130, 1133.
[3]Span. Cal. IV, ii, 630.

to us, but medieval ideas lingered in men's minds and Fisher was a living link between the later Middle Ages and what we call Modern History. So Chapuys' talk of the "secular arm" would win his acceptance. This was treasonous talk, and had any inkling of it come to Henry's ears, Fisher would have had short shrift.[4] Queen Catherine herself blocked Chapuys' plans by declaring, as he honestly reported to her nephew, that "she would consider herself damned eternally were she to consent to anything that might provoke a war".[5] That was undoubtedly Thomas More's attitude. He was more of a man of affairs than his old friend John Fisher, and he must have dreaded the prospect (and it was not entirely out of the question) of the Emperor landing in England with his troops. Such an intervention could only bring misery to the country. If we link this with his abhorrence of war, we can understand his decision to remain silent in an explosive situation.

Chapuys was right in saying that Queen Catherine had considerable popular support, though he certainly exaggerated its extent in the way all conspirators do, and it is not unfair to call him a conspirator. Nor was he in a position to gauge public opinion; it is doubtful if he spoke English when he arrived in the autumn of 1529; he moved in a restricted circle, and while some disgruntled nobles may have whispered to him in corners, he did not sense that they were not prepared to go further; they lacked a determined leader.

Henry married Anne Boleyn towards the end of January 1533; this was not officially recognized until, four months later, Archbishop Cranmer, Warham's successor, declared the marriage valid. A few days earlier, on 23 May, he had presided over a special court at Dunstable at which, in the absence of Queen Catherine, he pronounced her marriage with Henry to be nullified.

When Thomas More heard that Henry and Anne were married, he made the prescient remark to Roper, "God give grace, son,

---

[4]Those who condemn Bishop Fisher must also condemn Bishop Compton for signing the letter that brought William of Orange to England in 1688. The difference was that the Bishop of Rochester was on the losing side, and the Bishop of London on the winning side.

[5]Span. Cal. IV, ii, 649.

that these matters within a while be not confirmed with oaths".[6]

He himself, as Roper tells us, had to make a difficult decision when Anne was to be crowned in Westminster Abbey on Whit Sunday, 1 June 1533.

He received a letter from the Bishops of Durham, Bath and Winchester [Tunstal, Clerk and Gardiner] requesting him both to keep them company from the Tower to the Coronation, and also to take twenty pounds that by the bearer thereof they had sent him to buy him a gown with; which he thankfully receiving, and at home still tarrying, at their next meeting said merrily to them, "My lords, in the letters which you lately sent me, you required two things of me, the one whereof, since I was so well content to grant you, the other therefore I thought I might be the bolder to deny you. And like as the one, because I took you for no beggars, and myself I knew to be no rich man, I thought I might the rather fulfil, so the other did put me in remembrance of an Emperor that had ordained a law that whosover committed a certain offence (which I now remember not) except it were a virgin should suffer the pains of death, such a reverence had he to virginity. Now so it happened that the first committer of that offence was indeed a virgin, whereof the emperor hearing was in so small perplexity, as he that by some example fain would have had that law to have been put in execution. Whereupon when his council had sat long, solemnly debating this case, suddenly arose there up one of his council, a good plain man, among them and said, 'Why make so much ado, my lords, about so small a matter? Let her first be deflowered, and then after may she be devoured.' And so though your lordships have in the matter of the matrimony hitherto kept yourselves pure virgins, yet take good heed, my lords, that you keep your virginity still. For some there be that by procuring your lordships first at the coronation to be present, and next to preach for the setting forth of it, and finally to write books to all the world in defence thereof, are desirous to deflower you; and when they have deflowered you, then will they not fail soon after to devour you. Now, my lords," quoth he, "it lieth not in my power but that they may devour me, but God being my good lord, I will provide that they shall never deflower me."[7]

Tunstal and More may have met for the last time at this period.

[6]Roper, p. 57.

[7]Roper, p. 57. The story seems based on that told by Tacitus (*Annals*, 9) of the daughter of Sejanus.

The King, while recognizing and using Tunstal's great abilities, was not too sure of him. In 1531 the Bishop's houses were searched by orders of the King. Tunstal was kept in the north and not summoned to Parliament during the four years 1531-4. He came to London for the coronation, but returned to Durham afterwards. He and More were kept apart.[8] Even when Tunstal was sent to Fisher in the Tower he was not allowed to see More.

Many must have remarked on the absence from the coronation of the former Lord Chancellor who was still one of the Council. The new Queen, so quick to see reproach, must have read it as a deliberate slight. Why did Thomas More avoid the coronation? No doubt he was sick at heart at the thought of how Catherine of Aragon had been discarded, but so were many others who had enjoyed the society of that unhappy woman, yet they did not scruple to watch the triumph of her successor. As he told the bishops, mere presence at the coronation implied approval of what had been done. There may have been another thought in his mind. The coronation was a religious act taking place in the great Benedictine Abbey with the Archbishop as the chief officiant. After the anointing, Mass was said and the new Queen "kneeled before the altar where she received of the Archbishop the Holy Sacrament".[9] This was something more than an act of State; it was the sanctification of a union made in defiance of the Pope who had not yet pronounced his decision on the validity of the King's first marriage. It may have been some such view that kept Thomas More away.

On 11 July 1533 the Pope excommunicated Henry and declared his marriage with Anne Boleyn invalid; the enforcement of this was held in abeyance until September in the hope that Henry would retrace his steps. That month saw the birth of the Princess Elizabeth. On 23 March 1534 the Pope gave his decision on the marriage between Henry and Catherine; it was declared valid. The news reached London on 4 April, but seems to have been received coolly by the populace. Seven years had passed since Henry had first raised the question. This long delay undoubtedly weakened the prestige of the papacy in English eyes.

[8] See C. Sturge, *Cuthbert Tunstal*, pp. 190-1.   [9] Hall, II, p. 238.
K*

Writing to Cromwell on 5 March 1534 before the Pope's decision was given, More referred to Anne Boleyn as "this noble woman really anointed Queen". Was this a phrase used in a moment of human frailty? Who dare blame him if, as his pen moved across the paper, he tried to ward off the blow that he knew was coming, with smooth words? By that date, as we shall see presently, his days of immunity were over, and first in one way and then in another he was being harassed. His experience of Council affairs during the past fifteen or sixteen years had shown him that, once out of favour, an officer of State could expect little sympathy. Yet, he had the King's word! We need not doubt that, at the time, Henry was quite sincere in his regrets at More's resignation and in the public testimony he ordered to be paid in Parliament. What changed his mind? Or, should we say, "Who"?

The tradition in the More family was that Anne Boleyn was the cause of Thomas More's persecution. William Roper wrote of her "importunate clamour" that did "exasperate the King against him".[10] This belief was also stated by William Rastell[11] and echoed by Stapleton.[12] There can be no definite confirmation of this suspicion but it was not implausible.

It is a hopeless task now to try to read the character of Anne Boleyn for she is obscured by a fog of legend and scurrility. Thomas Gray's egregious couplet,

> When love could teach a monarch to be wise,
> And gospel-light first dawn'd from Bullen's eyes,

is probably as far from the truth as the scandal put out by Catholic propagandists after her death. Contemporary testimony seems, however, to agree that, as Queen, she became increasingly arrogant and vindictive. Sir Thomas More would be among those against whom her resentment was directed; he had refused to support the King against Queen Catherine, and he had refused to attend the coronation of the new Queen. While her influence lasted, a period of less than two years, she could vent her spite on those she regarded as her enemies and Henry was becoming more and more suspicious of those who did not wholeheartedly support him. As we look back on the events of those years, they seem part

[10]Roper, p. 74.   [11]Harpsfield, p. 235.   [12]Stapleton, p. 191.

of a planned policy but it was a stumbling from expedient to expedient. The King had got himself into a dangerous position. He could not but fear the repercussions of his actions. There was not only the mood of the country to cause concern, there was also the nagging question of what Charles V and Francis I might do. Henry had lost Thomas Wolsey and now Thomas More; the third Thomas, Cromwell, was not yet firmly established as an adviser, and the fourth Thomas, Cranmer, was serving his apprenticeship. It was no wonder that in such a time of strain, the King accepted the insinuations of his exigent wife. At the same time, it must be remembered that, without his approval, tacit or spoken, no move could have been made against Sir Thomas More.

Thomas More seems to have borne no ill-will to Anne Boleyn; he pitied her. When he was in the Tower, he once asked Margaret how Queen Anne did. "In faith, father, never better." "Never better, Meg!" quoth he. "Alas, Meg, alas, it pitieth me to remember into what misery, poor soul, she shall shortly come."[13]

At the end of 1533 an official statement in justification of the King's divorce and re-marriage was printed with the title *Articles devised by the Whole Consent of the King's Council*, more usually spoken of as *The Book of Nine Articles;* the ninth of these declared that the Pope was by birth illegitimate, that he was guilty of simony at his election, and of heresy in refusing the King's appeal. Early in the new year came More's *Answer to . . . the poisoned book*. William Rastell, the printer, was called before Cromwell, and accused of publishing a reply to *The Book of Nine Articles*.[14] Presumably Cromwell, or some official, had read More's book and it is difficult to see how it could be regarded as having anything to do with the Council's apologia. One can only assume it was a way of attacking More himself. William Rastell was able to point out that, although the book was dated 1534, it was, in fact, in print by Christmas 1533 and had, therefore, been composed before the *Articles* book was available. When he repeated this to his uncle, Sir Thomas More wrote to Cromwell.

[13]Roper, p. 77.
[14]See A. W. Reed, *Early Tudor Drama* (1926), p. 79.

The letter is dated from Chelsea, 1 February 1534. He stated the facts again and then referred to the *Articles* book.

> For of many things which in that book be touched, in some I know not the [canon] law, and in some I know not the fact. And therefore would I never be so childish nor so play the proud arrogant fool, by whomsoever the book had been made, and to whomsoever the matter had belonged, as to presume to make an answer to the book, concerning the matter whereof I never were sufficiently learned in the [canon] laws, nor fully instructed in the facts.[15]

No further action seems to have been taken.

The next move was a direct attack. An accusation was made, apparently by the new Queen's father, the Earl of Wiltshire, that More had taken bribes while he was Lord Chancellor. The charge was a safe one to make in days when gifts and other benefits were normally offered to, and often accepted by, judges. Even seventy years later, another Lord Chancellor, Francis Bacon, could be brought down by a similar charge. Thomas More, however, effectively dealt with each instance that was put by the Council. Yes, he had received a gilt cup from the wife of a successful litigant. "Then the Lord of Wiltshire (for hatred of his religion the preferer of this suit) with much rejoicing said unto the lords, 'Lo, did I not tell you, my lords, that you should find this matter true?'"[16]

He spoke too soon, for Sir Thomas went on to say that he had had the cup filled with wine; he drank to her and she to him, and then he had, with some difficulty, persuaded her to take the cup back to her husband as a New Year gift from the Chancellor. A similar case of the gift of a cup had a different ending; Sir Thomas, liking the fashion of the cup, accepted it in exchange for one of his own. A third case was that of a rich widow who, after a successful suit, sent Sir Thomas a pair of gloves with forty pounds in gold. He had accepted the gloves but had returned the money. Roper added: "Many things more of like effect for the declaration of his innocency and clearness from all corruption or evil affection could I rehearse besides".

A far more serious matter came up in January 1534. This

---

[15]Rogers, 194 (49).   [16]Roper, p. 62.

concerned the relations of Bishop John Fisher, Sir Thomas More and others with Elizabeth Barton, the Nun (or Maid) of Kent.[17]

Elizabeth Barton was born about 1506 in the parish of Aldington, Kent, on Romney Marsh. This was the living to which Archbishop Warham had presented Erasmus; his vicar, Richard Master, paid the scholar a pension of £20. He was described by Erasmus as a skilled theologian and man of upright character.[18] Elizabeth was a domestic servant and a severe illness in 1525 affected her personality. For long periods at a time she lay in a trance and would then give utterance to warnings against sin and vice. Her master and the neighbours considered that either she was possessed of the devil or was divinely inspired. In that day such a phenomenon was not regarded with the complete scepticism of today, nor would it be accepted immediately as a spiritual manifestation. The English mystics of the fourteenth and fifteenth centuries had accustomed people to the possibility of the supernatural being revealed through the natural. Richard Master listened to what Elizabeth said and he watched her; eventually he became convinced that she was an instrument of God. He at once reported the matter to Archbishop Warham who, after some inquiry, accepted the genuineness of the young woman's messages. Here it may be noted that all who were concerned acted correctly, either by referring the matter to superiors, or by instituting inquiries. Moreover, these manifestations continued for more than eight years before the clash with authority brought them to an end.

Inevitably the fame of Elizabeth's utterances spread widely, and in 1526 the Archbishop thought it wise to make a more thorough investigation, and he sent two monks of Canterbury, Edward Bocking and William Dering, to see the young woman. Both were men of good reputation. It is important to know something of Bocking. He was probably in his early forties. He had taken his doctorate at Oxford in 1518, and for a time had been warden of Canterbury College, and from there went to the Benedictine

[17]A recent survey is Ch. XV in D. Knowles, *The Religious Orders in England*, Vol. III (1959).

[18]An inventory of his property which was forfeited for misprision of treason, shows that he had 113 books, 42 of them Greek—a considerable library for those days.

monastery at Canterbury where he was cellarer. He was therefore a scholar and a man who had positions of responsibility. Fisher's early biographer described him as "a learned and virtuous man". In what followed, Dr Bocking may have exercised undue influence over a young woman of unstable temperament without realizing the dangers of the power a strong personality can have over an unformed mind. This is not, however, to say that he was a cunning rogue. He was convinced that Elizabeth was divinely inspired, and he gave her more careful instruction in her faith than she had previously had. Her prophetic sayings began to attract wider attention and many consulted her on their personal problems. It was wise to remove her from Aldington and to place her with the nuns at St Sepulchre's, Canterbury, where Dr Bocking became her confessor and spiritual director. He wrote down her sayings and gave a copy to Archbishop Warham who showed them to the King. Henry was only mildly interested and asked Sir Thomas More for his opinion; he reported that there was nothing noteworthy: "a right simple woman might, in my mind, speak it of her own wit well enough". There the matter might have rested had it not been for the wide aversion to the King's desire to free himself from his marriage. The Nun of Kent, as Elizabeth was commonly known, voiced this feeling in her prediction that if the King persisted in his intention, he "should no longer be King of this realm" and "should die a villain's death". Even here it is not necessary to see any sinister plotting to inflame public opinion; in her support for Queen Catherine she was voicing sentiments that were commonplace and could be heard in any pot-house.

When she was allowed to move about, her influence increased. Earlier she had had an interview with Wolsey but he was not impressed. She was at Calais in October 1532 when Anne Boleyn, Marquess of Pembroke,[19] was there during Henry's meeting with King Francis. Did something happen at Calais to rouse the resentment of the would-be queen? On Henry's return, the Nun spoke to him at Canterbury and upbraided him for deserting Catherine. She was also the guest at times of the Brigittines at

[19]This odd title had just been conferred on her.

Syon and it was there that Sir Thomas More was persuaded to see her.

The Nun became the symbol in Southern England of the popular support given to Queen Catherine. If discredit could be brought upon the Nun and her associates, then opposition to the King would be blunted and other grumblers would be warned of what might happen to them. The King therefore instructed Cromwell to look into the matter, and he, in turn, asked Cranmer to carry out an inquiry. The Archbishop interviewed the Nun about the middle of July 1533, and, in the course of several interrogations, under the prodding of Cromwell, he got from her a confession of simulation. During this prolonged questioning, the names of a number of important persons were mentioned, including Bishop John Fisher and Sir Thomas More. Attempts to implicate Queen Catherine failed. By November the Nun and her associates were in the Tower. Then followed a series of interrogations before the Council, and an augmented Council debated the matter for three days. At that time spoken words could not be made treasonous, so some other way had to be found to deal with these unfortunates. The Nun and her associates made a public confession of their duplicity at St Paul's on 23 November. Thomas More was there and was then convinced of the Nun's hypocrisy. It was decided to proceed by a Bill of Attainder[20] and in this were included the names not only of the immediate suspects but of John Fisher, Thomas More and others, who were accused of misprision of treason for not warning the King of what the Nun had predicted. The charge was as absurd as the one of praemunire against the clergy, for, as we have seen, the King had actually discussed the Nun with Thomas More; Fisher claimed that what she said to him had, according to her, been already said to the King, and he therefore saw no point in making a report; a reasonable explanation. The Bill was first brought into the Lords on 21 February 1534. When More had news of this he at once wrote to Cromwell giving him a full

[20]An Act of Attainder was just like any other statute; it had to go through the usual process of a Bill through Parliament. There was no trial; there was no necessity for legal proof of guilt. It avoided awkward testimony by witnesses for the defence.

account of his relations with the Nun and enclosing a copy of a letter he had sent to her.[21] He recalled the opinion he had earlier given the King that the Nun's words were those of a "right simple woman". Two friars, Risby of Canterbury and Rich of Richmond, had spoken to him about her, but, as soon as they mentioned her references to the King, he had refused to listen further and had warned Friar Rich that he was foolish to take any notice of such talk. Then later, during a visit to the Brigittines at Syon, he was asked to see the Nun who was staying there.

> We talked no word of the King's Grace or any great personage else, nor in effect, of any man or woman, but of herself, and myself, but after no long communication had for or ever we met, my time came to go home, I gave her a double ducat, and prayed her to pray for me and mine, and so departed from her and never spake with her after.

Later he had some misgivings when he heard of unwise conversations she was having with her many visitors. This was the reason for his letter to her. It contains the following passage:

> Good Madam, I doubt not but that you remember that in the beginning of my communication with you, I showed you that I neither was, nor would be, curious of any knowledge of other men's matters and least of all any matter of princes or of the realm, in case it so were that God had . . . any things revealed unto you, such things, I said unto your ladyship, that I was not only not desirous to hear of, but also would not hear of.

He reminded her of the fate of the Duke of Buckingham who had given ear to foolish prophesyings. He went on:

> I nothing doubt your wisdom and the spirit of God shall keep you from talking with any persons, specially with lay persons, of any such manner of things as pertain to princes' affairs, or the state of the realm, but only to commune and talk with any person high and low, of such manner things as may to the soul be profitable for you to show and for them to know.[22]

Cromwell may have questioned the authenticity of this letter, for there is a letter to him, perhaps from one of the friars, Rich or Risby, stating that he had seen the letter (which he summarized

---

[21]Rogers, 197 (51).   [22]Rogers 192 (47).

from memory) and had "counselled and desired Master Gold [one of the priests involved] also the woman, to keep it safe for the discharge of the said Master More".[23]

It may have been at Cromwell's suggestion that Thomas More then wrote to the King. The letter is dated 5 March.[24] More first reminded Henry of the promise made to be his "good and gracious lord" after his resignation, and referred him to the full account he had written to "your trusty councillor Master Thomas Cromwell" of his dealings with "the wicked woman of Canterbury".[25] More begged the King not to believe "the fallible opinion or soon spoken words of light and soon change-able people". He trusted that

> Our Lord for his mercy send you I should once meet with your Grace again in heaven, and there be merry with you, where among mine other pleasures this should yet be one, that your Grace should surely see there then that (howsoever you take me) I am your true beadman now and ever have been, and will be till I die, howsoever your pleasure be to do by me.

Beneath the formal phrasing here there is a quiet reminder of earlier intimacy when they had been "merry" together; no ordinary petitioner would have presumed to write of being "merry" in eternity with the king.

When the Bill of Attainder was read a third time in the Lords on 6 March, the section condemning "Elizabeth Barton, nun and hypocrite" was passed, but the lords asked for further considera-tion of the case against Sir Thomas More and suggested he should come before the Council to defend himself. John Fisher, who was ill at Rochester, had written a long letter to the Lords exonerating himself. He had asked to be judged by the normal process of law in the courts and not by this exceptional method of a Bill of Attainder; then he warned them, "to look upon your own perils which may happen to you in like cases. For there sitteth not one lord here but the same and other like may chance until himself that now is imputed to me." It was a warning that several

---

[23]L.P., VI, 1467.   [24]Rogers, 198 (52).
[25]When William Rastell printed this letter in E.W., he changed this to "the nun of Canterbury".

of the peers and Thomas Cromwell had good reason to recall within a few years.

Instead of a Star Chamber hearing, the King preferred an examination by a commission of four—Cranmer, Audley, Norfolk and Cromwell. The date of this interrogation is not known. Before More set out from Chelsea, William Roper "earnestly advised him to labour unto those lords for the help of his discharge out of that Parliament Bill [Attainder]; who answered me he would".[26]

The remarkable fact about this examination was that, according to Roper's account, the Nun of Kent was not mentioned. First of all Audley urged More, as an acknowledgement of the King's many favours to him, to "add his consent" to that of Parliament, the bishops and the universities to the marriage proceedings. More's reply was that, as the King had allowed him freedom of judgment and was fully aware of his opinions, he had hoped the subject was closed. Then the lords began to threaten him with the King's extreme displeasure, especially, so they alleged, because More had incited the King to maintain the Pope's authority in his book on the Seven Sacraments. "These terrors be arguments for children", replied More, echoing the words used by St Basil to the Emperor Valens, *Minare ista pueris*. More's answer to this ridiculous charge has already been quoted.[27] Thereupon, as Roper noted, "thus displeasantly departed they".

More, however, was far from displeased.

Then took Sir Thomas More his boat towards his house at Chelsea, wherein by the way he was very merry, and for that I was nothing sorry hoping that he had got himself discharged out of the Parliament Bill. When he was landed and come home, then walked we twain alone into his garden together, where I, desirous to know how he had sped, said, "I trust, sir, that all is well because you be so merry".

"It is so indeed, son Roper, I thank God", quoth he.

"Are you then put out of the Parliament Bill?" said I.

"By my troth, son Roper," quoth he, "I never remembered it."

"Never remembered it, sir?" said I. "A case that toucheth yourself so near, and us all for your sake. I am sorry to hear it, for I verily

trusted, when I saw you so merry, that all had been well."
Then said he, "Wilt thou know, son Roper, why I was so merry?"
"That would I gladly, sir," quoth I.

"In good faith, I rejoiced, son", quoth he, "that I had given the devil a foul fall, and that with those lords I had gone so far as without shame I could never go back again."

Had the Nun of Kent been mentioned, More would have remembered that his name was in the Bill of Attainder. The interrogation had shown that the real intention of the King was to frighten More into accepting the divorce; the matter of the Nun was a pretext for bringing pressure to bear on him. He now knew what lay before him; the uncertainties of his position had been swept away by this plain revelation of the King's mind. He felt renewed confidence, too, in the fact that he had been able to withstand the threats made by the Councillors. He once admitted to his daughter Margaret that "a fainter heart than thy frail father hath, thou canst not have". This first clash had shown that when the time came God would "stay me with his holy hand".[28]

Henry was angry when this failure was reported to him. At first he declared his intention of forcing the Bill of Attainder through with More's name in it, even if it meant going to the Lords himself. Audley and Cromwell knew that this might wreck the Bill, for Thomas More's reputation and popularity were such that discontent would increase if he were condemned on such slender evidence, and they may have especially feared the effect on the City where More was held in particular regard. It was with the greatest difficulty that they persuaded the King to delete More's name; as some slight solace to his feelings, the King stopped More's salary as a Councillor. John Fisher was condemned for misprision of treason which meant imprisonment during the King's pleasure and forfeiture of goods. This penalty was remitted for a fine of £300, one year's revenue of his poor bishopric.

Elizabeth Barton and four of her associates suffered at Tyburn on 21 April 1534, by which time both John Fisher and Thomas More were in the Tower.[29] What is one to say of this unsavoury affair? We have to remember that nearly all our information

[28]Rogers, 211 (61).   [29]Richard Master was pardoned.

comes from the case for the prosecution, and that during the long imprisonment in the Tower the Nun may have broken down under the many interrogations she had to suffer; we can put little value on her confessions for in our own century we have learned their worthlessness. The comment made by Fisher's early biographer during the reign of Queen Mary holds good. "For mine own part, I will not for certain affirm anything either with her or against her, because I have heard her diversely reported of and that of persons of right good fame and estimation."[30]

What part did Cromwell play in this attack on Thomas More? It has been said that it was he who "sought to include More"[31] in the Bill, but there is no clear evidence of this. No doubt Cromwell was intent on stifling the popular support of Queen Catherine and the indiscretions (to use no harsher term) of the Nun provided the material, and he pursued the case in his usual methodical and determined way. If John Fisher and Thomas More were implicated, it was regrettable, but any personal regard (he certainly had none for Fisher, neither had the King) must give way to State security. There is one undated entry in what are usually called Cromwell's "Remembrances"—jottings of things to be done—that reads: "Eftsoons to remember Master More to the king".[32] This can be twisted to imply that Cromwell was set on More's destruction, but this is straining a mere note too far. It may mean simply that Cromwell wanted to make sure of the King's intentions as regards More.

That Cromwell was probably not personally antagonistic to More is shown by the following incident related by Roper.

> Master Cromwell, meeting me in the Parliament House, willed me to tell my father [father-in-law] that he was put out of the Parliament Bill. But because I had appointed to dine that day in London I sent the message by my servant to my wife to Chelsea. Whereof when she informed her father, "In faith, Meg," quoth he, "*quod differtur non aufertur* (what is put off is not laid aside)".[33]

This news could have been given in half-a-dozen different ways, but Cromwell chose to announce it himself; there was nothing

[30]*Life of Fisher* (E.E.T.S.), p. 82.   [31]Bridgett, p. 322.
[32]L.P., VII, 50.   [33]Roper, p. 71.

to be gained by doing so, for there was not the slightest chance that Thomas More would ever again be in favour. We can give Cromwell the benefit of the doubt, and believe that it was a spontaneously friendly gesture. The seeming inconsistencies in his actions lie in his view of his function. He would not allow sentiment to interfere with policy. The King's will, even his whim, must be obeyed. He could suggest policies to the King and, if approved, plan their carrying out and sweep all obstacles aside. So if Thomas More became an obstacle, he must go, however contrary that may have been to Cromwell's private feelings about the man. The time was to come when Cromwell, having become perhaps over-confident, forgot the strength of the King's will, then he too was swept aside.

Roper added the following incident to his record.

> After this, as the Duke of Norfolk and Sir Thomas More chanced to fall in familiar talk together, the Duke said unto him, "By the Mass, Master More, it is perilous striving with princes. And therefore I would wish you somewhat to incline to the King's pleasure. For by God's body, Master More, *Indignatio principis mors est* (the wrath of the king is death)." "Is that all, my lord?" quoth he. "Then in good faith is there no more difference between your Grace and me, but that I shall die today, and you tomorrow."

Thomas More was not here playing the prophet, but Norfolk, after a lifetime of service, was to experience the wrath of the King. In 1547 he and his son, Surrey, were convicted of treason; Surrey was executed, but Norfolk escaped the block because Henry VIII died a few hours before the time of execution. Did Norfolk in those days recall the words of Thomas More?

CHAPTER XXVII

The Oath

THOMAS MORE had taken fully into consideration the possible, indeed probable, consequences that would follow his resignation. Had it been simply a matter of ill-health, he could have looked forward to a period of retirement in which he could "make his soul". The ill-health was genuine, but the King must have known that something more meaningful lay underneath. It may be noted that, although he had public tribute paid to Sir Thomas More's services, he did not bestow on him any of those honours that were customary on such an occasion. We do not know how often they talked of the marriage problem; our only guide is More's statement when he refused to accept a letter from the Emperor. To do so, he said, "might deprive him of the liberty he had always used in speaking boldly to King Henry in those matters which concerned Charles and Queen Catherine".[1] More's perception of the dangerous under-tow in the King's character warned him that sooner or later he would be caught up in the current and swept away. Something of this would be in his mind when he teased his family about the poverty they might have to face. It was the same consideration that led him to settle his property while it was his to settle.[2]

Roper does not make it clear when this decision was made. "After Sir Thomas More had given over his office . . ." is a vague statement and may not mean immediately after the resignation but as soon as he was convinced that his fears were well-founded. Perhaps the declaration of the marriage of Henry to Anne in May 1533 was the sign for which he waited. The first arrangement he made was "a conveyance for the disposition of all his lands, reserving to himself an estate thereof only for the term of his own life, and after his decease assuring some part of the same

[1]See above, p. 245.
[2]The legal points are explained by J. D. M. Derrett in *Moreana*, No. 5 (1965).

to his wife".[3] This would give him and his wife, should she survive him, life interests. The only reference More himself makes to this business comes in the last letter he wrote from the Tower. In a message for his son John, he wrote, "Our Lord bless him and his good wife my loving daughter, to whom I pray him to be good, as he hath great cause, and that if land of mine come into his hand, he break not my will concerning his sister Daunce [Elizabeth]".[4] Anne [Cresacre] More had her lands in Yorkshire. By the time More wrote these words, his own property had been forfeited, but "if land of mine come into his hand" suggests that he was hoping his Attainder might be reversed, as others had been in the past, and so something might be salvaged.

Roper tells us that two days after the first conveyance, reserving a life interest, Thomas More made a fresh conveyance of the land he had devised for William and Margaret Roper. As this was an unconditional gift, that is with no life interest involved, it escaped the later confiscations. The Roper portion was the south-east corner of the Chelsea estate, next to the church. It may have included More's New Building which could be adapted as a residence.

"God give grace", More had said, "that these matters within a while be not confirmed with oaths."[5] The announcement of the marriage of Anne on 28 May 1533 had prompted that comment. Parliament was not recalled until the middle of January 1534. During its adjournment, Anne Boleyn had become Queen and the Princess Elizabeth had been born. Henry still hoped for a son. He decided that the succession must be fixed by law. He would not depend on the Act passed after Bosworth Field declaring the inheritance of the Crown to "be, rest and remain and abide in the most royal person of our new Sovereign Lord Henry VII and in the heirs of his body lawfully comen perpetually". The problem lay in that one word "lawfully". The Princess Mary had been bastardized, and Henry must have been alive to the fact that many old adherents of Queen Catherine now regarded the Princess Elizabeth as a bastard. Here was all the material for a disputed accession should no son be born. So a new and drastic

---

[3]Roper, p. 79.   [4]Rogers, 218 (66).   [5]See above, p. 279.

Succession Act was passed early in 1534. It is an extraordinary document and has been described by one historian as "a treatise on the canon law, a constitutional enactment and a political manifesto".[6]

Only a sixth of the text[7] is concerned with the actual line of succession. The lengthy preamble points out the troubles that had occurred in the past by "ambiguity and doubts" regarding the succession. Such doubts, it was argued, gave "the Bishop of Rome" an excuse for interfering. The marriage between Catherine and Henry was then examined. One passage should be read carefully.

> . . . that the marriage heretofore solemnized between your highness and the Lady Katherine, being before lawful wife to Prince Arthur, your elder brother, which by him was carnally known, as does fully appear by sufficient proof in a lawful process had and made before Thomas, by sufferance of God, now archbishop of Canterbury and metropolitan and primate of this realm, shall be, by authority of this present Parliament, definitively, clearly, and absolutely declared, deemed and adjudged to be against the laws of Almighty God, and also accepted, reputed, and taken of no value nor effect, but utterly void and annulled, and the separation thereof, made by the said archbishop, shall be good and effectual to all intents and purposes; any licence, dispensation, or any other acts going afore, or ensuing the same, or to the contrary thereof, in any wise notwithstanding; and that every such licence, dispensation, act or acts, thing or things heretofore had, made, done, or to be done by the contrary thereof, shall be void and of none effect; and that the said Lady Katherine shall from henceforth be called and reputed only dowager to Prince Arthur, and not queen of this realm; and that the lawful matrimony had and solemnized between your highness and your most dear and entirely beloved wife Queen Anne, shall be established, and taken for undoubtful, true, sincere, and perfect ever hereafter, according to the just judgement of the said Thomas, archbishop of Canterbury, etc.

The Act surprisingly then went on to deal with all marriages within the prohibited degrees, a matter that had hitherto been

[6]H. A. L. Fisher, *History of England*, 1485-1547, p. 326.
[7]The full text is given in H. Gee and W. J. Hardy, *Documents illustrative of English Church History*, pp. 232-43.

controlled by canon law; it was as if Henry was determined that no one should make the mistake he claimed he had made. The point of this section was that in future such matters would be settled not by "the Bishop of Rome" but by "any archbishops, bishops, or other ministers of the Church of England".

At last the Act came to the succession. After Henry's death, the Crown was to go to his eldest surviving son; failing a son, to the Princess Elizabeth. Thus the Princess Mary was set aside.

1 May 1534 was fixed as the date for the proclamation of the "tenor and contents of this Act". The rest of the text, nearly a third of it, dealt with penalties for infringements. First of all came those guilty of high treason. They were defined as those who by writing or printing or by act imperilled the life of the King, or brought about any disturbance against the Crown; this was also applied to slandering the marriage with Queen Anne, or slandering the heirs to the Crown. The penalty was forfeiture of possessions and death. Those who spoke words of this kind, but did not go further, were guilty of misprision of treason; the penalty was imprisonment at the King's pleasure, and forfeiture of goods.

Finally came the provision for the oath to the succession. Here was something new in legislation; oaths had always been imposed for special purposes on individuals, but this Act applied to the whole population.[8] The wording of the clause calls for careful study.

> And, for the more sure establishment of the succession of your most royal majesty, according to the tenor and form of this Act, be it further enacted by authority aforesaid, that as well all the nobles of your realm spiritual and temporal, as all other your subjects now living and being, or that hereafter shall be, at their full ages, by the commandment of your majesty or of your heirs, at all times hereafter from time to time, when it shall please your highness or your heirs to appoint, shall make a corporal oath[9] in the presence of your highness or your heirs, or before such others as your majesty or your heirs will depute for the same, that they shall truly, firmly,

[8]This was the beginning of what may be termed a riot of oaths. For a generation, men swore and forswore themselves so many times that oaths lost all meaning.

[9]A corporal oath was one taken with the hand on a sacred object, such as the Gospels.

and constantly, without fraud or guile, observe, fulfil, maintain, defend and keep, to their cunning, wit, and uttermost of their powers, *the whole effects and contents of this present Act.*

Those last italicized words should be noted. The oath covered not only the succession, but everything else in the Act—the annulment of the marriage with Catherine, the validity of the marriage with Anne, the rejection of the authority of the Pope in matters of marriage—everything in it.

Those who "obstinately refused" to take the oath were guilty of misprision of treason. In the first draft of the Bill, this offence was made high treason, but Parliament modified this to "misprision", so instead of the death penalty the offender was liable to imprisonment at the King's pleasure with loss of goods. This change, in effect, postponed the executions of Fisher and More by a year. Before Parliament was prorogued on 30 March, the members of both Houses "most lovingly accepted and took such oath as was then devised in writing". Note the words "as was then devised". The Act itself did not give the words of the required oath.

On Low Sunday, 12 April 1534, Sir Thomas More and William Roper went to hear the sermon at St Paul's. Afterwards they walked to the Old Barge in Bucklersbury to see John and Margaret Clement who had gone to live their after their marriage. There it was, in his old home, that Thomas More received the summons to appear the next day at Lambeth before the Commissioners to take the oath to the Succession. He at once returned to Chelsea; he must have been comforted to have visited the house that had meant so much to him; his marriage, his children, and the happy meetings with Erasmus and John Colet and his many friends of those earlier, more care-free days, before he became engaged in "the busy trifles of princes".

Roper's own account of the last hours at Chelsea must be given:

> Then Sir Thomas More, as his accustomed manner was always, ere he entered into any matter of importance, as when he was first chosen of the King's Privy Council, when he was sent Ambassador, appointed speaker of the Parliament, made Lord Chancellor, or

when he took any weighty matter upon him, to go to church and be confessed, to hear Mass, and be housled, so did he likewise in the morning early the selfsame day that he was summoned to appear before the lords at Lambeth.

And whereas he evermore used before at his departure from his wife and children, whom he tenderly loved, to have them bring him to his boat and there to kiss them all, and bid them farewell, then would he suffer none of them forth of the gate to follow him, but pulled the wicket after him, and shut them all from him, and with an heavy heart, as by his countenance it appeared, with me and our four servants there took he his boat towards Lambeth. Wherein sitting still sadly awhile, at last he suddenly rounded me in the ear, and said, "Son Roper, I thank Our Lord the field is won". What he meant thereby I then wist not, yet loath to seem ignorant, I answered "Sir, I am thereof very glad". But as I conjectured after, it was for that the love of God wrought in him so effectually that it conquered all his carnal affections utterly.[10]

Why was More called so early to take the oath? He was not a Member of Parliament; he was no longer a Councillor; he held no official position. Yet, as far as the records show, he seems to have been the only layman called before the Commissioners on 13 April, more than a fortnight before the Act came into force. The others there whose names he noted were clergy such as Rowland Philips, Hugh Latimer and Nicholas Wilson. The King must have felt it desirable to get this leading layman to set an example to others; this confrontation with the members of the Council would bring things to a head one way or the other. It may be assumed that Henry expected More to capitulate when faced with the awful consequences; if so, the King had failed to read his former Chancellor's character aright.

Fortunately Thomas More wrote a letter to Margaret telling her what happened.[11]

The Commissioners were Archbishop Cranmer, Audley (Lord Chancellor), Thomas Cromwell (now Principal Secretary), and William Benson (Abbot, later Dean of Westminster). When Thomas More was asked by them to take the oath,

[10]Roper, p. 72.
[11]Rogers, 200 (54); perhaps this should follow, not precede, 201 (55).

I desired the sight of the oath, which they showed me under the
Great Seal. Then desired I the sight of the Act of Succession, which
was delivered me in a printed roll. After which read secretly by
myself, and the oath considered with the Act, I showed unto them
that my purpose was not to put any fault either in the Act or any man
that made it, or in the oath or any man that sware it, nor to condemn
the conscience of any other man. But as for myself in good faith my
conscience so moved me in the matter, that though I would not deny
to sware to the succession, yet unto the oath that there was offered
me I could not sware, without the jeoparding of my soul to perpetual damnation.

It was with a lawyer's eye that More would carefully read the
Act and then compare the oath with it. Roper tells us that More
said to Margaret, "I may tell thee, Meg, they that have committed
me hither [the Tower] for refusing this oath not agreeable with
the statute, are not by their own law able to justify my imprisonment". This point calls for examination. We have noted that no
oath was prescribed in the Act. The one offered to More "under
the Great Seal" had not been authorized by Parliament. Nor can
we be certain of the terms of that oath used at Lambeth. It may
have been the oath recorded in the Journals of the House of Lords
(I, 82), and confirmed by Letters Patent. This reads:

Ye shall swear to bear your faith, truth and obedience, alonely to
the King's Majesty, and to the Heirs of his body, according to the
limitation and rehearsal within this Statute of Succession above
specified, and not to any other within this realm, *nor foreign Authority,
Prince or Potentate;* and in case any oath be made, or hath been made,
by you to any other person or persons, that then ye to repute the
same as vain and annihilate; and that, to your cunning, wit and
uttermost your power, without guile, fraud, or other undue means,
ye shall observe, keep, maintain, and defend this Act above specified,
and all the whole contents and effects thereof, and all other Acts and
Statutes made since the beginning of the present Parliament, in
confirmation or for due execution of the same, or of anything
therein contained; and thus ye shall do against all manner of persons,
of what estate, dignity, degree or condition soever they be, and in no
wise do or attempt, nor to your power suffer to be done or attempted,
directly or indirectly, anything or things, privily or apertly, to the

let, hindrance, damage, or derogation thereof, or of any part of the same, by any manner of means, or for any manner of pretence or cause. So help you God and all Saints.

The defect of the first Act of Succession was remedied in the next session of Parliament by the passing of "An act ratifying the oath. . . ". This varies from the above in some ways; it begins with an oath of obedience to Queen Anne as well as to the King and his heirs, and at the end it adds "the holy Evangelists" to those whose help is invoked.

To what did More object in the oath? As it covered the whole Act, it implied repudiation of Papal authority, and the addition in the oath of "any . . . foreign Authority, Prince or Potentate" was clearly aimed at the Pope and was outside the wording of the Act. The reference to "all other Acts or Statutes made since the beginning of this present Parliament in confirmation or for due execution of the same" was another addition. While no such Acts had been passed bearing directly on the succession, there were others that struck at the Pope. The Acts passed had been the Statute of Appeals (24 Hen. VIII, c. 12) which forbad appeals from English to foreign courts; the Ecclesiastical Appointments Act (25 Hen. VIII, c. 20) which barred the Pope from having anything to do with the appointments to benefices; the Dispensations Act (c. 21), which denied the Pope's authority to grant dispensations; and the Heresy Act (c. 15) which curbed the powers of the bishops. The Act of Supremacy, the operative Annates Act, and the Treason Act, had not yet been made.

We must return to Lambeth. The Commissioners tried to frighten More with the threat of the King's "great indignation"; such a threat had not deterred him in the Nun of Kent business and it did not this time. Then, "I was in conclusion commanded to go down into the garden, and thereupon I tarried in the old burned chamber that looketh into the garden and would not go down because of the heat".

The Commissioners may have hoped that if he met others who had taken the oath while in the garden he might be influenced by their example, or they may have been nonplussed as to the next move.

Thomas More passed the time watching what went on in the garden.

> In that time saw I Doctor [Hugh] Latimer come into the garden, and there walked he with divers other doctors and chaplains of my Lord of Canterbury, and very merry I saw him, for he laughed, and took one or twain about the neck so handsomely that, if they had been women, I would have went [thought] he had been waxen wanton. After that came Master Doctor [Nicholas] Wilson forth from the lords and was with two gentlemen brought by me, and gentlemanly sent straight into the Tower. What time my Lord of Rochester [Fisher] was called in before them, that cannot I tell. But at night I heard that he had been before them, but where he remained that night and so forth till he was sent hither [the Tower], I never heard. I heard also that Master Vicar of Croyden, and all the remnant of the priests of London that were sent for, were sworn, and that they had such favour at the Council's hand that they were not lingered nor made to dance any long attendance to their travail and cost, as suitors were sometimes wont to be, but were sped apace to their great comfort, so far forth that Master Vicar of Croyden, either for gladness or for dryness, or else that it might be seen (*quod ille notus erat pontifici*) went to my Lord's buttery bar and called for a drink, and drank (*valde familiariter*).

We have already met the Vicar of Croydon, Rowland Philips, as Ralph Robinson's candidate for missionary labours in *Utopia*. More was evidently amused at Philips' exuberance on this occasion. The words, *quod ille notus erat pontifici*, are a quotation from St John's Gospel 18, 15: "And Simon Peter followed Jesus, and so did another disciple. And that disciple *was known to the high priest*."[12] This may be nothing more than an apt quotation referring to Philips' relations with Cranmer, who, as Archbishop of Canterbury, had a palace at Croydon where he frequently stayed. It is straining the application too much to suggest that More was seeing himself in the position of St Peter being tempted to deny his Lord.

More was called in again to the Commissioners and they tried to impress him with the list of those who had taken the oath. They wanted to know to what parts of the oath he objected and his

[12]See J. D. M. Derrett, *Moreana*, No. 8 (1965), pp. 67-70.

reasons for doing so. As before, and frequently in later days, he
refused to give the grounds of his objections.

> And that if I should open and disclose the causes why, I should
> therewith but further exasperate his Highness, which I would in no
> wise do, but rather would I abide all the danger and harm that might
> come toward me, than give his Highness any occasion of further
> displeasure.

He offered, however, to set out his reasons in writing to the King
if Henry on his part would not see further offence in such a
statement. It was pointed out to him that no such declaration by
the King could stand against the application of the statute.

Cranmer then argued that since More had said that he did not
condemn any who took the oath, he must have some doubts on
the matter and, in such a case, he should obey the King as a matter
of duty. This argument for a moment made More hesitate, but
he replied,

> that in my conscience this was one of the cases in which I was
> bounden that I should not obey my prince, since that, whatsoever
> other folk thought in the matter (whose conscience and learning I
> would not condemn nor take upon me to judge), yet in my conscience
> the truth seemed on the other side.

The Abbot of Westminster then suggested that More should
defer to the opinions expressed by the Parliament and the Council.

> To that I answered, that if there were no more but myself upon my
> side, and the whole of Parliament upon the other, I would be sore
> afraid to lean to mine own mind only against so many. But on the
> other side, if it so be that in some things for which I refuse the oath,
> I have (as I think I have) upon my part as great a council and a
> greater too, I am not then bounden to change my conscience, and
> confirm it to the council of one realm against the general Council
> of Christendom.

This too was an argument that More was to repeat in later
interrogations and at his trial.

> Upon this Master Secretary [Cromwell] (as he tenderly favoureth
> me) said and sware a great oath that he had lever that his own only
> son . . . had lost his head than that I should thus have refused the
> oath. For surely the King's Highness would now conceive a great

suspicion against me, and think that the matter of the nun of Canterbury was all contrived by my drift [influence]. To which I said that
the contrary was true and well known.

The letter ends:

As touching the whole oath, I never withdrew any man from it, nor
never advised any to refuse it, nor never put, nor will, any scruple
in any man's head, but leave every man to his own conscience. And
methinketh in good faith that so were it good reason that every
man should leave me to mine.

The Commissioners were puzzled by More's refusal to state his
reasons for not accepting the Act and the oath, nor were they sure
how best to proceed. So for a few days they committed him to
the charge of the Abbot of Westminster in the monastery.

Meanwhile they had put the oath to Bishop John Fisher. He
had come up from Rochester a very sick man; he too asked for
time to study the wording of the oath, and he was allowed to go
to his own palace close to Lambeth. Four days later, 17 April, he
was brought before the Commissioners again. His position was
the same as that of Sir Thomas More; he was willing to take the
oath to the succession, but not to "the whole effects and contents
of this present Act". He was at once sent to the Tower. Dr
Nicholas Wilson had refused to take the oath at the first hearing
and had at once been sent to the Tower.

Cranmer had been seeking for a way out of the difficult position in which the Commissioners found themselves. He wrote to
Cromwell suggesting that both More and Fisher should be allowed
to take the simple oath to the succession but that this modification
should not be made public so that people would assume that the
two had in fact subscribed to the whole oath. He thought this
would quieten not only the "Princess-Dowager" (Catherine) but
the Emperor as well and "many other within this realm".
Cromwell put the proposal to the King who instructed him to tell
Cranmer that the Bishop and Sir Thomas must swear to the whole
oath otherwise "it might be taken not only as a confirmation of
the Bishop of Rome's authority, but also as a reprobation of the
King's second marriage".

On 17 April 1534 Sir Thomas More again came before the

Commission and refused to take the oath. He was at once conveyed to the Tower.

As he was going thitherward, wearing, as he commonly did, a chain
of gold about his neck, Sir Richard Cromwell,[13] that had the charge
of his conveyance thither, advised him to send home his chain to his
wife, or to some of his children. "Nay, sir," quoth he, "that I will
not; for if I were taken in the field by my enemies, I would they
should somewhat fare the better by me."

At whose landing Master Lieutenant[14] at the Tower gate was ready
to receive him, where the porter demanded of him his upper
garment. "Master Porter," quoth he, "here it is", and took off his
cap, and delivered it him saying, "I am very sorry it is no better for
you." "No, sir," quoth the porter, "I must have your gown."

It was this kind of persiflage that made more solemn men like
Edward Hall shake their heads and murmur that it was "to his
gravity a great blemish".

And so was he by Master Lieutenant conveyed to his lodging, where
he called unto him John à Wood his own servant, there appointed to
attend him, who could neither write nor read; and sware him before
the Lieutenant that if he should hear him or see him, at any time,
speak or write any manner of thing against the King, the Council or
the State of the Realm, he should open it to the Lieutenant, that the
Lieutenant might incontinent reveal it to the Council.[15]

That precaution shows how Sir Thomas knew he would have to
watch every word he said lest he fall into a trap that would bring
him within the law; his own opinion, as expressed to his daughter
Margaret, was that he had been committed without legal cause.

The hesitations of the Commissioners in dealing with More
were due not only to a humane desire to spare a man of such
eminence among whose friends they had been glad to be counted,
but to fears of repercussions abroad where the name of Thomas
More was greatly honoured. This wider political aspect is shown
in an interview Eustace Chapuys had on 16 May with an unusually

[13]Son of Cromwell's sister who had married a Morgan Williams. Richard took his
uncle's name and did not relinquish it even when his uncle was executed. It is said he
dared to appear in court in mourning. His great-grandson was the Protector Oliver.
[14]Sir Edmund Walsingham, lieutenant of the Tower, 1525-1547.
[15]Roper, p. 74.

L

impressive gathering of the Council; there were present both archbishops, three bishops (including Tunstal), the Chancellor, the King's Secretary (Cromwell), the Duke of Norfolk and other peers and "chief magistrates of the Realm". The purpose was to justify to the Emperor the Act of Succession, not an easy task for it closely concerned his aunt, Queen Catherine, and his cousin, the Princess Mary. It was a long and inconclusive discussion, and Chapuys was clearly not impressed by the force of the arguments. He commented that the lightness with which Cranmer had regarded his oath of fidelity to the Pope at his consecration as archbishop had lowered the sanctity of an oath. He added:

> People swore because they dared not offer opposition, the penalty being forfeiture of life and property, and no one in these times wished to become a martyr; besides which, several reconciled themselves to the idea by the notion that oaths taken by force, against morality, were not binding.[16]

Chapuys believed that should Queen Catherine and her daughter refuse to take the oath, they too would be sent to the Tower. It was therefore no wonder that the King and his Council were apprehensive of what action the Emperor might take.

[16]S.P. (S), 5, i, No 58; L.P., 7, i, No 690.

Chapter XXVIII

Papal Primacy

The Lambeth Commissioners must have understood why Sir Thomas More declined the oath even if they were puzzled at his refusal to give his reasons. Certainly Cromwell had no cause for doubt on this point. He had recently received a letter from More, which must be considered in detail presently as it is a key-document, putting forward the writer's views on the issues.[1] This letter was intended for the King for it would have been Cromwell's duty to show it to Henry; indeed, it may be that its contents and implications occasioned the decision to have More called up to take the oath. The other Commissioners—they may have seen the letter or been told of its gist—could put two and two together. Apart from the decision about the succession, two questions remained. The first was the annulment by Cranmer of the marriage with Queen Catherine; the second was the implied rejection of papal authority. While there was no specific statement on this matter, the acceptance of the competence of the Archbishop of Canterbury to adjudicate was a direct denial of hitherto recognized papal prerogative. More would also have in mind the Submission of the Clergy, when, as John Fisher said, "The fort is betrayed even by them that should have defended it".[2] The recently passed Heresy Act[3] must have been as disturbing; it placed restrictions on the trial of heretics by the bishops' courts, and stated that "No manner of speaking against the Bishop of Rome, or his pretended power", or his decrees, was to be deemed heresy, and it was further declared that the authority of the Pope "was never commonly accepted or confirmed to be any law by God or man within this realm".

Thomas More refused, and continued to refuse, to make any

---

[1] Rogers, 199 (53).

[2] It should be kept in mind that the Act of Supremacy (as distinct from the declarations by the Convocations) did not become law until eight or nine months after More's appearance at Lambeth.

[3] 25 Hen. VIII, c. 14.

spoken statement on the nature of his objections. He knew that his one chance of escape was to avoid speaking words that could be quoted against him; it was at best a slender chance, but as a lawyer he knew it was his remaining hope. Not only would he not answer direct questions put to him by the Commissioners at Lambeth and later by members of the Council in the Tower, but he would not discuss the matter with his family and friends. This left them bewildered. He several times stressed that he judged no man who felt able to take the oath; he thus cleared himself of any suspicion that he was forming a party to oppose the will of the King and Parliament. In an ultimate question of this kind he believed that each must consult his own conscience after a careful study of the issues. An example of his personal detachment is seen in a report[4] by Christopher Chaytor, Tunstal's Registrar. One of Tunstal's servants named Burton came to see More and Fisher in the Tower on behalf of his master. More asked him whether Tunstal was likely to join them in the Tower. Burton replied that he did not know the Bishop's mind in the matter. To this More replied, "If he do not, no force [matter], for if he live he may do more good than to die with us".

It is important to appreciate Thomas More's attitude towards the papacy. No one could have been blamed in those days for having doubts about papal supremacy. The zenith of papal prestige had been reached under Innocent III who died in 1216; the nadir was reached by the death of Alexander VI (Borgia) in 1503, when Thomas More was twenty-five years old. That Pope was followed by the warrior Julius II (1503-13), and he in turn by the Medici Pope, Leo X, whose main interest was his own pleasure. Alexander VI's vicious life was a public scandal, and it needed a firm separation in men's minds of the office from the man to retain their loyalty to the Holy See. Earlier there had been the Babylonish Captivity at Avignon of 1305 to 1378, followed by the Great Schism of 1378-1417 when there were two, and even three, rival Popes. Is it surprising that many devout Christians began to wonder if the papacy was indeed of divine institution and inspiration?

[4]Dated 1539. See C. Sturge, *Cuthbert Tunstal*, p. 372.

This shameful state of the papacy led those who longed for a truly apostolic Church to seek ways of regeneration. So arose the Conciliar movement the purpose of which was to control the Pope through the General Council. The Council of Constance (1414-18) decreed that a General Council "holds an authority directly derived from Christ", an authority that "everyone of whatever status or dignity, even the Pope, is bound to obey". The question, "Is the Pope subject to the General Council?" was to agitate the Church for a long time. There can be little doubt that the degradation of the papacy was one cause of the Reformation.

Thomas More was acutely aware of all these abuses, and like John Colet and Erasmus and many others in Christian lands, he longed for a true reform. The ridicule of Erasmus' *Moria* and the satire of *Julius Exclusus*[5] infuriated the clergy and delighted the laity. The Lateran Council of 1512-17 passed pious resolutions that were never acted upon. Wolsey showed some concern in his early days of office, but, once he was a Cardinal, he became too involved in State affairs and in his own ambitions to make any resolute effort to face the problems of internal Church weaknesses. A kind of lethargy and a sense of helplessness had settled on the Church; only heroic measures would have been effective and, unhappily, there was no one who could take resolute command. Then came Luther. It should not be forgotten that Luther's initial appeal was to the multitude of those who were sick with disappointment; his later theological innovations, while holding many, drove away some early adherents.

We have seen how quickly Thomas More understood the new situation. The old problem of reform of abuses remained, but it had to give place in his mind to the more serious threat of disruption through heresy, and it was to combating heresy that he gave his thoughts and devoted his pen. The urgent need, he was convinced, was to reassert the paramount importance of preserving the unity of the Church under the Pope as its head on earth. This did not mean that he came to minimize the personal defects,

---

[5]Erasmus had been horrified at seeing the entry of Julius II at the head of his victorious troops into Bologna in 1506.

even vices, of the men who held the office, for, whoever was Pope, that man inherited the powers, the *potestas jurisdictionis*, given by our Lord to St Peter; outside the Church there could be no salvation.

The question of papal authority had arisen when in 1520 Thomas More discussed the *Assertio Septem Sacramentorum* with its royal author; it was the King's astonishing full commitment to the papacy that led More to study, quite apart from the marriage problem, the nature of the papacy. In the important letter to Thomas Cromwell, to which reference was made at the beginning of this chapter, More stated that he had studied the question of the primacy of the Pope "these ten years since and more", which brings us near to 1520. He further admitted that "I was myself sometime not of the mind that the primacy of that see should be begun by the institution of God". That he had such doubts is confirmed by an incident recorded by Cardinal Pole.[6] Antonio Bonvisi told Reginald Pole of a conversation he had had with Thomas More, and the Cardinal narrated this in the course of a sermon during the reign of Queen Mary Tudor. The subject of the primacy of the Pope had been mentioned and More had expressed the opinion that the supremacy was a matter of organization and not of divine origin. Some days later he sought out Bonvisi and said, "Whither was I falling, when I made that answer of the primacy of the Pope? I assure you, that opinion alone was enough to make me fall from the rest, for that upholdeth all." "He began", added the Cardinal, "to show him what he had read and studied therein, which was so fixed in his heart that for the defence of the same, he willingly afterward suffered death."

On this very question, Tunstal and More differed. The Bishop held the opinion that the papal primacy was a comparatively recent innovation and was not of divine institution. It seems that Tunstal seriously studied the historical claims of the papacy after his exchange of views with the King on the Royal Supremacy. His conclusions were set down in a correspondence with Reginald Pole in 1536. Pole reproached Tunstal for not having followed

[6]Strype, *Memorials*, III, ii, pp. 491-3.

the examples of More and Fisher. Tunstal replied that his reading of history had led him to take a different view from theirs. He may have been influenced by his memory of a visit to Rome in 1505 when he had been shocked at what he saw of the papal court.[7] Bishop John Clerk shared Tunstal's views.

The earliest statement of More's mature attitude to the papacy comes in his answer, as Rosseus, to Luther's reply (1522) to the *Assertio*.

I am moved to obedience to that See not only by what learned and holy men have written, but by this very fact especially, that we shall find that on the one hand every enemy of the Christian faith makes war on that See, and that, on the other hand, no one has ever declared himself an enemy of that See who has not also shortly after shown most evidently that he was the enemy of the Christian religion. Another thing that moves me is this, that if, after Luther's manner, the vices of men are to be imputed to the offices they hold, not only the papacy will fall, but royalty, and dictatorship and consulate and every other kind of magistracy, and the people will be without rulers, without law, and without order. Should such a thing ever come to pass, as indeed it seems imminent in some parts of Germany, they will then feel to their own great loss how much better it is for men to have bad rulers than no rulers at all. Most assuredly as regards the Pope, God, who set him over his Church, knows how great an evil it would be to be without one, and I do not think it desirable that Christendom should learn that by experience. *It is far more to be wished that God may raise up such Popes as befit the Christian cause and the dignity of the Apostolic office:* men who, despising riches and honour, will care only for heaven, will promote piety in the people, will bring about peace, and exercise the authority they have received from God against the 'satraps and mighty hunters of the world', excommunicating and giving over to Satan both those who invade the territories of others and those who oppress their own. With one or two such Popes the Christian world would soon perceive how much preferable it is that the papacy should be reformed than abolished.

This passage can be dated 1522 or 1523; it seems evident that the question More raised in reading the King's *Assertio* had led him to examine the position of the papacy with some care; it will be

[7] C. Sturge, *Cuthbert Tunstal*, pp. 193, 207-9.

noted that he did not shirk the problem of the personal morality of the Pope who, when More was writing, was Adrian VI; like his countryman and friend Erasmus, he had been educated by the Brethren of the Common Life, and he tried to persuade Erasmus to join him in Rome. Much was hoped of him, but he died in September 1523 before he could effect any of the reforms he saw were necessary. He was followed by the irresolute Clement VII, another Medici Pope.

The paragraph before the one just quoted begins, "As regards the primacy of the Roman Pontiff, the Bishop of Rochester has made the matter so clear. . . ." More was here referring to Fisher's *Assertionis Lutheranae confutatio*, which was published in Antwerp in January 1523 but seems to have been in circulation before that date; More had probably read it in manuscript. It was reprinted in 1537, 1545, 1558 and 1564, an indication of the impact Fisher made on theologians and scholars by his arguments.

The next statement on the papacy that can be dated comes in More's *Dialogue Concerning Heresies* (1528). It reads:

> This is the very Church; and this hath begun at Christ and hath had him for their head, and saint Peter his vicar, and after him, the head under him, and alway since, the successors of him continually—and have had his holy faith, and his blessed sacraments, and his holy scriptures delivered, kept, and conserved therein by God and his holy spirit.[8]

In the letter to Cromwell, More recalled his talk with the King about the *Assertio*[9]; he continued:

> But surely after that I had read his Grace's book therein, and so many other things as I have seen in that point by this continuance of these ten year since and more have found in effect the substance of all the holy doctors from St Ignatius [of Antioch], disciple to St John the Evangelist, unto our own days both Latins and Greeks so consonant and agreeing in that point, and the thing by such general councils so confirmed also, that in good faith I never neither read nor heard anything of such effect on the other side, that ever could lead me to think that my conscience were well discharged, but rather in right great peril if I should follow the other side and deny the primacy to

---

[8]E.W., p. 185.   [9]See above, p. 95.

be provided by God, which if we did, yet can I nothing (as I showed you) perceive any commodity [advantage] that ever could come by that denial, for that primacy is at leastwise instituted by the corps of Christendom and for a great urgent cause in avoiding of schisms and corroborate [confirmed] by continual succession more than the space of a thousand year at least, for there are passed almost a thousand year sith the time of holy St Gregory.

It must be admitted that that is not one of More's clearest statements, but it repays careful reading.

The letter then dealt with the delicate question of the King's claim to be Supreme Head of the Church in England, but More was careful to avoid a direct reference. "And therefore sith all Christendom is one corps, I cannot perceive how any member thereof may without the common assent of the body depart from the common head."

Those important words were to be repeated by Thomas More at his trial.

He then went on in this letter to express his approval of the King's appeal in November 1533 to a General Council. In view of this, More thought it would be unwise,

if his Highness should in his realm before, either by laws making or books putting forth, seem to derogate and deny not only the primacy of the see apostolic but also the authority of the general councils too, which I verily trust his Highness intendeth not, for in the next general council it may well happen that this Pope may be deposed and another substituted in his room with whom the King's Highness may be very well content.

More did not see any contradiction between an appeal to a General Council, which might overrule, or even depose the Pope, and his belief in the primacy of the papacy. So he stated:

Albeit that I have for mine own part such opinion of the Pope's primacy as I have showed you, yet never thought I the Pope above the general council nor never have in any book of mine put forth among the King's subjects in our vulgar tongue, advanced greatly the Pope's authority.

That was certainly true, for in reading More's controversial works

L*

we may note how he avoided any detailed discussion of the papacy. The Conciliar movement had accustomed men to this seeming contradiction between the primacy and the General Council, and it was one that was not resolved for many years.

CHAPTER XXIX

The Prisoner

SIR THOMAS MORE was in the Tower for fifteen months with Bishop John Fisher and Dr Nicholas Wilson as his fellow prisoners.[1] They could have been brought to trial in the King's Bench with the certainty that, having refused the oath, they would be condemned for misprision of treason, the penalty for which was life imprisonment and the loss of all possessions. There was nothing exceptional in this imprisonment without trial especially for those committed to the Tower; they were State prisoners and were the concern of the King and Council. The King may have hoped that even Thomas More would yield after a period of imprisonment, or he wanted him and Fisher (Wilson was of small account) out of the way and so be unable to influence public opinion; out of sight, out of mind!

It is important to be clear on one point; in these early months the question of the Royal Supremacy did not arise; there was no reference to it in the Act of Succession. The Convocations had accepted the title on behalf of the clergy, but this did not give the title statutory force. It was not until the end of 1534 that the Act of Supremacy was passed by Parliament. As we shall see, this had grievous consequences for the prisoners.

For the first twelve months, Thomas More was not harassed. After a time, Dame Alice and Margaret Roper were allowed to visit him, and the three walked together in the Tower garden. He was allowed to have books and facilities for writing, and, at his own expense, to make his cell as comfortable as possible. His personal servant, John à Wood, attended him.[2]

[1] They were joined later in the year by Dr Edward Powell, one of the theologians who defended Queen Catherine, and Dr Richard Fetherstone, who had been tutor to the Princess Mary. Two others, who are little more than names, were Canon Miles Willen of Windsor, and Prebendary Christopher Plummer of Chichester. Thomas Abel, a valiant defender of Queen Catherine, was already in the Tower.

[2] One tradition is that he was imprisoned in the Beauchamp Tower, another gives the Bell Tower, but there are no records to tell us where each prisoner was shut up.

The following passage from *A Dialogue of Comfort* probably refers to his cell. The visitor was no doubt Dame Alice.

I wist a woman once that came into a prison to visit of her charity a poor prisoner there, whom she found in a chamber, to say the truth, meetly fair, and at leastwise it was strong enough; but with mats of straw the prisoner had made it so warm both under the foot and round the walls that in these things for the keeping of his health she was on his behalf glad and very well comforted. But among many other displeasures that for his sake she was sorry for, one she lamented much in her mind, that he should have the chamber door upon him by night made fast by the jailor that should shut him in. For, by my troth, quoth she, if the door should be shut upon me I would ween it would stop up my breath. At that word of hers the prisoner laughed in his mind, but he durst not laugh aloud nor say nothing to her, for somewhat indeed he stood in awe of her and had his finding [expenses] there much part of her charity for alms; but he could not but laugh inwardly, why he wist well enough, that she used on the inside to shut every night full surely her own chamber to her, both door and windows too, and used not to open them of all the long night.[3]

Dame Alice had to pay fifteen shillings a week "board-lodgings", as she called it, for the support of her husband. Bishop Fisher, who ranked as a lord, had to pay a pound a week. Roper records one conversation she had during a visit to her husband.[4]

At her first coming, like a simple ignorant woman, and somewhat worldly too, with this manner of salutation bluntly saluted him.

"What the good year, Master More," quoth she, "I marvel that you, that have been always hitherto taken for so wise a man, will now so play the fool to lie here in this close, filthy prison, and be content thus to be shut up amongst mice and rats, when you might be abroad at your liberty, and with the favour and good will of the King and his Council, if you would but do as all the Bishops and best learned of this realm have done."

She then went on to contrast his prison with his home at Chelsea. This has already been quoted. She continued:

"I muse what a' God's name you mean here still thus fondly to tarry."

[3] *Dialogue of Comfort*, p. 385.
[4] There was little love lost between Roper and Dame Alice, and perhaps this friction between them has unfairly coloured our picture of her.

After he had a while quietly heard her, with a cheerful countenance he said unto her:

"I pray thee, good Mistress Alice, tell me one thing."

"What is that?" quoth she.

"Is not this house", quoth he, "as nigh heaven as my own?"

To whom she, after her accustomed homely fashion, not liking such talk, answered, "Tilly-vally, Tilly-vally!"[5]

"How say you, Mistress Alice," quoth he, "is it not so?"

"Bone Deus, bone Deus, man! Will this gear never be left?" quoth she.

"Well, then, Mistress Alice, if it be so," quoth he, "it is very well. For I see no great cause why I should much joy either of my gay house or of anything belonging thereunto, when, if I should but seven years lie buried under ground, and then arise and come thither again, I should not fail to find some therein that would bid me get me out of doors, and tell me it were none of mine. What cause have I then to like such an house as would so soon forget its master?"[6]

Margaret was her father's confidante during these months of waiting. She herself was not able to share his objections to the oath. Her cousin, William Rastell, says that she "took the oath with this exception, as far as would stand with the law of God". This must have been a mental reservation, but it would certainly not have been permitted as a spoken addition. Her father did not attempt to impose his views on his family.

As soon as possible after his arrival in the Tower, Thomas More sent a note to his daughter Margaret. As he had not yet any ink, he wrote this "with a coal", presumably a stick of charcoal; Cresacre More said that his grandfather (John More) at once inked over such letters to preserve them. This first one ends: "Recommend me to your shrewd Will and mine other sons, and to John Harris my friend, and yourself knoweth to whom else, and to my shrewd wife above all, and God preserve you all, and make and keep you his servants all."[7]

[5]Probably from Tityvallus, the demon in Mysteries, who collected in a sack idle vows spoken in church; hence 'idle words', or 'what nonsense!'

[6]Roper, p. 84. This passage is a good example of Roper's skill as a writer, a skill that has not been recognized as it should have been.

[7]Rogers, 201 (55). Shrewd here means clever. Was Cresacre More referring to letters written by More to his son? None have been preserved, nor have any to Dame Alice and the children other than to Margaret.

Margaret wrote a letter to her father in which she urged him to submit to the King's wishes. According to her cousin, William Rastell, she wrote this in order to "win credence with Master Thomas Cromwell that she might the rather get liberty to have free resort to her father". This is, however, not in accordance with later evidence, as we shall see. When Cromwell found that she was ready to take the oath and to persuade her father to do so as well, he gave the necessary permission for her to enter the Tower. More's answer shows that, for the first and last time, he was deeply hurt. Her letter came as a shock to him; he had made no attempt to persuade her, or any of his family, one way or the other, and he expected them to respect his decision in the same way. So he wrote:

> If I had not been, my dearly beloved daughter, at a firm and fast point (I trust in God's great mercy) this good great while before, your lamentable letter had not a little abashed me, surely far above all other things, of which I hear divers times not a few terrible toward me. But surely they all touched me never so near, nor were so grievous unto me, as to see you, my well-beloved child, in such vehement piteous manner labour to persuade unto me, that thing wherein I have of pure necessity for respect unto mine own soul, so often given you so precise answer before. Wherein as touching the points of your letter, I can make none answer, for I doubt not but you well remember, that the matters which move my conscience (without declaration whereof I can nothing touch the points) I have sundry times showed you that I will disclose them to no man. And therefore, daughter Margaret, I can in this thing no further, but like as you, labour me again to follow your mind, to desire and pray you both again to leave such labour, and with my former answers to hold yourself content.

He then turned to a thought that was to find expression in other letters.

> A deadly grief unto me, and much more deadly than to hear of my own death . . . is that I perceive my good son your husband, and you my good daughter, and my good wife, and mine other good children and innocent friends, in great displeasure and danger ot great harm thereby. The let [hindering] whereof, while it lieth nof

in my hand, I can no further but commit all unto God.[8]
Margaret did not then pursue the argument. What is probably
her next letter was full of her warm affection. It ended:

Your own most loving and obedient daughter and beadswoman,
Margaret Roper, which desireth above all worldly things to be in
John Wood's stead to do you some service. But we live in hope that
we shall shortly receive you again. I pray God heartily we may, if
it be his holy will.

We may wonder why More's family did not follow his
example. All of them must have taken the oath. Why, indeed,
did the people of the country, with so few exceptions, accept so
placidly the new order of things? Almost the only way of reaching the commonalty, especially in the country towns and villages,
was through their parish priests whose guidance they would
accept, however critical they might be of the clergy. So it was
that when all the bishops (except John Fisher) and the majority
of the clergy accepted Henry as Supreme Head, and later the
various changes in religion, the people, as a whole, followed
them. For them, such matters as the relations between the King
and the Pope, or the validity of Henry's marriage, were outside
their range of interest; these were problems for priest and noble.
Their personal regard for Queen Catherine did affect their attitude, but it was a sentiment that could not find an outlet. As to
the Act of Succession, how many knew what it contained? They
had to swear to "the whole effect and present contents of this
Act". It seems unlikely that the Act was expounded by the
commissioners to each person, nor would many, even of the
literate, ask to see a copy of the Act to examine it at leisure.

The More family could not be described as ordinary folk but
they must have been puzzled at what was happening. For them,
too, the acquiescence of the bishops, especially of their father's
close friend, Cuthbert Tunstal, must have carried great weight.
No doubt had Thomas More explained all the implications of
the Act of Succession, he could have persuaded them to accept
his opinion, but he would not force their consciences, and, as we
have just seen, even when Margaret put their case to him, he still

[8]Rogers, 202 (56).

refused to debate the fundamental issues. He was true to his decision to "leave every man to his own conscience" and would not pass judgment on the decision others might take.

More's family and friends were doing what they could to help him. His step-daughter, Alice Alington, seized the chance of a meeting with the new Lord Chancellor, Audley, to ask him to "be still good lord unto my father". Audley said that he had indeed been so in the matter of the Nun of Kent, but the position now was more serous; "he marvelled that my father is so obstinate in his own conceit, as that everybody went forth with all save only the blind Bishop and he". Then he laughingly related two fables, one of them being Wolsey's tale of the fools and the rain. "I was abashed of this answer", Alice wrote to Margaret, "and I see no better suit than to Almighty God."[9]

When Margaret next went to the Tower, she took Alice's letter with her for her father to read. The talk they had is recorded in a remarkable letter from her to Alice Alington. Its form is that of a dialogue with Alice's letter as a theme. We can imagine them sitting together in More's cell, or perhaps walking in the Tower garden. As they talked so the shape of the letter was decided. When she got back to Chelsea Margaret wrote the whole down. We can regard the result as the joint work of father and daughter.[10]

The first part of the reply gives us information of the state of More's health:

When I had a while talked with him, first of his diseases both in his breast of old, and his reins now by reason of gravel and stone, and of the cramp also that divers nights grippeth him in his legs, and that I found by his words that they were not much increased, but continued after their manner that they did before, sometime very sore and sometime little grief, and that at that time I found him out of pain, and (as one in his case might) meetly well-minded, after our seven [Penitential] Psalms and the Litany [of the Saints] said, to sit and talk and be merry, beginning first with other things of the comfort of my mother, and the good order of my brother, and all my sisters, disposing themself every day more and more to set little by the world, and draw more and more to God. . . .

[9]Rogers, 205.   [10]Rogers, 206.

She then gave him the letter, at the same time gently urging him to reconsider his decision. Evidently the distress her earlier letter had caused him had passed and they were able to discuss the matter without any trace of bitterness.

With this my father smiled upon me and said, "What, Mistress Eve, hath my daughter Alington played the serpent with you, and with a letter set you a-work to come tempt your father again, and for the favour that you bear him labour to make him swear against his conscience, and so send him to the devil?"

After reading the letter through twice, he said:

Forsooth, daughter Margaret, I find my daughter Alington such as I have ever found her, and I trust ever shall, as naturally minding me as you that are mine own. Howbeit, her I take verily for mine own too, since I have married her mother, and brought up her of a child as I have brought you up, in other things and learning both, wherein I thank God she findeth now some fruit, and bringeth her own up virtuously and well.

They went on to discuss Audley's fables; it was in comment on one of these that More told the story of Wolsey and the Council that has already been quoted. Margaret may have pressed the point that Audley had made—that More and Fisher were at variance with the opinions of many worthy and learned men. Thomas More declared that if the Bishop of Rochester himself now took the oath, this would not affect his own decision. Nor had he been influenced by Fisher.

For albeit, that of very truth, I have him [Fisher] in that reverent estimation, that I reckon in this realm no man, in wisdom, learning and long approved virtue together, meet to be matched and compared with him, yet that in this matter I was not led by him, very well and plainly appeareth, both in that I refused the oath before it was offered him, and in that also his lordship was content to have sworn of that oath (as I perceived since by you when you moved me to the same) either somewhat more, or in some other manner than ever I minded to do. Verily, daughter, I never intend (God being my good lord) to pin my soul at another man's back, not even the best man that I know this day living; for I know not whither he may hap to carry it.

Evidently More was under the impression that John Fisher had been prepared to take the oath on certain conditions; as far as the records go, these conditions were exactly the same as those which More put to the commissioners.

He went on to consider the reasons why many had taken the oath.

> Some may do for favour, and some may do for fear, and so might they carry my soul a wrong way. And some might hap to frame himself a conscience and think that while he did it for fear, God would forgive it. And some may peradventure think that they will repent, and be shriven thereof, and that so God shall remit it them. And some may be peradventure of that mind, that if they say one thing and think the while the contrary, God more regardeth their heart than their tongue, and that therefore their oath goeth upon what they think, and not upon what they say. . . . But in good faith, Margaret, I can use no such ways in so great a matter.

Margaret was not willing to give up her hope of influencing her father. She urged that a law made by Parliament should be obeyed.

> "Marry, Margaret," quoth my father again, "for the part that you play, you play it not much amiss. But Margaret first, as for the law of the land, though every man being born and inhabiting therein, is bound to the keeping in every case upon such temporal pain, and in many cases upon pain of God's displeasure too, yet is there no man bounden to swear that every law is well made, nor bounden upon the pain of God's displeasure, to perform any such point of the law, as were indeed unleaful [not permissible]."

Margaret was saddened at her failure to move her father. He saw this and rallied her with, "How now, mother Eve? Where is your mind now?"

> "In good faith, father," quoth I, "I can no further go, but am (as I trow Cresyde said in Chauser) come to Dulcarnon,[11] even at my wit's end. For since the example of so many wise men cannot in this matter move you, I see not what to say more, but if I should look to persuade you with the reason that Master Harry Patenson made. For

[11] Bk. III, 931. "At Dulcarnon right at my wittes end". A corruption from the Arabic meaning "two-horned", or a non-plus. O.E.D.

he met one day one of our men, and when he asked him where you
were and heard that you were in the Tower still, he waxed even
angry with you and said, 'Why? What aileth him that he will not
swear? Wherefore should he stick to swear? I have sworn the oath
myself.' And so I can in good faith go now no further neither, after
so many wise men whom you take for no example, but if I should
say like Master Harry, 'Why should you refuse to swear, father, for
I have sworn myself?'"

She presently brought up another point that had been put to her
by Thomas Cromwell.

"But yet, father," quoth I, "by my troth, I fear me very sore, that
this matter will bring you in marvellous heavy trouble. You know
well that as I showed you, Master Secretary sent you word, as your
friend, to remember that the Parliament lasteth yet."

This presumably was a hint that Parliament might pass an Act of
Attainder against More.

"Margaret," quoth my father, "I thank him right heartily. But as I
showed you then again, I left not this gear unthought on."

He then gave a glimpse of what his decision had cost him.

I forgot not in this matter the counsel of Christ in the Gospel, that
ere I should begin to build this castle for the safeguard of mine own
soul, I should sit and reckon what the charge would be. I counted,
Margaret, full surely many a restless night, while my wife slept and
went [thought] that I slept too, what peril was possible for to fall to
me, so far forth that I am sure there can come none above. And in
devising, daughter, thereupon, I had a full heavy heart. But yet (I
thank our Lord) for all that, I never thought to change, though the
uttermost should hap me that my fear ran upon.

So he ended:

And therefore, mine own good daughter, never trouble thy mind for
anything that ever shall hap to me in this world. Nothing can come
but that that God will. And with this, my good child, I pray you
heartily, be you and all your sisters, and my sons too, comfortable
and serviceable to your good mother my wife. And I right heartily
pray both you and them, to serve God and be merry and rejoice in
him. And if anything hap to me that you would be loath, pray to
God for me, and trouble not yourself, as I shall full heartily pray

for us all, that we may meet together once in heaven, where we shall be merry for ever, and never have trouble after.

The full flavour of this remarkable letter cannot be tasted by these few passages. The reader should study the whole in detail; there is no writing of comparable length that can give such a clear picture of More and of his daughter Margaret.

For some six months, Thomas More was allowed whatever privileges were possible in the Tower, but, after that, he was subjected to more severe conditions. This may have come with the opening of a new session of Parliament on 3 November 1534. The greatest deprivation for him was that he could no longer go to Mass in one of the Tower Chapels, St Peter ad Vincula or St John's. Margaret wrote in great distress:

> Father, what moved them to shut you up again, we can nothing hear. But surely I conjecture that when they considered that you were of so temperate mind, that you were contented to abide there all your life with such liberty, they thought it were possible to incline you to their will, except it were by restraining you from the Church, and the company of my good mother your dear wife and us children and beadsfolk.[12]

Her father replied:

> . . . so doth my mind always give me that some folk yet ween that I was not so poor as it appeared in the search, and that it may therefore happen, that yet eftsoons ofter than once, some new sudden searches may hap to be made in every house of ours as narrowly as is possible. Which thing, if ever it so should hap, can make but game to us that know the truth of my poverty, but if they find my wife's gay girdle and her golden beads. Howbeit I verily believe in good faith, that the King's Grace of his benign pity will take nothing from her. I thought and yet think again that I was shut up again upon some new causeless suspicion, grown peradventure upon some secret sinister information, whereby some folk haply thought that there should be found against me some greater things.

He came nearer the truth when he later wrote:

> Now have I heard since that somesay that this obstinate manner of

12Rogers, 209.

mine in still refusing the oath, shall peradventure force and drive
the King's Grace to make a further law for me. I cannot let [hinder]
such a law to be made. But I am very sure that if I died by such a law,
I should die for that point innocent afore God.[13]

It had probably already been decided to bring in a Bill of Attainder
against him.

[13]Rogers, 210 (60).

CHAPTER XXX

Parliament: Seventh Session

THE SEVENTH SESSION of Henry VIII's fifth Parliament opened on 3 November 1534 and was prorogued on 18 December. The legislation of those six weeks sealed the fates of Bishop John Fisher and Sir Thomas More. They had been in prison for nearly seven months; the charge that could have been brought against them was that they had refused to take the oath to the Succession; this was misprision of treason for which the penalty was life imprisonment and loss of goods. They were not brought before a court of law but were shut up in the Tower until the King and Council could decide what to do with them.

It may be asked, "Why were formal proceedings not taken against the prisoners?" The King and Cromwell may have felt that, until they were more certain of the mood of the country, it would be unwise to give prominence to two such notable and reputable persons as Fisher and More. We cannot know if their deaths were already contemplated; what we can be certain of is that the King was determined to have his own way; they *must* take the oath! It may be that Cromwell urged that everything should be done according to law and the will of Parliament. The legislation of this seventh session made it possible to put both prisoners to death.

The first Act was that of the Supremacy. It stated that, although the King had been "recognized by the clergy of this realm in their Convocations" as Supreme Head, yet "for the increase of virtue in Christ's religion within this realm of England" it was desirable to give statutory authority to this new title. The qualifying phrase, "as far as the law of Christ allows", was dropped. Few Acts of comparable brevity have given such comprehensive powers to the crown. The King now had complete control of the Anglican Church; he could carry out visitations, repress heresies, and "enormities which by any manner spiritual authority or

jurisdiction ought or may lawfully be reformed, etc." The Act
ended by repudiating all "foreign authority".

It should be noted that the Act of Supremacy imposed no oath,
nor were any penalties laid down for any offence against it; it was
simply declaratory. It has sometimes been said that Thomas More
refused to take the oath to the Supremacy; there was no oath to
take. As we shall see presently the matter was more subtle than
that.

By a further Act, first fruits and tenths (that is, the first year's
income from a benefice, from archbishop to parish priest, and an
annual tax of one tenth) were in future to be paid to the crown
and not to Rome. The clergy, who had hoped to be relieved of
these payments, found that they had merely changed masters;
some must have felt they had been double-crossed.

A Second Act of Succession followed; this was necessary to
regularize the oath which had been exacted under the previous
Act of Succession in which no oath had been formulated. The
new Act also made it clear that "every of the King's subjects . . .
shall be obliged to accept and take the said oath".

Having tidied up the business of the Succession oath, Parliament
turned to consider a new Act of Treasons.[1] Such an Act had been
under consideration since the beginning of 1531. There are five
drafts with Cromwell's annotations. Hitherto the law had been
that of 1352 (Edward III). The main grounds for an accusation
were compassing the King's death, levying war against him, and
adhering to his enemies. Some overt or outward action was
necessary to support the charge. The judges, however, had always
interpreted the Act, which was narrowly drawn, rather widely,
but spoken words alone were not accepted; there had to be some
evidence of intention to proceed from words to action. The
crucial innovation made by the 1534 Act comes in the following
extract:

> . . . that if any person or persons . . . *do maliciously wish, will, or
> desire, by words or writing,* or by craft imagine, invent, practise, or

[1] See "Treason Legislation of Henry VIII", by I. D. Thorney, in *Trans. R. Hist. Soc.*,
3rd series, xi. Also *The Tudor Constitution; Documents and Commentary*, ed. G. R. Elton
(1960), pp. 59–63.

attempt any bodily harm to be done to the king's most royal person, the queen's, or their heirs apparent, or *to deprive them or any of them of their dignity, title, or name* of their royal estates, or slanderously and maliciously publish and pronounce, *by express writing or words,* that the king our sovereign lord should be a heretic, etc.

The italicized phrases should be particularly noted.

There has been misunderstanding about the word "maliciously".[2] This is due to a statement made by Bishop John Fisher when he was interrogated in the Tower on 12 June 1535. He said:

> When the Act by the which words were made treason was a-making Robert Fisher, his brother [M.P. for Rochester], came to him to the Tower and said that there was an Act in hand in the Common House by which speaking of certain words against the king should be made treason. And because it was thought by divers of the said House that no man lightly could beware of the penalty of the said statute, therefore there was much sticking at the same in the Common House, and unless there were added in the same the words should be spoken maliciously, he thought the same should not pass.[3]

In fact the word "maliciously" is found in earlier drafts of the Bill. Evidently Robert Fisher had misunderstood the trend of the debate. Unfortunately no other report is extant. It may be conjectured that the "sticking" point for the Commons was the making of words alone treasonous. It opened the door wide for unscrupulous informers. Cromwell himself recognized that this would cause hesitation and perhaps opposition. In a note he made early in 1534 he jotted down, "To touch the word, writing or deed. They [the Commons] be contented that deed and writing be treason, and word by misprision with a declaration what the misprisions shall do."[4] The Commons had made such a distinction in the Act of Succession; it was not, however, made in the Act of Treasons. This interpretation of their attitude is supported by the fact that, by the time the Act was repealed in 1547 (Edward VI), it had become known as the "Act of Words".

Fisher, at his trial, argued that he had never spoken "mali-

---

[2] I have been guilty of this error myself; see *The Trial of St Thomas More,* pp. 60-1.
[3] This is the full version of that calendered in L.P., VIII, No. 858.
[4] L.P., VII, i, No. 51.

ciously" against the King, though More had warned him that this plea would not carry any weight. He was answered by his judges:

The word maliciously in the Statute is but a superfluous and void word, for if a man speak against the King's Supremacy [i.e. depriving him of one of his titles] by any manner of means, that speaking is to be understanded and taken in law as *maliciously*.[5]

For the prisoners in the Tower the most threatening part of the Act was this denying to the King of one of his titles, and the penalty was to "suffer such pains of death and other penalties, as is limited [specified] and accustomed in cases of high treason". Here was the means of entrapping Fisher and More and their fellows.

Towards the end of the session, Acts of Attainder were passed against Bishop John Fisher and others, and against Sir Thomas More. With Fisher were joined five priests, Nicholas Wilson, Richard Fetherston, Miles Willin, Christopher Plummer and Edward Powell They were accused of refusing to take the oath to the Succession, and were condemned to life imprisonment and loss of goods. A special clause deprived Fisher of his bishopric, a startling example of the new powers the King now had over the Church, for this was done outside the authority of the Archbishop of Canterbury.[6] Fisher thus became a commoner.

Nicholas Wilson later took the oath, and possibly so did Willin and Plummer as we hear nothing further of them. Richard Fetherston and Edward Powell were kept in the Tower, without trial, until 1540 when both were hanged at Smithfield on 30 July in company with some heretics. They should have as much honour in our thoughts as Fisher and More; for six years they resisted all attempts to get them to conform, and their deaths were not swift executions by the axe, but the long agony of being hanged, drawn and quartered.[7]

It is not clear why Thomas More was attaindered separately. The charge against him was that he had "obstinately, frowardly and contemptuously" refused to take the oath; he was further

[5]*Life of Fisher*, p. 117.
[6]In later documents he is described as "Mr John Fisher, D.D." In some he was "John Fisher, clerk", for even Henry VIII could not deprive him of his priesthood.
[7]They are not among the forty martyrs for whom canonization is sought.

reproached for having acted ungratefully and unkindly to his royal benefactor. He too was condemned to life imprisonment and the loss of goods.

On 16 December, a corody More held at Glastonbury Abbey was granted to a Richard Snell; the manor of South in Kent went to George Boleyn, the Queen's brother, and, later, one of More's judges, while the manors in Oxfordshire went to Henry Norris.[8] Apart from the land that had fortunately been given outright to the Ropers, his Chelsea property passed to William Paulet, later Marquis of Winchester.[9]

Many must have thought, and hoped, that the Attainders were the end of the affair. John Fisher was sixty-five years of age and had long suffered from serious illnesses; in the nature of things, his life was nearing its end. Thomas More, as his daughter Margaret had written, was suffering from a number of complaints. Both were now in prison for life and both had been reduced to penury. What further could be exacted of them? Only their lives remained at the mercy of the King.

One question must have been raised in the reader's mind. What part did More's sons-in-law play as Members of Parliament? His brother-in-law, John Rastell, as far as indications show, had become one of Cromwell's men. But what of William Roper, Giles Heron, William Daunce and Giles Alington? They all took the oath, but did they oppose any of the Bills in the Commons? There are no official reports of the debates. Edward Hall was a Member but he has little to say on what went on in Parliament. For instance the legislation of November-December 1534 is summed up in the sentence, "In this year on the third day of November, the King's Highness held his high court of Parliament, in which was concluded and made many and sundry good, wholesome and godly statutes." He did not mention these statutes or attempt to group them under these heads. Nor is William Roper, who could have told us so much, any more

---

[8] A corody was an annuity purchased from the monastery. See L.P., VII, 1601; VIII, 149/16; 162/13. Both Boleyn and Norris were executed on 17 May 1536.

[9] He was one of the judges of Fisher and More. He contrived to stick to office under Henry, Edward, Mary and Elizabeth. "I was born of the willow, not the oak", was his explanation for his survival.

informative about what actually took place in the debates. So we are left in the dark as to what share Thomas More's sons, as he called them, had in the making of the Acts of Supremacy and Treasons and in the Attainders of him and John Fisher and other prisoners in the Tower.

Here it will be helpful to set out the chronology of events as their sequence should be kept in mind.

1534
Parliament: Jan-March
    First Act of Succession   25 Hen. VIII, c. 22.
            17 April   More and Fisher sent to the Tower
Parliament: Nov.-Dec.
    Act of Supremacy   26 Hen. VIII, c. 1
    Second Act of Succession   26 Hen. VIII, c. 2
    Act of Treasons   26 Hen. VIII, c. 13
    Attainder of Fisher *et al.*   26 Hen. VIII, c. 22
    Attainder of More   26 Hen. VIII, c. 23

Chapter XXXI

The Interrogations

Soon after the Act of Attainder of Sir Thomas More had been passed, Dame Alice made an appeal on behalf of the family to the King.[1] This was a despairing and fruitless petition for her husband's release on the grounds of his "great continual sickness of body". The letter gives us some information of the situation in which she found herself. Until the Attainder, she had been allowed to retain her husband's movable goods and to receive the rents from his lands. These were now forfeited.

> And thus (except your merciful favour be showed) your said poor beadswoman his wife, which brought fair substance to him, which is all spent in your Grace's service, is likely to be utterly undone and his poor son, one of your said humble suppliants, standing charged and bounden for payment of great sums of money due by the said Sir Thomas unto your Grace, standeth in danger to be cast away and undone in this world also. But over all this the said Sir Thomas himself, after his long true service to his power diligently done to your Grace, is likely to be in his age and continual sickness, for lack of comfort and good-keeping, to be shortly destroyed, to the woeful heaviness and deadly discomfort of all your said sorrowful suppliants.

More had evidently had loans from the King which were still outstanding; for these John More was now liable. He, presumably, as we do not hear of his employment, was dependent on his wife's income from her Yorkshire lands. Dame Alice also pointed out that she still had to pay for her husband's keep in the Tower.

We have noted that the Acts of Supremacy and Treasons had put new weapons into the hands of the Council. If Thomas More would now say, in the presence of witnesses, or even one witness,

---

[1] Rogers, 212. On 16 March 1537, Dame Alice was granted an annuity of £20, and in 1542, the lease of a dwelling in Chelsea at twenty-one shillings a year. For eight years after her husband's death, she was also allowed to hold some land in Battersea leased from the Abbot of Westminster in 1529. See Roper, p. xli; also J. D. M. Derrett, *Moreana*, No. 6 (1965).

that the King could not be Supreme Head of the Church in England, then the Act of Treasons could be used against him for denying to the King one of his statutory titles. As the months passed, so the hope that imprisonment would weaken his resolve grew fainter. It was therefore decided to confront him with a point-blank demand for a statement on the Supremacy before commissions of Councillors in interrogations at the Tower.

On 16 April 1535 three Carthusian Priors were imprisoned in the Tower; one was John Houghton of the London Charterhouse; with them were Richard Reynolds, a learned Brigittine monk of Syon Abbey and a close friend of Thomas More, and John Haile, vicar of Isleworth in which Syon Abbey was situated. They were brought to trial on 28 April and condemned to be hanged, drawn and quartered because they refused to accept Henry VIII as Supreme Head. This dreadful example of what might happen to him if he proved obdurate, led to More's first interrogation on 30 April.[2] His account is in a letter to Margaret a day or two afterwards.[3]

> I doubt not but by the reason of the Councillors resorting hither, in this time (in which our Lord be their comforter) these fathers of the Charterhouse and Master Reynolds of Syon that be now judged to death for treason (whose matters and causes I know not) may hap to put you in trouble and fear of mind concerning me being here prisoner, specially for that it is not unlikely but that you have heard that I was brought also before the Council here myself. . . . On Friday the last day of April in the afternoon, Master Lieutenant came in here unto me and showed me that Master Secretary [Cromwell] would speak with me. Whereupon I shifted my gown, and went out with Master Lieutenant into the gallery to him. Where I met many, some known and some unknown in the way. And in conclusion coming into the chamber where his Mastership sat with Master Attorney, Master Solicitor, Master Bedyll, and Master Doctor Tregonwell, I was offered to sit with them, which in no wise I would.

[2] There is some difficulty about dates. More's indictment refers to two interrogations, 7 May and 3 June. More's letter is definite—"the last day of April". Roper (p. 80) refers to a visit from Cromwell; perhaps this was on 7 May. The indictment does not mention the one on 30 April, but this yielded no useful material for the case.

[3] Rogers, 214 (63).

The attorney-general, Sir Christopher Hales, was one of the capable agents of Henry's policy who reaped their reward when the monasteries were dissolved. The solicitor-general, Sir Richard Rich, was a more sinister time-server. Thomas Bedyll, "that smooth, sedate archdeacon",[4] was clerk of the Privy Council. Dr John Tregonwell (knighted 1553) had been proctor for the King in the marriage proceedings, and he was to be the least unscrupulous of the monastic visitors.

Thomas Cromwell opened the interrogation.

Master Secretary showed unto me that he doubted not but that I had by such friends as hither had resorted to me, seen the new Statutes made at the last sitting of the Parliament. Whereunto I answered: yea, verily. Howbeit, forasmuch as being here, I have no conversation with any people, I thought it little need for me to bestow much time upon them, and therefore I redelivered the book shortly and the effect of the statutes I never marked nor studied to put in remembrance. Then he asked me whether I had not read the first statute of them, of the King being Head of the Church. Whereunto I answered yes. Then his Mastership declared unto me, that since it was now by Act of Parliament ordained that his Highness and his heirs be, and ever right have been, and perpetually should be, Supreme Head in earth of the Church of England *under Christ*, the King's pleasure was that those of his Council there assembled should demand mine opinion, and what my mind was therein.

It will be noted that the words "under Christ" are used here. Did Cromwell slip them in knowing that More had not studied the Act in detail?

Whereunto I answered that in good faith I had well trusted that the King's Highness would never have commanded any such question to be demanded of me, considering that I ever from the beginning well and truly from time to time declared my mind unto his Highness, and since that time I had, I said, unto your Mastership, Master Secretary, also, both by mouth and by writing. And now I have in good faith discharged my mind of all such matters, and neither will dispute King's titles nor Pope's, but the King's true faithful subject I am and will be, and daily pray for him and all his, and for you all

---

[4]David Mathew, *The Reformation and the Contemplative Life* (1934), p. 237. For Tregonwell, see A. L. Rowse, *Tudor Cornwall* (1941), pp. 187-93.

that are of his honourable Council, and for all the realm, and otherwise than this I never intend to meddle.

Cromwell urged that the King was anxious to release More provided he would submit himself.

Whereunto I shortly (after the inward affection [state] of my mind) answered for a very truth, that I would never meddle in the world again, to have the world given me. And to the remnant of the matter, I answered in effect as before, showing that I had fully determined with myself, neither to study nor meddle with any matter of this world, but that my whole study should be upon the passion of Christ and mine own passage out of this world.

More was then asked to withdraw awhile, and, on his return, Cromwell tried a new argument, this time with a threat behind it. Did not More still think it his duty, though a prisoner condemned to a life sentence, to obey the King "who would follow the course of his law toward such as he shall find obstinate"? He added a significant remark, "that my demeanour in that matter was a thing that of likelihood made now other men so stiff therein as they be". Here is a hint of one reason for the increased pressure on More; others would be encouraged to persist in their objections to the new law. He replied: "I do nobody harm, I say none harm, I think none harm, but wish everybody good. And if this be not enough to keep a man alive, in good faith I long not to live."

One other fact had now become apparent; the King would have More's submission or his life.—"My poor body is at the King's pleasure, would God my death might do him good".

A note of impatience may be seen in these answers to the repetition of the old questions; it was as if More felt weary of the whole senseless business of trying to break down his resolution, a resolution that had been reached after much prayer and meditation. It was as if the world, after his year's imprisonment, had passed beyond his awareness; all that remained was his soul and God.

So he returned to his cell, "and here am I in such case as I was, neither better nor worse".

Having failed in her appeal to the King, though that may have got no further than the Secretary's office, Dame Alice now appealed to Cromwell directly and begged for some alleviation of her distress.[5] "I have been compelled of very necessity, to sell part of mine apparel for lack of other substance to make money of." She begged him "to show your most favourable help to the comforting of my poor husband and me, in this our great heaviness, extreme age, and necessity". There is no record of a reply.

Margaret was given permission to see her father again. The day was carefully chosen; it was 4 May, the day when the three Carthusian fathers, Richard Reynolds and John Haile were to be drawn to Tyburn from the Tower. It was probably hoped that the daughter might influence her father by her distress at what was taking place within view of his cell window. Roper recorded his wife's recollections.

He, as one longing in that journey to have accompanied them, said unto my wife then standing there besides him, "Lo, dost thou not see, Meg, that these blessed fathers be now as cheerfully going to their deaths as bridegrooms to their marriage? Wherefore thereby mayest thou see, mine own good daughter, what a great difference there is between such as have in effect spent their days in a straight, hard, penitential, and painful life religiously, and such as have in the world, as thy poor father hath done, consumed all their time in pleasure and ease licentiously. For God, considering their long continued life in most sore and grievous penance, will no longer suffer them to remain here in this vale of misery and iniquity, but speedily hence taketh them to the fruition of his everlasting Deity; whereas thy silly father, Meg, that like a most wretched caitiff hath passed forth the whole course of his miserable life most sinfully, God, thinking him not worthy so soon to come to that eternal felicity, leaveth him here yet still in the world, further to be plunged and turmoiled with misery."[6]

Far from weakening his resolution, this piteous sight had only strengthened it.

Roper records a visit from Cromwell to More that seems to have been less formal than an official interrogation.

Within a while after, Master Secretary, coming to him in the Tower from the King, pretended much friendship towards him, and for his

[5]Rogers, 215.   [6]Roper, p. 80.

comfort told him that the King's Highness was his good and gracious lord, and minded not with any matter wherein he should have any cause of scruple, from henceforth to trouble his conscience.[7]

What are we to make of this extraordinary change of attitude on the King's behalf? Was it a momentary memory that came to Henry of the happiness he had once found in More's company? We cannot tell, but it must have been a passing mood of a kind to which the King was subject. Thomas More took it at its true value, for he made some verses on the occasion.

> Eye-flattering Fortune, look thou never so fair,
> Nor never so pleasantly begin to smile,
> As though thou wouldst my ruin all repair,
> During my life thou shalt not me beguile,
> Trust shall I God, to enter in awhile
> His haven of heaven sure and uniform.
> Ever after thy calm look I for a storm.

The storm was not long delayed.

At the end of May, news reached England that the Pope had created Fisher a Cardinal. Paul III had succeeded Clement VII (the Pope of the Divorce) in October 1534. He was greatly concerned about the fate of Bishop Fisher whose writings he knew "were held in great esteem, especially in Germany and Italy". Moreover, he was planning the long-desired General Council and he wanted England to be represented.[8] To make Fisher a Cardinal would surely safeguard his life and perhaps secure his release. This action of the Pope has been described as maladroit; its weakness lay, however, in the Pope's ignorance of the character of Henry VIII. This was a puzzle to many. For instance, about this time Francis of France declared, "In effect he is the strangest man in the world, and I fear I can do no good with him". The Pope's well-intentioned action misfired.

Chapuys reported to the Emperor:

As soon as the King heard that the Bishop of Rochester had been created a Cardinal, he declared in anger several times that he would give him another hat, and send the head afterwards to Rome for the

---

[7]Roper, p. 81.

[8]It took him nearly ten years to overcome all the obstacles before the Council of Trent could meet.

M

Cardinal's hat. He sent immediately to the Tower those of his Council to summon again the said Bishop and Master More to swear to the King as Head of the Church, otherwise before St John's day [St John the Baptist, 24 June] they should be executed as traitors. But it has been impossible to gain them, either by promises or threats, and it is believed they will soon be executed. But as they are persons of unequalled reputation in this kingdom, the King, to appease the murmurs of the world, has already on Sunday last caused preachers to preach against them in most of the churches here, and this will be continued next Sunday.[9]

This was dated 16 June and referred to the interrogation of 3 June. By that date three more of the Carthusians were in the Marshalsea and another ten were in Newgate where they were left to starve in chains. Margaret Clement (Giggs) did her utmost to succour them, but her valiant efforts were at length thwarted.

On 3 June, Thomas More had to face a commission of Thomas Cranmer, Archbishop of Canterbury, Thomas Audley, Lord Chancellor, the Duke of Suffolk, the King's brother-in-law, the Earl of Wiltshire, the Queen's father, and Thomas Cromwell. In writing to Margaret about this interview, More showed how clearly he saw the intention that lay behind the questioning; they wanted to trap him into saying aloud that he did not accept the King's Supremacy.

Cromwell once more pointed out that More's obstinacy was causing "much grudge and harm in the realm", and the King's command was that he should make "a plain and terminate answer". To this More replied:

For if it so were that my conscience gave me against the statutes (wherein how my mind giveth me I made no declaration) then I nothing doing nor nothing saying against the statute, it were a very hard thing to compel me to say either precisely with it against my conscience to the loss of my soul, or precisely against it to the destruction of my body.[10]

Cromwell, who seems to have directed the proceedings, then tried another line of attack. He pointed out that in matters of

[9]L.P., VIII, 876. Another version of the King's words reads, "Well, let the Pope send him a hat when he will, but I will so provide that whensoever it cometh, he shall wear it on his shoulders, for head shall he have none to set it on". *Life of Fisher*, p. 112.
[10]Rogers, 216 (64).

heresy More had compelled men to make precise answers concerning the Pope's authority, so the King, as Supreme Head by law, could "compel men to answer precisely to the law here".

> I answered and said that I protested that I intended not to defend any part or stand on contention, but I said there was a difference between those two cases because that at that time, as well here as elsewhere, through the whole corps of Christendom the Pope's power was recognized for an undoubted thing, which seemeth not like a thing agreed in this realm and the contrary taken for truth in other realms. Whereunto Master Secretary answered that they were as well burned for denying of that, as they be beheaded for denying of this, and therefore as good reason to compel them to make precise answer to the one as to the other.

No doubt More as a lawyer admired the way in which Cromwell handled the case. Two questions were then put to him.

> The first whether I had seen the statute. The other whether I believed that it were a lawful made interrogatory or not. Whereupon I refused the oath and said further by mouth, that the first I had before confessed, and to the second I would make no answer. . . . I meddle not with the conscience of them that think otherwise, every man *suo domino stat et cadit.*[11]

Thomas More saw that the end could not long be delayed. His thoughts turned with gratitude to his old friends; among these was Antonio Bonvisi. More described himself "almost this forty years not a guest, but a continual nursling in Master Bonvisi's house". It was probably through his friendship with Thomas Cromwell that Bonvisi had been allowed to send gifts to Fisher and More in the Tower; to More he had sent a warm gown, and to Fisher food and wine. So at the end of a letter to this old friend More made his prayer to God "that for his mercy sake, he will bring us into his rest where shall need no letters, where no wall shall dissever us, where no porter shall keep us from talking together".[12]

The interrogations had failed of their purpose; the prisoner had

[11]Rom. 14, 4. "It is not for you to condemn someone else's servant: whether he stands or falls it is his own master's business: he will stand, you may be sure, because the Lord has power to make him stand."
[12]Rogers, 217 (65).

made no statement that could be used against him. Three servants
were, therefore, questioned. They were—Richard Wilson,
Fisher's servant; John à Wood, More's servant, and George Gold,
a servant of the Lieutenant. The result was meagre.

There had been some exchange of notes and gifts between the
two prisoners. Wilson "had sent Master More's servant half a
custard on Sunday last, and long since, green sauce [salad]. More
sent him [Fisher] an image of St John and apples and oranges after
the snow that fell last winter. On New Year's Day, More sent a
paper with writing, £2,000 in gold, and an image of the Epiph-
any". The £2,000 "in gold" must have been one of More's bits
of fun; perhaps the sum in figures, or a drawing of a money bag,
was on a scrap of paper; was there, too, a play on George Gold's
name? The latter admitted carrying letters between the two
prisoners but these had been burned "as there was no better
keeper than fire". John à Wood said that messages between
Fisher and More were about the answers each had given to the
members of the Council.

On 12 June, the Bishop was questioned. He admitted that notes
had passed between him and Sir Thomas, but he denied that
there was any discussion of how each should conduct himself;
each wanted to know how the other was faring. Two days later
More was also examined on the letters.[13] He said he wanted George
Gold to show the letters to a friend (probably Gold could not
read) to see that they were harmless, but Gold had preferred to
burn them. There had been no attempt to concert answers.
When Fisher had suggested that the word "maliciously" would
exempt them as both spoke without malice, More had warned
him (rightly as it proved) that the word would not be interpreted
in that way. He acknowledged writing letters to Margaret as
soon after each interrogation as possible as she was with child
and her anxiety for him might prove harmful. He ended his
statement by saying:

And saith that she had written to him before divers letters to exhort
him and advertise him to accommodate himself to the King's
pleasure, and, specially, in the last letter, *she used great vehemence*

[13]For these interrogations, see L.P. VIII, 856, 858, 859, 867.

and obsecration to persuade this examinat to incline to the King's desire.[14]

On 12 June, the day of John Fisher's last interrogation, the Lieutenant of the Tower, Sir Edmund Walsingham, came to More's cell to tell him that the Council had decided he must be more rigorously treated. With the Lieutenant were Sir Richard Rich, solicitor-general, and Richard Southwell,[15] sheriff of Norfolk and one of the Duke's followers. Two of Cromwell's servants, named Palmer and Berleght, were instructed to collect and remove More's books, papers and writing materials. Thomas More's suspicions must have been roused when he saw the solicitor-general, a man for whom he had small regard. What was he doing there?

More did not know that Rich had visited John Fisher on 7 May and had tricked the Bishop into saying the fatal words, "The King cannot be Supreme Head of the Church in England". Rich had pretended, or had been instructed to say, that he came from the King who was not yet fully satisfied in his conscience that he could be Supreme Head, and he appealed to John Fisher, as a priest, to give him his opinion, which, Rich declared, should it be unfavourable, would not be used against Fisher. The Bishop, feeling unable to refuse a request made to him as if in the confessional, guilelessly spoke his opinion. This was, in spite of Rich's assurances, brought up at his trial, and was sufficient to condemn him.

There can be no doubt that Rich hoped to play a similar trick on Sir Thomas More, but he was now dealing with one of the leading lawyers of the day, not with a "simple" priest.

Let us first read Roper's account of their conversation.[16]

Master Rich, pretending friendly talk with him, among other things, of a set course, as it seemed, said thus unto him:

"Forasmuch as it is well known, Master More, that you are a man

[14]S.P., I, pp. 434-5.
[15]Holbein painted a fine portrait of Southwell (Florence); he was a man of flexible principles, who, with one brief period of imprisonment, managed to adjust himself to the religious changes. He died in Elizabeth's reign, a wealthy man. He was the grandfather of Blessed Robert Southwell. Palmer was one of Cromwell's servants (L.P., VIII, 732), so probably was Berleght.
[16]Roper, pp. 84-6.

both wise and learned as well in the laws of the Realm as otherwise, I pray you therefore, sir, let me be so bold as of good will to put unto you this case. Admit there were, sir," quoth he, "an Act of Parliament that all the Realm should take me for King, Would not you, Master More, take me for King?"

"Yes, sir," quoth Sir Thomas More, "that would I."

It will be noted that Rich was here following the method so familiar to both of them at the moots at the Inns of Court, where imaginary cases, as well as actual ones, were posed for the consideration of the students.

"I put case further", quoth Master Rich, "that there were an Act of Parliament that all the Realm should take me for Pope. Would you then, Master More, take me for Pope?"

"For answer, sir," quoth Sir Thomas More, "to your first case, the Parliament may well, Master Rich, meddle with the state of temporal Princes. But to make answer to your other cause, I will put this case: Suppose the Parliament would make a law that God should not be God. Would you then, Master Rich, say that God were not God?"

"No, sir," quoth he, "that would I not, since no Parliament may make any such law."

"No more", said Sir Thomas More, *as Master Rich reported of him* [i.e. at the trial], "could the Parliament make the King Supreme Head of the Church."

The actual words in the indictment at the trial read, "the cases are not similar, since the King can be made or unmade by Parliament; to which every subject being at the Parliament may give his consent; but, as to the supremacy, the subject cannot be bound, since he cannot give his consent in Parliament, and though the King be accepted as such in Parliament, there are many other countries that do not agree".

In 1963 a document came to hand that had been overlooked by More's biographers (including myself) that throws new light on this crucial conversation.[17] It is in a dilapidated condition and

---

[17]P.R.O., S.P. 2/R, folios 24 and 25. I must give myself the credit for having noticed this document. A full transcription will be found in Ap. II. The points (. . .) indicate lacunae but not their extent.

consists of two sheets that have suffered from damp and rats. Enough can, however, be deciphered to make sense. It is not dated, but it may with confidence be claimed as having been written between the time of the conversation and the drawing up of the indictment; it is thus the earliest record we have of what was said.

It opens with the passage in the indictment in which More said, "Your conscience will save you, and my conscience will save me". Then comes a fuller version of Rich's remark. "Whereupon the said Richard . . . said to the said More, 'Sir, for me to give you advice or counsel being a . . . experience, learning and wisdom, it were like as a man should take . . . of water and cast it in the Thames by cause it should be. . . . .'" This well-oiled compliment (it is easy to guess its trend) is followed, as in the indictment, by Rich's statement, "Sir, protesting with you that I have no commission or commandment to . . . with you of the matter ye wot of, nevertheless with your favour I ask . . . you this case". It is unlikely that More was taken in by this disclaimer. A solicitor-general does not visit a prisoner in his cell out of curiosity; it was not as if Rich had been one of More's friends. Then comes the hypothetical case of Parliament declaring Rich to be King. More's reply, as far as it is legible here, is on the lines of the indictment.

According to Roper, the next "case" was "that all the realm should take me for Pope". There is no mention of this in the document which goes on to give More's "case" of Parliament decreeing that "God were not God", thus emphasizing that there were limits to the power of Parliament. Here there is a considerable lacuna so we cannot be sure of the exact words used by Rich; the word "England" can be deciphered. More's reply in the best-preserved part of the document shows that Rich had at length put the question of the Supremacy. "Whereunto the said More said that the cases were not like by cause that a King . . . y be made by Parliament and a King deprived by Parliament to which act any . . . Subjects being of a Parliament may give his consent but to the case . . . a Subject can not be bound by cause he cannot give his cause [sic, consent?] . . . him . . . Parliament. Saying further that although the King were accepted in England yet most utter parts [i.e. outer or foreign countries] do not affirm the same."

We now come to the last passage of this report, and it is this that is of importance, as it adds to Roper's account and to the indictment. The document gives Rich's final words as:

Well, Sir, God comfort you, for I see your mind will not change which I fear will be very dangerous to you for I suppose your concealment to the question that hath been asked you is as high offence as other that hath denied. And thus Jesus send you better grace.

This surely means that Thomas More had continued to conceal his opinion, and this silence, Rich warned him, was as dangerous as an outright denial.

Two days after the conversation with Richard Rich, More was again questioned by a commission of the Council. Three questions were put to him.

1. *Whether he would obey the King as Supreme Head?*
   He can make no answer.
2. *Whether he will acknowledge the King's marriage with Queen Anne to be lawful, and that with lady Catherine invalid?*
   Never spoke against it, nor thereunto can make no answer.
3. *Where it was objected to him that by the said statute he, as one of the King's subjects, is bound to answer the said question and recognize the King as Supreme Head, like all other subjects?*
   He can make no answer.[18]

It will be noted that the matter of the King's marriage was also brought up.

Did the Council hope that he would repeat the words he was alleged to have spoken to Rich two days earlier? In fact, had More spoken against the Supremacy to Rich (before witnesses), what point would there have been in maintaining silence? The indictment had therefore to fall back on Rich's report.

Stapleton recorded that after the removal of his books, Thomas More closed the shutters of his window; when he was asked why he did so, he replied, "Now that the goods and the implements are taken away, the shop must be closed".

[18]L.P., VIII, 867.

CHAPTER XXXII

"While he was a prisoner"

THE LAST four hundred pages of Sir Thomas More's *English Works* contain the writings made "while he was a prisoner in the Tower". Some are unfinished or consist of fragments preserved by his children.

The most considerable of these writings is the *Dialogue of Comfort against Tribulation*. It was printed first by Richard Tottel[1] in 1553. The copy was provided, it may be assumed, by William Rastell, who had returned from exile on the accession of a Catholic Queen. He did not leave Louvain until after 17 July 1533 when his wife died and was buried there. The work must have been put in hand at once for it was published on 18 November. It was again printed in 1573, this time by John Fowler in Antwerp. He had married Alice the daughter of John Harris, More's secretary, and Dorothy Colley who had been Margaret Roper's maid. This family piety is understandable as the book was, in a sense, Thomas More's testament to his children.

We do not know how the manuscript was smuggled out of the Tower; the Council, after More's attainder, would not have permitted a manuscript of some 150,000 words to pass out of its control had it been among the papers removed in June 1535. Perhaps Margaret Roper took home portions as they were written, and no doubt John à Wood had his share in saving the precious book. There would be little difficulty during the first six months of More's imprisonment in passing out manuscripts and letters; moreover, bribery could do much.

We cannot be sure at which period of his imprisonment More wrote the book, but it is reasonable to place it in the months before the passing of the Act of Treasons, for once that was on the statute book, the prisoner was more closely watched.

---

[1]This was among the earliest books printed by Tottel who also had a share in the printing of the *English Works*.

It was a book of comfort for his family, but it was also one of comfort for himself, even if written before he was in danger of being convicted of high treason. His long experience as a councillor and his close association with the King and knowledge of his character, would warn him that he had no hope of gaining his freedom, and small hope of keeping his life. There was a slender chance that the King might relent and set free his former faithful servant.

Thomas More never doubted the rightness of his decision to refuse the oath, a decision reached after much agony of mind and spirit, but he did doubt his courage in facing physical pain. This comes out in two of his letters to Margaret.[2]

> I found myself (I cry God mercy) very sensual and my flesh much more shrinking from pain and from death than methought it the part of a Christian man.

> Surely Megge, a fainter heart than thy frail father hath, canst thou not have. And yet I verily trust in the great mercy of God that he shall of his goodness so stay me with his holy hand that he shall not finally suffer me to fall wretchedly from his favour. . . . I am of nature so shrinking from pain that I am almost afeared of a fillip.

And in a letter to an unknown priest named Leder he wrote in January 1535: "And I trust both that they will use no violent forcible ways[3] and also that if they could, God would of his grace and the rather a great deal through good folks' prayers give me strength to stand."[4]

The fear he had to overcome was the spectre of the fate awaiting a commoner condemned for treason; to quote that to be passed on John Fisher:

> You shall be led to the place from whence you came, and from thence shall be drawn through the City to the place of execution at Tyburn, where your body shall be hanged by the neck; and, being half live, you shall be cut down and thrown to the ground, your bowels to be taken out of your body, and burnt before you, being

---

[2]Rogers, 210 (60); 211 (61).
[3]Was he here thinking of torture? Under Common Law, torture was not permissible in England, but was used with the consent of the Council in cases of suspected treason.
[4]Rogers, 213 (62).

alive; your head shall be smitten off; and your body be divided into
four quarters; and after, your head and quarters be set up where the
King shall appoint, and God have mercy upon your soul.

The fear would pass and return, but each time he was able to
recover his strength of soul; the thought he expressed to Margaret
would recur: "It is a case in which a man may lose his head and
yet have none harm, but instead of harm, inestimable good at the
hand of God."

If the reader of the Dialogue of Comfort will keep in mind the
conditions in which it was written, the fears that beset the
uncertainties of his fate, and his anxiety for his family and friends,
and, perhaps least in his mind, his bodily infirmities, the book's
unevennesses,[5] its occasional repetitiveness and excursiveness
will be conceded. He was not writing in the quiet of his library
at Chelsea, but in a prison cell. He probably had no time to give
his book a careful revision, perhaps he had no inclination to do
so; this of itself will account for some lack of finish.

Most readers, unless intent on literary analysis, will not be
aware of these inequalities, that is because the spirit of the book
soon takes charge and we feel we are in the presence of a man
who had come to terms with life and death, yet had kept his
cheerfulness of mind. His fears were very human and we can
share them. The theme of pain, suffering and death runs through
the book like a dark thread, and it may be these reflect his variations in mood at a time when he did not know what each day
might bring. Not that these subjects were new in More's writings.
Thoughts on death and preparation for death will be found
throughout his writings. But now, in the Tower, he was face to
face with it himself, and so in this Dialogue of Comfort he reverts
time and again to the Four Last Things.

The title-page tells us that the book was written "by an
Hungarian in Latin, and translated out of Latin into French and
out of French into English". This elaborate pedigree was part of
the make-believe that appealed to the author. The two speakers
are the aged Anthony and his nephew Vincent; they discuss the

---

[5]For a stimulating study of the Dialogue of Comfort, see the version edited by Dean
Leland Miles of Bridgeport University (Indiana, 1965).

danger threatening Christendom by the advance of the Turks into Hungary under Suleiman the Magnificent, who, the year before More went to the Tower, had once more advanced to Belgrade. This historical setting was used as analogous to the advance of heresy in Europe. In this period of danger, Vincent seeks comfort from his uncle. If the Turks conquer, will their prisoners be forced by torture to renounce their Christianity? Vincent, representing the younger generation, points out that his uncle is nearing the end of his life, "but us here shall you leave of your kindred a sort of sorry comfortless orphans". What comfort had he to give in these perilous times? His uncle replies, "How can you be comfortless in any tribulation, when Christ and his Holy Spirit, with them their inseparable Father (if you put full trust and confidence in them) be never neither one finger breadth of space nor one minute of time from you?" So the scene is set and the subject defined.

This is not a controversial work but it contains much that has a bearing on the heresies of the times. Thus on good works, Anthony says:

As for the merit of man in his good works, neither are they [the heretics] that deny it full agreed among themself, nor any man is there almost of them all that since they began to write hath not somewhat changed and varied from himself. . . . And, as we grant them also that no man may be proud of his works for his own unperfect working, and for that in all that man may do he can do God no good, but is a servant unprofitable and doth but his bare duty; as we, I say, grant unto them these things, so this one thing or twain do they grant us again, that men are bound to work good works if they have time and power, and that whoso worketh in true faith most, shall be most rewarded.[6]

It will be noted that Thomas More here somewhat modifies his criticism of the Lutheran doctrine of justification by faith alone; instead of the kind of outright attack to be found in the *Dialogue Concerning Heresies*, he is looking for common ground. "Therefore will I let God work and leave off contention; and nothing shall I now say, but that with which they that are

[6]pp. 175-6.

themself of the contrary mind shall in reason have no cause to be discontented."

Such a development in More's thought should not surprise us, for now his dominating desire was the maintenance of the unity of the Church. It would, indeed, be astonishing if a man of his acute intelligence and sensibility had become fixed in the opinions he had held in his younger days. Had he written *Utopia* in 1530 instead of in 1515, he would have produced a different sketch for an ideal commonwealth. It is pointless, as some have done, to charge More with "inconsistencies"; like all men of vigorous mind, he advanced in his thinking and could not rest satisfied with the opinions he held in earlier years. His religious faith remained secure, indeed it became deeper with time and experience of men and affairs.

Any attempt to summarize the contents of the *Dialogue of Comfort* would not be helpful; it lacks a carefully developed argument that can be set down schematically. One or two aspects may, however, be considered.

The reader will soon note Thomas More's love of the Bible. Part of this *Dialogue* is a commentary on the Compline Psalm (Vulgate, 90), *Qui habitat in adiutorio Altissimi*, with its application to the life of a prisoner under threat of severe penalties. Apart from general references to biblical characters and incidents, there are over a hundred quotations, many from the Psalms, which, it may be surmised, Thomas More knew by heart, for they were interwoven with his thoughts. There are a few passing references to Juvenal, Terence, Martial and Pliny, but not the frequent appeals to the Early Fathers, his "old interpreters of Scripture", that one expects in More's writings. Even his "Holy Saint Austin" is mentioned only four or five times, the *De Civitate Dei* being named. There is one reference to St Jerome. Of later writers St Thomas Aquinas is mentioned once and there is a more extended use of the writings of John Gerson, one of the leaders of the Conciliar movement. This paucity of quotations from authorities —they are paraphrased rather than given verbatim—suggests that while he was writing this *Dialogue*, More had few books with him; his study was on the Bible.

There are many recollections of his experience of life in the world, sometimes put into the form of one of those "merry tales" he enjoyed telling; at other times we get a straight account of some incident. For instance, the story in Book III, ch. 10, of "a great man of the church" probably refers to Wolsey, but we cannot be sure; the basic fact may have been played on by More's imagination. Occasionally the identification is more certain; thus the account in Book II, ch. 4, of how "a young girl" cured a fever that had defeated the physicians, was surely a reference to Margaret Giggs. Where Harpsfield uses such material, the attribution is more likely to be correct as he was closely in touch with the Roper-Rastell-Clement circle. It would certainly be rash to assume, as some have done, that every tale of a wife was drawn from Dame Alice. Her husband's references to her in his Tower letters are evidence of his affection for her: "my shrewd wife above all", "my good wife", "your good mother my wife", and, "my good bedfellow".

The prisoner's thoughts must often have gone back to Chelsea. There is a passage in Book II, ch. 16, that calls up Roper's words:

And because he was desirous for godly purposes sometime to be solitary and sequester himself from worldly company, a good distance from his mansion house, builded he a place called the New Building, wherein there was a chapel, a library and a gallery; in which, as his use was upon other days to occupy himself in prayer and study together. So on the Fridays there usually continued he from morning till evening, spending his time only in devout prayers and spiritual exercises.[7]

So he wrote in the *Dialogue of Comfort*:

Let him also choose himself some secret solitary place in his own house, as far from noise and company as he conveniently can, and thither let him sometime secretly resort alone, imagining himself as one going out of the world even straight into the giving up his reckoning unto God of his sinful living.[8]

At the end of the *Dialogue*, the problem of a painful death is again faced and resolved:

Let us therein conform our will unto His, not desiring to be brought

[7]Roper, pp. 25-6.   [8]p. 287.

unto the peril of persecution (for it seemeth a proud, high mind to desire martyrdom), but desiring help and strength of God if He suffer us to come to the stress. . . . When we feel us too bold, remember our own feebleness. When we feel us too faint, remember Christ's strength. In our fear let us remember Christ's painful agony that Himself would for our comfort suffer before His Passion to the intent that no fear should make us despair, and ever call for His help such as Himself list to send us. And then need we never to doubt but that either He shall keep us from the painful death or shall not fail so to strength us in it that He shall joyously bring us to heaven by it.

So in his cell, Thomas More meditated upon the Passion of Christ. At his interrogation on 30 April 1535, he declared that henceforth "my whole study should be upon the Passion of Christ and mine own passage out of this world". Before his arrest in April 1534, he had completed in English a History of the Passion.[9] A year later, in the Tower, he began an *Expositio Passionis*, this time in Latin. It was published in his *English Works* in a translation by his grand-daughter Mary (Roper) Bassett. In the margin was the note, "My grandfather's copy was for lack of leisure never well corrected". What is with little doubt "my grandfather's copy" was recognized in 1963 at the Royal College of Corpus Christi at Valencia. The manuscript is described as follows:

The MS comprises about one hundred and seventy folios of octavo size written on both sides and bound in green velvet. The first one hundred and fifty-six leaves contain the Latin *Passion* (from the going to the Mount of Olives to the seizure of Jesus). The rest of the volume contains rough notes and drafts of passages for this work, also for the short piece of exhortation *Quod pro fide fugienda mors non est* and for the *Precatio ex Psalmis collecta* in which More brought together passages from the psalms relevant to his situation.

The *Passion* is heavily corrected, and the final revisions agree closely with the text published in the Latin *Works* in 1565. It throws light on his method of composition. Apparently he first made rough notes and wrote out suitable quotations from the Bible. He then composed rapidly, so rapidly that at times he wrote a word

[9] A letter to John Harris of early 1534 asked him to make some corrections in this History of the Passion; see Rogers (48).

Manuscript of the *Passion*

twice, then corrected it, or revised a phrase before completing a sentence. Later he would go over the whole section, insert improvements in clarity and emphasis, and sometimes cross out passages with which he was dissatisfied.[10]

A note by William Rastell in the *English Works* reads:

A work of truth full of good and godly lessons which he began being then a prisoner, and could not achieve and finish the same, as he that ere he could go through therewith (even when he came to the exposition of the words *Et incecerunt manus in Jesum*) was bereaved and put from his books, ink and paper, and kept more strictly than before, and soon after was put to death himself.

Thomas More did not altogether avoid controversial points in this treatise; indeed that would have been impossible with such a subject. He excused this in the following note:

Now albeit (as I suppose) few men have less lust to move great questions, and put manner of dispicions [disputations] in unlearned man's mouths than I, which rather would wish every man to labour for good affections, than to long for the knowledge of less necessary learning, or delight in debating of sundry superfluous problems, yet of some such demands as I now see many men of much less than mean learning, have oft right hot in hand, I shall not let one or twain myself here a little to touch.

Another Tower composition was *A Treatise to receive the Blessed Body of our Lord sacramentally and virtually both*. It is a short (some five thousand words) and clearly written exhortation evidently intended for ordinary folk, like the *Dialogue Concerning Heresies*. Indeed the style is unusually simple and it is regrettable that More did not more often write in the same manner. One passage is surely based on his memories of the visits Henry VIII used to pay to Chelsea.

For if we will but consider, if there were a great worldly prince which for special favour that he bare us would come visit us in our house, what a business we would then make, and what a work it would be for us, to see that our house were trimmed up in every

---

[10]The happy discoverer was Professor Geoffrey Bullough of King's College, London. The above description is taken from an article by him in *The Tablet*, 21 Dec. 1963. We must await the publication of the Yale edition for a full study. See p. 352.

point, to the best of our possible power, and everything so provided and ordered, that he should by his honourable receiving what affection we bear him, and in what high estimation we have him; we should soon by the comparing of that worldly prince and his heavenly prince together (between which twain is far less comparison than is between a man and a mouse) inform and teach ourself with how lowly mind, how tender loving heart, how reverent humble manner we should endeavour ourself to receive this glorious heavenly king, the king of all kings, almighty God himself, that so lovingly doth vouchsafe to enter, not only into our house (to which the noble man Centurio acknowledged himself unworthy) but his precious body into our vile wretched carcase, and his holy spirit into our poor simple soul.

This little treatise, one might say tract, is followed by "certain devout and virtuous instructions, meditations, and prayers, made and collected by Sir Thomas More". The first piece is entitled "Imploratio"; this is a cento of verses gathered from the Psalms. The last to be quoted is Psalm 66; so evidently what must have been a congenial occupation had to be broken off.

The prayers printed in the *English Works* include one headed "A Devout Prayer"; this, or part of it, was composed by Margaret More and sent to her father. In answer he thanked her for the prayer and quoted a sentence or two from it; "it doth me good here to rehearse your own words"; he continued:

> I beseech our Lord, my dearly beloved daughter, that wholesome prayer that he hath put in your mind, it may like him to give your father the grace daily to remember and pray, and yourself as you have written it, even so daily devoutly to kneel and pray it.[11]

Copies of these prayers were circulated among friends of the family, and some were included in manuals of prayers used by Catholics in penal times.

Of all the prayers the one that brings us nearest to Thomas More is that written in the margins of his Book of Hours.[12] This was a Paris edition of 1530 of the Sarum Usage. More wrote his meditations in the top and bottom margins of nineteen successive pages. It is here given in the original spelling.

[11]Rogers, 211 (61).
[12]Now at Yale. For a description with facsimiles, see *Moreana*, No. 5. (1965). See p. 356.

Gyve me thy grace good lord
To sett the world at nought

To sett my mynd faste uppon the
And not to hange vppon the blaste
of mennys mowthis

To be content to be solitary
Not to long for worldely company

Lytle & litle Vuurely to caste of the world
And ridde my mund of all the bysynes thereof

Not to long here of eny worldely thyngis
But that the heryng of worldely fantesyes may
be to me displeasant

Gladly to be thinkyng of god
Pituously to call for his helpe

To lene vn to the cumfort of god
Bysyly to labour to love hym

To know myn awne vilite & wrechednesse
To humble & meken my selfe vnder the
myghty hand of god

To bewayle my synnys passed
ffor the purgyng of theym patiently to
suffre adversite

gladly to bere my purgatory here
To be ioyfull of tribulations

To walke the narow way that ledeth to life
To bere the crosse with christ

To haue the laste thing in remembraunce
To have ever a fore myn yie my deth that ys
ever at hand

To pray for perdon byfore the Iudge come
To haue continually in mynd the passion that
christ suffred for me

ffor his benefitys vncessauntly to geve hym thankys
To by the tyme agayn that I before haue loste

gyve me thy grace gad lord

Ad primam de. b. Maria.   Fo. rbij.

Eus in adiutoriu meum intende.
Dñe ad adiuuãdum me festina.
Gloria patri et filio: et spũi sctõ.
Sicut erat in prin. ꝛc. Hymnus.
Saz.   cj

to sett the world at nought

The Book of Hours

356

To adstayn from vayne confabulations
To estew light folysh myrth & gladnesse

Recreationys not necessary to cutt off
Of worldely substauns frendys libertie life and
all to sett the losse at right nowght for the wynnyg of christ

To thynke my mooste enemys my best frendys
for the brethern of Ioseph could never haue done
hym so mych good with theire love & favour as
they did hym with theire malice & hatered.

These myndys are more to be desired of
every man than all the treasore of
all the princes & kyngis christen & hethen
were it gathered & layed to gether all vppon one hepe.

NOTE

The commonplace book (Bodleian, MS. Lat. th.d. 15) of Robert Parkyn (d. 1570), curate of Adwick-le-Street, Doncaster, contains a long prayer ascribed to Sir Thomas More. It is, in fact, the composition of John Fisher, the holograph original of which is in the Public Record Office (S.P.I.; 93, ff. 99-102). A transcription is given as Appendix A of my *Saint John Fisher*. Adwick is within a few miles of Barnburgh, the home of John and Anne More; it was presumably from them that Robert Parkyn got his copy of the prayer. We can only speculate as to how it came into their hands. Did Fisher send a copy to his fellow-prisoner who passed it on to his son John? No other copy is known.

CHAPTER XXXIII

The Indictment

JOHN FISHER was brought to trial on 17 June 1535. The evidence against him was that he had declared before witnesses that "the King our sovereign lord is not Supreme Head in earth of the Church of England". The verdict of "Guilty" was a foregone conclusion and he was condemned to death as a traitor; he was beheaded on Tower Hill on 22 June. His naked body was left on the scaffold until the evening when some soldiers gave it perfunctory burial in the churchyard of All Hallows by the Tower.

Three monks of the Charterhouse, Humphrey Middlemore, William Exmewe and Sebastian Newdigate, had suffered at Tyburn a week before St John Fisher.

Sir Thomas More would, doubtless, be informed of these sorrowful events; it may have been hoped that even then his resolution might be shaken by the knowledge of what lay ahead of him if he remained obdurate.

On "Monday next after the feast of St John the Baptist", 28 June, a Grand Jury at Westminster returned a true bill against Thomas More, late of Chelsea; the date of the trial was to be on the "Thursday next after the morrow of St John the Baptist", 1 July.[1]

Before we discuss the trial itself, it is necessary to study the Indictment,[2] which might be called "the case for the Crown".

The Indictment opens with a recital of the relevant parts of the Acts of Supremacy and Treasons. Parliament had enacted that the King, his heirs and successors, should be accepted as the only Supreme Head in earth of the Church of England; to deprive

---

[1] The Feast (Birthday) of St John the Baptist is 24 June; by "morrow" is meant presumably the Octave.

[2] P.R.O., *Baga de Secretis*, Pouch 7, Bundle 3 m.7. The Latin text is given in Harpsfield, pp. 269-76; a translation is given in *English Historical Documents*, Vol. V (1967).

him of this, or of any of his other titles, in word or writing, was high treason.[3]

Then follows a detailed account of the grounds on which the charge of treason was based. In conclusion it is stated that

the aforesaid jurors declare that the aforesaid Thomas More, falsely, traitorously and maliciously, by craft imagined, invented, practised and attempted, wholly to deprive our sovereign lord the King of his dignity, title and name stated in the above mentioned statute, namely of his dignity, title and name of Supreme Head in earth of the Church of England, to the manifest contempt of the King and in derogation of his royal crown, against the form and effect of the aforsaid statutes, and against the peace of our lord the King.

The charge was supported by four statements of evidence; it is convenient to call these "counts".

I. The first count was that on 7 May 1535, Thomas More remained obstinately and maliciously silent when asked if he accepted the King as Supreme Head.

II. The second count was that on 12 May Thomas More sent a number of letters to John Fisher to encourage him in his refusal and to say that he himself kept silence. At his interrogation that day he had said, "The Act of Parliament is like a sword with two edges, for if a man answer one way, it will confound his soul, and if he answer the other way, it will confound his body".

III. The third count is really an extension of the second. Collaboration between the two prisoners was shown by the fact that both had declared at interrogations that "the statute is like a two-edged sword". Thus it was hoped to establish that they were "aidors, counsellors, consenters and abettors" within the law of treason.

IV. This fourth count was the crucial one. Thomas More, it was claimed, had declared to Sir Richard Rich that the King could not be Supreme Head, thus he "maliciously" persisted in his treason.

We shall return to these allegations when reviewing the trial itself. Perhaps it should be pointed out that they were not four

[3]The absurdity of the charge may be gauged by the fact that one of Henry's official titles was King of France. Everyone knew he was no more King of France than he was of Spain, yet, to say he wasn't, was treason!

separate charges; the charge was of having committed treason by refusing to recognize one of the King's titles.

Something needs to be said of how these trials were then conducted. One disadvantage under which we labour is the scantiness of what records there are of treason trials under Henry VIII. We cannot even be sure of the procedure. The unofficial reports of More's trial give us the best account we have of the proceedings, yet all there is to go upon is only a tithe or less of what took place. For Fisher's trial we have to rely on William Rastell's account written some years later; this does not invalidate it, but time is apt to blur details. This was incorporated in the early Life of Fisher compiled during the reign of Mary Tudor.[4] This has all the marks of a carefully prepared work by a conscientious writer. Rastell mentioned that he had been at Fisher's execution and he may have been at the trial. From such meagre documentation, we can at least gather some idea of how these cases were conducted.

We must forget our present-day notions of what constitutes a fair trial. In Tudor times it was assumed that anyone accused of treason was guilty; it was a political rather than a judicial act. The prisoner does not seem to have been given a copy of the indictment to study beforehand; this meant that he did not know the exact charges against him until he came into court. He was not allowed counsel nor could his witnesses (if they were admitted) be heard on oath. The testimony of one person was sufficient. Under Edward VI, two witnesses were required, but this was soon abrogated; there had been no such provision in previous reigns. The trial amounted to a verbal duel between the accused and the Crown with all the advantages in favour of the prosecution. Our strict rules of evidence were unknown.

Nor were juries expected to bring in a freely-considered verdict; it took more than another century for that principle to get established. The jury was expected to bring in a verdict in accordance with the wishes of the bench.

Trials were held in the King's Bench Court, or at sessions, but for important cases a special commission of *oyer* and *terminer* was

[4]E.E.T.S. (1921).This early Life should be studied in the Bollandist edition of 1891-3, by Fr Van Ortroy. The Rastell account is in Harpsfield, pp. 221-52.

issued; the members of this exceptional court were not all judges or lawyers, and it gave the Crown an opportunity for selecting commissioners of the right colour. This packing of the bench was not then regarded as scandalous; it was normal.

The commission for the trial of Sir Thomas More was directed to: Sir Thomas Audley (More's successor as Lord Chancellor), the Duke of Norfolk (Anne Boleyn's uncle), the Duke of Suffolk (the King's brother-in-law), the Earl of Huntingdon, the Earl of Cumberland (Lord Privy Seal), the Earl of Wiltshire (Anne Boleyn's father), Lord Montague, Lord Rochford (Anne Boleyn's brother), Lord Windsor (Keeper of the King's Wardrobe), Thomas Cromwell (the King's Secretary), the two Chief Justices and other judges; nineteen in all, thirteen of whom had presided at the trial of John Fisher a fortnight earlier. Hardly an impartial bench!

The trial took place in Westminster Hall and More was brought before the King's Bench. The visitor to the Hall today will need to use his imagination to reconstruct the scene. He must dismiss from his mind the dramatic spectacles presented by the later trials of Strafford, Charles I, and Warren Hastings. At the south end of the Hall, where the broad flight of steps now leads into St Stephen's, there were two courts, one on either side of the present doorway. There was no door at that period. The King's Bench was on the left and Chancery on the right. For the accommodation of so many "judges", the two courts were probably thrown into one at More's trial. A high barrier separated the courts from the main body of the Hall, and it may be doubted if anyone out there could have heard what was going on beyond the barrier. Plate 24 shows what the Hall looked like early in the seventeenth century and this probably was as it appeared in the previous century. It is not known if the public was permitted in the body of the Hall; probably lawyers would be allowed to be there as it was their usual place of meeting one another and their clients. We know that no member of the More family was there, not even William Roper who had an official position in the King's Bench Court. Their absence may have been in response to a wish expressed by Sir Thomas himself, but it is equally likely that the King had given instructions to exclude them.

CHAPTER XXXIV

The Trial

JOHN FISHER'S JOURNEY to and from Westminster on 17 June for his trial had been made partly by land, and, as he passed, many knelt for his blessing and showed their sympathy with him. Thomas More was therefore taken by the river on 1 July so that such demonstrations could not be repeated.[1] Had his judges any stirrings of compassion as they saw the prisoner slowly coming towards them up the Hall, walking with the aid of a staff? Those who had not seen him for many months must have been shocked at the change in his appearance; his feeble steps, his whitening hair and long beard and his drawn features were unlike the man who had been the King's companion and one they had counted it a privilege to know. As soon as the preliminaries had been completed, a chair was brought for him.

After the reading of the Indictment, which More now heard for the first time, Audley, as Lord Chancellor, offered him the King's pardon "if you will revoke and reform your wilful, obstinate opinion". Norfolk, as the senior councillor present, confirmed this offer. They would not be surprised that the pardon was not accepted on the terms proposed. Presumably the attorney-general would then state the case for the Crown; Sir Christopher Hales[2] had preferred the indictment against Cardinal Wolsey and had led the case against John Fisher, as he was to do against Anne Boleyn. There is no record of his opening speech but it would follow the lines of the indictment.

It would be a mistake to assume that the narratives of the trial give us the exact wording used, and, it may be, the recorder (whoever he was) got arguments in their wrong order; however,

[1]For a detailed study of the authorities for our knowledge of the Trial, the reader may be referred to the author's *The Trial of St Thomas More* (1964). The account in the present chapter follows, in the main, Harpsfield's recension (pp. 183-198), and quotations not otherwise noted are from those pages.

[2]He succeeded Cromwell as Master of the Rolls in 1536.

362

we have to use what we have, and be grateful that we have anything at all!

In his first reply, Thomas More at once mentioned the King's "late marriage", which is not mentioned in the Indictment, but he and his listeners knew quite well that this was at the root of the trouble. He said, "Of malice I never spoke anything against it, and that whatsoever I have spoken in that matter, I have none otherwise spoken but according to my very mind, opinion and conscience". He then pointed out that "for this mine error, I have not gone scot free". He was in prison for life and all his possessions had been confiscated. This led him to point out that he was now being tried under Acts passed while he was imprisoned, and during that time he had kept silent on all matters of State. "Touching, I say this challenge and accusation, I answer that, for this my taciturnity and silence, neither your law nor any law in the world is able justly and rightly to punish me, *unless you may besides lay to my charge either some word or some fact in deed*." There we have the lawyer's argument and also the explanation of why he had doggedly refused to answer questions on the Supremacy.

The attorney-general made the point that this silence was in itself a "sure token and demonstration of a corrupt and perverse nature, maligning and repining against the Statute". A faithful subject, when questioned, would "without any dissimulation, confess the Statute to be good, just and lawful".

Thomas More took up this point by saying that, by common law, "he that holdeth his peace seemeth to consent", or, as the saying goes, "Silence gives consent". Not that More wanted his silence to be interpreted as consent, but he was making a valid point. Words alone were now to be regarded as treasonous, but was silence also to be so regarded? He went on:

For as for that you said, that every good subject is obliged to answer and confess, ye must understand that, in things touching conscience every true and good subject is more bound to have respect to his said conscience and to his soul than to any other thing in all the world besides, namely, when his conscience is in such sort as mine is, that is to say, where the person giveth no occasion for slander, of tumult and sedition against his Prince, as it is with me; for I assure you that I have not hitherto to this hour disclosed and opened my conscience and mind to any person living in all the world.

More was voicing his fundamental objection to being compelled to accept the King's new title of Supreme Head; it was an invasion of the prerogative of conscience that is part of the Divine Law. Statute law under Henry VIII began to encroach on the territory ruled by the law of God, since it applied man-made law to the deeply held religious convictions of the individual. In this light we can see More's case as a protest against the increasing powers assumed by the King and Parliament to regulate men's inmost beliefs.

As to his claim that he had kept his own counsel, we have already seen the truth of this; he even refused to discuss the question with his favourite daughter Margaret. We are not told how the court dealt with this argument. The record passes on to the second and third counts given in the Indictment; these were concerned with the letters or notes that had passed between More and Fisher; they could not be produced as evidence as they had been destroyed at the suggestion of George Gold.

"Would God", quoth Sir Thomas More, "that these letters were now produced and openly read. . . . In one of them there was nothing in the world contained but certain familiar talk and recommendations [information], such as was seemly and agreeable to our long and old acquaintance. In the other was contained my answer that I made to the said Bishop, demanding me what thing I answered at my first examination in the Tower upon the said Statute [of Supremacy]. Whereunto I answered nothing else but that I had informed and settled my conscience, and that he should inform and settle his."

As to the fuss made in the third count about both having used the expression "a two-edged sword", More claimed that this was purely coincidental, "by reason of the correspondance and conformity of our wits, learning and study, not that any such thing was purposely concluded upon and accorded betwixt us".

Again we are left in ignorance of how the prosecution dealt with the rejoinder. Clearly the absence of the letters took much of the substance out of the charge of collaboration. When he was asked the rather pointless question why he wrote the letters to Fisher, More gave the obvious answer, "Considering they were both in one prison, and for one cause, he was glad to send unto him and to hear from him again". This brought the matter down to human terms; two old friends wondering how the other was faring.

According to Harpsfield's narrative, it was at this point that More pleaded "Not Guilty", but he must surely have done so after the reading of the Indictment. He added that if the terms "maliciously, traitorously and diabolically" were removed from the Indictment, there would be no grounds for his condemnation.

The trial had now reached a consideration of Rich's evidence of his conversation with Sir Thomas More in the Tower. Unfortunately we do not know exactly what Rich said in Court.

> Wherefore, for the last cast and refuge, to prove that Sir Thomas More was guilty of this treason, Master Rich was called for to give evidence to the jury upon his oath as he did. Against whom thus sworn, Sir Thomas More began in this wise to say . . . .

It seems that Rich must have stated categorically that More had denied to the King his title of Supreme Head.

The wording of the Indictment follows closely the first draft of the report of the conversation. In translation, the Indictment gives the words as:

> The King can be made or unmade by Parliament, to which every subject being at the Parliament may give his consent; but as to the Supremacy, the subject cannot be bound, since he cannot give his consent in Parliament, and though the King be accepted as such in Parliament, there are many other countries that do not agree.

More's argument was that while Parliament can decide who is, or who is not King, it is not competent to make the King Supreme Head as this is not a matter that can possibly be decided by one country; it affects all Christian countries and only a General Council can deal with such a proposal. We have seen that, *at the time*, Rich did not consider this to be an outright denial of the new title.[3] The first draft reads:

> Well, Sir, God comfort you, for I see *your mind will not change*

[3] See above, p. 344.

which I fear will be very dangerous to you for I suppose *your concealment to the question that hath been asked* of you is as high offence as other that hath denied.

It is clear that Rich's evidence made More very angry; it is the only time in the trial when his usual composure was seriously ruffled. He put three points in his defence.

1. Rich was a hostile witness of discreditable character. "You were esteemed very light of your tongue, a common liar, a great dicer, and of no commendable fame"—a description that must have made Rich wince.
2. Was it likely that he (More) would have spoken words to a visitor, not even a friendly one, that he had refused to speak when time and again the direct question was put to him by the Councillors?
3. Whatever was said to Rich, was in answer to hypothetical cases such as lawyers discussed in their moots.

Thomas More went on to clear himself of any malicious intent. He felt sure that the Lords and Commons could not have meant that a man in whom no malice could be found should be condemned to death. Moreover, he asked, was it conceivable that he who had been so trusted and honoured as he had been by the King, "by the space of twenty years and more showing his continual favour towards me"—was it conceivable that he would now act maliciously against such a Prince?

Richard Rich had evidently been stung by Thomas More's attack on him, so he called two witnesses to confirm his own report of what was said. Both Richard Southwell and Cromwell's servant, Palmer, declared that they had been so busy that they had not listened to the conversation. They were thus unable to support Rich's evidence.

Not that this made any difference to the inevitable verdict. There is no further record of More's defence nor of the solicitor-general's reply.

The jury brought in the foreseeable verdict of guilty. Lord Chancellor Audley then began to pronounce sentence, but Sir Thomas, who had recovered his equanimity, interrupted him:

My lord, when I was toward the law, the manner in such case was to ask the prisoner, before judgement, why judgement should not be given against him.

Audley's lapse may have been sheer nervousness at having to condemn his predecessor to the cruel death of a traitor. He must have been intimate with Thomas More for he had been made attorney of the Duchy of Lancaster when More was its Chancellor. Even in those perilous times human feelings could not be suppressed completely. An alternative explanation is that the King had given instructions that More should not be allowed to justify himself apart from answering the evidence brought against him. To stay a convicted prisoner from speaking against the verdict was to rob him of a cherished privilege of unburdening his mind. Thomas More must have been looking forward to the opportunity of liberating his spirit after so many months of silence during which he must often have been tempted to speak out. His speech must have been carefully thought out in those long days of solitude in his cell. It is so important for an understanding of his mind and spirit that it must be given in full.

"Seeing that I see ye are determined to condemn me (God knoweth how) I will now in discharge of my conscience speak my mind plainly and freely touching my Indictment and your Statute withal.

"And forasmuch as this Indictment is grounded upon an Act of Parliament directly repugnant to the laws of God and his Holy Church, the supreme Government of which, or of any part whereof, may no temporal Prince presume by any law to take upon him, as rightfully belonging to the See of Rome, a spiritual pre-eminence by the mouth of our Saviour himself, personally present upon earth, only to St Peter and his successors, Bishops of the same See, by special prerogative granted; it is therefore in law, amongst Christian men, insufficient to charge any Christian man."

The report continues in indirect speech:

And for proof thereof, like as among divers other reasons and authorities, he declared that this Realm, being but one member and small part of the Church, might not make a particular law disagreeable with the general law of Christ's Universal Catholic Church, no more than the City of London, being but one poor member in respect of the whole Realm, might make a law against an Act of Parliament to bind the whole Realm. So further showed he that it was contrary both to the laws and statutes of our own land yet unrepealed, as they might evidently perceive in Magna Charta, *Quod Anglicana ecclesia libera sit et habeat omnia jura integra, et libertates suas illaesas.*[4] And also contrary to the sacred oath which the King's Highness himself, and every other Christian Prince always with great solemnity received at their coronations; alleging, moreover, that no more might this Realm of England refuse obedience to the See of Rome than might a child refuse obedience to his own natural father.

Thomas More was here affirming an essential principle of "Christ's Universal Catholic Church", as he liked to call it, a principle that has been part of Christian teaching since the foundation of the Church. There are limits set by Divine Law to the authority of princes and states. No single one of them can legislate for the whole Church, or, without injustice, demand of the individual anything contrary to Christian teaching. When the state goes beyond these limits, the Christian has a duty to follow his conscience in obedience to God and the Church.

Few men have been as scrupulous as Thomas More in serving their king with complete faithfulness; his whole public life was evidence of true loyalty. Whatever More may have come to feel about the personal character of Henry, he did not allow this to affect his devotion to the Crown. This makes his final refusal of obedience all the more impressive. Moreover, he recognized that his decision had to be a personal one, a matter of his own conscience, and, in that sense, private. Had Henry been more perceptive and more magnanimous, he would have left this faithful servant in untroubled retirement, knowing full well that Thomas More was not a sedition-monger.

We can see More's protest as directed against the rapid extension of Royal and Parliamentary authority into a field that had hitherto been reserved to the Church. There was a good case for a readjustment of their relations and there was undoubted need to define more closely the powers of the Church over men's daily lives. Instead of a reasonable reform, all the powers of the papacy were transferred to the Crown between 1533 and 1536. Not the

[4]That the English Church shall be free [i.e. from interference by the King], and shall have all its rights undiminished and its liberties unimpaired. (First clause of the Charter.)

least significant of the changes was the ban on the teaching of Canon Law in the universities. As yet the new Supreme Head had not attempted to define doctrine by declaration or statute, but now there was nothing to stop him doing so. Even the authority of the Convocations was in abeyance. Where could men look for the ultimate authority in religion? It was one of More's distinctions that, from the early days of the King's Matter, he had sensed how far Henry might go.

Thomas More's speech was interrupted by Chancellor Audley, who asked him if he set his judgment against that of so many learned men, the bishops and the universities. The same point had been made in the interrogations; More now elaborated his reply

> If there were no more but myself upon my side, and the whole of Parliament upon the other, I would be sore afraid to lean mine own mind only against so many. But if the number of Bishops and Universities be so material as your Lordship seemeth to take it, then see I little cause, my Lord, why that thing in my conscience should make any change. For I nothing doubt but that, though not in this Realm, yet in Christendom about, of these well-learned Bishops and virtuous men that are yet alive, they be not the fewer part that are of my mind therein. But if I should speak of those that are already dead, of whom many be now holy saints in heaven, I am very sure it is the far greater part of them that, all the while they lived, thought in this case that way that I think now; and therefore am I not bounden, my Lord, to conform my conscience to the Council of one Realm against the General Council of Christendom. For of the aforesaid holy Bishops I have for every Bishop of yours, above one hundred, and for one Council or Parliament of yours (God knoweth what manner of one) I have all the Councils made these thousand years. And for this one kingdom, I have all other Christian Realms.

The Duke of Norfolk now broke in to say, "We now plainly perceive that ye are maliciously bent". It is difficult to see how this applies to what More had just been saying. There may, however, be some displacement of material here. More's reply reads:

> Nay, nay, very and pure necessity, for the discharge of my conscience, enforceth me to speak so much. Wherein I call and appeal to God, whose only sight pierceth into the very depth of man's heart, to be my witness.

N

Then he added abruptly—and here again the report may be confused—"Howbeit, it is not for this supremacy so much that ye seek my blood, as for that I would not condescend to the marriage".

Then followed a curious incident reported by Roper.

The Lord Chancellor, loath to have the burden of that judgement wholely to depend on himself, there openly asked advice of the Lord Fitzjames, then Lord Chief Justice of the King's Bench, and joined in Commission with him, whether this Indictment were sufficient or not. Who, like a wise man, answered, "My lords all, by St Julian" (that was ever his oath), "I must needs confess that if the Act of Parliament be not unlawful, then is not the Indictment in my conscience insufficient."[5]

What are we to make of this? It was rather late in the day to question the sufficiency of the Indictment, and Fitzjames's very cautious answer, in place of a plain "Yes", is still more perplexing. Can it be that both Audley and Fitzjames had doubts of the legality of the charge, or that both would have liked to find some way out of an embarrassing business?[6]

As Fitzjames did not offer an escape route, Audley had no option but to condemn Sir Thomas More to death at Tyburn.

Roper has another surprise for us. After sentence had been passed, More was asked "if he had anything else to allege for his defence" and the Commissioners said they would "grant him favourable audience". This was surely a most irregular proceeding. The trial was over; the prisoner condemned; what more was there to say? One again gets the impression that the Commissioners regretted the whole affair and still hoped for an excuse to recommend mercy. More's reply was like the "two-edged sword" about which so much fuss had been made; it could only have made his listeners more uncomfortable.

More have I not to say, my lords, but that like the Blessed Apostle

[5]Roper, p. 95.
[6]As a Chief Justice, Fitzjames must have worked closely with Lord Chancellor More. Roper would be intimate with Fitzjames of whose court he was clerk of the Pleas. The reference to his customary oath suggests familiarity. It is inconceivable that the two did not discuss More's Trial.

Paul as we read in the Acts of the Apostles, was present and consented to the death of St Stephen, and kept their clothes that stoned him to death, and yet be they now both twain Holy Saints in heaven, and shall continue there friends together for ever, so I verily trust, and shall therefore right heartily pray, that though your lordships have now here in earth been judges to my condemnation, we may hereafter in heaven merrily all meet together, to our everlasting salvation. And thus I desire Almighty God to preserve and defend the King's Majesty, and to send him good counsel.

CHAPTER XXXV

"The Field is Won"

IN HIS REPORT of the trial of the Duke of Buckingham in 1521, Hall wrote after the verdict, "Then was the edge of the axe turned towards him, and so led into a barge". There was no such symbolic gesture after Sir Thomas More's condemnation; he was a commoner and was to suffer like the basest criminal. He was taken in charge by the Constable of the Tower Sir William Kingston, "his very dear friend, who, when he had brought him from Westminster to the Old Swan towards the Tower, there with an heavy heart, the tears running down his cheeks, bade him farewell". Sir William later said to William Roper, "In good faith, I was ashamed of myself, that, at departing from your father, I found my heart so feeble, and his so strong, that he was fain to comfort me, which should rather have comforted him".[1]

The Old Swan stairs (now Old Swan Wharf) was just above the Bridge. The narrowness of the arches and the size of the piers and starlings made the passage dangerous at flood and ebb tides. From the stairs the rest of the journey would be on foot along Thames Street (now Lower Thames Street) to the Lion Tower that guarded the drawbridge over the moat. It was probably near here that Margaret and John More with Margaret Clement were waiting. William Roper was surely there for his account of the meeting is so charged with feeling that it suggests the memories of an eyewitness. He wrote:

> When Sir Thomas More came from Westminster to the Towerward again, his daughter, my wife, desirous to see her father, whom she thought never to see in this world after, and also to have his final blessing, gave attendance about the Tower Wharf where she knew he should pass by before he could enter the Tower, there tarrying for his coming. As soon as she saw him, after his blessing on her knees reverently received, she, hasting towards him, and, without con-

[1]Roper, p. 97.

372

sideration or care of herself, pressing in among the middest of the throng and company of the guard that with halberds and bills went round about him, hastily ran to him, and there openly in the sight of them all, embraced him, took him about the neck and kissed him. Who, well liking her most natural and daughterly affection towards him, gave her his fatherly blessing and many godly words of comfort besides. From whom after she was departed, she, not satisfied with the former sight of him, and like one that had forgotten herself, being all ravished with the entire love of her dear father, having respect neither to herself, nor to the press of people and multitude that were there about him, suddenly turned back again, ran to him as before, took him about the neck and divers times together most lovingly kissed him, and at last, with a full heavy heart, was fain to depart from him, the beholding whereof was to many of them that were present thereat so lamentable that it made them for very sorrow thereof to mourn and weep.

Roper makes no mention of John More and Margaret Clement, but Stapleton tells us that she "embraced and kissed him", and that John, "after receiving his father's blessing, kissed him and received his kiss in return". This must have been the bitterest part of More's ordeal; he had seen the last of his family.

Four full days passed between the trial and the execution. Margaret sent her maid Dorothy Colley (Stapleton's informant) to the Tower each day to take and receive messages; on her last visit she brought back to her mistress Thomas More's hair shirt and scourge with this letter:

Our Lord bless you good daughter and your good husband and your little boy and all yours and all my children and all my godchildren and all our friends. Recommend me when you may to my daughter Cecily, whom I beseech our Lord to comfort, and I send her my blessing and to all her children and pray her to pray for me. I send her an handkercher and God comfort my good son her husband [Giles Heron]. My good daughter Daunce hath the picture in parchment that you delivered me from my Lady Conyers, her name is on the back side. Shew her that I heartily pray her that you may send it in my name again for a token from me to pray for me.

I like special well Dorothy Colley, I pray you be good to her. I would wit whether this be she that you wrote me of. If not I pray you be good to the other, as you may in her affliction and to my good

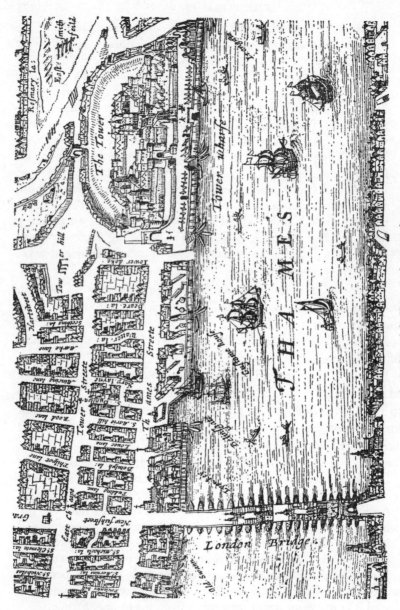

London Bridge and the Tower in the sixteenth century

daughter Joan Allen to give her I pray you some kind answer, for she sued hither to me this day to pray you be good to her.

Nothing has been discovered about Lady Conyers. The second paragraph seems to refer to some domestic trouble Margaret had been having with her maids. More's anxiety to smooth over such frictions even at such a time was typical of him. The letter continues:

> I cumber you good Margaret much, but I would be sorry, if it should be any longer than tomorrow, for it is St Thomas Eve and the utas of St Peter[2] and therefore tomorrow long I to go to God, it were a day very meet and convenient for me. I never liked your manner toward me better than when you kissed me last for I love when daughterly love and dear charity hath no leisure to look to worldly courtesy.
> Farewell my dear child and pray for me, and I shall for you and all your friends that we may merrily meet in heaven.
> I thank you for your great cost.
> I send now unto my daughter Clement her algorism stone and I send her and my good son [John Clement] and all hers God's blessing and mine.
> I pray you at time convenient recommend me to my good son John More. I liked well his natural fashion. Our Lord bless him and his good wife my loving daughter, to whom I pray him be good, as he hath great cause, and that if the land of mine come to his hand, he break not my will concerning his sister Daunce. And our Lord bless Thomas and Austen and all that they shall have.[3]

"Your great cost" does not refer here to expenses Margaret had incurred, but to the time she had given to her father in his prison days. The "algorism stone" was a slate used for calculations but perhaps used by More when he no longer had pen and paper. John More's "natural fashion" refers to that last meeting when the son knelt for his father's blessing. "Thomas and Austen" were the sons of John and Anne More. Thomas was born in 1533; he is shown in the composite picture of the More family. All his life he had to suffer the penalties exacted from Catholic recusants.

[2]7 July was the anniversary of the translation of the body of St Thomas of Canterbury in 1220 from the Cathedral crypt to the shrine. "Utas" means "Octave"; 6 July.
[3]Rogers, 218 (66).

He died in 1606. His youngest son was Cresacre More. Nothing further is known of Austen; presumably he died in youth.

This last extant letter from Thomas More shows the signs of hurried composition; he jotted down whatever came into his mind; perhaps Dorothy Colley could snatch only a few minutes and so he wrote quickly. There is no message to Dame Alice, but she would have had a separate letter, or, it may be, as his wife, she was allowed a last meeting in the Tower.

His wish that he might suffer on 6 July was granted. Early that morning, Thomas Pope,[4] "his singular friend", came to tell him that he was to be executed at nine o'clock. The King had already commuted the Tyburn hanging to execution by the axe. This may not have been out of regard for his old servant and friend; there would have been public demonstrations on the long way through the city to Tyburn. Pope also brought the message that the King's wish was that "at your execution you shall not use many words". Thomas More then asked that Margaret should be allowed to arrange for his burial; this was granted as well as permission for other members of the family to be present. More expressed his deep gratitude to the King for this concession. Presumably the King would not give permission for them to be present at the execution, and we know that only Margaret Clement was there.

Thomas More decided to wear the fine gown that had been given him by Antonio Bonvisi, but the Lieutenant persuaded him to choose something less valuable as it would be the perquisite of the executioner. So he wore a coarse, grey gown belonging to John à Wood.

The earliest account of the execution is very brief.[5]

The Wednesday [sic. Tuesday] following, he was beheaded in the great square in front of the Tower, and said little before execution only that the people there should pray God for him and he would pray for them. Afterwards, he exhorted them and earnestly beseeched them to pray God for the King, so that He would give him

[4]He had been an official in the Chancery Court. He used his later wealth to found Trinity College, Oxford.
[5]Harpsfield, p. 266.

good counsel, protesting that he died his good servant, but God's first.

The next account, chronologically, was written by Edward Hall in his *Chronicle* published in 1542. Hall is an important witness; as an Under-sheriff in 1535 of the City he was probably present at the execution; even if he was not there, he was in a position to collect first-hand information. He was an ardent Henrician and had no sympathy with Thomas More's opposition to the King's Church policy. He gives us a view that must be taken into account when we try to assess contemporary opinion: "Also the 6th day of July was Sir Thomas More beheaded for the like treason before rehearsed, which as you have heard was for the denying the King's Majesty's Supremacy."

Hall had just recorded the execution of John Fisher and had made the comment, "wonderful it is that a man being learned should be so blind in the scriptures of God that proveth the supreme authority of princes so manifestly." To continue his account of Thomas More's execution:

This man was also counted learned, and as you have heard before he was Lord Chancellor of England, and in that time a great persecutor of such as detested the Supremacy of the Bishop of Rome, which he himself so highly favoured that he stood to it until he was brought to the scaffold on the Tower Hill where on a block his head was stricken off and had no more harm.

The last words recall to mind More's comment in a letter to Margaret, "it is a case in which a man may lose his head and yet have none harm".[6] Perhaps it was a saying of the times.

I cannot tell whether I should call him a foolish wise man, or a wise foolish man, for undoubtedly he, beside his learning, had a great wit, but it was so mingled with taunting and mocking that it seemed to them that best knew him, that he thought nothing to be well spoken except he had ministered some mock in the communication, insomuch as at his coming to the Tower, one of the officers demanded his upper garment for his fee, meaning his gown, and he answered he should have it and took off his cap, saying it was the uppermost garment that he had. Likewise, even going to his death

[6] See above, p. 347.

at Tower Gate, a poor woman called unto him and besought him to declare that he had certain evidence of hers in the time that he was in office (which after he was apprehended she could not come by) and that he would entreat she might have them again, or else she was undone. He answered, "Good woman, have patience a little while, for the King is good unto me that even within this half hour he will discharge me of all my business, and help thee himself". Also when he went up the stair on the scaffold, he desired one of the Sheriff's officers to give him his hand to help him up, and said, "When I come down again, let me shift for myself as well as I can". Also the hangman kneeled down to him asking him forgiveness of his death (as the manner is) to whom he said, "I forgive thee, but I promise thee that thou shalt never have honesty [credit] of the striking off my head, my neck is so short". Also even when he should lay down his head on the block, he having a great gray beard, striked out his beard and said to the hangman, "I pray you let me lay my beard over the block lest ye should cut it"; thus with a mock he ended his life.[7]

Stapleton added some particulars given him by Dorothy Colley (Harris). On his way to the scaffold a woman proffered him some wine, which he refused, saying, "Christ in his passion was given not wine but some vinegar to drink". That may be a later embellishment; we are on safer ground with the next story. It is of "a certain citizen of Winchester"—the name suggests an authentic source. This man had sought More's advice in happier times on some kind of temptation that beset him. He too was in the crowd at the execution. He called out, "Do you recognize me, Sir Thomas? Help me, I beg you: for that temptation has returned to me and I cannot get rid of it." More's reply was, "I recognize you perfectly. Go and pray for me, and I will pray earnestly for you." Yet another woman spoke to him, this time to complain that when he was Chancellor he had given a wrong judgment against her. More replied, "I remember your case quite well, and if I had to pass sentence again, it would be just the same as before".

How are we to judge the reliability of such stories? The only test we can use is to consider if they are in character. The story of

7Hall, II, pp. 265-6.

the woman and the wine, or, rather More's answer, is suspect
for that reason. The others are in keeping with what we know of
his character. Perhaps one or other of Stapleton's incidents may
have occurred at some other period, for he certainly gives More
a busy time during his walk of some two hundred yards from the
Tower. Not that there was anything exceptional in such conversations; we have seen how More himself was involved in an exchange of remarks with Edmund Dudley on the way to execution.[8]

Stapleton adds some particulars of what happened on the
scaffold. After declaring that he died "the faithful servant of God
and the King and in the faith of the Catholic Church", he knelt
down and recited the *Miserere*. When the executioner wished to
bind his eyes, More said, "I will cover them myself".

None of the records tell us whether a priest was present on the
scaffold. Thomas More died without the presence of any relative
or friend. He was unaware that Margaret Clement was in the
crowd. He would know that his daughter Margaret would be
somewhere near waiting to carry out her last sad duty to him.
We always think of Thomas More as the centre of a very lively
family circle and of a multitude of friends. He died a lonely man
separated from all those he loved. He himself may have willed it
that way.

Our only information about the burial comes from Stapleton,
who recorded Dorothy Colley's recollections. The burial was to
be in the church of St Peter-ad-Vincula within the Tower. On
her way with Dorothy, Margaret visited a number of churches
and gave alms to the poor so that by the time they reached the
Tower, her purse was empty. Then she realized that she had
forgotten to bring a winding-sheet but she had no money to buy
one.

Her maid Dorothy suggested that she should get some linen from a
neighbouring shop. "How can I do that", she answered, "when I
have no money left?" "They will give you credit", replied the maid.
"I am far away from home", said Margaret, "and no one knows me

St Peter ad Vincula in the Tower

here, but yet go and try." The maid went into a neighbouring shop
and asked for as much linen as was needed; she agreed on the price.
Then she put her hand into her purse as if to look for the money,
intending to say that unexpectedly she found herself without money,
but that if the shopkeeper would trust her she would obtain the price
of the linen as quickly as possible from her mistress and bring it back.
But although the maid was quite certain that she had absolutely no
money, yet in her purse she found exactly the price of the linen, not
one farthing more or less than the amount she had agreed to pay.
Dorothy Harris [Stapleton concluded], who is still living in Douai,
has told me these details again and again. With this winding-sheet,
so strangely obtained, the two Margarets and Dorothy most
reverently buried the body.[9]

Shortly afterwards, the body of St John Fisher was removed from
All Hallows churchyard and reburied near that of St Thomas
More.[10]

In 1876 the little church was subject to thorough "restoration".
When the stone flags were removed it was found that as a result

of burials during more than three hundred years, the subsoil was chock-a-block with the bones of hundreds of the dead. Not all were victims of the axe; most were of those who had died in the Tower parish of which St Peter-ad-Vincula was the church. All these bones were carefully gathered together; they were reburied in a new vault to the north of the chapel. Among them are the bones of the two saints.

More's head, having been parboiled, was displayed on London Bridge. Margaret bribed the executioner, who was in charge, to let her have the head before it was flung into the river as John Fisher's had been. During her lifetime (she died in 1544) the head remained in her care. It is said that she left it to her eldest daughter, Lady Elizabeth Bray, who died in 1558. She it was, it is assumed, who had it placed in the Roper vault in St Dunstan's, Canterbury. It was last seen in 1837. The head or skull is behind an iron grille in a niche; it is in a leaden box shaped like the mail coif of chain armour.

The Roper vault was sealed, and the chantry is now the chapel of St Nicholas. A tablet set in the floor reads:

BENEATH THIS FLOOR
IS THE VAULT OF THE
ROPER FAMILY IN WHICH
IS INTERRED THE HEAD OF
SIR THOMAS MORE
OF ILLUSTRIOUS MEMORY
SOMETIME LORD CHANCELLOR
OF ENGLAND WHO WAS
BEHEADED ON TOWER HILL
6TH JULY 1535

ECCLESIA ANGLICANA LIBERA SIT

*   *   *

When Erasmus received the news of the executions, he wrote to a friend, "From the extract I enclose from a letter, you will earn of the fate of the Bishop of Rochester and Thomas More, than whom England never had two men more saintly or more learned. I feel as if I had died with More so closely were our two souls united."

He arranged for the publication of the *Expositio fidelis de morte Thomae Mori*, which was based on a newsletter[11] issued in Paris in August. In the preface to his new book *Ecclesiastes*, he lamented the loss of several of his old friends, and most of all "of the Bishop of Rochester and of Thomas More, whose heart was whiter than snow, a genius such as England never had before, nor ever will have again."[12]

[11]For the text of the Paris Newsletter, see Harpsfield, pp. 254-265.
[12]Erasmus died almost exactly twelve months after Thomas More.

Appendix I

Date of Birth

The years of the births of most Tudor notabilities are conjectural; luckily, the choice for the date of Thomas More's birth is limited to 6 or 7 February 1477 or 1478, and it doesn't really matter which is preferred.

The solution (if there is one) lies in the interpretation of an entry by Sir John More in a manuscript now at Trinity College, Cambridge. This is a record of the dates of his marriage and of the births of his children. The entry for Thomas reads, in translation:

> Memo. *That on the Friday next after the Feast of the Purification of the Blessed Virgin Mary, between two and three in the morning, was born Thomas More, son of John More, gentleman, in the seventeenth year of King Edward the Fourth after the Conquest of England.*[1]

Had Sir John left it at that, all would have been clear, but, unfortunately, he added between the lines (to be inserted before "between two and three") the words, "namely, on the 7th of February".

The 17th year of Edward IV ran from 4 March 1477 to 3 March 1478 inclusive. February 1477 did not therefore fall within that regnal year, but February 1478 did, and that would be conclusive. However, there is the complication that 7 February 1478 was not a Friday but a Saturday. I think Fr Bridgett's view was reasonable—"the birth took place soon after midnight of the Friday," so both days, Friday and Saturday, were in Sir John's mind when he made his note—hence the confusion. Fr Bridgett decided for 1478, as did R. W. Chambers (upon second thoughts). This year is accepted as a working hypothesis in this present book.

All this trouble would not have arisen if only we could be certain in which year Hans Holbein made the drawing of the More family that went to Erasmus. As we have seen,[2] the age of each person was given (though not by Holbein). Was the drawing made in 1526 or 1527? We don't know.

---

[1] The reference to the Conquest may puzzle the reader. It means the fourth Edward after Edward the Confessor.

[2] See above, p. 190.

Those who have a taste for this kind of conundrum should consult’ to begin with, Harpsfield, pp. 298–303; Chambers, *Thomas More*, pp. 48–9, and Marc'hadour, *L'Univers de Thomas More*, pp. 34–41. The inquirer will take up a number of promising clues only to find that each leads to a dead end.

Conversation between Sir Thomas More and Sir Richard Rich, 12 June 1535

Reference: P.R.O., S.P. 2/R, folios 24 and 25

N.B. The series of dots indicates only roughly the extent of the lacunae.

f.24. The effect of the . . . between Rychard . . ./ and the sayd Sir Thomas More in the presence of . . ./ Edward Walsyngham Rychard Southewell/ *blank* Palmer and *blank* Berleght.

. . . . charitably movyd the seyd Sir Thomas More to be conformable/ . . . . lawes as wer made concernyng the case that he knew of / upon the condycion that yf the seyd More wold so be that he wold . . . on his / f. 25 . . . . to whome the seyd More gave thanks saying that your Cons . . . ./ Save you and my conscience shall save me. Wheruppon the seyd Rychard / . . . to the seyd More Sir for me to gyve you advyse or counsell beyng a / . . . experyence lernyng & wysedome yt were lyke as yf a man wold take / . . . . of water and cast yt in to Temmys by cause yt shold not be / . . . Sir protestyng with you that I have no commission or commaundement to / . . . with you of the mater ye wott of Nevertheless with your favour I ask / . . . you this case If it were inactyd by Parlyament that I should be King / . . . and who so ever sayd nay shold .t.d. what offence were yt to y . . . / If ye seyd h . . . I were King for sothe . . . my conseyence yt werre none off. . / . . . ye were bound to say and to .ccept me for so muche as your consent/. . . . . whereunto . . . seyd More sayed that he shold offende . . / . . . ., for he . . . bound by the act by cause he myght gyve his / . . . . And he sayd further that the same case was a . . . case / . . . . . putt a nother hyer case whiche was this Sir I put case / . . . , by Parlyment that God were not God And if any Repug . . . /same act that yt shold be treason yf the questyon were askyd of your . . . / . . . ye say that God were not God according to the Statute And if he dyd, dyd / you

affende yea for sothe wherunto the seyd Ryche sayd that act was not /
possyble to be made to make God ungod but Syr by cause your case
ys . . . . . / . . . to you & me witys Syr . . . to be pl. . . . . . . Ingland
. . . . / . . . affirme & accept . . . so as welle as in the
case that I were made Kyng . . . / . . iche case ye agre that ye were
bound so to affirme & accept me to be Kyng . . . / whereunto the seyd
More sayd that the cases were not lyk by cause that a Kyng / . . . y be
made by parlyament and a Kyng depryved by Parlyament to whiche
act any / . . . Sybyettes beyng of the parlyment may gyve his concent
but to the case . . . . a Subyett can not be bound by cause he cannot
gyve his cause [*sic*, consent?] . . . / . . . hym . . . Parliament Saying
further that although the Kyng were acceptyd / in Ingland yet moste
Utter partes doo not affirme the same Whereunto the sayd / Ryche
sayd Well Sir God comfort you for I see your mynd wyll not change /
which I fere wyll be very daungerous to you for I suppose your
concelement to the / questyon that hath been askyd of you ys as high
offence as other that hath denyd / . . and thus Jesu send you better grace.

The More Family Circle

DAME ALICE MORE lived at Chelsea after Sir Thomas's execution. She had disputes about land with William Roper and with a John Lane.[1] We do not know when she died; she would presumably be interred in the More vault.

At the death of his step-mother in 1545,[2] Thomas More would have inherited Gobions, but it was forfeited to the Crown. The lease was granted in June 1546 for twenty-one years to William Honnyng, one of the Clerks of the Council, at a rental of £50. 9s. 8d.[3] In 1557 the reversion was assigned to the Princess Elizabeth for life, so, although Queen Mary restored Gobions to the Mores, the estate did not come under their control until the death of Queen Elizabeth in 1603.

Margaret Roper was called before the Council (date not known) for having her father's head and his papers in her possession. She begged to be allowed to keep these "for her consolation" and her plea was granted. She and the rest of the family were watched. The Ropers' house at Butclose was searched at a later date to no purpose. Questions about her and Margaret Clement were asked when Sir Geoffrey Pole was interrogated in the Tower in October 1538, but again with no effect. John More was imprisoned for a short period, but as his grandson, Cresacre, wrote, "because they had sufficiently fleeced him before", he was released.

The first of the family to suffer death was Giles Heron who was hanged at Tyburn on 4 August 1540 but the details of the high treason for which he was condemned are not recorded. During the investigation of what is known as the Plot of the Prebendaries of Canterbury against Cranmer in 1541, witnesses were asked if they had had any communications with William Roper, John More, John Clement and John Heywood. Unfortunately their answers were not recorded.

William Roper was imprisoned in the Tower for a short period and fined £100 in February 1543 for having given alms to John Beckenshawe who was accused of plotting with Cardinal Pole.

[1]See above, p. 232. Roper, p. xli; *Moreana*, No. 4 and No. 5.
[2]See above, p. 266.
[2]L.P., XXI, i. No. 1166 (38).

O*

William Daunce, husband of Elizabeth More, got into trouble in 1544 but received a pardon in April of that year for "all treasonable words against the King's Supremacy". On the same day, John More also received his pardon. Others involved in this "round-up", as it may be called, were John Heywood, John Ireland (chaplain to the Ropers at Eltham), John Larke (parish priest at Chelsea) and Germain Gardiner (a relative of Bishop Gardiner of Winchester). John Heywood submitted at the last moment, but the other three were hanged at Tyburn on 7 March 1544.[4]

Margaret Roper died at Christmas 1544 and was buried in the More vault. Her brother John died three years later; as the last reference to him described him as "of Chelsea" it seems likely that he died there. His widow, Anne, married George West and they settled at the Cresacre estates at Barnburgh, Yorkshire, with Thomas and Austin and the other six children of John More. She died in 1577.

When Edward VI came to the throne and the Protector Somerset and Archbishop Cranmer were able to strengthen Protestantism, the position of Catholics became more and more irksome. The issue of the new Book of Common Prayer in 1549 was a sign of the times. Many Catholics preferred to go into exile. Among them was John Clement who left in July 1549; Antonio Bonvisi followed him two months later. Margaret Clement with her children, Thomas and Margaret, joined her husband in October. William Rastell and his wife (Winifred Clement) crossed in December. They all settled at Louvain where other refugees joined them, including young Nicholas Harpsfield, the future biographer of Sir Thomas More. William Roper did not leave the country but sent his eldest son, Thomas, to be educated at Louvain. Roper's official position no doubt sheltered him.

With the accession of Mary Tudor in July 1553, the exiles returned, save for Winifred Rastell who died that month. William Rastell became a judge of the Queen's Bench in 1555. William Roper was sheriff of Kent in 1553 and represented Rochester in Parliament. John Clement resumed his practice as a doctor and was closely associated with the College of Physicians; he got back the Old Barge which had been forfeited when he fled the country.

The new reign meant it was possible to print Thomas More's works again, and to this task William Rastell devoted himself. The project for a life of More led to William Roper's vivid record which was used (and all but smothered) in the expanded biography written by Harps-

[4]L.P. XX. i. 444. 812, 853.

field. The folio of the English Works was published in April 1557. The death of Queen Mary in the following year meant a resurgence of Protestantism, but it was not until 1563 that the position of Catholics became oppressive; the penalties under the Acts of Uniformity and Supremacy of 1559 were then made more severe. The Clements and William Rastell again went into exile, this time, permanently. They were joined by John Heywood and by Thomas More's secretary, John Harris with his wife Dorothy Colley who had been Margaret Roper's maid. They brought with them many of More's letters and papers, and it was from these and from Dorothy Colley's recollections and those of the other exiles that Thomas Stapleton was able to write his life of More in 1588.

William Rastell died at Louvain on 23 August 1565; Margaret Clement died at Mechlin on 6 July 1570 and John Clement on 1 July 1572. John Harris died at Namur on 11 November 1579 in the same year as his son-in-law, John Fowler, the printer. Dorothy Harris was still alive in 1588. John Heywood survived into old age until 1580. His two sons, Ellis and Jasper, were distinguished Jesuits.

William Roper chose to remain in England and continued in his office as protonotary of the Queen's Bench, a position he handed on to his son Thomas. Roper got into trouble in 1568 for "having relieved with money certain persons who have departed out of the realm, and who, with others, have printed books against the Queen's supremacy and government". This tells us that he was one of those who financed the Catholic apologists in exile at Douai and elsewhere. That he was an active supporter of the seminary at Douai (Douay) is shown by the fact that a month after his death, a Solemn Requiem was sung at the college for the repose of his soul. The College Diary recorded that he would be "missed most greatly by all Catholics living here and in England".

When, in 1569, William Roper was required to accept the Act of Uniformity, he declared his loyalty to the Queen but asked not to be pressed to sign what was counter to his conscience. In the same year the Eltham magistrates reported him for failing to attend his parish church. Again in 1577 his name with that of his son Thomas and his grandson Philip Basset was on a list of those members of Lincoln's Inn who had not taken Communion according to the Act. The outcome of these complaints is not known.

His will is dated 10 January 1577; in it he made generous provision for prisoners of the Queen's Bench and for his clerks and servants. The will ended, "And my body to be buried at Chelsea in the vault with the body of my dearly beloved wife (whose soul our Lord pardon), where my father-in-law, Sir Thomas More (whose soul Jesus bless), did mind to be buried".[5] He died on 4 January 1578, but in spite of his declared wish, he was buried in the family vault at St Dunstan's, Canterbury. His epitaph there (not extant) gave his age as eighty-two, and recorded that he was the husband of Margaret, the daughter of Sir Thomas More, Chancellor of England. He was described as a munificent benefactor to the imprisoned, the oppressed and the poor. Then came a statement that struck an unusual note in an epitaph—that he had lived a widower for thirty-three years. Surely this means that he remained entirely devoted to the memory of Margaret. Nor, as one reads his masterly tribute to the father, can one doubt his deep affection for the daughter.

The last male descendant of Sir Thomas More was Fr Thomas More, S.J., who died in 1795. The Eystons of East Hendred are descended from his sister Bridget. The male line from William and Margaret Roper ended in the eighteenth century. The present representative of the family is Lord St Oswald who owns the Locky version of the group portrait.[6] A considerable number of people can claim descent from Sir Thomas More on the distaff side.

---

[5] This should dispose of two stories still current: (1) that Margaret Roper was buried at St Dunstan's, and (2) that Sir Thomas More's body was removed to the Chelsea vault.

[6] The Lords Teynham (Roper-Curzon), and the Trevor-Ropers, are descended from William Roper's younger brother, Christopher.

Index